ORGANIZATIONAL PSYCHOLOGY

ORGANIZATIONAL PSYCHOLOGY

Foundations and Applications

Robert B. Lawson
Zheng Shen

New York   Oxford
OXFORD UNIVERSITY PRESS
1998

OXFORD UNIVERSITY PRESS

Oxford   New York
Athens   Auckland   Bangkok   Bogota   Bombay   Buenos Aires
Calcutta   Cape Town   Dar es Salaam   Delhi   Florence   Hong Kong
Istanbul   Karachi   Kuala Lumpur   Madras   Madrid   Melbourne
Mexico City   Nairobi   Paris   Singapore   Taipei   Tokyo   Toronto

and associated companies in

Berlin   Ibadan

Library of Congress Cataloging-in-Publication Data
Lawson, Robert B.
Organizational psychology: Foundations and applications   /   Robert
B. Lawson, Zheng Shen.
    p.   cm.
    Includes bibliographical references and index.
    ISBN 0-19-511069-2
    1. Psychology, Industrial.   I. Shen, Zheng.   II. Title.
HF5548.8.L32   1998   96-29599
158.7—dc21   CIP

9 8 7 6 5 4 3 2 1
Printed in the United States of America
on acid-free paper

To all those who hope and strive
continuously to be stewards
for each other and our earth

Contents

Preface

This book focuses on people and their performance in organizations. An organization, whether for profit or in the service of the public as a governmental or nonprofit organization, does many things, all of which are done by people. Likewise, almost all of us will spend the major portion of our adult lives working in organizations, virtual or otherwise. Thus, it is extremely valuable to know about people at work and their interactions with each other in work organizations, which are the primary foci of organizational psychology.

The major purpose of this book are (1) to promote an understanding of how to lead, manage, and work in a wide variety of organizations; (2) to teach you strategies to sharpen and guide your organizational actions, experiences, and aspirations; and (3) to help you appreciate those organizational forces that shape individual and organizational lives in the global marketplace.

Organizational Psychology: Foundations and Applications is intended primarily for advanced undergraduate and graduate students in psychology, business administration, public administration, and related disciplines, as well as interested professionals and practitioners. Just as the authors have come to work together from opposite sides of the world, so we believe fervently that people from these different disciplines will all benefit by coming together, when possible, to work as a team to understand and manage people better in a wide variety of organizations.

Organizational Psychology: Foundations and Applications is unique because we present a theoretical framework or model for each major topic, related empirical findings, and specific applied interventions for a variety of organizational situations. Throughout the book, we use a transcultural approach to promote the understanding of a wide variety of persons in a wide variety of organizations by identifying the common shared features and those that make different groups and organizations unique. In addition, we balance the forces of the global marketplace with the concomitant forces and mandates of the local environment in which the organization is a community member. Also, we present throughout the book specific applied strategies that with some appropriate modifications to fit specific demands of a given situation can be used in a variety of organizations. These applied strategies have been harvested from a sound platform of theory and empirical evidence, when possible, to provide a solid grounding for their application. Last, in each chapter, we begin with an overview, a list of learning objectives, and conclude with a summary of the material presented. In short, the material is designed to engage your imagination and to be used in a wide variety of organizations around the world.

Our framework for understanding organizations and managing members of those organizations consists of three fundamental components—People, Processes, and Adaptation. We have divided the book into three sections with these titles to help you become familiar with the framework and apply it in your organizational activities.

The first section is People, since organizations are crafted from people who come together because they believe and eventually test the belief that they can accomplish something more effectively and efficiently together than anyone could do alone. This section contains four chapters. Chapter 1, an introduction to organizational psychology, includes definitions of organizations, approaches to studying organizations, and the framework for understanding organizations. Chapter 2 focuses on the nature of people and organizations, organizational variables, methods for studying organizations and their members, and a specific strategy for getting a preliminary sense of an organization.

Chapter 3 discusses organizational culture, which can affect all members of an organization and is thus an influential force in the performance of individual members and the organization as a whole. It presents a model of organizational culture, some empirical findings of financial and psychological outcome measures, and a specific applied strategy to change an organizational culture.

Chapter 4 explores workforce diversity. It presents the dynamics and demographics of the global workforce, along with a variety of strategies for enhancing diversity in the workplace and in the leadership teams of organizations. It also includes specific strategies to fix the mix and describes the many challenges and advantages of diversity in organizations.

Part 2, Processes, which includes five chapters, focuses on what people and groups do in organizations to relate to each other, namely, teaming, motivating, leading, deciding, and resolving conflicts. All these processes or patterned activities shape the relationships among organizational members and with their customers or clients and consequently strongly influence the performance and productivity of organizations. Chapter 5 discusses groups at work, group dynamics, and teams in organizations as a fundamental response to the major mantra of this period, namely, Do more with less. Chapter 6 examines individual and organizational motivation and makes plain the fundamental shift in emphasis from individual to organizational motivational forces caused, in large measure, by the intense competitive pressures of the global marketplace, the unrelenting demands of global customers and clients for the best quality goods and services at the lowest price, and the widespread implementation of quality-im-

provement programs. It also explores models of motivation, specific motivational levers and strategies (they work!), and the relationship between culture and motivation.

Chapter 7 presents models of leadership and power, as well as specific strategies to get and keep each in dynamic organizational contexts. In addition, it reviews the sources of power, influence tactics, organizational politics, and a variety of issues related to gender, diversity, and dysfunctional leadership (how to avoid it!).

Chapter 8 focuses on decision-making models for individuals and organizations, clarifies that decision making in organizations is primarily a social process, and presents specific strategies to avoid the land mines of group decision making, such as Groupthink and the Abilene Paradox. The chapter concludes with specific applied strategies for obtaining good ideas and perspectives for effective organizational decision making. Chapter 9 defines conflicts, discusses the sources of conflict and styles of reacting to conflict, and presents specific strategies for conducting negotiations with many different kinds of organizations based in different cultures around the world.

Part 3, Adaptation, consists of three chapters that emphasize the changes that individuals and organizations must manage daily as they perform in the global marketplace. Chapter 10, on individual change, examines the changing role of work in people's lives; the evolving contract between organizations and their members; and the stream of forces that leadership of a diversified workforce must address, such as aging, role juggling, and sex and drugs in the workplace. It includes empirical findings and specific applied strategies to enhance individuals' adaptation in the global marketplace which operates 24 hours per day and has an impact on organizations and their members everywhere. Chapter 11 focuses on organizational change and presents a model of planned organizational change that is extremely challenging to cultivate and sustain. It covers a variety of organizational plans for change, the importance of organizational vision, and the needs of the evolving global organization, as well as the new rules for work in organizations that will be more common in the 21st century.

Chapter 12 is a brief summary of the major principles and guidelines developed in the other chapters. It underscores the fundamental and universal need to promote wholesome human relationships in dynamic and productive organizations that perform in the incessantly driven global marketplace. We suggest that the systematic application of competence, grace, and compassion in organizations can lead to more effective, efficient, and noble organizations.

We are grateful and indebted to many people, including our students and our universities that have challenged and supported us in this project. We are especially indebted to our colleagues and friends, Drs. Zenglo Chen and Zhenhua Ma, who brought us together for periods of study and work in both Beijing and Burlington. We are also indebted to our families and friends who encouraged us constantly to keep going, especially when the way became less clear, hypercomplex, and, at times, confusing. Thank you Mona and Shu-Zi for believing in us and standing by us over the years.

We are particularly indebted to Jennie Marcotte, who kept us on schedule, word processed countless revisions, and brought us our horoscope each day so we could get a sense of the big picture. We are grateful for her welcome friendship and support during periods of turbulence as we proceeded along the way.

Lastly, we thank our anonymous reviewers, the editorial staff, and especially Gioia Stevens of Oxford University Press for her thoughtful and gracious leadership.

PART I

PEOPLE

1

An Introduction to Organizational Psychology

CHAPTER OVERVIEW

In these times, more people are being born each day, are getting into increasingly closer electronic and real contact with each other, and are doing business with each other more and more each day, regardless of where they work and live. These immutable events have an impact on and shape all organizational and personal lives each day at the dawn of the 21st century. To embrace the challenges and opportunities of today and tomorrow, you will be well served if you are educated in the theory, data, and applications of organizational psychology. Such a grounding will enhance your flexibility, serve as a source of hope and encouragement, and infuse quality in all you do.

This chapter discusses the visible and invisible hands of the global marketplace. It defines the constructs of organizations and global organizations throughout the world, discusses organizational psychology approaches to understanding organizations, indicates in what type of organizations organizational psychologists are primarily employed and how much they are paid, and identifies critical skills for working effectively in organizations. It presents a framework for understanding organizations that focuses on people, processes, and adaptation. The American, Asian, and European cultural economic blocks are briefly described to provide a global context for the framework for understanding organizations anywhere. The chapter concludes by emphasizing the importance of applied knowledge grounded in solid data sets and theory. The bottom line of organizational psychology is becoming increasingly clear: It is not where you do it but how well you do it with whatever you have to do it with.

LEARNING OBJECTIVES

- identify three immutable global forces that affect organizations and people's work lives
- define the constructs of organization and global organization
- identify what organizational psychologists do, where they work, what they get paid, and the critical skills they need to work effectively
- describe a theoretical framework for understanding organizations wherever they are located that includes information about *people* (organizational culture and workforce diversity), key organizational *processes* (such as group dynamics, motivation, leadership, power and politics, decision making, and conflict resolution), and *adaptation* at the individual and organizational levels
- identify and describe briefly the American, Asian, and European cultural-economic blocks that are shaping the global economy
- indicate the importance of being grounded in the theory, data, and applications of organizational psychology
- get your organization going, rather than staying stuck in repetition, compared to creative adaptation.

Never forget you and I are a part of the world.

OUR WORLD

All people everywhere are experiencing more and more each day what has been called a New World Order, although it is still difficult to define clearly all the features of this new era that marks the global ascent of humanity to the 21st century. Three features that appear to have a significant influence on each person and organization around the world are *increasing contact, the global marketplace,* and *invisible and visible hands.*

Increasing Contact

Each day brings people closer and closer to each other as a result of their increasing virtual (electronic) and real-time (actual) contact with others throughout the world. Today, it is possible to communicate almost anywhere in the world in one minute and to travel to almost any place in one day. This multiple and diverse crossing of the boundaries of space and time requires all persons and organizations to update their assumptions about themselves, humanity, and our home, the Earth (Boyacigiller & Adler, 1991; Naisbitt, 1994; Naisbitt & Aburdene, 1990). Although the authors of this book are drawn from opposite ends of the globe, we have worked together almost as if we lived in the same city of Beijing or Burlington, Vermont, as a result of electronic and real-time linkages.

The global population (births minus deaths) increases 237,748 persons each day or 2.8 persons each second. As Table 1–1 indicates, the world population was 5.6 billion in 1994, and the United Nations estimated that it will reach 6.0 billion in 1998, 8.5 billion in 2025, and 10.0 billion in 2050. Approximately 98%, of the population growth will be in Africa, Asia, and Latin America, with only 2% in the more economi-

Table 1–1. World Births, Deaths, and Population Growth, 1994

Characteristic	World	Developed	Developing
Population	5,642,151,000	1,240,354,000	4,401,797,000
Births	139,324,000	16,944,000	122,380,000
Deaths	52,514,000	11,715,000	40,799,000
Natural Increase	86,810,000	5,229,000	81,582,000

Three People Each Second	Where in the World Do They Live?
Every two seconds around the world nine infants are born and three people die. The net increase of three people each second results in a growth in a world population of 10,600 per hour, or 254,000 per day.	According to the U.S. Bureau of the Census, 75 of each 100 persons in the world today live in only 22 countries. The other 25 live in any of the remaining 184 countries. Thirty-seven people out of every 100 live in China and India.

Timely updates available from U.S. Bureau of Census, International Programs Center off the World Wide Web at http:// www.census.gov/cgibin/popclockw.

cally developed regions of the world. In fact, by 2050, Europe is projected to shrink from its 1994 population of 498 million to 486 million persons. China had a population of 1.2 billion in 1994 (21% of the world's population), which is projected to peak in 2035 at 1.54 billion and decline thereafter. The populations of Russia and the other independent republics of the former Soviet Union and Soviet Bloc are projected to expand from 289 million in 1994 to 344 million by 2025. Last, the population of the United States is projected to increase from 261.6 million in 1995 to 392 million in 2050.

Not only will Asia be one of the big three areas of population growth in the world for the next 50 years, it is also the current home of the top 10 of the world's 50 largest banks, ranked by assets in 1994 (Wright, 1995). Obviously, development in Asia will continue to unfold dramatically in the years ahead in terms of both human and financial resources and opportunities.

No matter how much one may try to be apart from the world, each one of us is a part of the world. Organizational psychology encompasses some valuable fundamental principles and specific practices that allow different people to work together efficiently (to do things right) and effectively (to do the right things), no matter where in the world they live and work.

The Global Marketplace

Another important feature of the times is the global marketplace—the daily, diversified, and increasingly dense interactions among people throughout the world that are focused on the exchange of goods and services. Although no precise definitions are universally accepted, most discussions of the global economy contain two fundamental components: *developed* (industrial/electronic information-based economies that are capable of generating high income levels) and *developing* (agriculture-based economies with low income levels) continents, regions, or countries (Wright, 1995). The wealthiest nations are located mainly in Western Europe and North America, with only Japan, Australia, and New Zealand representing the Pacific region. These nations are at the center of the global marketplace and are responsible for promoting trade among the peoples of the world, for helping to finance development in poor countries, and for maintaining a stable economic world.

The major economic powers are loosely joined in the so-called Group of Seven, or G-7: Canada, France, Germany, Italy, Japan, the United Kingdom, and the United States. These nations produce about 75% of the world's total output of goods and services. The leaders of the G-7 countries meet once a year to discuss international economic policy. In recent years, the G-7 has focused on mechanisms to eliminate or minimize barriers to the expansion of the global economy, for example, the General Agreement on Tariffs and Trade (GATT), the 1993 agreement among 125 countries (responsible for 85% of the world's trade) to minimize tariffs and quotas in the trade exchanges between its signatories. Also, specific regional alliances have emerged around the globe that are identified as the Asian, American, and European cultural-economic blocks (Humes, 1993). Later sections of this chapter will examine how the theories, data, and applied strategies of organizational psychology are expressed in each of these three cultural-economic blocks.

As people in different countries have more and more contact with each other, issues of similarities and differences among people across national, ethnic, racial, social, and other boundaries move to the forefront. The responses to these issues will have an impact on everyone's daily life in relation to peace or war, jobs or no jobs, open or closed futures, and the nature of families and educational, business, and governmental enterprises. As global citizens, we all must come to grips with ourselves, each other, and the world. There are no isolated places to hide, our actions are reflected on our computer screens or terminals, and we are stressing the carrying capacity of each other and the Earth.

We must think logically and act compassionately to advance each other, our organizations, and the world.

Last, it is becoming increasingly clear that organizations in the global marketplace must create and deliver the best net value to customers, regardless of their geographic location (Stahl & Bounds, 1991). Basically, customers everywhere want three primary things from a product or service: *quality*, *cost*, and *rapid delivery or response time*. People want the best products and services at the lowest possible prices now! A study of the priorities of 200 manufacturing firms indicated that quality and dependable delivery topped the list of these competitive organizations (Miller & Roth, 1988). A major challenge for global organizations and citizens is to give the best of themselves to each other. Organizational psychology can provide a critical knowledge base about how to bring out the best in organizations and organizational members, regardless of where they work and live in the world.

Invisible and Visible Hands

Another significant feature of the world is that unregulated competitive forces in the marketplace and in organizations can lead to dysfunctional conflict and even chaos, while unbridled pervasive cooperative forces can lead to collusion and even oligarchic control. Accordingly, sound and balanced regulatory forces will continue to be necessary for the effective management of markets, organizations, and organizational members. Such regulatory forces arise primarily from governmental actions at the local, state, national, and international levels (such as the North American Free Trade Agreement of 1993 and GATT) and indicate that just as private-sector business firms are players in the global marketplace, so, too, are governmental organizations.

In the global marketplace, there must be two hands at work, one invisible (market forces, Smith, 1776/1937) and the other visible (governmental regulation), for one without the other

will get only half the job done and can create dysfunctional systems and enterprises. Just look at different places in the world where one of these forces is primarily operative at the expense of the other to see that two hands are better than one. In our view, market and regulatory forces are not mutually exclusive, yet for the two to operate effectively requires global organizations in both the private and public sectors. It is increasingly clear that in the global marketplace, open-market economies flourish more readily with democratic governments than with socialist governments, some of which are associated with centrally planned economies (Weitzman, 1993).

We embrace and affirm the centrality of the bottom line of financial performance, reflected by operating at profit levels or maintaining balanced budgets, cost cutting, and enhancing business and public service organizations. We contend that you can only get to the bottom line of financial performance measures with and through people in your organization. Your own experiences probably support the perspective that it is more effective, efficient, and rewarding to get to the bottom line with wholesome competition and cooperation, management of conflict, and recognition of the value of people and stewardship than with a focus only on the accumulation of power and on control over the lives of people.

Organizational psychology provides practical insights on motivation and conflict management that are grounded in sound data for getting people to work efficiently and effectively with each other and in a wide variety of organizations. These insights can be applied in both private for-profit business firms and public sector organizations, including governmental and nonprofit organizations.

DEFINITIONS OF ORGANIZATION

There are hundreds of definitions of the concept of organization in the management, psychological, and sociological literatures, and these definitions are being constantly updated and revised (Galbraith, 1987; Mowday & Sutton, 1993; Offerman & Gowing, 1990; Reed & Hughes, 1992).

Organization

Some representative definitions of *organization* are as follows:

- "social arrangements for the controlled performance of collective goals" (Buchanan & Huczynski, 1985, p. 5)
- "the planned coordination of the activities of a number of people for the achievement of some common, explicit purpose or goal" (Schein, 1988, p. 15)
- "a collection of people and materials brought together to accomplish purposes beyond the means of individuals working alone" (Wagner & Hollenbeck, 1995, p. 47)
- "a group of individuals who work together toward common goals" (Lewis, Goodman, & Fandt, 1995, p. 5).

Common elements that run through these definitions include the fact that organizations involve

individuals banding together to form a group

sustained interpersonal interactions

the belief that the group can achieve what an individual cannot

the pursuit of a common goal or goals

coordination of actions.

The definitions and common elements apply to for-profit (business firms), public (governmental), or nonprofit organizations, regardless of whether the organizations are located in Bangkok, Beijing, Boston, Buenos Aires, Johannesburg, Moscow, or Tel Aviv. If you were to visit an organization in any of these places or

anywhere else around the world, you would most likely find that in almost all instances, organizations

are hierarchical

distribute authority systematically

involve teamwork

make decisions, exhibit conflict, have an organizational culture, socialize members, have a increasingly diverse workforce, motivate members, and solve problems

are influenced by economic, political, and legal forces.

Although these features of an organization are constantly changing—for example, organizations move from less hierarchical (fewer managerial layers) to flatter hierarchies (empowered teams)—they are usually present, to various degrees, in all organizations. In short, over time, features of an organization do not change as much as does the expression of any given organizational feature.

Our definition of *organization* is a group of two or more persons who believe they can achieve some goal or goals together that no member can achieve alone or as well. The goal can be anything from meeting basic human needs, such as food, shelter, and safety, to the production or delivery of sophisticated and complex products or services. In all instances, people in an organization must communicate, decide, act, resolve conflict, and learn together if there is to be an organizational advantage relative to the individual who works alone.

The Global Organization

We define *global organization* as one, regardless of size, resources, and geographic location, that aspires to or has sustained access to the global marketplace and is or will be influenced by it over time. The *global marketplace* is a person or group of persons anywhere in the world who are willing and capable of purchasing a product or service, regardless of the place of origin of the product or service, provided it meets customers' or clients' specifications of the highest quality at the lowest possible price delivered as quickly as possible. Just as the wall dividing Berlin was dismantled in 1989, the global marketplace is not defined primarily by fixed structural features, such as geographic location or homogeneous workforces or customers. Rather, it is defined by functional features like preparing a high-quality product or service, delivering it in a timely and price-sensitive way, and following through with any extended needs of customers or clients that are associated with the product or service. What counts is what you do, rather than where you do it, and it is important to bear in mind that this guideline applies or will apply to all organizations sooner or later. If you need an immediate image of the global marketplace, look at the diversity of your colleagues at work, as well as of your customers and clients.

APPROACHES TO ORGANIZATIONS

All around the world, there are various types of organizations, from transnational organizations spanning many continents to microbusinesses located in remote villages, with people, who are the sine qua non of any organization. Thus, a sound set of foundational principles of how organizations and people work, interact, and grow professionally and personally in organizations and applied strategies to achieve efficiencies are essential for working in the global marketplace.

The origins of organizational psychology, or management psychology, as some Chinese colleagues call it, can be traced back more than 3,000 years to the Chinese, who developed written, oral, and martial arts tests for Confucian or public service personnel that were used until 1905 (DuBois, 1965, 1970; Wang, 1993). According to Katzell and Austin (1992), organizational psychology in the United States is ex-

tremely diverse; must promote a global perspective; needs to integrate the science and practice of organizational psychology; and must serve the needs of managers, as well as of employees and the larger surrounding communities in which organizations are nested.

Types of Professionals

There are many scholarly and professional approaches to the systematic study of organizations, most of which look at organizational activities expressed at the individual (micro), group (meso), or organizational system (macro) level. Thus, for example, organizational psychologists may be interested in studying and managing an individual's motivation and empowerment (a microlevel focus), enhancing group or team performances (a mesolevel focus), or examining organization-wide features like organizational culture or organizational learning (a macrolevel focus). Most professionals who study and work with organizations are interested in enhancing organizational performance by adopting a management perspective, which focuses on the efficiency of groups and organizational systems, or a human relations perspective, which stresses the well-being and development of individuals, or most likely by embracing both organizational and individual issues.

Management is a process of administering and coordinating resources effectively and efficiently to achieve organizational goals (Lewis et al., 1995). *Effectiveness* involves the organizational pursuit of appropriate goals (doing the right things), while *efficiency* is the use of minimum input to yield maximum output (doing things right). Inasmuch as all organizations have people, it is imperative to have a solid understanding of human nature and actions, especially in organizational settings. To obtain such knowledge about people and organizations, the executive, manager, union leader, or any member of an organization can turn to a variety of types of professions that come under the heading human resources, industrial-organizational psychology, organizational behavior, or organizational psychology.

In general, human resource professionals focus on practical and effective ways to manage employees' behaviors. Many organizations have a vice president for human resources, a human resources manager, a small human resources unit, or at least a person who deals with such issues as staffing (recruitment, hiring, and retention), training, performance appraisal, and compensation programs for employees (Ferris, Rosen, & Barnum, 1995).

In general, *industrial-organizational psychology* is defined by two interrelated strands. Industrial psychology, the older strand, tends to take the management perspective of seeking strategies to promote organizational efficiency and encompasses topics like the design of jobs and the selection, training, and performance appraisal of employees. Organizational psychology, the newer strand, grew out of the human relations movement in organizations and adopts the perspective of enhancing employees' well-being in the workplace. In addition to topics such as the design of jobs and appraisal of employees' performance, it focuses on group and contextual influences on individuals and organizational processes like leadership, decision making, motivation, and individual and organizational change. Many industrial-organizational psychologists tend to identify themselves primarily as organizational, rather than industrial-organizational, psychologists, given the many references to the present as the postindustrial or information era.

Organizational behavior is a field of study that seeks to understand, explain, predict, and change human behavior in the organizational context. In general, it emphasizes observable behaviors at the individual, group, and organizational systems levels. The basic notion is that behavioral change is critical to individual and organizational change and that cognitive and affective changes in members will follow behavioral changes. In general, organizational behavior draws on concepts and ideas from many disciplines, including political science, sociology, and psychology, whereas organizational psychology draws primarily on psychology. However, the types of topics, concepts, and interventions embraced by organizational psychology are broadening, so the fields of organizational behavior and organizational psychology are becoming fused.

Organizational Psychology

We define *organizational psychology* as the systematic study of dispositional (trait) and situational (contextual) variables that influence the actions or behaviors and experiences (thoughts and feelings) of the individual, as well as the group aggregation of such behaviors and experiences. Examples of dispositional or trait variables are gender, age, and race, and examples of situational variables include a reward system, management style, or organizational culture, any of which—alone or in combination—influences both individual and aggregated group-level actions, thoughts, and feelings.

We view *organizational psychology* as the development of theories of organizationally based human actions and experiences, the search for quantitative and qualitative data about organizational activities, and systematic applications of strategies to enhance organizational and individual productivity and well-being. Whether one is interested in understanding and working with organizations in the American, Asian, or European cultural-economic blocks, such endeavors will be of most value when they are grounded in theory, data, and applications from organizational psychology, rather than in only one of these facets. Theory and data without applications promote pedantry, while applications without a grounding in theory and data prompt the endless adoption of the newest techniques or fads in an attempt to understand organizations and the people within them.

It is crucial to understand how to work and live more fully and effectively, especially since work responsibilities continue to consume larger and larger chunks of people's lives. Our focus in organizational psychology is on the global organization, whether it is a two-person operation in the remotest village in the world or a mammoth transnational organization composed of thousands of persons. Although these two examples are different, as organizations they share the fundamental properties of people working together and deciding on organizational alternatives and are connected to each other because they are both parts of the same world. As the 21st century approaches, the geographic location of the workplace is assuming less and less importance in contrast to one's access to the global marketplace. The global marketplace requires that all members of the workforce must integrate local cultural norms and practices with the demands and norms of global organizations to deliver high-quality products and services in a timely fashion anywhere in the world. The balancing of local cultural identity with the pressing demands of the global marketplace, held together by the demands of faceless customers for the highest-quality products or services at the lowest possible prices delivered quickly, is one of the most important defining features of the world.

Work Sites and Salaries

Figure 1–1 presents the work sites of organizational psychologists, based on the results of a survey from Division 14 of the Society for Industrial and Organizational Psychology (SIOP) of the American Psychological Association (APA) (Howard, 1990). As you can see, most organizational psychologists are employed in universities, management consulting firms, and private organizations. A solid grounding in the theory, data, and systematic applied strategies of organizational psychology can prepare them well to work in a wide variety of sites.

For a wide variety of specializations in psychology, the Research Office of the APA found that of the 2,029 respondents (a 57% return rate) who had just earned doctoral degrees in 1993, the highest 11–12 month (annual) median starting salary was earned by applied psychologists ($49,000), especially those who were working in businesses or private organizations ($52,000) (Kohout, 1995). Those entering clinical psychology reported a median annual starting salary of $40,000. In contrast, for those who took faculty positions in universities or colleges, the median 9–10 month (academic) salary was $34,000.

For organizational psychologists, Zickar and Taylor (1996) reported salary data for 1,486 respondents (a 58.3% return rate) of members of Division 14 of SIOP. They noted that in 1994, the median annual income for respondents who had doctoral degrees for at least five years was $71,000, that 25% of the respondents earned more than $100,000, and that 10% earned more than $150,000. The median income for respondents with master's degrees was $59,500. The

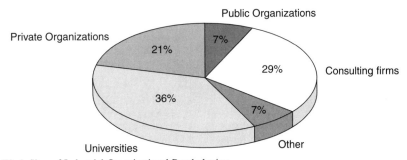

Figure 1–1 Work Sites of Industrial-Organizational Psychologists.
Adapted from A. Howard (1990). *The Multiple Facets of Industrial Organizational Psychology.* Arlington Heights, IL: Society of Industrial and Organizational Psychology. p. 9.

median annual income of men was considerably higher than that of women in 1994 ($75,000 versus $58,500) partly because significantly fewer women had doctoral degrees and men had much more experience (an average of 16.9 years versus 10.6 years). In short, salaries for organizational psychologists are clearly competitive with those of other psychologists and reflect substantial gender disparities that remain to be addressed in this profession as well as others.

Organizational Skills

To be an effective member of a global organization, one must be a continuous learner and possess some fundamental skills to address the many current organizational challenges, as well as those that lie ahead. Table 1–2 presents a list of critical skills or competencies that most organizational psychologists would agree are needed for effective participation in organizations. In addition, individuals will need to bring to their organization personal qualities or traits, such as conscientiousness (hard work and personal discipline), openness to experience, extroversion (the capacity to be sociable as well as ambitious), agreeableness (a sense of cooperation), and emotional stability (Mount, Barrick, & Strauss, 1994).

TABLE 1–2. Organizational Skills for Effective Participation in the Workforce

---

Interpersonal skills: Working in teams, teaching and learning from others, serving customers, communicating, leading, negotiating, and working well with people from culturally diverse backgrounds.

Informational and conceptual skills: Acquiring and evaluating data, organizing and managing data sets or files, interpreting data and communicating information, and using a vast array of electronic instruments to access and use effectively the increasing electronic infrastructure and data warehouses being developed daily around the world.

Technological and system skills: Applying technological tools to specific tasks and understanding social, organizational, and technical systems for enhancing individual and organizational performances.

Clearly, a sound knowledge of the theories, (for instance, models of motivation), specific data sets (such as the effects of goal setting on productivity), and applied strategies (like techniques for setting individual and team goals) of organizational psychology can enhance substantially the levels of critical skills needed to function effectively in organizations. For example, the following brief list of some of the key questions addressed by organizational psychology clearly indicates the centrality of organizational psychology for the development and refinement of these skills:

- What are the best ways to motivate people—intrinsic (satisfaction and flow experiences), extrinsic (money and other benefits), or a mix of these reward systems?

- What specific strategies exist for enhancing the creativity and productivity of diverse work teams?

- Can there be a similar organizational culture that is shared by local organizational units dispersed around the globe and is staffed by persons from different national or regional cultures?

- What is the best way to make effective and efficient decisions, resolve conflicts, and lead an increasingly diversified workforce?

- What is the most effective use of electronic instruments and systems in actual as well as virtual offices and organizations?

- What are the most effective strategies or systems for enhancing the well-being, productivity, and organizational citizenship of organizational members?

ORGANIZATIONAL PSYCHOLOGY: A FRAMEWORK

Our framework for understanding the actions and experiences of organizational members consists of three basic components: *people, processes,* and *adaptation*. Figure 1–2 presents the major components and the facets of each component and indicates the mutual relationship among the three components. The nine organizational issues that all organizations face each day—organizational culture, workforce diversity, group dynamics, motivation, leadership, decision making, conflict resolution, individual change, and organizational change—are subsumed under the three components.

People, Processes, and Adaptation

Inasmuch as people are at the heart of any organization, we treat first two forces that have a profound impact on an organization and its members and the organization: organizational culture and workforce diversity. Organizational culture is a macrolevel variable that affects all members of an organization (see Chapter 3). Likewise, workforce diversity (see Chapter 4) is an ex-

tremely important influence on organizations around the globe, and its importance will increase in the 21st century, as indicated by the data on the global population presented earlier in this chapter. An organizational culture that promotes competencies, learning, hard and smart work, and an openness to ideas and people will have a substantial competitive advantage, especially when it has the wisdom and skills to harness the benefits of workforce diversity.

Most organizations anywhere in the world undergo fundamental organizational processes that are key to the development of individuals and the organizations as a whole. Since work in organizational settings usually involves groups and teams, rather than individuals working alone, organizational processes, such as decision making, leadership, and conflict resolution, are primarily social processes. Accordingly, in Chapter 5, we examine the forces governing the formation, maintenance, and performance of ef-

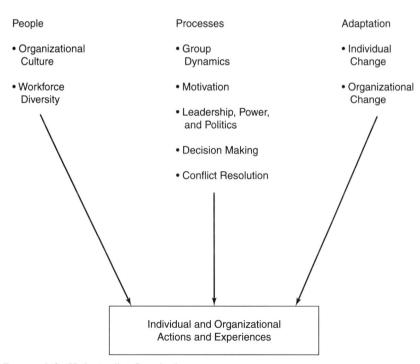

Figure 1–2   Framework for Understanding Organizations.

fective groups and teams. In Chapter 6, we discuss individual- and group-based theories of human and organizational motivation and the fundamental change in the primary source of motivational forces from the individual to groups, reflected by the importance of service to customers or clients.

Chapter 7, on leadership, power, and politics, focuses on various theories and applied strategies for leading diversely populated organizations and for clarifying the importance of emotional forces that shape leadership and the dynamics of power in organizations. Decision making is another fundamental organizational process that has been researched extensively; in Chapter 8, we examine the major findings of decision-making studies, as well as electronically based decision making and creativity. Inasmuch as conflict is inevitable in every organization, we examine various applied strategies to manage conflict at the individual and group levels in Chapter 9.

The third major component of our framework is adaptation, which we examine at the levels of individual (Chapter 10) and organizational (Chapter 11) change. Our treatment of individual change focuses on work-life issues, such as the changing nature of work, family responsibilities, mentoring, the 24-hour work day, the contingent workforce (temporary employees), and substances in the workplace, and examines organizational-level change across the Asian, American, and European cultural-economic blocks.

Cultural-Economic Blocks

As others have suggested (Fowler, 1996; Humes 1993; Katzell & Austin, 1992), we believe that psychology in general and organizational psychology in particular must embrace and evolve a global perspective by studying organizations and organizational activities from the world. Accordingly, we examine organizational issues that are associated with the American, Asian, and

European cultural-economic blocks, given the importance of these three blocks in the global economy (Humes, 1993). Much of the material we examine is derived primarily from American and European organizations and, to a lesser extent, Asian organizations. However, since we discuss the global organization, which is characterized by universal structures and processes that are expressed in terms of the regional or local cultural contexts in which such organizations operate, we also include organizational information from other parts of the world.

Economically, the American cultural-economic block includes Canada, Mexico, and the United States. In general, U.S. management focuses on organizational structure, as reflected in concerns about levels of managerial control and the systematic distribution of formal authority or reporting lines in an organization. It also strongly emphasizes quantitative data, the importance of rationality for decision making, and the pursuit of quantitative outcome measures of performance at all levels of the organization. American managers have been mesmerized by new managerial techniques and facts because of their belief that management involves fundamental concepts that apply anywhere in the world. Another fundamental feature of U.S. management is the specialist or expert, reflected in MBA programs that include specialist concentrations like finance, marketing, and human resources (European graduate programs do not) (Humes, 1993). In short, American management strategies stress clearly defined organizational structures and job descriptions, quantifiable standards, and clear prescriptive manuals for individual and organizational actions, in contrast with European and Asian approaches to management.

The European cultural-economic block includes the Continental countries of Western Europe (Belgium, France, Germany, Italy, Spain, and the Scandinavian countries), the United Kingdom (England, Northern Ireland, Scotland, and Wales), the emerging countries of Eastern

Europe (Hungary, Poland, the Baltics, Russia, and newly independent states like Byelorussia). The major forces of economic integration across these diverse national cultures and a more fluid, open European economy, coupled with the emergence of open market economies in countries that formerly had centrally planned economies, are dramatically influencing organizations in this block. Typically, the Western European management style emphasizes rationality, accommodation to differences, and less clearly defined and articulated management manuals and styles. In general, the British style of management focuses on common sense, pragmatism, and adaptability and is often perceived by others as non-European in outlook (Humes, 1993). On the European continent, French management stresses logic, rationality, and class; German management emphasizes order, discipline, and efficiency; and Italian management values charisma, spontaneity, and flair (Barsoux & Lawrence, 1990; Humes, 1993). More so than Americans and Asians, Europeans have tolerated and appreciated greater variety in their lives and organizations.

The Asian cultural-economic block includes Japan, People's Republic of China (or mainland China); India; the Four Little Dragons (Hong Kong, Singapore, South Korea, and Taiwan); Thailand; emerging South Asian countries, such as Vietnam and Cambodia; and Australia and New Zealand, with the arc of the Pacific Rim countries completed by the western coasts of Canada and the United States. In general, the major Japanese firms that dominate the global marketplace have evolved from the *zaibatsu*, or pre–World War II megacompanies, including many that were owned by wealthy and powerful clans built around vertical ladders of obligation (Wagner & Hollenbeck, 1995). After World War II, the zaibatsu were reconfigured into six industrial conglomerates (Dai-Ichi Kangyo, Fuyo, Mitsui, Mitsubishi, Sanwa, and Sunitomo) that are now centered on Japanese banks, rather than feudal clans. Independent

firms, such as Nissan, Sony, and Toyota, were also founded. Japanese management style stresses hierarchy, seniority, loyalty, and continuous learning. Chinese firms also stress hierarchy and loyalty, and many practice as much as possible the iron rice bowl philosophy of employment for life that, of course, is more and more difficult, if not impossible, to maintain in China or anywhere in the world owing to significant and frequent changes in the global economy. In Asia, as elsewhere, there is growing interest in the development of at least some universal management practices for the global organization, focuses on accountability, employee empowerment and responsibilities, an openness to new ideas, and a more heterogenous workforce in terms of gender, racial, and ethnic-cultural differences (Humes, 1993). There is, of course, a wide diversity of organizations within each of the three cultural-economic blocks, and the similarities among the blocks are often more striking than are those among the countries within a block.

Foundations to Applications

We conclude this chapter by pointing out that we will emphasize, when possible, theory, empirically derived data, and application strategies that emerge from organizational psychology. In many instances, we find students in psychology and sociology with a solid grounding in data and theory, respectively, yet with little exposure to applied strategies and business students who are well versed in applied strategies but are less well grounded in the theory and data sets of organizational psychology. As the social psychologist and student of organizations Kurt Lewin said, "There is nothing more practical than a good theory," to which we would add: especially when theory and practice are connected by data. Persons who are interested in or working in organizations need to be grounded in organizational theory, data, and applications, regardless of whether they are students of business, psychology, sociology, or whatever and regardless of what type of organization (public, private, or nonprofit) is of concern to them.

SUMMARY

Always remember the fundamentals: People live and work in different places, are both different and similar in many ways, are always changing, and share the same Earth. Through a recognition and appreciation of diversity, you can also find similarities, since almost all people live and work in organizations that are always made up of people. Accordingly, to be an effective participant in the global economy, it is important to have an understanding of organizations and the people who work in them, no matter where the organizations are located.

Basically, organizations are social enterprises of people coming together to achieve some shared goals that they believe they can achieve more effectively and efficiently together than alone. All organizations are global organizations to the extent that they participate or aspire to participate in the global economy in which customers and clients anywhere are served anytime, quickly, cheaply, and with the highest-quality goods and services.

Organizational psychology focuses on understanding people especially in their workplaces. In our treatment of organizational psychology, we stress the importance of a sound knowledge of theory, data, and applied strategies to work effectively with and in organizations. Also, our framework for understanding organizations is grounded in the belief that there are both important similarities and differences in organizations located in the American, Asian, or European cultural-economic blocks, as well as in other parts of the world. In particular, we will examine similarities and differences in organizational culture and workforce diversity and the fundamental organizational processes of group dynamics, motiva-

tion, leadership, power, politics, decision making, and conflict resolution. Last, we will explore the relationships between change in individual members and organizations, both of which seek value-added enhancements, rather than a primary focus on the accumulation of individual power and organizational dominance, respectively.

We aspire to understand more fully ourselves, others, and organizations. We invite you to join us in this pursuit and hope this book will be of value to you in your personal and organizational journeys.

CHAPTER REFERENCES

Barsoux, J. L., & Laurence, P. (1990). *Management in France*. London: Cassell.

Boyacigiller, N. A., & Adler, N. J. (1991). The parochial dinosaur: Organizational science in a global context. *Academy of Management Review, 16,* 262–290.

Buchanan, D., & Huczynski, A. (1985). *Organizational behavior*. London: Prentice Hall International.

DuBois, P. H. (1965). A test-dominated society: China, 1115 B.C.–1905 A.D. In *Proceedings of the 1964 invitational conference on testing problems* (pp. 3–11). Princeton, NJ: Educational Testing Service.

DuBois, P. H. (1970). *A history of psychological testing*. Boston: Allyn & Bacon.

Ferris, G. R., Rosen, S. D., & Barnum, D. T. (Eds.). (1995). *Handbook of human resource management*. Cambridge, MA: Blackwell.

Fowler, R. D. (1996). 1996 editorial: 50th anniversary issue of the American Psychologist. *American Psychologist, 51,* 5–7.

Galbraith, J. R. (1987). Organization design. In J. W. Lorsch (Ed.), *Handbook of organizational behavior*. Englewood Cliffs, NJ: Prentice Hall.

Howard, A. (1990). *The multiple facets of industrial organizational psychology*. Arlington Heights, IL: Society for Industrial and Organizational Psychology.

Humes, S. (1993). *Managing the multinational: Confronting the global-local dilemma.* Englewood Cliffs, NJ: Prentice Hall.

Katzell, R. A., & Austin, J. T. (1992). From then to now: The development of industrial-organizational psychology in the United States. *Journal of Applied Psychology, 77,* 803–835.

Kohout, J. (1995). *Doctorate employment survey 1993: Highlights.* Washington, DC: American Psychological Association.

Lewis, P. S., Goodman, S. H., & Fandt, P. M. (1995). *Management: Challenges in the 21st century.* Minneapolis: West.

Miller, J. G., & Roth, A. V. (1988). *Manufacturing strategies: Executive summary of the 1988 North American manufacturing futures survey* (research report). Boston: Boston University School of Management.

Mount, M. K., Barrick, M. R., & Strauss, J. P. (1994). Validity of observer ratings of the big five personality factors. *Journal of Applied Psychology, 79,* 272–280.

Mowday, R. T., & Sutton, R. I. (1993). Organizational behavior: Linking individuals and groups to organizational contexts. *Annual Reviews of Psychology, 44,* 195–229.

Naisbitt, J. (1994). *The global paradox.* New York: William Morrow.

Naisbitt, J., & Aburdene, P. (1990). *Megatrends 2,000.* New York: William Morrow.

Offermann, L. R., & Gowing, M. K. (1990). Organizations of the future. *American Psychologist, 45,* 95–108.

Reed, M., & Hughes, M. (Eds.). (1992). *Rethinking organization.* London: Sage.

Schein, E. (1988). *Organizational psychology* (3rd ed.). Englewood Cliffs, NJ: Prentice Hall.

Smith, A. (1937). *An inquiry into the nature and causes of the wealth of nations.* New York: Modern Library. (Original published 1776)

Stahl, M. J., & Bounds, G. M. (1991). *Competing globally through customer value: The management of strategic suprasystems.* Westport, CT: Quorum Books.

Wagner, John A. III, & Hollenbeck, J. R. (1995). *Management of organizational behavior.* Englewood Cliffs, NJ: Prentice Hall.

Wang, Z. M. (1993). Psychology in China: A review dedicated to Li Chen. *Annual Review of Psychology, 44,* 87–116.

Weitzman, M. L. (1993). Capitalism and democracy: A summing up of the arguments. In S. Bowles, H. Gintis, & B. Gustafison (Eds.), *Markets and democracy: Participation, accountability, and efficiency* (pp. 306–315). Cambridge, England: Cambridge University Press.

Wright, J. W. (1995). *The universal almanac: 1996.* Kansas City, MO: Andrews & McMeil.

Zickar, M., & Taylor, R. (1996). Income of SIOP members in 1994. *The Industrial Organizational Psychologist: TIP, 33,* 63–70.

SUGGESTED REFERENCES

After most chapters, we suggest some key books, specific journal articles, or other materials that we believe will assist you in understanding more fully some of the theories, data, and applied strategies of organizational psychology.

The major journals or periodicals presented next provide a thorough treatment of the wide variety of issues addressed in organizational psychology. It should be noted that the list is suggestive rather than exhaustive.

Academy of Management Journal
Academy of Management Review
Administrative Science Quarterly
American Journal of Sociology
American Political Science Review
American Review of Public Administration
American Sociological Review
Annual Review of Psychology
California Management Review
Columbia Journal of World Business
Harvard Business Review
International Review of Industrial and Organizational Psychology
Journal of Applied Behavioral Science
Journal of Applied Psychology
Journal of Economic Behavior and Organization
Journal of International Business Studies
Journal of Personality and Social Psychology
Management Science
Managing

Organizational Behavior and Human Decision Processes (1985 on)
Organizational Behavior and Human Performance (1966–84)
Organizational Dynamics
Organization Science
Psychological Bulletin
Psychological Review
Public Administration Review
Sloan Management Review
Strategic Management Journal

Books

Bray, D. W., & Associates (1991). *Working with organizations and their people.* New York: Guilford Press.

Collins, E. G. C., & Devanna, M. A. (1992). *The portable MBA.* New York: John Wiley & Sons.

Dunnette, M. D., & Hough, L. M. (Eds.). (1993). *Handbook of industrial and organizational psychology* (2nd ed., Vol. 4). Palo Alto, CA: Consulting Psychologists Press.

Ferris, G. R., Rosen, S. D., & Barnum, D. T. (Eds.). (1995). *Handbook of human resource management.* Cambridge, MA: Blackwell.

Gitlow, H. S., & Gitlow, S. J. (1987). *The Deming guide to quality and competitive position.* Englewood Cliffs, NJ: Prentice Hall.

Kets de Vries, M., & Miller, D. (1984). *The neurotic organization: Diagnosing and changing counterproductive styles of management.* San Francisco: Jossey-Bass.

Lorsch, J. (1987). *Handbook of organizational behavior.* Englewood Cliffs, NJ: Prentice Hall.

Journal Articles

Goldstein, I. L., & Gilliam, P. (1990). Training system issues in the year 2,000. *American Psychologist, 45,* 134–143.

Kerr, S. (1975). On the folly of rewarding A, while hoping for B. *Academy of Management Journal, 18,* 769–783.

2

Nature of Organizations and Methods of Study

CHAPTER OVERVIEW

In this chapter we explore the features of human nature and the nature of organizations, the methods of collecting organizational data, and the kinds of data collected about organizations and present a brief protocol or process that will help you get a sense of an organization. We focus on tools and tool sets for studying individual and aggregated or organizational actions and experiences, so you can get from one place of understanding and managerial efficacy to another place of deeper appreciation of people and organizations.

Since organizations around the globe are made up of people, knowledge of interpersonal and social processes is essential for understanding and managing organizations. We identify five fundamental features that influence and shape human nature and organizations. Some of these features include the influence of dispositional (trait) and situational (context) variables on the actions and experiences of individuals and organizations, individual and organizational learning, and the role of rationality and emotionality in organizations. To help you understand more fully organizations and people who work in them, we examine the types of organizational data that can be collected and the levels of analysis of the organizational data (micro- or macro databases) and identify key independent and dependent variables in organizational psychology. Thereafter, we discuss four fundamental methods for studying organizations and then descriptive and inferential statistics as tools that allow you to present a richer description of individuals at work and the nature of organizations. We then examine an inquiry process or protocol that focuses on organizational architecture, demography, geometry and politics, and networks to help you get a feel or sense of an organization that can be refined into a more detailed profile of an organization employing one or more of the basic methods of study presented in this chapter.

LEARNING OBJECTIVES

When you finish studying this chapter, you will be prepared to

- identify five fundamental features of human nature and the nature of organizations that are related to enhanced competitive advantage
- identify important dispositional and contextual variables that influence the actions and experiences of individual members and organizations, such as the personality trait of conscientiousness and job autonomy, respectively
- define and distinguish between individual learning and organizational learning and describe how each relates to organizational culture
- identify and distinguish between robust independent and frequently studied dependent variables in organizational psychology
- identify four frequently used methods of study in organizational psychology and explain the advantages and limitations of each

- define measurement and distinguish between descriptive statistics (shrinking data chunks into meaningful wholes) and inferential statistics (reaching beyond limited observations to larger groupings or populations)
- define four key domains of organizational data sets—organizational architecture, demography, geometry and politics, and networks—to get a feel for any organization
- configure specific tool sets—levels of data, types of variables, and methods of study—to describe, measure, and interpret data derived from observations of individuals, groups, and organizations.

To get somewhere, you need to start from somewhere.

THE NATURE OF US AND OUR ORGANIZATIONS: FIVE FUNDAMENTALS

As you well know from your own experiences, it is important for a new member of an organization to learn quickly and accurately about the people in the organization and to figure out how the new organization actually works. As you move into an organization as a new employee or an organizational psychologist, it is helpful to be grounded in the basic forces that influence people and organizations in most places in the world. Learning how to work and live in a new organization is perhaps similar, although less poignant, than learning to live as a bicultural or culturally competent individual at the juncture of two cultures as the result of being raised in one culture and now living or working in another (La Fromboise, Coleman, & Gerton, 1993). An organizationally competent person works effectively and efficiently in a given organization and needs to know about the values and beliefs of the organization, exhibit sensitivity to the affective (emotional) side of the organization, and perform organizationally sanctioned behaviors. In addition, he or she negotiates the architectural or structural, demographic, political, and communication networks of the organization. Such a person also needs to

know the extent to which the actions, values, and emotions of individuals in the organization arise from universal and contextual or cultural forces, especially as the workforce becomes increasingly diversified around the world. What forces define all of us as persons, what do we have in common, and what forces define us as uniquely different individuals or groups? (Mesquita & Frijda, 1992).

Pfeffer (1994) suggested that the traditional sources of competitive advantage for an organization have been eroded with the construction of the global marketplace. For example, the advantages of product and process technology, captured by patents and copyrights, respectively, are less enduring, given the pace of technological change. Likewise, once protected and regulated markets are opened to competition, they are difficult to close or regulate again. As these and other sources of competitive advantage (including the movement from large to fragmented market shares) undermine the advantages of economies of scale, the centrality of competent, committed, and flexible organizational members emerges as the engine for competitive economic advantage. Accordingly, it is essential to have a facile knowledge of the nature of persons and organizations to promote the economic viability and the effective and healthy functioning of organizations and their members.

To help you develop a coherent understanding of people and organizations, we first address some fundamental features of human nature (the essence of being human) and organizations (the essence of being a group). We identify five forces that shape and determine individual and organizational actions and experiences: *dispositional and situational forces, variation, problems, learning*, and *rationality-emotionality* (see Table 2–1). Our assessment of each agent influences our notions of the causes of specific individual and organizational actions and experiences and the applied strategies one may choose to deal with these actions and experiences. Ours is, of course, a selective and focused list of causal agents, so you may wish to modify it as you see fit.

Dispositional and Situational Forces

If you assumed that people around the world are fundamentally the same and that their behaviors are influenced primarily by such traits as age or personality, you would manage people by focusing on these common traits. Such a state of affairs would allow you to proceed as if all people have similar personalities and what holds for one employee also applies to all employees, regardless of their racial, ethnic, or cultural group. In short, you would focus only on people's immutable demographic traits (like age, gender, and personality) or mutable personal traits (learned skills or behaviors), or *dispositional variables*, as the primary determinants of per-

TABLE 2–1. Five Fundamental Features of Human Nature and Organizations

---

- Individual and organizational actions and experiences arise from dispositional and situational forces.

- Variation is a part of each person and all organizations.

- All people and organizations have problems.

- All people and organizations have the capacity to learn.

- All people and organizations behave rationally and emotionally, and both types of behavior are essential for effective functioning.

---

formance in the workplace (Levin & Stokes, 1989). The notions that younger employees are more open to change and learning new skills than are older employees, that women manage better than do men, or that less educated workers are not as good an employment bet as are more educated workers are examples of a dispositional approach to understanding and managing people. Thus, if you wanted to change some organizational process, you would apply strategies that focus on replacing an employee with another who has the target dispositional trait or educating or forcing the incumbent to change the target mutable personal trait (for example, to obtain more education).

Organizational psychologists who have extensively studied the influence of the dispositional variable of personality on job performance have found that personality is the relatively stable pattern of individual traits or characteristics that an individual brings to a variety of situations (Barrick & Mount, 1991, 1993; Basic Behavioral Science Task Force, Health Council, 1996; Goldberg, 1993). That is, these personality traits do not change even though situations may change dramatically. In fact, five personality traits—*the big five*—appear to be all that is needed to explain most variations in personality among individuals (see Table 2–2). There is a growing store of incontrovertible evidence that conscientiousness, coupled with extroversion, especially for work with a large social component, is an excellent predictor of success in a job. Mount, Barrick, and Strauss (1994) found that personality, as assessed by the target person who completes a personality inventory (such as the Gordon Personality Inventory) and then by others (like a supervisor, co-worker, and customer) who complete the same inventory on the basis of their knowledge of the person were both valid methods of predicting job performance, specifically sales work. Furthermore, they found that the personality traits of conscientiousness and extroversion were excellent predictors of job performances based on these assessments.

TABLE 2–2. The Big Five Personality Factors

Conscientiousness—responsible, dependable, persistent, organized, achievement oriented
Extroversion—sociable, assertive, ambitious, and active
Agreeableness—good-natured, cooperative, and trusting
Emotional Stability—calm, secure, at ease
Openness to Experience—imaginative, sensitive

M. K. Mount, M. R. Barrick, & J. P. Strauss, "Validity of observer ratings of the big five personality factors," *Journal of Applied Psychology, 79*, p. 272. Copyright © 1994 by the American Psychological Association, Washington, DC. Adapted with permission.

People usually provide accurate descriptions of their capabilities, actions, and experiences at work. Most organizations use the common selection practices of employment interviews and checking references for potential new hires (assessment by others). When these data are coupled with self-assessments by the candidates that focus on the dispositional variables of conscientiousness and extroversion, their predictive validity for job performance is high (McDaniel, Whetzel, Schmidt, & Maurer, 1994; Mount et al., 1994). Thus, 360-degree performance appraisal systems that include assessments by self, supervisor, peers, and clients yield more accurate predictions of successful performance than do any one assessment alone. Also, as organizations rely more and more on self-directed teams, interpersonal skills become increasingly important and the dispositional variable of extroversion assumes greater importance, along with conscientiousness, as a valid predictor of job performance.

Of course, everyone knows from experience that people differ widely, more so within groups than among large groups, regardless of the dimension (such as age, gender, or race) that defines any particular group. Accordingly, variation among people suggests that situational or contextual variables can generate or contribute substantially to the behavioral and experiential differences (beliefs and values) among people from different groups. Thus, the beliefs that any person, regardless of age, is open to change, provided there is an environment or context that

promotes change; that women and men are equally good managers, depending on whom they have to manage; and that with appropriate training and educational programs, any person will be a good employment bet are examples of a primarily situational approach to understanding and managing people. Either the dispositional or the situational perspective, like almost everything in life, can become distorted and dysfunctional if it is carried to the extreme. In fact, in managing people in the workplace, one must manage as if people are the same, as well *as if* they are different, for they are both. It is this inherent paradox that is a fundamental feature of human nature.

It is not easy to manage and lead effectively in any organization. Effective management requires one to think logically, act compassionately, and appreciate that dispositional and situational variables alone or in combination influence significantly the behaviors and experiences of organizational members. For example, it has been suggested that the extent to which personality or trait variables drive behavior differs, depending on the degree to which the context, situation, or environment inhibits freedom to act in idiosyncratic ways. Strong situations are those in which there are considerable demands or pressures to yield to conformity, whereas weak situations are those in which there are relatively few demands to conform (Mischel, 1977). Accordingly, in weak situations, differences in personality are more likely to be expressed and to influence the specific behavior that people adopt. In organizations, jobs vary in the amount of autonomy employees have or the extent to which employees can select appropriate work behaviors, decide on the order and pace of tasks, and so forth; thus, autonomy constitutes a potentially powerful situational variable. Barrick and Mount (1993) reported that the personality or dispositional variables of conscientiousness and extroversion were highly predictive of supervisors' rating of the job performance of managers in jobs that were high in autonomy. Hence, the degree of autonomy in a job (situational variable) moderates the predictive validity of conscientiousness and extroversion (dispositional variables). In short, almost all behaviors are determined by both situational and dispositional variables, although some researchers believe that situational variables are more influential than dispositional variables (Davis-Blake & Pfeffer, 1989; Newton & Keenan, 1991).

Let us now consider some of the complications of examining an organization relative to the concepts of dispositional and situational variables. You pick the organization, one of which you are now a member or aspire to become a member, to make the concepts come alive for you. Suppose you were interested in values (defined here as preferences) in the organization that can be expressed as weak (cold-button) or strong (hot-button) values. And suppose you believed (as do many, including the authors) that there are universal or consensual human values that all members bring to an organization—a dispositional approach to understanding the functioning of individuals and organizations. Table 2–3 lists some of the universal human values about which there is a fair amount of agreement, including truth telling (honesty), promise keeping (integrity), fair play (equity), and mutual respect.

Thus, in the conduct of human and organizational affairs, you would conclude that people value or prefer to be treated and to treat other members of the organization, as well as customers and clients, according to these values. Inasmuch as you would believe that these values are dispositional variables that are expressed in all cultures or societies around the world, you would expect to find them enacted in any organization and by all members of the organization. Yet this is not always the case, which suggests that in some fashion, the organizational context, culture, or environment somehow moderates or influences the behavioral expression of these values (Davis-Blake & Pfeffer, 1989; Newton & Keenan, 1991). In other words, contextual or situational variables are operating, so one would need to search for the organizational processes that may be moderating these fundamental values. Perhaps the organization is grossly under-staffed, is under extreme financial pressures, or is experiencing turbulent changes as a result of its falling market share, or there is high turnover of leaders and employees. Such a state of affairs indicates that fundamental human values can be moderated to fit a situation or that such values are not expressed in behaviors reflecting denial and conflict, which cumulatively can have dysfunctional effects on the members and the organization.

In summary, if you adopt a dispositional perspective of individual and organizational actions and experiences, you find people with all the "right stuff," hire them, and pay little attention to the situation or context in which they work, assuming that they will shape their context, rather than be shaped by it. On the other hand, if you adopt a situational perspective, you focus on analyzing the situation or context and changing one or more features of it, assuming that the situation or context will shape an individual. Obviously, it is essential to remember that in actual organizations, both dispositional and situational forces contribute to individual and organizational actions and experiences. Therefore, when looking at an organization, you must keep one eye on people and the other eye on the situations or contexts in which they work.

TABLE 2–3. Suggested Universal Human Values

- Truth telling or honesty
- Promise keeping or integrity
- Fair play or equity
- Mutual respect and caring

Variation

A system is a collection of components, each of which performs a specific function or set of functions and contributes to and is influenced by the operation of the other components, as well as by the overall functioning of the system. There are many categories or types of systems, including physical, biological, behavioral, and social systems. Our primary interest here is *behavioral systems* and *social systems*—the interactive activities of an individual and a group of individuals, respectively. An inherent property of all systems is variation, flux, or change, which can be thought of as instances of common and special variation. For example, assume that punctuality is an important personal trait. In general, there will be slight variations in punctuality from day to day but relatively few instances of people arriving at work very early or very late. The many small instances of variation are called *common variation* and reflect a lot of little flux or variation (trivial many). However, the few but large instances of variation are examples of *special variance* (vital few). Almost every system exhibits this pattern, or what is known as the Pareto principle, of many small and few large instances of variation (Gitlow & Gitlow, 1987; Walton, 1986). This same line of reasoning can be extended to a social system, such as a work organization, when one considers, for example, the promised delivery time of a product or service to customers in the global marketplace, which usually yields small variations in the time of delivery, peppered periodically with a few instances of large variations in the time of delivery. The former reflects common variation and the latter reflects special variation of the organizational social system.

In both instances, the system, whether an individual or an organization, is said to be in control in that the behavior or action of the system is highly predictable and there are frequent, albeit small, variations and infrequent large variations. Such a system is predictable, reliable, stable, highly repetitive, and incapable of moving beyond effectiveness (high-quality outcome) and efficiency (optimization of resources). Such a system is also stereotyped and unlikely to drift or change much, which is desirable as long as there is no major change in the need or demand

for the product or service from the customer or client base. A system that is in control does the same thing better and better if it is continuously improved, but it never does anything new. It provides a stable platform for the operation of the organization, but can get the organization stuck in a rut.

Variation arises everywhere in an organization, from the different functional business areas, such as manufacturing, marketing, finance, engineering, and personnel, to the increasingly diversified workforce. Because no one can know or do everything in an organization, it is important to harvest the diversity or variation by promoting shared goals, behaviors, beliefs, and values among the members. An effective manager appreciates and values variation or diversity because it affords the opportunity to change and do different things and to promote organizational stability by constructing, when appropriate, systems with low variability.

Problems

Most persons and organizations are reluctant to acknowledge that they have problems and then to address them, hoping instead that they will go away. We have yet to encounter an organization or an individual anywhere that is "problem free," although organizations may be in denial or unaware of their organizational selves, as reflected by their lack of attention to feedback from customers, clients, or members or by their ignoring internal management information systems. As we are sure you realize, variation at both the individual (within and among individuals) and organizational levels creates problems as well as opportunities. In general, problems are perceived as negative and opportunities are framed as positive even though both involve decision making from among perhaps ambiguous alternatives and risk about the accuracy of forecasting outcomes of decisions. In many respects, whether individuals or organizations perceive a situation as a problem or an opportunity depends on such factors as their sense of efficacy or capacity to deal with specific tasks; outlook on life (pessimistic or optimistic); and, what is most important, what they have learned or not yet learned (Bandura, 1986).

It is important to keep in mind that an organization always has problems, given the dynamic, nondeterministic nature of systems and events that are beyond the control of individuals, although the culture of an organization strongly influences whether such problems are constructed as opportunities. If an organizational culture does not promote learning, optimism, and efficacy (a sense of capability or confidence in oneself and the organization), then changing a chief executive or operating officer, manager, or individual employee will not fix the particular problem. Because the organizational culture is usually shared by most members of the organization, change must focus on systemic processes and the shared beliefs, values, and actions of the members. As we discuss in Chapter 3, changing an individual and an organizational culture involves learning, which is another fundamental feature of humans and organizations.

Learning

We define *learning* as a relatively permanent change in the behavior and cognitive operations of an individual or organization as a result of experience. This definition implies that what is learned can be unlearned and thus that actions are flexible and can be adapted to changing environmental conditions.

Organizational learning arises from learning by individual members of the organization. Individual or organizational learning serves as a bridge from the past through the present to the future, since as an organization learns, it builds on experiences and then decides in the present whether to continue the same historical actions or move into new activities, such as new products, markets, services, or ways of doing business (Nystrom & Starbuck, 1984). Given a dynamic, changing environment with variation

giving rise to problems that require choices, the capacities to learn and unlearn are critical for organizational competitiveness and well-being. In fact, so long as an organization (or an individual) has the two vital behavioral signs of problems and learning, one knows it is functioning and has the capacity to adapt and grow.

Organizational learning is based on individual learning, which is then captured and shared with other members of the organization in organizational policies, standard operating procedures, cultural norms, and organizational stories and ceremonies (Argyris & Schon, 1978; Jelinek, 1979). Low-level organizational learning is based on repetition and routine and takes "place in organizational contexts that are well understood and in which management thinks it can control situations" (Foil & Lyles, 1985, p. 807). For example, if organizational members attend a weeklong seminar on new management practices or new technologies and share what they have learned with other members, and if the other members put this new information into practice and incorporate it in standard operating manuals and other organizational memory systems, then organizational learning has taken place.

If the new material focused on making "more efficient" current organizational operations or systems, then this is an example of single-loop organizational learning, making the same product or providing the same service, just now doing it better (Argyris & Schon, 1978). However, if the new material required changes to different organizational norms, products, or services, such as from toy maker to software manufacturer, then this is an example of double-loop organizational learning in which the focus is upon doing the right thing (market wise) or becoming more effective (Argyris & Schon, 1978; Lawson & Ventriss, 1992). Once the new material is deposited, encoded, and embraced in the organizational memory systems (manuals, procedural guidelines, mission statement), then organizational learning endures even if the original learners leave the organization because the new practices or norms are part of the organization; they are not restricted to an individual or a small band of individuals who first learned them (Lawson & Ventriss, 1992).

Rationality and Emotionality

Both individuals and organizations sometimes act in a manner that makes plain that they are not governed by strictly rational principles of action. Feelings, fears, hopes, and prejudices influence actions and decisions; this cluster of affective, emotional, or nonrational influences is a fact of individual and organizational life (Goleman, 1994; George, 1990; George & Brief, 1992). Rather than deny or control these affective forces, we encourage the coupling of nonrational with rational processes, including planning, problem solving, and a focus on data-based management. It is just as important to know the numbers about an organization as to know the emotional responses of members to those numbers, especially key quantitative indexes of the organization's financial performance.

All people learn through emotions as well as through thoughts, so to ignore one fails to recognize the fundamental nature of humans and organizations (National Advisory Mental Health Council, 1995). Members of an organization experience the full range of adult emotions—anger, anxiety, fear, serenity, belonging, identity, joy, and sadness—and use these emotional experiences as a base for guiding their interactions with other members of the organization and for learning about the organization. Thus, they need to remain alert to organizational politics and appreciate that political activities represent the intersection of the powerful and pervasive rational and emotional forces of the organization. We suspect that there has never been a meeting at which all emotionality was checked at the door. Such a state of affairs is as unthinkable as a meeting at which all rationality is checked at the door, although some meet-

ings sure seem as if rationality is absent, which reinforces the importance of being aware of and sensitive and responsive to the emotional side of people and organizations.

In the arena of organizational politics, an organizational issue may draw coalitions of a number of formal groups in an organization that would not normally join together. In addition, organizational politics is observable in the pursuit of individual power and goals, coupled or in conflict with organizational authority (legitimated power by position in the organization). It is also seen in the co-opting, or neutralizing, of real or perceived opponents by offering them membership in a decision-making group, so their individual voices and influence are moderated by group norms of conformity and decision making by consensus, which may be expressed as majority or unanimous votes by the group. In leading and managing people in organizations, it is essential to harness political forces and to understand that they are a reflection of the fundamental nature of humanity and organizations, not intrinsically negative.

Political sensitivity is as important as is keeping an open mind, especially when it is grounded in data-based approaches to management, a commitment to principles that promote equality of opportunities for those who want to work, fairness, justice, and compassion. Likewise, power in an organization is a resource to be cultivated and ideally deployed to advance organizational and congruent individual goals. In general, people are willing to empower and be empowered by others, but are seldom willing to forfeit power without some acceptable rationale or exchange relationship. Most power exchanges involve some form of quid pro quo or something for some desired resources.

Leading and managing in the global marketplace requires an awareness and appreciation of some fundamental features of the nature of humans and organizations. We identified five features, *dispositional and situational variables, variation, problems, learning,* and *rationality-*

emotionality that we believe are central to understanding people and organizations anywhere in the world and that shape and influence applied strategies for managing effectively. This is not a fixed list of features, and we encourage you to modify the features as your circumstances and situations require. In so doing, you will appreciate the key role of situational or contextual variables in influencing applied management strategies.

ORGANIZATIONAL DATA, LEVELS OF ANALYSIS, AND VARIABLES

When possible, we encourage observation and inquiry focused on systematically acquired organizational data on human actions or behaviors and experiences that can be expressed at the individual (micro), work-team or small-group (meso), and organizational (macro) levels of analyses. Organizational experiences include cognitive and affective experiences (thoughts and feelings) that serve to define and distinguish individuals, small groups, or particular organizations. We also encourage an emphasis on collecting organizational data by making systematic observations at both the individual (micro) and aggregate (meso or macro) levels of analysis to determine the relationship, if any, among these levels of organizational data that can indicate whether an applied strategy of prevention or intervention is better framed at the individual, group, or combined levels of organizational analysis.

A data-based approach is preferable to guesswork or the appeal to intuitive and engaging opinion, for it is usually grounded in quantitative measures, such as absenteeism rates, the number of projects completed successfully on time, types and frequency of various types of conflict, as well as a range of financial measures that are the cumulative actions and experiences of the organizational members. In addition, qualitative or focused descriptive data of observed organizational actions and experiences can enrich and enhance the meaning assigned to the quantitative data.

An example of the collection of simple quantitative and qualitative data on decision making in an organization may be an observation of decision making by a five-person work team during which the assigned leader spoke for 10 of the 15-minute meeting advocating one proposal, rebutted the alternatives suggested by three other members without allowing further discussion by the team, and then called for a decision based on a majority (three out of five) vote for that proposal, rather than a full consensus or unanimous vote by all five members. Throughout the meeting, the leader stood while the other members sat and shuffled papers or fidgeted while the other members spoke. If you observed this pattern over time, canvassed each member individually, and found that the four other members believed that the leader behaved autocratically and felt left out of the decision, you could conclude with some confidence that this pattern exemplifies directive, rather than participative, leadership. Furthermore, if you observed the same pattern of group and individual behaviors and experiences in other work teams in the organization, you could conclude that the organizational culture promotes directive leadership in decision making. Obviously, from these observations, you know only about the decision-making process, not about the outcomes of the decision. Nevertheless, quantitative and qualitative data can be of great value in that they allow one to describe and then modify organizational actions and experiences.

Last, when possible, we encourage the adoption of the experimental method of hypothesis testing to determine the relationships, if any, within organizational data sets. In many respects, organizational actions and experiences can be considered a form of experimentation when, for example, an organizational member says, "If we do this action, we can expect this outcome or pattern of outcomes." Obviously, the confidence or accuracy of the expected relationship is enhanced when you have repeated observations of actions and experiences and control over the dispositional and situational variables that may influence a particular outcome. Accordingly, it is best to start with a small, focused experiment to achieve "small wins," such that if the organization does this (Variable A), then you can expect to observe this outcome (Variable B). This type of experiment is the essence of the hypothesis-testing method in which you vary the *independent (manipulated) variable* and observe the consequences, if any, on the *dependent (measured) variable* (Weick, 1984).

Table 2–4 presents a sample of some of the important and frequently studied independent and dependent variables in organizational psychology. Knowing the relationship, if any, among these variables for an organization is important for effecting or maintaining organizational effectiveness and productivity.

It is difficult to isolate and manipulate a single independent variable at a time in a functioning organization because other variables may be changing (covariance) during the period of observations and those variables may be the primary source of variation or change in a dependent or measured variable. This situation may give rise to error or random variation, rather than experimental variation that results from the manipulation of the independent variable. Thus, although hypothesis testing is not the only method or always the most appropriate method,

TABLE 2–4. Examples of Independent (Manipulated) and Dependent (Measured) Variables in Organizational Psychology

Independent Variable	Dependent Variable
Dispositional	*Dispositional*
Motivation, educational level, age, sex, race, ethnicity, interpersonal skills, and coping skills	Job performance, production or service output, job satisfaction, stress and wellness, absenteeism, turnover, and organizational citizenship
Contextual	*Contextual*
Open and communicative organizational environment	Frequency, quality, and consequences of communications
Compensation: Salary, wages, benefits program	Individual and work-team performances and outputs
Opportunities for promotion	Organizational competitiveness, productivity, and/or quality of product or service
Respectful, challenging, safe, and clean work environment	Organizational innovation
Job security	Financial indexes of profitability and community development
Functional systems, such as financing, marketing, and production	

it affords the opportunity to discover causal relationships between independent and dependent variables and hence allows you to predict and gain control over specific organizational behaviors and experiences, which, in turn, can promote organizational stability and productivity.

METHODS OF STUDY

In organizational psychology there is a vast literature on organizations, with data located in many places, including textbooks, journals, electronic list servers (bulletin boards), World Wide Web home pages, and organizational archives and manuals. In large measure, the value and applicability of any of these data sets is determined by the method of inquiry used to obtain the data, usually expressed in numerical and verbal normative formats (general prescriptive guidelines or algorithms). Regardless of the method of study, the focus of data collection may be on individuals (for example, searching for the dispositional variable that is the best predictor of job performance), small groups (such as studying the quality of decisions, reflected in resources saved, made by a small group of

TABLE 2–5. Advantages and Disadvantages of Four Methods of Study

	Advantages	Disadvantages
Case study	Generates new topic areas	Affords little control of variables
	Provides insights	Makes determinants of actions and experiences difficult to discern
	Suggests hypotheses	
Field experiment	Permits causal inferences	Affords a limited degree of control of variables
	Makes it easier to generalize results	Does not allow for subjects to be randomly selected
	Enhances realism	
Laboratory experiment	Allows for a high degree of control and precision	Results are often artificial and unrealistic
	Permits strong causal inferences	Results have limited generalizability
	Involves the random assignment of subjects to treatment conditions	Arouses suspicion in subjects
Archival research	Is unobtrusive	Is limited to using available data
	Is relevant to the topic of interest	Yields correlational data

knowledgeable persons, compared to the decision made by an expert), or the entire organization (like determining turnover rates for all members of an organization in response to a 20% pay cut for all employees).

In most instances, you would want to design a study or project in which you had the tightest possible control over the independent (manipulated) and dependent (measured) variables, so you could have confidence in your findings of the relationships, if any, between, say, a pay cut (independent variable) and the turnover rate or actual departure from the organization (dependent variable). In many instances, you can use almost all the standard research methods in organizational psychology to study a relationship like this, although each method has advantages and disadvantages (Eisenhardt, 1989; Glaser & Strauss, 1967; Yin, 1984).

Table 2–5 presents the four primary methods of study that are used most often in organizational psychology. In general, as you move from case study to laboratory experiment, you gain increasing control over the independent and dependent variables at the expense of losing realism, ecological validity, or touch with the actual organization, members, or events that are internal and external to an organization.

Case Study

This method focuses on understanding the dynamics of a single organization or multiple organizations (Eisenhardt, 1989). In general, case studies use a combination of data collection methods, such as interviews, surveys, questionnaires, and observations involving qualitative (words), quantitative (numbers), or both types of evidence. In these studies, researchers observe, measure, and record whatever they find without experimentally manipulating the independent variables. Case studies can be used to provide detailed descriptions, test theory, or generate theory. For example, a detailed study of Organization Alpha may be designed to determine if participative decision making is ef-

fective in an actual organizational setting. Or on the basis of detailed descriptions of the organization, an hypothesis may emerge that can be tested in a field or laboratory based experiment. The limitations of this method include little, if any, control over independent and, to a lesser extent, dependent variables, and the difficulty of determining what independent variables—dispositional, contextual, or both—are responsible for whatever dependent measures are part of the study.

Field Experiment

This method involves systematic observations of events in real-life organizations and situations in which it is usually possible to manipulate some independent variables and measure some dependent variables. However, it may not be possible to assign subjects randomly to treatment conditions and to control other variables that may have a significant impact on the dependent measures. Compared to the laboratory experiment, the trade-off is realism for reduced control of the conditions of observation.

An example of a field experiment would be an examination of the effects of procedural justice or an explanation by management of a pay cut or reduction in force on employees' job satisfaction and turnover or voluntary departure from the organization (Schaubroeck, May, & Brown, 1994). Since the researcher may not have control over the magnitude of the pay cut (independent variable), he or she has to take whatever is there in the field. Likewise, there may be limited opportunities to select dependent variables because the employees may be resentful and overworked and refuse or attempt to sabotage any data collection processes.

Laboratory Experiment

This method allows the greatest opportunities for controlled observations in response to manipulations of the independent variables and measurement of the dependent variables. In general, laboratory experiments are conducted in artificial environments in which the phenomena under study are created by the researcher. About 29% of organizational studies published each year in major journals are laboratory experiments (Dipboye, 1990). Laboratory experiments can involve the systematic study of any aspect of organizations or actions within organizations, such as decision making or conflict resolution, because the researchers simulate or create the testing conditions.

In the "in-basket technique," which is frequently used in laboratory experiments in organizational psychology, participants are presented with a series of incoming communications about a specific topic and must decide on a specific course of action on the basis of their analysis of these communications. Usually, the contents of the incoming communications, task instructions, or task goals are manipulated across subjects, and such manipulations serve as the independent variable. Also, some measure is taken for the dependent variable, such as the number of alternatives considered before a decision is made or the quality of the decision. Although the results of a laboratory experiment may have limited generalizability, the trade-off is that the researcher has a high degree of control over the major variables and the results are precise.

Archival Research

In this method, the data that are collected are limited to whatever is available from the organization. Measures of absenteeism, turnover, sales performance, and team performance may be part of the data sets maintained by an organization. Archival research is a relatively unobtrusive procedure that seldom has an impact on the current behavior of organizational members because the major focus is on analyzing existing data sets that have been collected over time, rather than on analyzing the results of questionnaires or other survey instruments that have been completed by current employees.

An example of archival research would be a study designed to determine accident rates among different types of employees (new employees versus those who have been working for three or more months, years, or whatever) at different times of the day or as a function of the amount of work required in a fixed period. The archival method can be used to test a hypothesis—for instance, more accidents occur late in the day or work shift than early in the day or shift because of fatigue. The findings of an archival study may also generate hypotheses that can be tested by one of the other methods of study.

An important point to keep in mind is that each method has distinct advantages and disadvantages and a working knowledge of all four methods will definitely be of value to an organizational psychologist.

Measurement

Almost regardless of what method of study is used, measurement, or the assignment of numbers to people, actions, or things, is just about inevitable and serves to distinguish quantitative from qualitative methods that usually capture recorded observations in narrative form (Strauss & Corbin, 1990).

Researchers seek measures that are *reliable*—that yield the same repeated measured values over time or across subjects. They also seek *valid* measures in which there is a significant relationship between the predictor or test and criterion or performance scores. For example, if a person scores high in conscientiousness on a personality test and her or his job performance is high at a subsequent time (say, three weeks or years later) and, in fact, is higher than other persons whose personality scores were lower, one can conclude that this measurement of personality has high predictive or criterion-related validity. Content validity arises when the measurement of a selection procedure is justified by showing that it samples representatively significant parts of the job under study. Construct validity involves identifying the psychological trait (the construct) that underlies the successful performance of a job and then devising a selection procedure to measure the presence and magnitude of that construct; for example, measures of conscientiousness (the construct) always relate positively to enhanced job performance.

In almost all instances, the quantitative data are subject to some kind of statistical treatment for data analysis. In general, *descriptive statistics* allow researchers to take large quantities of data and package them into meaningful wholes, such as means or medians (measures of central tendency, that is, the average and middle value of the data set, respectively). Also, variance (a dispersion measure) is helpful in approximating, in part, how robust or powerful a particular independent variable might have been on a particular dependent variable. Thus, if manipulation of an independent variable known as X always produces Y scores of 8, 9, or 10 out of a range of 1 to 20, then the variance is low compared to measures that produce Y scores of 2, 10, or 18. Measures of central tendency and dispersion are useful for summarizing observations of a single dependent variable.

Correlation is another descriptive statistic that indicates the degree (magnitude) and direction (positive or negative) of a relationship between two dependent variables and is most frequently measured by the Pearson product-moment correlation coefficient. Thus, if productivity increases as pay increases, then the relationship is positive. However, it is not possible to determine if increased pay causes increased productivity this way. To get a better handle on causal relationships between pay and productivity, a researcher would have to conduct a systematic study in which pay was varied systematically from decrease through no increase to various degrees of increase.

Regression analysis is still another descriptive statistical technique that allows you to determine how well or poorly a given predictor or test variable (like conscientiousness) influences or determines a criterion or performance outcome measure (such as sales or absenteeism).

Inferential statistics afford researchers the opportunity to generalize data and summaries of data beyond the sample or the actual measures from a limited sample of subjects (for instance, 1,000 women all aged 21) to larger groupings or populations of subjects (like all 21-year-old women or all women in China or in the world). To make such generalizations, one uses statistical tests that are based on probabilities. Furthermore, inferential statistics allow a researcher to determine if the observed measures of the dependent variable are the result of error variance (are due to chance or some other systematically changing condition beyond the researcher's control), of the experimental treatment, or of the researcher's manipulation. Thus, for example, if you varied pay levels and observed no systematic impact on productivity while all the participants (unbeknownst to you) received large sums of cash from other sources or were resentful and angry with their employer for other reasons, you might conclude erroneously that pay level had no significant effect on productivity. You can control, in part, for these extraneous influences by asking the participants to keep a critical-incidents journal during the study. If you have control over all or almost all the other influential variables and find a substantial mean difference in productivity levels between high and low pay conditions, with the probability of finding such a mean difference by chance of less than 1 in 20 (.05), you would conclude that the difference in productivity levels is due to the treatment conditions (pay levels), rather than chance. Such an outcome has statistical significance because the probability of finding the observed value of the statistical test (t-test—difference between two groups or analysis of variance, ANOVA—difference between two or more groups) is less than .05, 1 in 20, or 5 in 100.

Last, *meta-analysis* has become an increasingly popular statistical tool in organizational psychology (as well as other disciplines) because it allows researchers to summarize data from the findings of many studies, rather than just one study. For example, 50 studies based on 10,000 subjects may have reported a high positive correlation between level of pay and productivity. If you take a mean or average of the reported correlations across these 50 studies that may have involved widely different types of subjects, organizations, and/or tasks, you are now in a stronger position to indicate less equivocally that pay and productivity are correlated and, most likely, causally related.

Many of the studies presented in subsequent chapters involve one of the four methods of study and some type of statistical treatment presented in this section. Thus, you are now in a more solid position to get a better sense of the utility and limitations of each study on the basis of your understanding of the methods of study and issues of measurement in organizational psychology.

GETTING A FEEL FOR AN ORGANIZATION

As presented in Table 2–6, there are four domains of organizational knowledge that are helpful for getting an initial sense of an organization. For most organizations, most of the requisite data are readily available in organizational handbooks, public relations materials, and personnel department publications and, most important, by moving through the organizations and listening with an open mind and heart—a skill that can be strengthened and refined with practice, practice, and more practice! The basic idea is to find out what is on the minds of the organizational members and the "shared mind" of the organization. Therefore, it is critical to listen, observe, and inquire respectfully about organizational actions or experiences, especially those that appear surprising or confusing to you yet are readily accepted by the members. Such surprises provide glimpses of the organizational culture that we will treat in Chapter 3. In short, you need to know about the *structural* (divisions, departments, units, and work teams), *human* (workforce mix), *relationships* (authority and power), and *networks* (how and what members communicate) influences of both the internal and external environment of the organization.

Organizational Architecture

Table 2–7 presents a summary of key informational items about organizational architecture that give a sense of whether the structure of the organization is big and bulky, small and nimble, or some other combination of these features. Obviously, if the structure is large, unchanged for years, and lacks coherence, you will have your hands full in changing the organization. Even if the organizational structure is not the sole determinant of organizational functions, it is most certainly an influential factor.

TABLE 2–6. A Brief Outline of Data Sets that Are Needed to Get a Feel for an Organization

Organizational architecture: structural patterns of the arrangement of people into units within the organization and with the external environment

Organizational demography: defining features of organizational members and clusters of clients, or customers

Organizational geometry and politics: spatial and functional influence relationships in the internal and external organizational environments

Organizational networks: communication patterns within the organization and with the external environment

TABLE 2–7. Organizational Architecture

Focus on the structural patterns of organizing people and activities within the organization and with the external environment.

- How many divisions, departments, or units exist; how long has each existed; what is the size of the expense and income budgets; and how many employees are there per unit?

- How and why are units created, merged, and eliminated?

- Are there any task forces or matrix groupings that focus on specific issues or processes that cut across organizational structures, such as divisions or departments? If so, what are the task foci, and how and why have they been created, merged, and eliminated?

- What are the units and the positions within the units that interact systematically with the external environment? What are the patterns of interaction, and how is the externally collected information dispersed within the organization?

Information about these structural patterns can provide some preliminary indices of the *relative* power and influence of the different units in an organization. In general, the larger the budget and number of employees of a unit, the more the potential influence. The rationale for creating, modifying, and eliminating units provides some preliminary indices of the forces that shape the organization, such as a customer focus or a technical focus. The structural patterns of interaction with the external environment can provide useful information about the relationships between the organization and the external environment if such interaction is systematic, localized, or dispersed throughout the organization. The magnitude of the interaction and internal communication efforts can indicate the value of this set of activities.

Organizational Demography

Table 2–8 outlines some suggested demographic indices with a variety of other suggested dimensions that may help define an organizational workforce, as well as the customer or client base and potential new market clientele. In general, diversity or variation on a variety of dimensions can enhance the possibilities of cultivating and strengthening a nimble organization and its presence in the global marketplace because variation is inherent in all systems. Obviously, diversity

around an evolving core of a clearly stated and internalized organizational mission, processes, and practices is a goal that requires constant attention and nurturance.

Organizational Geometry and Politics

This domain provides a sense of influence relationships, allows a perspective on the nonrational, affective side of the organization and can provide suggestions about possible levers for instituting organizational change expressed by in-

TABLE 2–8. Organizational Demography

Focus on the composition and distribution of the organizational members and clusters of clients or customers and any noteworthy changes in them over the past three to five years.

- What are the average age, education, length of employment, and salary-wage features that describe the overall organization and the members of each of the major structural units (divisions or departments) in the organization?

- What are the major or noteworthy differences between managers and nonmanagers or among levels of management in reference to gender, race, ethnicity, or any other definable attribute?

- What common features, if any, do members of the highest and lowest levels of the organization share, including organizational beliefs, values, and actions? What is the income or overall compensation ratio between the highest and lowest paid persons in the organization?

- What features define and distinguish the customer or clientele base, such as age, education, gender, race, ethnicity, and educational level, and have there been any major changes in these features over the past three to five years?

Demographic information about an organization can provide an initial sense of the membership and some of the major forces, such as age, race, gender, and educational level, that may be shaping organizational actions (or inactions) and experiences. Also, such information can be useful in constructing the membership of an intervention or leadership team, as well as of participants in continuing education and skill-upgrade programs. Demographic information on customers and any recent changes in it are important for determining the responsiveness and strategic planning programs of the organization.

fluential organizational positions, persons, policies, processes, or some mix of them. No matter how rational your proposed intervention, it is unlikely to be adopted by the organizational members unless you have a firm understanding of organizational politics, passion, and power relationships that will shape the acceptance and implementation of the proposed organizational change. Information about organizational politics is difficult to ascertain, for although authority (legitimate power inherent to a position in an organization) is usually expressed publicly, power relationships that are based on coalitions and emotional strata seldom are, especially to organizational outsiders. Table 2–9

TABLE 2–9. Organizational Geometry and Politics

Focus on the physical distribution or layout of the organization as well as patterns of influences reflected in nonverbal behaviors, gestures, and who gets invited and who participates in key meetings or other key organizational functions in which influence is exerted to direct organizational actions.

- What is the overall quality of the organizational facilities, cleanliness, and orderliness and the relative size of spaces assigned to different managers and organizational functions?

- What are the policies (written guidelines) and/or practices governing the assignment and use of physical facilities, from offices to equipment of all kinds?

- How is influence exercised (for modifying the actions and experiences of others), and what are the reactions to such exercises of influence?

- What are the symbols of influence and specific guidelines or policies governing authority (legitimate organizational influence)?

Information about organizational geometry and politics can suggest possible questions or hypotheses to be examined further to identify more clearly organizational loci of power and influence. It is important to remember that physical structures and distances between persons or groups have social meaning; for example, bigger offices may suggest more power than smaller or if all members in a group defer or recognize respectfully a particular group member. It is also important to remember that lines of influence may not be as visible as or similar to reporting lines in the organization.

presents the important features of organizational geometry and politics.

Organizational Networks

Last, Table 2–10 is a guide to obtaining overarching information about communication networks in an organization and about the processes through which an organization communicates with components of the external environment. Do members communicate primarily face to face or through phone calls, voice mail, and E-mail, that is, is it a virtual organization so there is little face-to-face communication within the organization? Also, what are the temporal patterns of dialogue, regardless of the medium of communication in the network: Do people get back to each other in a timely fashion or leave communication loops open and hanging? It is important to know if the chief executive officer, leader, or leadership team walks around the organization (practicing Management by Walking Around) really, virtually, or in some mix of the two. If the leader or leaders primarily do the former, then it is highly likely that decision making is open to influence by sensate, rather than filtered virtual or real, informational reports flowing to the key decision makers. Last, how and what does the organization communicate to customers and clients, and, if appropriate, how does the organization work with the press? Remember that the press almost always has the last word!

Obviously, the four domains of organizational knowledge provide only a skeletal database from which you will form initial assumptions about organizational dynamics that you will have to test and refine through continued data collection and authentic interactions with organizational members and constituents, keeping an open mind. Working in and with organizations can be a challenging, honorable, and important undertaking because you can influence the daily lives of many persons within and connected to the organization. Accordingly, we recommend

TABLE 2–10. Organizational Networks

Focus on who communicates with whom and how and the frequency, content, and outcomes of communication, both within and outside the organization.

- What are the methods of communication among members of the organization, such as electronic systems, periodic newsletters, and reports of critical financial and other organizational data on organizational performances?

- How are positive and negative emotions expressed, and are they valued or avoided by organizational members? How do members become aware of organizational hot-button issues (issues that generate intense emotions among members)? What are the formal and informal communication networks?

- How and what does the organization communicate with customers or clients? Does the organization regularly solicit feedback from customers, how does it do so, and what happens as a result of customers' or clients' complaints and compliments?

- What does the community know about the organization, and how is that information acquired? Are there key external persons, besides customers, with whom the organization communicates regularly?

Information about organizational networks can provide insight into members' and customers' level of awareness of important and emotionally charged organizational activities and functions.

that you examine the American Psychological Association's "Ethical Principles and Code of Conduct" (1992) or the ethical guidelines of other professional management associations.

SUMMARY

This lengthy chapter focused on tools and tool sets for gaining a better understanding of and managing organizations. The first set of tools consisted of five fundamental assumptions about organizations and individuals that define their basic natures and thus have important implications for what one studies about organizations, and how. We defined and examined dispositional (trait) and situational (contextual)

forces that influence powerfully individual and organizational actions and experiences. We noted also that organizations exhibit and require variation and have problems, which are the basis for organizational learning. Organizational learning arises from learning by individual members, since the individuals share what they have learned with other members and this information is embedded in the organization by its inclusion in standard operating manuals and procedures, as well as other forms of organizational documentation.

The second set of tools included four specific methods of study commonly used in organizational psychology: the case study, field experiment, laboratory experiment, and archival research. Each method of inquiry has particular strengths and weaknesses, and each can enrich the others. For example, the case study method is excellent for rich or detailed descriptions of a given organization or subset of organizations and can be a great source of hypotheses, which, in turn, can be tested using either the field or laboratory experiment or both.

The third set of tools was a detailed protocol for getting a preliminary feel for an organization that was structured around the systematic acquisition of information about organizational architecture, demography, geometry and politics, and networks. For instance, data on organizational demography such as the age, gender, educational levels, and distribution by unit or function of organizational members, and similar information about customers or clients can provide useful information about some of the challenges and opportunities faced by an organization. Organizational demography tells you who is doing the organizational work, while organizational architecture tells you the structural features of the organizational environment. In a similar fashion, organizational geometry, politics, and networks tell you how the members do their organizational work.

In the final analysis, the systematic use of all three tool sets can help you better understand

and manage organizations, provided that you continue to sharpen your skills of observation and listen to the verbal as well as nonverbal communications of the organization and its members. Since these skill-sharpening exercises require a great deal of practice, we encourage you to spend as much time as possible in your target organization and to meet with as wide a variety of organizational members as possible.

CHAPTER REFERENCES

Argyris, C., & Schon, D. (1978). *Organizational learning: A theory of action perspective.* Reading, MA: Addison-Wesley.

Bandura, A. (1986). *Social foundations of thought and action: A social cognitive theory.* Englewood Cliffs, NJ: Prentice Hall.

Barrick, M. R., & Mount, M. K. (1993). Autonomy as a moderator of the relationship between the big five personality dimensions and job performance. *Journal of Applied Psychology, 78,* 111–118.

Basic Behavioral Science Task Force of the National Advisory Mental Health Council. (1996). Basic behavioral science research for mental health. *American Psychologist, 51,* 22–28.

Davis-Blake, A., & Pfeffer, J. (1989). Just a mirage: The search for dispositional effects in organizational research. *Academy of Management Review, 14,* 385–400.

Dipboye, R. L. (1990). Laboratory vs. field research in industrial and organizational psychology. In C. L. Cooper & I. T. Robertson (Eds.), *International review of industrial and organizational psychology 1990* (pp. 1–34). Chichester, England: John Wiley & Sons.

Eisenhardt, K. M. (1989). Building theories from case study research. *Academy of Management Review, 14,* 532–550.

Ethical principles of psychologists and code of conduct. (1992). *American Psychologist, 47,* 1597–1611.

Foil, C. M., & Lyles, M. A. (1985). Organizational learning. *Academy of Management Review, 10,* 803–813.

George, J. M. (1990). Personality, affect, and behavior in groups. *Journal of Applied Psychology, 75,* 107–116.

George, J. M., & Brief, A. P. (1992). Feeling good—doing good. A conceptual analysis of the mood at work-organizational spontaneity relationship. *Psychological Bulletin, 112,* 310–329.

Gitlow, H. S., & Gitlow, S. J. (1987). *The Deming guide to quality and competitive position.* Englewood Cliffs, NJ: Prentice Hall.

Glaser, B., & Strauss, A. (1967). *The discovery of grounded theory: Strategies of qualitative research.* London: Wiedenfeld & Nicholson.

Goldberg, L. R. (1993). The structure of phenotypic personality traits. *American Psychologist, 48,* 26–34.

Goleman, D. (1994). *Emotional intelligence.* New York: Bantam Books.

Jelinek, M. (1979). *Institutionalizing innovation: A study of organizational learning systems.* New York: Praeger.

La Fromboise, T., Coleman, H. L. K., & Gerton, J. (1993). Psychological impact of biculturalism: Evidence and theory. *Psychological Bulletin, 114,* 395–412.

Lawson, R. B., & Ventriss, C. L. (1992). Organizational change: The role of organizational culture and organizational learning. *Psychological Record, 42,* 205–219.

Levin, I., & Stokes, J. P. (1989). Dispositional approach to job satisfaction: Role of negative affectivity. *Journal of Applied Psychology, 74,* 752–758.

McDaniel, M. A., Whetzel, D. L., Schmidt, F. L., & Maurer, S. D. (1994). The validity of employment interviews: A comprehensive review and meta-analysis. *Journal of Applied Psychology, 112,* 599–616.

Mesquita, B., & Frijda, N. H. (1992). Cultural variations in emotions: A review. *Psychological Bulletin, 112,* 179–204.

Mischel, W. (1977). The interaction of person and situation. In D. Magnusson & N. S. Endler (Eds.), *Personality at the crossroads: Current issues in interactional psychology* (pp. 333–352). Hillsdale, NJ: Lawrence Erlbaum.

Mount, M. K., Barrick, M. R., & Strauss, J. P. (1994). Validity of observer ratings of the big five personality factors. *Journal of Applied Psychology, 79,* 272–280.

National Advisory Mental Health Council. (1995). Basic behavioral science research for mental health: A national investment—Emotion and motivation. *American Psychologist, 50,* 838–845.

Newton, T., & Keenan, T. (1991). Further analyses of the dispositional argument in organizational behavior. *Journal of Applied Psychology, 76,* 781–787.

Nystrom, P. C., & Starbuck, W. H. (1984). To avoid organizational crises unlearn. *Organizational Dynamics, 12,* 53–65.

Pfeffer, J. (1994). *Competitve advantage through people: Unleashing the power of the work-force.* Cambridge, MA: Harvard University Press.

Schaubroeck, J., May, D. R., & Brown, F. W. (1994). Procedural justice explanations and employees' reactions to economic hardship: A field experiment. *Journal of Applied Psychology, 79,* 455–460.

Strauss, A., & Corbin, J. (1990). *Basics of qualitative research.* Newbury Park, CA: Sage.

Walton, M. (1986). *The Deming management method.* New York: Putnam.

Weick, K. E. (1984). Small wins: Redefining the scale of social problems. *American Psychologist, 75,* 378–385.

Yin, R. (1984). *Case study research.* Beverly Hills, CA: Sage.

3

Organizational Culture

CHAPTER OVERVIEW

Organizational culture is an important situational variable that influences all members of an organization to various degrees, so it is important to have a sound understanding of this construct to manage and work effectively in an organization. Organizational culture is learned as members construct strategies to solve problems of external adaptation (for example, how best to participate in the global marketplace) and internal integration (how best to coordinate and enhance processes and people inside the organization). As these learned strategies prove effective, they are taught to new members as the best practices to solve organizational problems and are even taken for granted by all members of the organization. Thus, by having the capacity to modify organizational culture, it is possible to change the actions, thoughts, and feelings of a large segment of members of the organization.

In this chapter, we present a directory for finding and describing an organizational culture, indicate levels of expressions of culture in an organization, and provide specific strategies or tools to modify organizational culture. We also treat the relationships between organizational culture and the impact of the larger societal culture, type of business, and the beliefs of the founder and leadership team on the contents of organizational culture. We conclude with a framework for developing an organizational culture based on competencies in the domains of organizational processes, people, and the environment.

LEARNING OBJECTIVES

When you finish studying this chapter, you will be prepared to

- define organizational culture and distinguish it from organizational climate
- identify the nature of cultural change and appreciate the pathways to change
- identify the core components of organizational culture: unifying and shared patterns of thoughts, feelings, values, and actions
- understand the relationship between organizational learning and organizational culture
- identify the origins of organizational culture and the major dimensions along which such cultures vary across the American, Asian, and European cultural-economic blocks
- describe and understand the function of organizational culture in relation to the problems of external adaptation and internal integration
- use a directory of organizational culture based on documents, manuals, ceremonies, rites, rituals, and stories
- identify the levels of organizational cultural and learn specific applied strategies to change an organizational culture
- evaluate the impact of organizational culture on organizational measures, including financial and productivity measures
- learn a framework for introducing an organizational culture based on competencies in organizational processes, people, and the environment.

Accept loss as a universal force.

INDIVIDUAL AND ORGANIZATIONAL CHANGE

The culture of an organization—the shared and unifying thoughts, feelings, values, and actions of organizational members in response to organizational issues and challenges—is a pervasive influence on everyone in an organization and thus merits systematic attention and development by effective leaders. When it is shared among organizational members, organizational culture is carried by all or a majority of the members; guides and predisposes the thoughts, feelings, and actions of members; and distinguishes members from outsiders. Organizational culture is a cohesive force that is expressed in the cognitions, affect or feelings, values, and actions of members, as well as in organizational ceremonies, stories, rituals, and artifacts or things that give physical structure to the shared thoughts, feelings, values, and actions of organizational members. Organizational culture is the way *all* members think, feel, and act in an organization, rather than just one or a few members. It is a collective, not an individual, organizational construct and force.

Organizational culture is vital and ubiquitous and carries information about what is permissible and what is not allowed in a particular organization. It is important to the individual because it can be a cohesive force during turbulent times, as well as a force that can be a barrier to innovation and the adoption of critical organizational change. Organizational culture is a powerful macrolevel situational or contextual variable that influences shared organizational actions and experiences. Therefore, it is essential that organizational leaders have systematic knowledge of the culture's core components, origins, functions, and processes for change and the effects of culture on individual- and organizational-level performances.

Cultural Awareness

For most members of organizations, the most poignant awareness of organizational culture usually arises when they perhaps inadvertently transgress some cultural code, norm, or belief even though culture is conveyed to them almost daily by organizational policies, standard operating procedures, organizational stories, and organizational ceremonies (Schein, 1985, 1990, 1992). Cultural awareness can be enhanced by systematic study of the culture and the organizational learning processes supporting the formation, maintenance, and modifications of the culture, (Siehl & Martin, 1984). Such an awareness can facilitate systematic changes in organizational behavior that can lead to enhancements of a variety of organizational performances, such as group productivity, collective efficiencies, and a sense of belonging and community (Davis, 1984; Deal & Kennedy, 1982; Kilmann, Saxton, Serpa, & Associates, 1985; Ouchi, 1981; Peters & Waterman, 1982; Sathe, 1985; Schein, 1985, 1990, 1992; Sethia & Von Glinow, 1985; Tichy, 1983; Wilkins & Ouchi, 1983).

Organizational climate and culture are sometimes conceptually interchanged (Lippitt, Langseth, & Mossop, 1985; Ott, 1989), with definitions of organizational climate usually focusing on an individual's perception or awareness of events, practices, procedures, and behaviors that are rewarded, supported, and expected in a given organization or unit in the organization (Burke, Borucki, & Hurley, 1992; Schneider & Gunnason, 1990; Schneider, Wheeler, & Cox, 1992). We think of organizational climate and culture as related concepts in that both are concerned with awareness of organizational context. However, like others (see, for example, Trice & Beyer, 1993), we consider organizational culture to go beyond individual awareness of organizational events and ambience. Organizational culture focuses on shared meanings by members of the organizational contexts, rather than individual perceptions, such that the former distinguishes members from nonmembers of an organizational culture although both members and nonmembers may be aware of the context or climate. In short, *climate* is an individual's awareness, while *culture* embraces shared awareness by members, coupled with shared meanings or interpretations of organizational events, practices, and actions.

Nature of Change

Cultural change in an organization is structural, requires time (three to five years), and is resisted because it is initially perceived as a loss at some level by almost all organizational members (Deal, 1985; Schein, 1992). When an organizational culture changes, there are concomitant changes in the ways members think, feel, value, and act in regard to critical issues, problems, and challenges facing their organization. If you have been through an organizational cultural change, you have a sense of the experiential magnitude and nature of the cognitive, emotional, and behavioral changes that are involved. If not, just ask some of your friends who work (or have worked) in the automotive, computer, or health care industries about their experiences and the nature of the change. Cultural change is not inherently bad, but it is initially difficult because it is perceived as a loss of stability, clarity, and predictability; appears inevitable; and has an impact on almost all organizational members. Organizational cultural change is the gateway to the future that may appear at first as a serious threat to many organizational members and then as a welcome change as the new unifying patterns of thoughts, feelings, values, and actions yield success as a result of the reengineering or re-creation of the organization (Hammer & Champy, 1993).

Once an organization learns to continue to manage loss as a universal and repetitive phenomenon, then it can be more open to change and the challenges that lie ahead for each organizational member. The nature of organizational cultural change is such that global organizations must continuously learn to manage loss to stay in business.

Pathway to Change

The first step on the pathway of individual and cultural change is the awareness and acceptance that loss is a universal force. We speak here of the perceived sense of loss of the unifying and shared patterns of knowing how to think, feel, value, and act in reference to important organizational issues. The sense of loss is perceived in many instances by those who are the most socialized to the current culture and usually by those who are in the most powerful organizational positions because they sense that they have the most to lose by finally accepting that the old ways no longer work. Thus, a new leader, a new technological process (a move to a paperless electronic communication system from a paper-based communication system), a more diversified workforce, increasing customer demands, expanding markets, or any combination of these organizational events give rise to new ways of thinking, feeling, and acting in relation to these changes that ultimately replace the shared and unifying thoughts, feelings, values, and actions of the former organizational culture that served as a cohesive force, binding the members together.

The second step on the pathway to change is the firm belief that the organization can be strengthened further and enhanced as a consequence of cooperative change efforts. Although individual and organizational change is perceived as both a threat and an opportunity, the latter perception is more prevalent if the organizational culture that the members shared accepts that perceived loss is part of the change process and is open to learning at the individual and group levels (Mowday & Sutton, 1993).

Cultural change is much more easily espoused than enacted. The down payment for cultural change is uncertainty and instability, which can yield many dividends of adaptability and a new stable pattern of shared beliefs, feelings, values, and actions that must be continuously updated. Your organization will be stuck doing the same things over and over if no acknowledged problems are being addressed and it has stopped learning. Likewise, individual members without problems and who have stopped learning are likely to be stuck as well.

ORGANIZATIONAL CULTURE

This section presents the variety of definitions of organizational culture and the shared features of the many definitions, identifies the core cultural components, and discusses the role of organizational learning in the formation and modification of organizational culture. Although a lot is known about organizational culture, all the mechanisms by which organizational culture influences individuals, groups, the overarching global performances of an organization, and the bidirectional influence of individuals and groups on organizational culture (and vice versa) are not fully understood.

Definitions of Organizational Culture

Since there are innumerable definitions of organizational culture, we include here only a few that have guided theory building and applied cultural change strategies over the past 10 or so years. Thus, we find the following paraphrased or quoted definitions of organizational culture as

- the shared values of organizational members (Peters & Waterman, 1982)

- the way we do things around here (Bower, 1966)

- familiar management tasks or practices (Siehl & Martin, 1984)

- values, heroes, rites, rituals, and communications—"a system of informal rules that spells out how people are to behave most of the time" (Deal & Kennedy, 1982, p. 15)

- "the shared and relatively enduring pattern of basic values, beliefs, and assumptions in an organization" (Sethia & Von Glinow, 1985, p. 403)

- a mind-set—"the realm of feelings and sentiments" (Allaire & Firsirotu, 1985, p. 26)

- "a pattern of shared basic assumptions that the group learned as it solved its problems of external adaptation and internal integration, that has worked well enough to be considered valid, and, therefore, to be taught to new members as the correct way to perceive, think, and feel in relation to those problems" (Schein, 1992, p. 12).

In *The Organizational Culture Perspective*, Ott (1989) included 38 representative definitions of organizational culture extracted from 58 books and articles on the subject. He described organizational culture as a socially constructed, unseen, and unobservable force behind organizational activities. Organizational culture is a social energy that moves organizational members to act and a unifying theme that provides meaning and direction to and mobilizes the members. It functions as an organizational control mechanism, informally approving or prohibiting behaviors. Last, Ott suggested that organizational culture is a concept, construct, energy, or idea, rather than a thing that can be directly observed, measured, and manipulated. In short, organizational culture is a hypothetical construct that must be inferred from the shared thoughts, feelings, values, and actions of organizational members.

Another way to conceptualize organizational culture is to think of it as analogous to the traditional construct of Chinese medicine, *Qi*, which is the vital universal energy that courses through each individual and consists of yin (dark force) and yang (bright force). When the Qi flows harmoniously and freely throughout an individual, the person enjoys a healthy, functional, and effective mind and body. However, when the flow of Qi is blocked or thwarted, the result may be dysfunction, illness, and eventually death. The Qi is a vital energy, universal, not directly observable, and an important explanatory construct of human events. We believe that organizational culture can be thought of as organizational Qi and that it serves the same functions and operates similarly in organizations as Qi is believed to do.

Core Cultural Components

From the foregoing definitions, we conclude that the core components of any organizational culture are the *unifying and shared patterns of thoughts, feelings, values, and actions* among organizational members that are related to important organizational issues and challenges. It is not just any thoughts, feelings, values, and actions that are the essence of an organizational culture but, rather, the unifying patterns that are *shared, learned, aggregated at the group level, and internalized* only by organizational members.

In many organizations, almost all the members are socialized to hold the same or similar thoughts, feelings, values, and actions about important issues the organization is confronting. The shared thoughts, feelings, values, and actions may be organization wide. However, the shared cultural components may differ from one major unit of the organization to another, such as among the finance, marketing, and production departments or between the upper and lower levels of the organization, reflecting subcultures by functional areas or by organizational architecture, respectively. In any organization, it is possible to observe both an organization-wide culture and a variety of subcultures (Martin, 1992). As Martin clearly indicated, subcultures can be enhancing or highly supportive of the organization-wide culture, expressed as countercultures in conflict with other subcultures or the larger organizational culture, or orthogonal subcultures that are neither positive nor negative toward management or each other.

Consider the case of IBM, a major global organization, and how the chief executive officer Louis V. Gerstner Jr. recognized the importance of sharing a unifying pattern of thoughts, feelings, values, and actions as a key feature of an organization-wide culture. According to Gerstner, IBM has eight principles (presented in Table 3–1) that its members must internalize and share to guide their organizational actions and experiences. He stated:

We have to be a company that bases its decisions on some very fundamental operating principles. If we all understand these principles, and we all work by them, then we will transform IBM into a leader and a winner. . . . It's a very simple recipe for success. And every person in IBM, must, and I know will, embrace this set of principles. There are no others. They're not to be added to, subtracted from, augmented or lost in translation. . . . Everyone will be expected to work by these principles and to actively implement them throughout the company. . . . Manage

TABLE 3–1. Example of a Patterned Set of Principles to Be Shared, Valued, and Acted on by Organizational Members

IBM Principles
1. The marketplace is the driving force behind everything we do.
2. At our core, we are a technology company with an overriding commitment to quality.
3. Our primary measures of success are customer satisfaction and shareholder value.
4. We operate as an entrepreneurial organization with a minimum of bureaucracy and a never-ending focus on productivity.
5. We never lose sight of our strategic vision.
6. We think and act with a sense of urgency.
7. Outstanding, dedicated people make it all happen, particularly when they work together as a team.
8. We are sensitive to the needs of all employees and to the communities in which we operate.

Reprinted by permission from *Think Twice.* Copyright 1993 by International Business Machines Corporation.

whatever you do against this set of principles, and we will trust your judgment. (Gerstner, 1993, pp. 4, 14)

As you are well aware, it is difficult to predict with great precision whether such principles as a set of independent variables will have a positive impact on individual and organizational performances, given all the other changes or covariation within and external to IBM or any other organization for that matter. What is clear is that at IBM, a cultural change framework and set of processes are in place and that billions of dollars and thousands of lives are at stake for this organization and its multitude of customers.

Organizational culture is learned by members as well as *modified* as a result of their individual learning. In other words, organizational culture changes and is changed by organizational members. This is an important point because it indicates that culture is malleable, dynamic, and an adaptive learning mechanism. New members acquire organizational culture by being socialized to it; by directly observing other members' actions (or inactions); and by otherwise being exposed to organizational stories, rituals, jokes, and reward systems, all of which are understood primarily by insiders. In effect, organizational culture can shape and direct members' shared patterns of beliefs, feelings, values, and actions, which, in turn, influence its continuing evolution. Schneider (1987) recognized the bidirectional influence relationship of organizational culture in the following excerpt from his presidential address to the Society for Industrial and Organizational Psychology of the American Psychological Association:

> We have been seduced into thinking that organizational structures and processes are the causes of the attitudes, feelings, experiences, meanings, and behaviors that we observe there. We attribute cause not to the people attracted to, selected by, and remaining within organizations, but to the signs of their existence in the organization: to structure, process, and technology.

Enough is enough. We are psychologists and behavioral scientists; let us seek explanation in people, not in the results of their behavior. The people make the place. (p. 451)

Organizational culture is a *group-* or *aggregate*-level phenomenon in that it influences many persons and so is a contagious and robust organizational force. Thus, for example, it has been shown that the specific work-related attitudes that organizational members form are strongly influenced by people with whom they have frequent contact (Rice & Aydin, 1991). Likewise, it has been reported that people who interacted with each other shared similar interpretations of events, whereas members of different interaction groups attached qualitatively different meanings to similar organizational events (Rentsch, 1990).

Last, it is important to appreciate that organizational culture is *internalized* in that it guides, directs, predisposes, and accentuates members' thoughts, feelings, and values and, in turn, their actions regarding important organizational issues. As members become more socialized in a given organizational culture, they tend to make sense of, attribute meaning to, and understand organizational events in a similar fashion, which serves to unify them as well as create cognitive and emotional boundaries between them as insiders and nonmembers as outsiders. A person becomes part of the organizational culture when he or she not only acts but, most important, thinks and feels like and has similar values to other organizational members about important organizational issues and challenges. Accordingly, cultural change strategies that are geared to primarily changing the behaviors or actions of a few or a focused group of members are most likely to be ineffective unless they also emphasize changing the members' shared thoughts, feelings, values, and actions.

In summary, organizational culture is a macrolevel variable and is expressed in organizations as unifying patterns of thoughts, feelings, values, and actions that are shared, learned, aggregated at the group level, and internalized by organizational members as the appropriate way to think, feel, and act in their organization.

Organizational Learning

As was discussed in Chapter 2, organizational learning is based on individual learning, which is then shared with other members of the organization in organizational policies, standard operating procedures, cultural norms, and organizational stories and ceremonies (Argyris & Schon, 1978; Jelinek, 1979). Lower-level organizational learning is acquired through repetition and routine and takes "place in organizational contexts that are well understood and in which management thinks it can control situations" (Foil & Lyles, 1985, p. 807). In other words, lower-level organizational learning involves the restructuring of practices and procedures without fundamentally changing existing cultural norms. Higher-level organizational learning, in comparison, "aims at adjusting overall rules and norms rather than specific activities or behavior." (Foil & Lyles, 1985, p. 808). This kind of organizational learning specifically tries to develop new skills, new knowledge, new cultural norms, and new insights. Moreover, one of its key characteristics is how an organization can *unlearn* previous behaviors and develop new cognitive frameworks or interpretive schemes in confronting problems that are ambiguous or ill defined (Nystrom & Starbuck, 1984; Ventriss & Luke, 1988).

Organizational learning serves as the mechanism for spreading and connecting members' shared patterns of thoughts, feelings, values, and actions. For example, when an organizational member learns a better way to think, feel, or act in relation to a given organizational problem and systematically shares what he or she has learned with other members by behavioral modeling and including it in written operating procedures, manuals, policy statements, and other key organizational documents or videotapes (such as those used to socialize new members), then organizational learning occurs because other members now have the opportunity to think, feel, and act like the original learner. It is interesting that even if the original learner and all her or his colleagues have left the organization, current members may still operate in the same fashion regarding the original organizational issue or challenge because the manuals and policy statements have not changed. In this situation, organizational learning and cultural absorption are a legacy to new members that are grounded in what individuals learned and shared with other organizational members, even when the original learners are no longer members of the organization.

ORIGINS OF ORGANIZATIONAL CULTURE

Organizations are located within larger societal cultures, such as the African, American, Chinese, European, or Japanese cultural contexts, yet almost all organizational cultures are unique to particular organizations. Obviously, there is variation not only among larger social cultures but within each society, depending on the region in which a particular organization is located. In fact, some estimates of the number of the different cultures that currently exist start at around 10,000, compared to the 186 nations that are affiliated with the United Nations, which indicates that most countries have many cultures (Triandis, 1995). In almost any organization around the globe, the organizational culture would consist of the uniquely patterned beliefs, feelings, values, and behaviors that connect the members to the organization and simultaneously distinguish that organizational culture from the cultures of other organizations. In general, any organizational culture arises from three primary sources:

- the broader societal culture in which the organization is nested

- the type of business or the business environment of the organization

- the beliefs, values, and basic assumptions about the nature of reality and human nature held by the founders or first-generation leaders of the organization.

As you might anticipate, different perspectives prevail regarding the relative robustness of these three primary forces, and it is difficult to determine precisely which factor or combination of factors is most influential in giving rise to organizational culture (Chatman & Jehn, 1994; Ott, 1989).

On the basis of his study of thousands of managers employed by a large transnational business, Hofstede (1980) identified four interpersonal dimensions, drawn from 40 countries, that appeared to differentiate managers. These dimensions, which some believe are related to organizational design and culture, are as follows:

- Power distance: the degree of power inequities or differences between two individuals. High power distance signals that the power holders or authority figures are entitled to privileges that are framed within strong and clear superior-subordinate relationships between organizational members.

- Uncertainty avoidance: the degree of organizational stability and predictability preferred by members. High uncertainty avoidance reflects members' strong preferences for written rules and regulations and consensus and susceptibility to high levels of anxiety and stress.

- Individualism: the preference for collective or individual action. High individualism is characterized by less emotional dependence on the organization; a preference for individual, rather than group, decisions, and a high value placed on individual initiative.

- Masculinity: the dominant sex-role pattern in which assertiveness is the male role, nurtu-

rance is the female role, and high masculinity favors larger organizations and an intense motivation to achieve.

Table 3–2 presents a taxonomy of organizational characteristics for the four interpersonal dimensions identified by Hofstede (1980). After an extensive study of 10 organizations in different countries, Hofstede, Neuijen, Ohayv, and Sanders (1990) concluded, on the basis of 180 in-depth interviews combined with 1,295 completed survey instruments, that organizational values are determined primarily by the larger societal culture entering the organization through the hiring process, while organizational practices are acquired as a result of the socialization of new members to the organizational culture.

Some researchers have emphasized that the types of business in which organizations are engaged and their general business environment are the primary determinants of organizational culture (Deal & Kennedy, 1982). Chatman and Jehn (1994) reported larger differences among the organizational cultures of service-based organizations in four different industries than within any one of the industries. Each organization faces a different set of forces that shape its organizational cultural, depending on its products or services, competitors, customers and clients, and governmental regulatory influences, and these forces are the primary determinants of culture. Likewise, it has been suggested that individual professions selectively attract people who are inclined to the beliefs, values, and actions that characterize them (Schein, 1978).

Other researchers have stressed that the primary determinants of an organizational culture are the basic assumptions, beliefs, and values of the founder or the leaders who are in place especially during organizational crises (see, for example, Schein, 1986, 1990, 1992). In our judgment, it is most important to be aware of all three of these fundamental determinants of organizational culture and to assess their relative influence for particular organizations on the basis of

TABLE 3–2. Taxonomy of Organizational Characteristics Based on Four Interpersonal Values for Different Countries

Power Distance

Low	High
(Austria, Denmark, Israel, Norway, Sweden)	(Brazil, India, Mexico, Philippines, Venezuela)
Decentralized, flat organization; small wage differentials among organizational levels	Centralized, tall organization; large wage differentials among organizational levels

Uncertainty Avoidance

Low	High
(Britain, Denmark, India, Sweden, United States)	(France, Greece, Japan, Peru)
Less structuring of activities fewer written rules, and prone to risk	More structuring of activities, more written rules, and aversive to risk

Individualism

Low	High
(Greece, Mexico, Taiwan, Venezuela)	(Australia, Britain, Canada, Netherlands, United States)
Personal organization that encourages loyalty, duty, and group participation	Impersonal organization that encourages individual initiative

Masculinity

Low	High
(Denmark, Finland, Sweden, Thailand)	(Austria, Italy, Japan Mexico, Venezuela)
Sex roles minimized and more women in more qualified jobs	Sex roles clearly differentiated and fewer women in qualified jobs.
Soft, yielding, intuitive skills rewarded; interpersonal support valued.	Aggression, competition, and justice rewarded; work valued

Adapted from Table 4.1 in *Managing Organizational Behavior*, by H. L. Tosi, J. R. Rizzo, and S. J. Carroll. Copyright © 1990 by Harper & Row, New York. Adapted with permission of Addison-Wesley Educational Publishers, Inc.

specific observations of the target organizational culture. The societal determinant requires knowledge of the larger contextual culture and is likely to "be most powerful in the processes of organizations [related] to authority, style, conduct, participation and attitudes and less powerful in formal structuring and overall strategy" (Child, 1981, p. 347). A focus on the business domain as the primary determinant of organizational culture requires knowledge of the values and practices of different professions or skills, and this source of organizational culture is likely to be highly influential for complex and innovative manufacturing or service domains. Furthermore, the influence of the founder is essential, particularly when you are trying to understand the unique features of a given organizational culture. For example, Biggart's (1989) investigation of sales organizations found that charismatic founders use their emotional expressiveness, linguistic ability, confidence, and vision to inspire their followers and build their organizational cultures.

Finally, regardless of which force or set of forces (such as the larger social cultural context; type of business; or beliefs, values, and assumptions of the founder-leader) shape organizational culture, pervasive themes seem to be addressed in almost organizational cultures. These themes focus on the issues and challenges of innovation, stability, the role of attention to detail, and orientation toward people, outcomes of results, and collaboration and teams (Chatman & Jehn, 1994; Hofstede et al., 1990; O'Reilly, Chatman, & Caldwell, 1991).

FUNCTION OF ORGANIZATIONAL CULTURE

The primary function of an organizational culture is to enhance the organization's responsiveness to the problems of external adaptation and internal integration (Schein, 1985, 1990, 1992). All organizations have to deal continuously with these two broad categories of problems, and the awareness of such problems and

adaptive organizational learning are two vital signs of the effectiveness of the organization. Table 3–3 presents some specific issues of external adaptation and internal integration that must be handled by organizational leaders and members.

External Adaptation

The mission is the raison d'être of the organization that is usually expressed in the mission statement, which must be publicized, reviewed, and updated periodically. In general, a short overarching mission statement is sound if it can be expressed readily by members of the organization and appears prominently in a variety of organizational communications. Such a mission statement affords the opportunity to accommodate more tailored mission statements for each of the main units in the organization. A mission statement provides a focus, gives a sense of grounding, and can evoke deep passions and tireless effort. Table 3–4 presents some illustrative mission statements and guidelines for constructing a mission statement.

The definition of organizational goals flows from the mission statement, provides specific statements of organizational purposes, and focuses the attention and energies of the organizational members. Also, the process of goal setting allows the organization to align its organizational capacities, reflected in its cultural, human, financial, and physical resources, with its organizational aspirations (Locke & Latham, 1990). In our judgment, goal setting is extremely important for shaping and changing organizational cultures, but it is not totally without risk (such as setting the wrong organizational goal because of the lack of information or premature decision making to reach a consensus). The details of goal setting are discussed more fully in Chapter 6.

The issues of the means, measurement, and correction of actions by systematic feedback are important components of the process of external adaptation that are shaped by the organiza-

TABLE 3–3. Problems of External Adaptation and Internal Integration

Problems of External Adaptation and Survival

Mission and Strategy. Obtaining a shared understanding of the core mission, primary task, and manifest and latent functions.
Goals. Developing a consensus on goals, as derived from the core mission.
Means. Developing a consensus on the means to be used to attain the goals, such as the organizational structure, division of labor, reward system, and authority system.
Measurement. Developing a consensus on the criteria to be used in measuring how well the group is doing in fulfilling its goals, such as the information and control system.
Correction. Developing a consensus on the appropriate remedial or repair strategies to be used if goals are not being met.

Problems of Internal Integration

Common Language and Conceptual Categories. If members cannot communicate with and understand each other, a group is impossible by definition.
Group Boundaries and Criteria for Inclusion and Exclusion. One of the most important areas of culture is the shared consensus on who is in and who is out and by what criteria one determines membership.
Power and Status. Every organization must work out its pecking order, its criteria, and rules for how one gets, maintains, and loses power; a consensus in this area is crucial to help members manage feelings of aggression.
Intimacy, Friendship, and Love. Every organization must work out its rules of the game for peer relationships, for relationships between the sexes, and for the manner in which openness and intimacy are to be handled in the context of managing the organization's tasks.
Rewards and Punishments. Every group must know what its heroic and sinful behaviors are; what gets rewarded with property, status, and power; and what gets punished in the form of withdrawal of the rewards and, ultimately, excommunication.
Ideology and "Religion." Every organization, like every society, faces unexplainable and inexplicable events, which must be given meaning so that members can respond to them and avoid the anxiety of dealing with the unexplainable and uncontrollable.

Adapted from *Organizational Culture and Leadership*, pp. 52, 56, by E. H. Schein. Copyright 1985 by Jossey-Bass, San Francisco. Used with permission.

tional goals. Systematic and sustained feedback about goal-oriented performances is essential to organizational members, so they can determine which actions to continue and which actions and goals need to be modified so as not to waste organizational resources. In general, external adaptation requires an awareness of and sensitivity to the larger societal culture; the global, regional, and domestic marketplaces; and issues for a particular type of business. *Macroknowledge*, or knowledge about the functioning of groups, organizations, governments, and larger societal cultures, is necessary for effective external adaptation.

Internal Integration

Problems of internal integration arise for every organization; must be addressed; and, in general, require an awareness of and sensitivity to intra- and interpersonal processes. *Microknowledge*, or knowledge about how people think, feel, act, and relate with others, is necessary for effective internal integration. When they are not engaged in specific activities, most people in most places around the world spend a fair amount of time thinking and talking to the most important person in their lives: themselves. It has been estimated that if human ideation about oneself was translated into a word-by-word script, one would find that people talk to themselves at the rate of about 1,200 words per minute. This self-talk can be positive and motivating or negative and paralyzing. Almost all people focus each day on thoughts about their self-efficacy or ability to execute a particular task or pattern of actions (Bandura, 1986). In general, the higher a person judges her or his ef-

TABLE 3–4. Illustrative Mission Statements and Guidelines for Constructing a Mission Statement

---

Illustrative Mission Statements

"We strive continuously to provide the highest quality in firm and refreshing support for our customers and each other." *Athletic Wear Company*

"We exist to give you the highest quality natural fertilizer so you can grow and we can come off smelling like a rose." *Organic Fertilizing Company*

"Our mission is to provide you with the highest quality evening wear anywhere." *TGIF Slipper Company*

Guidelines for Constructing a Mission Statement

The mission statement should reinforce the idea that the organization is something one should identify with and that deserves respect from employees, customers, vendors, and the community.

The mission statement should provide a rallying point, uniting people so they can feel satisfaction in working toward a common goal.

The mission statement should focus on quality, cost-effectiveness, continuous improvement, and customer satisfaction.

Avoid managerial zeal in completing the mission statement, behaving as if the mission statement is a done deal, getting stuck in writing the mission statement, acting as if the mission statement is cast in stone, forgetting the mission statement after it is written, and believing the mission statement will tell you how to behave in specific situations.

---

ficacy for a particular task, the more likely the person is to engage in that task; persist if not initially successful; choose alternate task-completion strategies if the original strategy is not successful; and, in the long run, gets more things done than does the person who judges her or his efficacy to be low (Bandura, 1986; Dvir, Eden, & Banjo, 1995; Eden & Aviram, 1993; Lawson & Ventriss, 1992). We discuss the construct of perceived self-efficacy more fully in Chapter 6.

Every organizational culture develops its own specialized language and the dictionary of meanings of organizational terms and the texts of organizational concepts, procedures, and stories vary from one organization to another. Organizational boundaries influence disclosure and levels of trust, which are usually higher with organizational members than with outsiders, es-

pecially in relation to important organizational issues and challenges. The issue of power is treated more fully in Chapter 7. Here, it is important to bear in mind that every organization includes information about who has power and how it is exercised under different conditions.

Last, the problems of social relationships in the workplace have taken on greater importance, given the increasing amount of time people spend at work and the widening diversity of the workforce, which increases the number of different cultural perspectives on such important issues as intimacy, friendship, and love.

Cultural Directory

Table 3–5 presents a brief directory of sources of cultural information on external adaptation

TABLE 3–5. Preliminary Directory of Organizational Culture

External Adaptation	Loci of Organizational Information
Mission	The charter, mission, and vision statements; annual reports; founders' documents and biographies; accreditation reports; recruitment materials; and minutes of board meetings.
Goals	Strategic planning documents, annual budget reports, and public relations materials.
Means	Technological reports, standard operating procedures, manuals, and organizational charts.
Performance Measures	Management information systems, personnel documents and performance-appraisal forms, and financial statements.
Correction Mechanisms	Strategic planning documents, personnel records, internal management documents, and records of retreats.

Internal Integration	Loci of Organizational Information
Language	Internal memorandums, electronic mail, records of management meetings, and public relations materials.
Boundaries	Employee recruitment and selection materials, orientation materials, organizational stories, and personnel management systems.
Power and Status	Organizational structures, annual budget reports, physical-plant documents, space and equipment budgets, strategic planning documents, and minutes of board meetings.
Peer Relationships and Intimacy	Personnel records and management systems, human resource materials, employee assistance program materials, informal memorandums, public bulletin boards, and electronic mail.
Reward System	Personnel records, performance-appraisal system, unit or departmental budgets, space and equipment inventories, and employee development programs.
Ideology	Charter, biographies of the founders, annual reports, organizational stories, strategic planning documents, and public relations materials.

and internal integration, which are major problems that every organizational culture confronts. The timeliness, content, and distribution of the documents identified in Table 3–5 are all sources of information about the organizational culture. Thus, for example, if the mission statement has not been reviewed and updated about every five years or only a few members can briefly state the mission of the organization, it may be an indication that the leaders need to pay closer attention to the cultivation of their organizational culture. If organizational members deny or ignore the problems of external adaptation and internal integration, the organization is

likely to be ineffective, dysfunctional, or on the verge of extinction.

When organizational psychologists work with organizations that focus on issues of organizational culture, we collect the kinds of documents, brochures, and other sources of information about culture presented in Table 3–5. In addition, organizational psychologists inquire and, if possible, observe organizational rites, ceremonies, and rituals to obtain a richer description and appreciation of the organizational culture. According to Trice and Beyer (1985), an organizational rite is a fairly elaborate, planned, and dramatic set of activities that consolidate various forms of cultural expressions into one event that is usually presented to an audience. Typical organizational rites include rites of passage (the socialization of new members or promotion parties), renewal (organizational development activities like retreats, workshops, and learning sessions), and integration (office holiday parties, picnics, or field trips). An organizational ceremony is a system of collected rites, such as the annual meeting of shareholders or annual budget and planning sessions. Organizational rituals are standardized sets of behaviors to manage anxieties that are practiced most often in departmental or unit meetings that frequently do not result in specific decisions or actions. Finally, we also seek any organizational stories, legends, humor, or gestures that reflect glimpses of the organizational culture. Organizational psychologists look for themes, patterns, trends, or idiosyncrasies that almost inevitably provide the direction for further and deeper inquiry into the organizational culture.

LEVELS OF ORGANIZATIONAL CULTURE

According to Schein (1985, 1990, 1992), organizational culture is discernible at three different levels that are presented schematically in Figure 3–1.

Artifacts

It is widely agreed that the most readily observable but least exact expression of the shared meanings of the culture are represented by *artifacts*. Artifacts include things and the arrangement of things in an organization, as well as observable behaviors captured by organizational stories and jokes, ceremonies (celebrations of values and basic assumptions, such as annual or major recognition meetings and graduation exercises), rites and rituals (habitual activities rooted in values and basic assumptions like weekly or monthly departmental meetings or

presentations), and norms (unwritten rules for appropriate and inappropriate behaviors). Artifacts of a culture are quickly detected, although in many instances, the shared meanings held by the members in relation to them are difficult to decipher readily. It is not the artifact or thing in itself but, rather, the shared meaning that is key for appreciating and becoming deeply aware of the organizational culture.

Values

Values, which we defined in Chapter 2 as preferences and that Schein (1992) defined as someone's sense of what ought to be, as distinct from what is, represent the second level of organizational culture. The basic issue at this level of organizational culture is the members' determination of what works or is successful for a given organizational problem. Thus, for example, when sales go into a nosedive, a firm may decide to do more advertising, which is followed by increased sales. If this pattern is repeated and continues to result in success, then the organizational members who shared in the experiences will come to value advertising as a sound investment of organizational resources. As the members begin to explain, mostly to themselves, why advertising worked and therefore is valued, they will develop focused and strongly held beliefs associated with particular values. Values can be both espoused and enacted; however, adults pay the greatest attention to enacted or operationalized values and are more inclined to modify their own values in response to them than to values that are solely expressed or espoused. In our judgment, a single enactment of a core organizational value is much more valuable than a thousand espousals of that value. The loudest words are those of the doer.

The validity of a given value is determined by testing the preferred solution against physical or social realities. For example, out of many comparable manufacturing processes, one is selected or valued because it yields the most

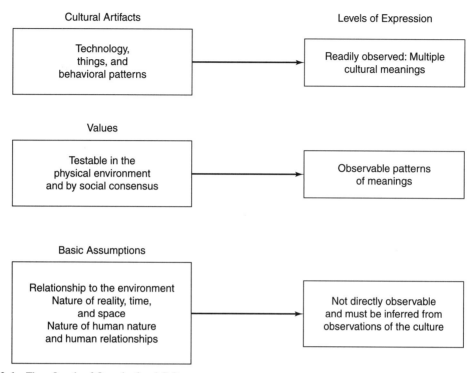

Figure 3–1   Three Levels of Organizational Culture.
Adapted from *Organizational Culture and Leadership*, p. 14, by E. H. Schein. Copyright 1985 by Jossey-Bass, San Francisco. Used with permission.

durable product or particular activities are performed in particular ways because they "feel right" or are accepted by a large majority of organizational members as the right thing to do. Hence, what works and what members agree works becomes the anvil against which values are hammered out for a particular organizational culture.

Basic Assumptions

According to Schein (1985, 1990, 1992), when the initial preferences for organizational problem solving continue to be successful, organizational members increasingly take the originally tentative solutions for granted and come to believe that their selected solutions actually reflect reality because they have continued to be successful. If a solution works repeatedly, it must be true, and any doubt about its efficacy is eliminated from the minds of the members and eventually from the cultural mind of the organization. We are, of course, not talking about trivial assumptions but about fundamental beliefs about the nature of reality. Thus, for example, if the members of an organization share the belief that they must first and foremost learn to harmonize human actions and desires with the elements of the world, such as clean air, water, open spaces, and respect for vegetation and other living creatures, it is most likely that they will be working for a "green organization" (Shrivastava, 1995). In contrast, those who fundamentally believe that the carrying capacity of the environment is infinite or relatively unimportant to "the business of business" will be found in a different organizational culture performing a different set of organizational activities.

Sooner or later, every individual and every organization must confront all or most of the fundamental assumptions listed in the lower panel of Figure 3–1 that, in the formative stages of an organizational culture, are consciously recognized and actively debated. As the members act on their fundamental beliefs about these issues and the organization succeeds, grows, and prospers, the fundamental beliefs are taken for granted and simply acted on without further reflection or regard. According to Schein (1992) and Ott (1989), when these fundamental beliefs are shared, taken for granted, and nondebatable, they become the basic assumptions of the culture. Table 3–6 presents some examples of basic assumptions that may be part of an organizational culture. If these basic assumptions

determine what organizational members pay attention to, act on, and express a range of intense feelings about, you can imagine the different kinds of organizations that may operate according to some of them. In fact, Schein (1992, p. 26) asserted that "the essence of a culture lies in the pattern of basic underlying assumptions, and once one understands those, one can easily understand the other more surface levels and deal appropriately with them."

Last, according to Argyris (1976), Argyris and Schon (1974), and Schein (1992), cultural change occurs only when the basic assumptions change. Changing basic assumptions is an anxiety-provoking and difficult process that involves double-loop organizational learning or basically changing the important things you

TABLE 3–6. Examples of Basic Assumptions Held by an Organizational Culture

Relationship to the environment

Earthly resources are infinite or can be replaced and are to be developed for profit.
Earthly resources are finite and are to be protected or developed sparingly.

Nature of reality, time, and space

Reality is based on social consensus, rather than on absolute truths.
Time is money.
Small is better than big.

Nature of human nature

People are basically honest, trustworthy, realistic, and enjoyable.
People are lazy, greedy, only interested in themselves, and cynical.

Nature of human activity

If you do what you love for a living, you will never have to work again.

Nature of human relationships

Never mix business and friendship.
People interact only out of self-interest.

have done and still do, rather than single-loop learning, which involves getting more efficient at what you now do (Argyris, Putnam, & Smith, 1985). Thus, especially at the level of basic assumptions, it is imperative to accept loss as a universal force.

CHANGING ORGANIZATIONAL CULTURE

According to Adler and Ghadar (1990), organizations evolve through four stages of development—*domestic*, *international*, *multinational*, and *global*—that are driven by the life cycles of their products (or services). In the domestic phase, the organization develops and produces unique new products primarily for the market in the country or territory in which the organization is housed. In the international phase, the organization markets products in other countries, which involves exporting products, assembling products in these countries, and finally producing products abroad. In the third phase, the organization operates in a competitive multinational environment, with a focus on pricing, sourcing, producing, and distributing products along integrated global lines of business. In the global phase, organizations, to survive, need nimble systems that are globally coordinated and integrated while highly differentiated and nationally responsive (Bartlett, Doz, & Hedlund, 1990; Bartlett & Ghoshal, 1989; Bartmess & Cerney, 1993; Humes, 1993; Prahalad & Doz, 1987).

Criteria for Cultural Change

Clearly, the organizational culture of a firm in the global phase will be different from that of a firm in the domestic phase, although both will consist of unifying patterns of shared beliefs, feelings, values, and actions. Whether an organization is serving a domestic or global market, it takes three to five years to make changes in an organizational culture at the level of basic assumptions, while changes at the level of artifacts

can be accomplished within a year at most (Ott, 1989; Schein, 1992). Given the magnitudes of time, personnel, and financial resources that can be invested in changing organizational culture, it is important to know if an organizational problem or pattern of problems is due to cultural issues or to more focused personnel or unit-based turbulence. Allen (1985) suggested that affirmative answers to the following three questions suggest that the pattern of problems are culture based or systemic and indicate that cultural change is probably needed:

- Is the problem or pattern of problems chronic?
- Is the problem or pattern of problems widespread or organization wide?
- Has the problem or pattern of problems resisted previous focused (departmental or unit) change efforts?

In the process of changing an organizational culture, it is essential to describe richly and understand the current organizational culture before one can set goals for changing the organizational culture and learning strategies. Organizations can remain stuck if the cultural change process includes mainly focused and unrelated goals and interventions that span organizational units and many key individuals. There is growing evidence that changing an organizational culture involves changing organizational learning strategies (Foil & Lyles, 1985; Schein, 1992) and systematically using goal-setting strategies (Lawson & Ventriss, 1992; Locke & Latham, 1990; Matsui, Kakuyama, & Onglatco, 1987).

Social Science Perspectives

According to Martin (1992), there are three social science perspectives, each of which serves as a framework for collecting and interpreting data on organizational cultures (see Table 3–7).

The *integration* perspective looks for cultural manifestations (artifacts and values) that con-

TABLE 3–7. Martin's Three Social Science Perspectives on Organizational Culture

Perspective	Integration	Differentiation	Fragmentation
Orientation to consensus	Organization-wide consensus	Subcultural consensus	Multiplicity of views (no consensus)
Relation among manifestations	Consistency	Inconsistency	Complexity (not clearly consistent or inconsistent)
Orientation to ambiguity	Exclusion	Ambiguities channeled outside subcultures	Focus on ambiguities

Adapted from *Cultures in Organizations: Three Perspectives*, p. 13, by J. Martin. Copyright 1992 by Oxford University Press, New York. Adapted with permission of the author.

sistently reinforce the basic cultural assumptions, promote organization-wide cultural consensus, and exhibit cultural clarity regarding members' beliefs, feelings, values, and actions. Integrated organizational cultures are consistent, clear, and consensual.

The *differentiation* perspective, according to Martin (1992), reveals systematic inconsistencies among actions, values, and assumptions and consensus by members of a subculture (for example, by functional area, such as accounting versus personnel, or by architectural levels for instance, those in the upper or lower level). It also reveals the absence of an organization-wide consensus and cultural ambiguities or uncertainties that are channeled outside the subculture to retain clarity within the subculture (as in the belief that "the folks in accounting are really fouling up the operations of this department because of their strange ways of counting things and people").

Finally the *fragmentation* perspective focuses on the multiplicity, complexity, and ambiguity of members' beliefs, feelings, values, and actions (lack of any consensus). Martin (1992) clearly indicated that the perspective, framework, or paradigm of the cultural observer or observers influences the description, interpreta-

tion, and intervention strategies of a given organizational culture. Most important, in our judgment, Martin has made plain that any organizational culture most likely reflects a mix of the three perspectives but that one perspective is more dominant than the other two.

Cultural Change Strategies

There are innumerable applied strategies for changing organizational culture (Kilmann et al., 1985). Schein's (1992) leader-centered change strategy is perhaps the most fully articulated. It is a strategy that involves a clinical (or helping) relationship between outside consultants and informed and cooperative insiders whose primary joint task is to identify and then change the basic assumptions of the organizational culture primarily by changing either the leaders' assumptions or changing the leaders. In general, Schein's approach reflects Martin's (1992) integration perspective in that there is a search for an organization-wide consensus, consistency, and clarity, which are determined primarily by the founder and extant leadership.

Schein (1992) identified specific primary strategies that can be applied to change an organizational culture. All these strategies focus on the formal (and, it is hoped, informal) organizational leader or leadership team and include, for example,

- what leaders pay attention to, measure, and control
- how leaders react to critical incidents and organizational crises
- observed criteria by which leaders allocate scarce resources
- deliberate role modeling, teaching, and coaching
- observed criteria by which leaders recruit, select, promote, retire, and excommunicate organizational members

Schein (1992) also identified secondary strategies and reinforcement mechanisms to change organizational culture that include modifying organizational rites, rituals, and stories; structuring reward systems to promote change; and revising formal statements, such as the organizational mission statement (what we do), vision statements (what we aspire to be), value statements, and recruitment materials. Schein's cultural change process focuses primarily on the leader or leadership team and involves the consultant working closely with organizational insiders who are committed to organizational change and have sufficient influence to have an impact on many members of the organization.

L and S Cultural Change Strategy

In this section, we present a cultural change strategy that combines features of different approaches that, in one way or the other, involve changing norms, or unspoken rules of behavior (Allen, 1985), reward systems (Sethia & Von Glinow, 1985), and organizational rites, or organized and planned activities that have both practical and expressive consequences (Trice & Beyer, 1985). Our culture change strategy has

been applied in public service organizations (Lawson & Ventriss, 1992) and in our consulting practice with business firms and is sufficiently flexible to be applied to a wide variety of organizations. Basically, there are three phases to our cultural change strategy that are presented in Table 3–8.

Phase 1, *assessment*, involves three steps: identifying the client, increasing cultural awareness, and establishing baselines. The first step focuses on *identifying the organizational processes* of motivational systems, leadership, decision making, conflict resolution, and individual-organizational change as the client for the change program, rather than a particular individual, group, or unit. It is important to indicate that these organizational processes will change *only if* individual members who give life to them change their shared and unifying patterns of thoughts, feelings, values, and actions about the critical issues before the organization and processes that address those issues. This step is intended to make plain that the cultural change process is not focused on a single individual or

TABLE 3–8. L and S Cultural Change Strategy

Phase 1	Assessment
	Identifying the client
	Increasing cultural awareness
	Establishing baselines
Phase 2	Construction and Implementation of Cultural and Learning Change Projects
	Two to three projects
	Specific goals, deadlines, and systematic feedback for each project
	Rite of enhancement
Phase 3	Organizational Outcome Measures and Project Modifications
	Synthesis and interpretation of changes in performance or identification of barriers to change
	Sustained participation by the leadership

cluster of individuals but, rather, is a systemic change process intended to include everyone.

The second step in Phase 1 involves *increasing cultural awareness* by assembling as many of the documents that serve as a preliminary directory of an organizational culture (see Table 3–5), meeting systematically with groups from the major levels or units of the organization, and walking around and talking informally with organizational members. It is also helpful to visit the organization at least once early in the day and late at night (or during the night shift) to get some unedited glimpses of the organization; also, whenever you can, obtain information about organizational stories (usually associated with organizational crises), jokes, ceremonies, and rituals (usually high-frequency regimented interactions, such as meetings); receive customers' or clients' complaints and compliments; and meet with external persons or organizations that interact regularly with the target organization.

The third step in Phase 1 is to *establish cultural baselines* by creating a short draft document that describes the current organizational culture. This is a delicate and critical step, and it is best to show the draft to the leadership and to emphasize the assets and benefits of the current culture while focusing on areas or activities that require revamping or refinement. In writing this description, it is valuable to follow the outline of problems of external adaptation and internal integration presented in Table 3–3. From the assessment document, the leadership, committed organizational members, and you (acting primarily as a facilitator) can identify the cultural baselines and focal processes around which you can begin to build cultural change projects.

Phase 2, *construction and implementation of cultural and learning change projects*, is the action phase. At this juncture, it is best to identify two or three organizational projects and initiate each sequentially and then gradually overlap the projects so that a stream of small wins accumulates that then is communicated systematically to all organizational members. Thus, for exam-

ple, it may be appropriate to construct or review the existing mission statement following the guidelines outlined in Table 3–4 and attempt to uncover some of the basic assumptions of the culture (see Table 3–6). Once the draft mission statement is completed, circulate it throughout the organization to obtain suggestions for revisions and discuss the document to give everyone an opportunity to participate in the process.

In addition, establish process-focused groups that examine some of the key organizational processes, such as decision making and conflict resolution, to identify what changes, if any, may be required in these processes so as to enact the new or revised mission statement. Here, it is appropriate to establish some learning experiments in which a current process that supports the new or revised mission statement is described and root causes of problems and barriers to change are identified and then to start implementing a change in a given process while monitoring changes in performance.

Last, it is important to initiate or reinforce an existing rite of enhancement (a public celebration of the positive accomplishments of the members of the organization; see Trice & Beyer, 1985). Some simple yet powerful rites include a casual dress day on the last day of the workweek, a dress-up day, or a weekly event in which ideas and actions toward continuous improvement are recognized and refreshments are served.

Phase 3, *organizational outcome measures and project modifications*, includes a synthesis and interpretation of performance or outcome measures for all cultural change projects and then decisions about what modifications of existing cultural change projects are required or if the new projects need to be firmly established as the way to do things in the organization. It is critical to provide systematic feedback to members so they become aware of their individual and collective sense of efficacy (capacities to execute specific patterns of actions), identify the extent of resistance to change, and help to identify barriers to change in the organizational culture. Some organizational-level measures include changes in the quality of products, or services or delivery times, cost savings, and measures of cohesiveness or conflict resolution.

EFFECTS OF ORGANIZATIONAL CULTURE

Cultural transformation requires time. Therefore, if the leadership is not prepared for a sustained campaign, then the focus will be lost and the transformation effort will dwindle and die (Stahl & Bounds, 1991).

Organizational culture influences the unifying pattern of what and how members think, feel, value, and act in reference to the key issues of the problems of external adaptation and internal integration. It transmits what is permissible and what is not allowed in an organization and sends a clear message to all members that those who do not adjust to the culture will not succeed, regardless of their competencies or achievements (Kets de Vries, 1993; Kets de Vries & Miller, 1984, 1986; Ott, 1989).

The specific impacts of organizational culture on organizational performances remain to be determined by careful empirically based studies. However, it is clear that many have assumed that the linkage exists (Allen & Kraft, 1982; Davis, 1984; Deal & Kennedy, 1982; Kilmann, 1984; Kilmann et al., 1985; Pascale & Athos, 1981; Peters & Waterman, 1982; Schein, 1985, 1990, 1992), and there is growing empirical evidence to support this assumption (Denison, 1984; Kotter & Heskett, 1992; Wilkins & Ouchi, 1983).

Barney (1985) suggested that organizational culture can be a source of competitive advantage, provided that the culture is valuable, in that it fosters actions by members that lead to high sales or low costs or add financial value to the organization in other ways. In addition, the organizational culture must be rare, in that it has features that are not common to the cultures of a larger number of organizations, and imperfectly imitable, so that other organizations cannot copy its unique features.

Organizational Outcomes

Kotter and Heskett (1992) studied the cultures of 207 major U.S. firms in 25 industries, including airlines, computers, financial products and services, pharmaceuticals, retail sales, and telecommunications. They measured the strength of the organizational culture based on their survey instrument and three measures of economic performance for the period 1977–88: average yearly increase in net income, average yearly return on investment, and average yearly increase in stock price. Perhaps, their most important finding was that adaptive organizational cultures have a significant impact on the long-term economic performance of firms in that the firms with adaptive cultures increased revenues by an average of 682% versus 166% for firms with unadapted cultures, expanded their workforces by 282% versus 36%, raised their stock prices by 901% versus 74%, and improved their net incomes by 756% versus 1%. In addition, Kotter and Heskett concluded that organizational culture will be an important factor in determining long-term financial performances well beyond the 1990s; unadaptive cultures that inhibit strong long-term financial performances are not rare, even though the membership of firms with these cultures is full of reasonable and intelligent people; and although difficult to change, corporate cultures can be made more performance enhancing. Table 3–9 presents the core values and common managerial behaviors shared by managers of adaptive and unadaptive cultures identified by Kotter and Heskett.

Cultures and Organizations

The authors have lived and worked briefly in each other's countries as well as in other countries around the globe, and we know from experience that there are fundamental social and psychological differences between the citizens of our respective countries in relation to freewill and determinism, individualism versus collectivism, and different orientations toward com-

TABLE 3–9. Adaptive versus Unadaptive Corporate Cultures

	Adaptive Corporate Cultures	Unadaptive Corporate Cultures
Core Values	Managers care deeply about customers, stockholders, and employees. They place a high value on people and processes that can create useful change.	Managers care about themselves, their immediate work group, or some product or technology. They value the orderly and risk-reducing management process.
Common Behavior	Managers pay close attention to all their constituencies, especially customers; initiate change when needed; and take risks.	Managers behave politically and bureaucratically. They do not change their strategies quickly to adjust to or take advantage of changes in their business environments.

Reprinted with the permission of The Free Press, a division of Simon & Schuster, New York, from *Corporate Culture and Performance*, by J. P. Kotter & J. L. Heskett. Copyright © 1992 by Kotter Associates, Inc., and James L. Heskett.

munication and understanding (Boyacigller & Adler, 1992; Hofstede, 1980). We also know from experience that larger societal cultures vary in their degree of oppressiveness and openness, both of which exist in all societal cultures. Accordingly, we value and respect the importance and impact of larger societal cultures on organizational cultures and encourage you to consider the cultural material presented in this chapter as a platform for models and applied strategies that must be shaped, revised, and perhaps jettisoned, depending on your judgment and appreciation of local situational or contextual forces.

TABLE 3–10. Ouchi's *Theory Z*, Derived from Features of Japanese and American Organizations

Japanese Organizations	U.S. Organizations
Lifetime employment	Short-term employment
Slow evaluation and promotion	Rapid evaluation and promotion
Nonspecialized career paths	Specialized career paths
Implicit control mechanisms	Explicit control mechanisms
Collective decision making	Individual decision making
Collective responsibility	Individual responsibility
Wholistic concern for employees	Segmented concern for employees

Theory Z Organizations

Long-term employment
Consensual decision making
Individual responsibility
Slow evaluation and promotion
Implicit informal control with explicit measures of performance
Moderately specialized career pattern

Conversely, we believe, as do others (Ouchi, 1981; Ouchi & Wilkins, 1985; Schein, 1992), that in conjunction with the potent contextual influence of the larger societal culture, it is also possible and appropriate to construct organizational cultures that can be highly valuable for global organizations. An early study by Ouchi (1981) (criticized by Sullivan, 1983), which focused on firms in Japan and the United States, found that organizations in both countries had organizational cultures that incorporated many of the core components of their larger societal cultures, as summarized in Table 3–10. Ouchi then concluded that selected features of both Japanese and American firms can and have been incorporated into organizations. These combined features constitute his Theory Z of organizational culture. As a consequence of subsequent recessionary developments throughout the world during the early 1990s, many Japanese and American firms have had to abandon some of the features of a Theory Z organization, such as a commitment to lifelong employment, although some firms did so reluctantly and with anguish (Gerstner, 1993; Naj, 1993; Ono, 1993; Schlesinger & Kanabayashi, 1992).

Competency Culture

We also believe, along with others (Barney, 1992; Lado & Wilson, 1994; Wright & Snell, 1991), that successful global organizations of the 1990s and the 21st will cultivate cultures that promote work competencies and compassion for persons and environments while they focus on the timely delivery of the highest-quality products or services at the lowest possible prices. The three domains of work competencies—*organizational*, *human*, and *environmental*—with a few actions for each one, are listed in Table 3–11. These competencies and associated actions are only suggestions, and we encourage you to consider them only as a point of departure for modification on the basis of your experiences and expectations for the future of your organization.

TABLE 3–11. Suggested Actions for Three Competency Domains to Be Cultivated in the Cultures of Aspiring or Established Global Organizations

Organizational Competencies

Choose nimble organizational processes to deliver the highest-quality products or services at the lowest possible prices now.

Treat customers or clients as partners.

Human Competencies

Promote teamwork, coupled with personal initiative and responsibility.

Promote trust, diversity, organizational security, and development of a corps of loyal and committed members.

Environmental Competencies

Promote wholesome work environments, processes, and a positive presence in the larger community.

Work as a partner with governments to promote just, expeditious, and minimal-barrier regulatory processes.

We close with the firm belief that the failure to plan and manage organizational culture is a plan to fail and that the secret of life is that there is no secret. Organizational cultures, like individual lives, are created as a consequence of beliefs, feelings, values, and actions that make each person responsible to himself or herself and to others. What is lost as a result of change can be found anew in continuing individual efforts expressed through shared and unifying societal and organizational cultures.

SUMMARY

It is essential to remember that organizational culture is a situational variable that influences, to various degrees, all members of an organization. Organizational culture is the unifying and shared pattern of thoughts, feelings, values, and actions that serve to bind together organizational members and distinguish them from nonmembers. It determines, in large measure, the responses of organizational members to problems of external adaptation and internal integration that confront all organizations around the globe. Furthermore, understanding the components of these two problems allows one to build a directory that will fully describe an organizational culture.

Organizational learning and organizational culture are intimately linked to each other, and this linkage provides the bases for instituting organizational cultural change. A specific change strategy and the detailed steps in implementing it were presented that can be applied in a wide variety of organizations, subject to specific refinements, depending on unique features of the target organization. That the organizational culture influences organizational financial and productivity outcomes indicates that it is an important factor for participating in the global marketplace. Last, the outline we presented for an organizational culture based on competencies in the domains of organizational processes, people, and environment can be applied to a wide variety of organizations.

A solid understanding of organizational culture yields many dividends by making plain what is acceptable and unacceptable in a given organization. Thus, it minimizes the unnecessary expenditure of attention and emotions regarding what, how, when, and why to think, value, feel, and act in the workplace.

CHAPTER REFERENCES

Adler, N. J., & Ghadar, F. (1990). International strategy from the perspective of people and culture: The North American context. In A. Rugman (Ed.), *Research in global strategic management: International business research for the twenty-first century* (pp. 261–289). Greenwich, CT: JAI Press.

Allaire, Y., & Firsirotu, M. (1985). How to implement radical strategies in large organizations. *Sloan Management Review, 26,* 19–34.

Allen, R. F. (1985). Four phases for bringing about culture change. In R. Kilmann, M. J. Saxton, R. Serpa, & Associates, *Gaining control of the corporate culture* (pp. 332–350). San Francisco: Jossey-Bass.

Allen, R. F., & Kraft, C. (1982). *The organizational unconscious: How to create the corporate culture you want and need.* Englewood Cliffs, NJ: Prentice Hall.

Argyris, C. (1976). *Increasing leadership effectiveness.* New York: John Wiley & Sons.

Argyris, C., Putnam, R., & Smith, D. M. (1985). *Action science.* San Francisco: Jossey-Bass.

Argyris, C., & Schon, D. A. (1974). *Theory in practice: Increasing professional effectiveness.* San Francisco: Jossey-Bass.

Argyris, C., & Schon, D. (1978). *Organizational learning: A theory of action perspective.* Reading, MA: Addison-Wesley.

Bandura, A. (1986). *Social foundations of thought and action: A social cognitive theory.* Englewood Cliffs, NJ: Prentice Hall.

Barney, J. B. (1985). Organizational culture: Can it be a source of sustained competitive advantage? *Academy of Management Review, 11,* 656–665.

Barney, J. B. (1992). Integrating organizational behavior and strategy formulation research: A resource-based analysis. In P. Shrivastava, A. Huff, & J. Dutton (Eds.), *Advances in strategic management* (Vol. 8, pp. 39–61). Greenwich, CT: JAI Press.

Bartlett, C. A., Doz, Y., & Hedlund, G. (1990). *Managing the global firm.* London: Routledge & Kegan Paul.

Bartlett, C. A., & Ghoshal, S. (1989). *Managing across borders: The transnational solution.* Cambridge, MA: Harvard Business School Press.

Bartmess, A., & Cerney, K. (1993). Building competitive advantage through a global network of capabilities. *California Management Review, 35,* 78–103.

Biggart, N. W. (1989). *Charismatic capitalism: Direct selling organizations in America.* Chicago: University of Chicago Press.

Boyacigiller, N. A., & Adler, N. J. (1991). The parochial dinosaur: Organizational science in a global context. *Academy of Management Review, 16,* 262–290.

Bower, M. (1966). *The will to manage.* New York: McGraw-Hill.

Burke, M. J., Borucki, C. C., & Hurley, A. E. (1992). Reconceptualizing psychological climate in a retail service environment: A multiple-stakeholder perspective. *Journal of Applied Psychology, 77,* 717–729.

Chatman, J. A., & Jehn, K. A. (1994). Assessing the relationship between industry characteristics and organizational culture: How different can you be? *Academy of Management Journal, 37,* 522–553.

Child, J. (1981). Culture, contingency and capitalism in the cross-national study of organizations. In B. M. Staw & L. L. Cummings (Eds.), *Research in organizational behavior* (Vol. 3, pp. 303–356). Greenwich, CT: JAI Press.

Davis, S. M. (1984). *Managing corporate culture.* Cambridge, MA: Ballinger.

Deal, T. E. (1985). Cultural change: Opportunity, silent killer, or metamorphosis? In R. Kilmann, M. J. Saxton, R. Serpa, & Associates, *Gaining control of the corporate culture.* San Francisco: Jossey-Bass.

Deal, T., & Kennedy, A. A. (1982). *Corporate cultures: The rites and rituals of corporate life.* Reading, MA: Addison-Wesley.

Denison, D. (1984). Bringing corporate culture to the bottom line. *Organizational Dynamics, 13,* 5–22.

Dvir, T., Eden, D., & Banjo, M. L. (1995). Self-fulfilling prophecy and gender: Can women be Pygmalion and Galatea? *Journal of Applied Psychology, 80,* 253–270.

Eden, D., & Aviram, A. (1993). Self-efficacy training to speed reemployment: Helping people to help themselves. *Journal of Applied Psychology, 78,* 352–360.

Foil, C. M., & Lyles, M. A. (1985). Organizational learning. *Academy of Management Review, 10,* 803–813.

Gerstner, L. V. (1993, December). A road map for the revolution: Defining the principles. In *Think Twice.* Armonk, NY: International Business Machines.

Hammer, M., & Champy, J. (1993). *Reengineering the corporation: A manifesto for business revolution.* New York: HarperCollins.

Hofstede, G. (1980). *Culture's consequences: International differences in work-related values.* Beverly Hills, CA: Sage.

Hofstede, G., Neuijen, B., Ohayv, D., & Sanders, G. (1990). Measuring organizational cultures: A qualitative and quantitative study across twenty cases. *Administrative Science Quarterly, 35,* 286–316.

Humes, S. (1993). *Managing the multinational: Confronting the global-local dilemma.* Englewood Cliffs, NJ: Prentice Hall.

Jelinek, M. (1979). *Institutionalizing innovation: A study of organizational learning systems.* New York: Praeger.

Kets de Vries, M. F. R. (1993). *Leaders, fools, and imposters.* San Francisco: Jossey-Bass.

Kets de Vries, M. F. R., & Miller, D. (1984). *The neurotic organization: Diagnosing and changing counterproductive styles of management.* San Francisco: Jossey-Bass.

Kets de Vries, M. F. R., & Miller, D. (1986). Personality, culture, and organization. *Academy of Management Review, 11,* 266–279.

Kilmann, R. H. (1984). *Beyond the quick fix: Managing five tracks to organizational success.* San Francisco: Jossey-Bass.

Kilmann, R., Saxton, M. J., Serpa, R., & Associates. (1985). *Gaining control of the corporate culture.* San Francisco: Jossey-Bass.

Kotter, J. P., & Keskett, J. L. (1992). *Corporate culture and performance.* New York: Free Press.

Lado, A. A., & Wilson, M. (1994). Human resource systems and sustained competitive advantage: A competency-based perspective. *Academy of Management Review, 19,* 699–727.

Lawson, R. B., & Ventriss, C. L. (1992). Organizational change: The role of organizational culture and organizational learning. *Psychological Record, 42,* 205–219.

Lippitt, G. L., Langseth, P., & Mosso, J. (1985). *Implementing organizational change.* San Francisco: Jossey-Bass.

Locke, E. A., & Latham, G. (1990). *A theory of goals and performance.* Englewood Cliffs, NJ: Prentice Hall.

Martin, J. (1992). *Cultures in organizations: Three perspectives.* New York: Oxford University Press.

Matsui, T., Kakuyama, T., & Onglatco, M. (1987). Effects of goals and feedback on performance in groups. *Journal of Applied Psychology, 72,* 407–415.

Mowday, R. T., & Sutton, R. I. (1993). Organizational behavior: Linking individuals and groups to organizational contexts. *Annual Review of Psychology, 44,* 195–229.

Naj, A. K. (1993, May 7). Some manufacturers drop efforts to adopt Japanese techniques. *Wall Street Journal,* p. 1.

Nystrom, P. C., & Starbuck, W. H. (1984). To avoid organizational crises, unlearn. *Organizational Dynamics, 12,* 53–65.

Ono, Y. (1993, April 20). Unneeded workers in Japan are bored, and very well paid. *Wall Street Journal,* p. 1.

O'Reilly, C., Chatman, J., & Caldwell, D. (1991). People and organizational culture: A Q-sort approach to assessing person-organization fit. *Academy of Management Journal, 34,* 487–516.

Ott, J. S. (1989). *The organizational culture perspective.* Pacific Grove, CA: Brooks/Cole.

Ouchi, W. G. (1981). *Theory Z: How American business can meet the Japanese challenge.* Reading, MA: Addison-Wesley.

Ouchi, W. G., & Wilkins, A. L. (1985). Organizational culture. *Annual Review of Sociology, 11,* 457–483.

Pascale, R. T., & Athos, A. G. (1981). *The art of Japanese management: Applications for American executives.* New York: Simon & Schuster.

Peters, T. J., & Waterman, R. H. Jr. (1982). *In search of excellence.* New York: Harper & Row.

Prahalad, C. K., & Doz, Y. L. (1987). *The multinational mission.* New York: Free Press.

Rentsch, J. R. (1990). Climate and culture: Interaction and qualitative differences in organizational meanings. *Journal of Applied Psychology, 75,* 668–681.

Rice, R. E., & Aydin, C. (1991). Attitudes toward new organizational technology: Network proximity as a mechanism for social information processing. *Administrative Science Quarterly, 36,* 219–244.

Sathe, V. (1985). How to decipher and change corporate culture. In R. Kilman, M. Saxton, R. Serpa, & Associates (Eds.), *Gaining control of the corporate culture.* San Francisco, CA: Jossey-Bass.

Schein, E. H. (1978). *Career dynamics: Matching individual and organizational needs.* Reading, MA: Addison-Wesley.

Schein, E. H. (1985). *Organizational culture and leadership.* San Francisco: Jossey-Bass.

Schein, E. H. (1990). Organizational culture. *American Psychologist, 45,* 109–119.

Schein, E. H. (1992). *Organizational culture and leadership* (2nd ed.). San Francisco: Jossey-Bass.

Schneider, B. (1987). The people make the place. *Personnel Psychology, 40,* 437–453.

Schneider, B., & Gunnarson, S. (1990). Organizational climate and culture: The psychology of the workplace. In J. W. Jones, B. D. Steffy, & D. Bray (Eds.), *Applying psychology in business: The manager's handbook* (pp. 542–551). Lexington, MA: Lexington Books.

Schneider, B., Wheeler, J. K., & Cox, J. F. (1992). A passion for service: Using content analysis to explicate climate themes. *Journal of Applied Psychology, 77,* 705–716.

Schlesinger, J. M., & Kanabayashi, M. (1992, October 8). Many Japanese find their "lifetime" jobs can be short-lived. *Wall Street Journal,* p. 1.

Sethia, N. K., & Von Glinow, M. A. (1985). Arriving at four cultures by managing the reward system. In R. Kilmann, M. J. Saxton, R. Serpa, & Associates, *Gaining control of the corporate culture* (pp. 400–420). San Francisco: Jossey-Bass.

Shrivastava, P. (1995). The role of corporations in achieving ecological sustainability. *Academy of Management Review, 20,* 936–960.

Siehl, C., & Martin, J. (1984). The role of symbolic management: How can managers effectively transmit organizational culture? In J. G. Hunt (Ed.), *Leaders and managers: International perspective on managerial behavior and leadership* (pp. 227–239). New York: Pergamon Press.

Stahl, M. J., & Bounds, G. M. (1991). *Competing globally through customer value: The management of strategic suprasystems.* Westport, CT: Quorum Books.

Sullivan, J. J. (1983). A critique of Theory Z. *Academy of Management Review, 8,* 132–142.

Tichy, N. (1983). *Managing strategic change: Technical political and cultural dynamics.* New York: John Wiley & Sons.

Triandis, H. C. (1995). *Individualism and collectivism.* Boulder, CO: Westview Press.

Trice, H. M., & Beyer, J. M. (1985). Using six organizational rites to change culture. In R. H. Kilman, M. J. Saxton, R. Serpa, & Associates, *Gaining control of the corporate culture* (pp. 370–399). San Francisco: Jossey-Bass.

Trice, H. M., & Beyer, J. M. (1993). *The cultures of work organizations.* Englewood Cliffs, NJ: Prentice Hall.

Ventriss, C., & Luke, J. (1988). Organizational learning and public policy. *American Review of Public Administration, 18,* 337–357.

Wilkins, A., & Ouchi, W. G. (1983). Efficient cultures: Exploring the relationship between culture and organizational performances. *Administrative Science Quarterly, 28,* 468–481.

Wright, P. M., & Snell, S. A. (1991). Toward an integrative view of strategic human resource management. *Human Resource Management Review, 1,* 203–225.

SUGGESTED REFERENCES

Some suggested survey instruments for various quantitative measures of organizational culture:*

The Norms Diagnostic Index (Allen & Dyer, 1980): This measure assesses seven dimensions of behavioral norms, such as performance facilitation, job involvement, training, leader-subordinate interaction, policies, and procedures.

Kilmann-Saxton Culture-Gap Survey (Kilmann & Saxton, 1993): This questionnaire measures actual operating norms and those that should be operating if performance, job satisfaction, and morale are to be increased.

Organizational Culture Profile (O'Reilly, Chatman & Caldwell, 1988): This inventory measures nine categories of values regarding what is important, how to behave, and what attitudes are appropriate.

Organizational Beliefs Questionnaire (Sashkin, 1984): This measure attempts to ascertain 10 values shared by the organization.

Corporate Culture Survey (Glaser, 1983): This instrument measures the strength and type of culture based on Deal and Kennedy's (1982) four types.

Organizational Values Congruence Scale (Enz, 1986): This measure examines the congruence between employee and management values.

---

*Adapted from A. Furnham & B. Gunter. (1993). "Corporate Culture: Definition, Diagnosis, and Change." In G. L. Cooper & I. T. Robertson (Eds.), *International review of industrial organizational psychology, 1993* (Vol. 8, pp. 233–261) New York: John Wiley & Sons.

4

Workforce Diversity

CHAPTER OVERVIEW

This chapter is about people throughout the world—their differences and similarities to each other. Most people have more difficulty with differences than with similarities owing, in large measure, to their proclivity for social relationships that promote communal sharing founded in a sense of similarities. People are drawn to groups because they seek others who are like them in one or more dimensions that they deem psychologically and physically important. The critical challenge for each person and each organization around the world is to learn that diversity is a bridge to finding deeper similarities and interests among all human beings.

Workforce diversity is an emotionally engaging and extremely important challenge that all global organizations face. In this chapter, we define diversity and examine briefly the organizational stages of promoting diversity, from affirmative action to valuing differences and managing diversity, each of which is designed to achieve specific diversity goals. We then examine global forces that are shaping workforce diversity around the world and specific issues for organizations in Asia, Europe, and the United States. The concept of the glass ceiling and the outcomes of this dysfunctional organizational feature are discussed next, followed by a detailed description of the positive and negative outcomes of affirmative action and the challenges and potentially positive outcomes of the multicultural organization and the process of managing diversity.

We then present a reality check for some of the asymmetries between majority and minority members of an organization around issues of position, power, and compensation. Thereafter, we discuss a promotion process for a diverse workforce that is based on studies in the United States and South Africa. We also outline a 360-degree performance-appraisal process that involves diverse raters of performance for all members of a workforce. Finally, we examine a model of human social relationships that suggests that all humans have the same basic inclination to engage in four basic types of interpersonal relationships, discuss the implications of the model for managing a diverse workforce, and conclude with specific strategies to enhance the management of diversity.

The bottom line is that all people need to respect and care for themselves and others so as to create wholesome and productive workplaces in which people can embrace their differences and similarities and achieve challenging and productive organizational goals.

LEARNING OBJECTIVES

After studying this chapter, you will be prepared to

- define workforce diversity and distinguish among affirmative action, valuing diversity, and managing diversity

- indicate clearly three major global forces that are shaping workforce diversity around the world

- describe why global organizations must manage diversity and know the demographics of and trends in workforces in Asia, Europe, and the United States

- define the glass ceiling as a barrier to diversification and identify the costs of such dysfunctional organizational features

- describe the stages of diversity of affirmative action, the multicultural organization, and managing diversity

- describe the laws of the land and people that address workforce diversity and make plain that diversity is a legal, moral, and business imperative

- identify some of the negative outcomes of affirmative action and specific strategies to promote a multicultural organization and indicate the positive outcomes of diversity for organizations and work processes in organizations

- describe a reality check for employment opportunities, indicating the extent of the asymmetry between majority and minority persons in organizational positions, power, and compensation

- identify a promotion process that can provide benefits to all individuals and organizations around the globe, based on studies in the United States and South Africa

- describe a 360-degree performance-appraisal process and indicate the contents and positive outcomes of diverse raters of performance for all members of a diverse workforce

- discuss the four-component model of human social interaction that appears universal and requires each person from any cultural, racial, or ethnic group to learn not the categories of social interaction but the rules for implementing them in a given organization or context

- implement specific strategies to enhance the management of diversity in your organization

- embrace more fully with your mind and heart the need, challenges, and benefits to all organizational members and customers or clients of a diverse workforce.

The walls that divide us from each other are within each one of us.

CHALLENGES FOR ALL

The globalization and increasing diversity of the workforce are inevitable, and both are a source of challenge and hope for all humanity. The fundamental guideline for harnessing the forces of diversity is to understand that working with an increasingly diverse workforce requires strategic, organizational, and personal risks and courage to gain the rewards of diverse productive organizational teams that can continuously improve the quality, value, and timely delivery of goods and services to global customers and clients.

R. R. Thomas (1995, p. 246) defined *diversity* "as any mixture of items characterized by differences *and* similarities." In line with this definition, individuals, groups, and organizations that want to promote diversity should focus on both the differences and the similarities between people; specify the dimensions of diversity (such as gender, race, sexual orientation, product line, and functional specialization); and emphasize the collective mixture, rather than one or two constituent members of the mixture.

Organizational actions to address diversity in the workplace have evolved through three phases: affirmative action, valuing differences, and managing diversity (Henderson, 1994). Regardless of what phase of diversification your organization is in, changes in both the organizational culture and individuals are inevitable if there is to be a diversified workplace. People often resist change by proposing that the culture must change first without defining clearly what is meant by organizational culture and what aspects of the culture must change. For this and other reasons, we introduced the topic of organizational culture in Chapter 3, so you are now better prepared to embrace the opportunities and difficulties of creating and maintaining a diverse workplace.

Table 4–1 compares the three phases of diversification of an organization. *Affirmative action*, the first phase, includes legally required plans and statistical procedures for recruiting, training, and promoting specific underutilized and competent members of a target group. The major goal is to assimilate qualified and underrepresented people into the organization. Affirmative action is a remedial strategy in that it attempts to correct previous wrongs, with progress usually indexed by the achievement of specific quantitative aims. *Valuing diversity* is driven by moral and ethical imperatives to promote pluralism, not assimilation, and the guiding philosophy that difference is better. This strategy encourages changing organizational members' perceptions of and attitudes toward minorities and women. *Managing diversity* focuses on developing managerial skills and policies to optimize every member's contribution to the organization's goals. This strategy is driven by the expectation that managing diversity will yield higher morale, productivity, and profits, rather than by legal or ethical mandates.

We turn now to the challenges that all organizations around the world face to some degree and the global developments and demographics that mark diversity in the workplace as one of the major opportunities and challenges for all people as the 21st century approaches.

Loss of Economic Sovereignty

As a consequence of the growing integration of the global economy, all nations have progressively lost control of their individual economic destinies. No nation can any longer unilaterally determine its own interest rates, balance export and import accounts, or finance its national debt without careful consideration of the policies and actions of other nations. Thus, for example, by the year 2,000, many countries will benefit from greatly expanded trade with China, India, and Latin America as they become more fully integrated into the global economy. Just as railroads and long-haul trucks along with radio, television, and telecommunications, have linked the domestic markets of all nations, so have container ships, jet aircraft, and satellite and fiber optic communications created the axial transportation and communication corridors to create the infrastructure of the global marketplace. Not only do goods and services travel along the global corridors, but, to a lesser extent, so do the members of the global workforce. Hence, manufacturing, services, and the labor force are no longer tied to a particular place. It is the increasing change in the composition of the global workforce and the dynamics of the domestic workforces of Asia, Europe, and the United States that are the primary focuses of this chapter.

Global Developments and Demographics

Three important global developments and demographics are shaping the global workforce (Johnston, 1991):

Women will continue to enter the workforce in great numbers, particularly in the developing countries. Women now make up one third of the global workforce, and that proportion is expected to reach 50% by the year 2,000. As a consequence, organizations will have to respond by providing greater day care, flextime, and parental leave options for child and elder care (L. T. Thomas & Ganster, 1995).

TABLE 4–1. Comparisons of Affirmative Action, Valuing Differences, and Managing Diversity

Affirmative Action	Valuing Differences	Managing Diversity
Quantitative. The achievement of equality of opportunity is sought sought by changing organizational demographics. Progress is monitored by statistical reports and analyses.	*Qualitative.* The emphasis is on the appreciation of differences and the creation of an environment in which everyone feels valued and accepted. Progress is monitored by organizational surveys of attitudes and perceptions.	*Behavioral.* The emphasis is on building specific skills and creating policies that get the best from every employee. Efforts are monitored by progress toward achieving goals and objectives.
Legally driven. Written plans and statistical goals for specific groups are used.	*Ethically driven.* Moral and ethical imperatives are the impetus for cultural change.	*Strategically driven.* Behaviors and policies contribute to organizational goals, such as increased profits and productivity.
Remedial. Specific target groups benefit as prior wrongs are addressed. Previously excluded groups have an advantage.	*Idealistic.* Everyone benefits by feeling valued and accepted in an inclusive environment.	*Pragmatic.* The organization benefits: Morale, profits, and productivity increase.
Assimilation Model. Assumes that groups that are brought into the system will adapt to existing organizational norms.	*Diversity Model.* Groups retain their own characteristics, shape the organization and are shaped by it to create a common set of of values.	*Synergy Model.* Diverse groups create new ways of working together effectively in a pluralistic environment.
Opens doors. The focus is on hiring and promotion decisions.	*Opens attitudes, minds, and the culture.* The emphasis is on inclusion not assimilation.	*Opens the system.* Managerial practices and policies are affected.
Resistance. Resistance arises from perceived limits to autonomy in decision making and fears of reverse discrimination.	*Resistance.* Resistance arises from the fear of change and discomfort with differences.	*Resistance.* Resistance arises from the denial of demographic realities, of the need for alternative approaches, and of the benefits of change.

From *Cultural Diversity in the Workplace: Issues and Strategies*, by G. Henderson. Copyright © 1994 by Quorum Books, Westport, CT. Reproduced with permission of Greenwood Publishing Group, Inc., Westport, CT.

The average age of the global workforce will continue to rise, especially in the developed countries. For example, by the year 2,000, 40% of the workforce in countries like Japan, Germany, the United Kingdom, and the United States will be under age 34, compared with 53% in China and 55% in Pakistan. Similarly, 15% or more of the population of industrialized nations will be aged 65 or older versus less than 5% in most developing nations. Clearly, the clarion call for young persons who are seeking employment opportunities is to go global. Likewise, more and more older persons from developed nations are likely to retire and travel to other countries during the 1990s; for instance, the Japanese will continue to retire in Hawaii, while older Americans and English pensioners will seek the warmth of Mexico and Spain, respectively.

The global workforce will become increasingly better educated, and developing countries will produce a greater share of the world's high school and college graduates. The mix of the world's skilled human capital is changing dramatically such that by the year 2,000, only 21% of the high school enrollees in the world will be found in developed countries, compared to 69% in developing countries. Likewise, by 2,000, three fifths of all enrolled college students in the world will be from developing countries. Overall, by 2,000, high school enrollments are expected to grow 60% (to 450 million students), while college enrollments could double again to more than 115 million students.

In general, high school graduates and unskilled workers—janitors, dishwashers, waiters—are recruited locally, college graduates are recruited nationally, and those with graduate degrees are recruited internationally. However, as the population ages in developed countries and more persons earn higher educational degrees in developing countries, it is likely that a wide variety of persons from around the world will be working in countries, especially developed countries, other than where they were born. The capacity to manage and derive added value from a diversified workforce is thus a cardinal requirement for effective global organizations.

Many physical, political, and economic barriers have been dismantled in the past few years around the globe, and more will be broken down in the future. In these new open places in various parts of the world, the seductive forces of isolationism and balkanization continue to divide and separate people. The challenge before each person is to continue to dismantle the interior psychological walls that can divide people from each other. These interior psychological walls are constructed from preconceived notions about groups of people with whom one may have little direct contact, as well as by uncertainty, ambiguity, and fear of the unknown. Accordingly, it is our humble perspective that managing and benefiting from diversity in the workforce is everyone's responsibility and will require each of us to be determined, compassionate, creative, and courageous risk takers. In other words, diversity in the workforce not only yields financial rewards for an organization, as we will demonstrate later, but, most important, provides the opportunity to bring out the best in each member of the organization. Managing, valuing, and benefiting from a diverse workforce requires the use of both the dispositional and situational forces that shape people and allow them to shape their workplaces and organizational cultures. It is our firm belief that one of the major paths to wholesome, productive, and harmonious relations among nations, organizations, and people is through the processes that harness the benefits of a diverse workforce, which will require a great deal of hard and creative work by everyone.

We now consider briefly some of the dynamics of various workforces in the world that have and will shape organizational developments through the early years of the new century.

WORKFORCE DYNAMICS AND DEMOGRAPHICS

As organizations position themselves to become leading participants in the global marketplace, their success will depend, to a large extent, on their capacity to cultivate and harness diverse high-performance work teams that will deliver the highest-quality goods and services for their global customers and clients in a timely manner. Each global organization must encourage and actively promote respect for and the value of diverse and competent members to build trust among its members, which is the cornerstone of high-performing individuals and work teams. When an individual trusts herself or himself, such a person knows well her or his capacities and is prepared to trust others, for you cannot trust another until you first trust yourself. Organizational trust and diversity are essential for global organizations, and if we believe in and trust ourselves and then others, we minimize psychological barriers among people (Mayer, Davis, & Schoorman, 1995).

In the next few sections, we briefly examine some dynamics and demographics of the workforces of the three sociocultural-economic blocks—Asia, Europe, and the United States—to observe some of the diversity issues that global organizations must confront in these countries.

Asia: Japan

According to some, Japan may well lose its global competitive edge by the beginning of the 21st century because of its changing demographics and its attitudes and practices toward a diverse workforce (Fernandez & Barr, 1993). For example, even after the economic slowdown that began around 1991, there were still 114 jobs for every 100 men and 92 jobs for every 100 women. This labor shortage will become greater because the population of Japan is aging more rapidly than in any other industrialized nation, the birthrate is not rising, and the national norm is for most women to leave the labor force when they marry. In addition, equal employment laws are not enforced, the immigration laws are restrictive, and the chasm between wealthy Japanese and average citizens is widening. Furthermore, an increasing number of Japanese workers are separating work from personal life and are thus leaving companies in midcareer for better pay, and Japanese companies are restructuring and downsizing (Fernandez & Barr, 1993). To be more competitive in the global marketplace, Japan will have to enhance the rights of minorities and immigrants and equalize opportunities for women and global international employees.

Asia: People's Republic of China

China is a nation of approximately 1.2 billion people and comprises an area of 9.6 million square kilometers (3.7 million square miles). It is exceeded in size only by Canada (9.9 million square kilometers, or 3.8 million square miles) and Russia (17.0 square kilometers, or 6.6 million square miles), but those two countries have much smaller populations (29 million and 148.2 million, respectively) (Johnson, 1996). In China, 20% of the population lives in urban areas and 80% lives in rural areas, and most Chinese are farmers (Smith, 1991).

The Chinese developed a civilization in relative isolation that has endured longer than any other in the history of the world. Its unique products—silk, porcelain, and tea—have long been well known. Not only has Chinese culture left its indelible mark on those of neighboring countries—Vietnam, Korea, and Japan—but Chinese inventions, such as the magnetic compass, gunpowder, paper, and printing, have had a far-reaching impact on the development of the West. Visitors, from Marco Polo in the 13th century to Matteo Ricci in the 16th century, reported favorably on a society that, in many respects, outshone the Europe of their times.

Today, China is the world's most populous nation, with one fourth of the world's people. Since the 1960s, the population has been expanding at an annual rate of 2.1%, or by an average of 17.4 million people per year (Smith, 1991).

China is a multinational country in which 93% of the population is Han, or ethnic Chinese. The remaining 68 million are distributed among 55 "minority nationalities," ranging in size from the 12 million Zhuang to some groups that number fewer than 1,000. Most of these minorities differ from the Han in language and customs. The Moslem Hui are distinguished only by religion, and the Manchu are almost completely assimilated. National policy encourages cultural continuity and limited political autonomy, and representatives are trained for local leadership at nationality institutes that also promote research on ethnic languages and history. Most of these groups are scattered in the sparsely settled border areas, five of which—Inner Mongolia, Ningxia, Xinjiang, Xizand (Tibet), and Guangxi—have been designated "autonomous regions" (local administrations similar to provinces but with more independence). Where significant concentrations of a particular minority exist, autonomous prefectures and counties have been created both within these regions and in western provinces, such as Yunnan and Guizhou. Minorities have been exempted from China's stringent birth control program of the one child per family, and their numbers have been increasing at a greater rate than the Han's.

One of the first and most important tasks of the Communist government, created in 1949, was to develop educational institutions. Before 1949, over 80% of the population was illiterate, and in rural areas, the illiteracy rate was over 95%. First, the government tried to provide primary education for as many as possible by conducting special campaigns to teach adults in factories and rural areas to read and write. Secondary and higher educational institutions were developed largely according to Soviet patterns. The results were quick and favorable—about 60% of school-age children were in school in 1952, and 96% were enrolled in 1976. Most university degree programs last four years. University education is free, and students with economic difficulties are provided grants by the state for education-related expenses, such as housing and food. The enrollment in regular colleges and universities rose from 315 million in 1985 to 550 million in 1987, or a 75% increase in five years.

In 1989, two events that were important for China and the world occurred: the Tiananmen Square demonstrations and deaths and the dismantling of the Berlin Wall. The repercussions of these events are still being experienced in the global marketplace. According to Shizhong, Zhang, and Larson (1992) these developments signal the following basic issues and trends that are shaping China and will continue to do so:

- great tension between central control by Beijing over economic and political developments and the desire of the provinces and distal regions to pursue their own economic and political goals

- the need to maintain a critical balance of control of the military and for the military to maintain stability

- the pursuit of technology, expertise, and markets in the global marketplace, coupled with an unwillingness by key governmental figures to accept some fundamental rules of the global community, especially the basic human rights of freedom of speech, movement, and the press.

A new generation of Chinese is moving into leadership positions. Despite periodic major setbacks, together with great lurches forward, it is known that China will be a major economic force in the 21st century as a result largely of its diverse population, which is united by the Chinese capacities for hard work, sacrifice, skill, experience, and genius.

European Community

It is clear that Europe is more culturally diverse than Japan or China. However, despite the 12-member European Community (EC)—Belgium, Denmark, France, Germany, Greece, Ireland, Italy, Luxembourg, the Netherlands, Portugal, Spain, and the United Kingdom—which is the largest trading block in the global marketplace, Europe must confront issues of the diverse workforce. For example, the EC, like Japan, is experiencing declining birthrates, coupled with a rapidly aging population and growing resentment toward a relatively small number of immigrants (Fernandez & Barr, 1993). Also, some EC members funnel women into lower-level management positions and traditionally female jobs and, in some cases, severely restrict women from taking certain service-sector jobs, such as in banking. Specifically, women hold only 3.3% of the executive positions in Italy, but constitute 34% of the workforce, while in Greece, only 11% of the 60% of women in public-sector jobs have high-level positions (Fernandez & Barr, 1993).

United States

In 1992, women in the United States made only 72 cents for every dollar earned by men, and it is projected that at the current pace, women will reach pay parity with men in the year 2017 (Fernandez & Barr, 1993). By 2,000 just about half the workforce will be female, and by 2040, half the U.S. population will be Americans of African, Latino, Asian, or Native American (ALANA) descent.

In their report *Workforce 2,000*, Johnston and Packer (1987) identified the following five fundamental demographic features that are shaping the U.S. workforce and will continue to do so in the 21st century:

The population and workforce will grow more slowly. The population will grow by only 0.7% per year by 2,000, compared with 1.9% annually since the 1950s. Also the workforce will expand by only 1% per year during the 1990s, which is one third the annual expansion rate of the past 25 years in the United States.

The population and workforce will grow older, and a shrinking pool of young persons will enter the workforce. The average age of the workforce will rise from 36 in the late 1980s to 39 by the year 2,000. In addition, there will be an 8% (2-million-person) decrease in the population of workers aged 16–24.

More women will enter the workforce. Approximately two thirds of the new entrants to the workforce during the 1990s will be women, and it is expected that 61% of all women of working age will have jobs by the year 2,000. Also, women will continue to be concentrated in lower-paying jobs than men and may still earn less than men even for comparable jobs.

Most of the new entrants to the workforce will be ALANAs. Almost one third (29%) of the new entrants to the workforce will be Americans of African, Latino, Asian, or Native American descent.

Immigrants will constitute the largest share of the increase in the population and workforce since the beginning of the 20th century. Annually, approximately 600,000 legal and illegal immigrants will enter the U.S. during the 1990s, and about two thirds of these immigrants who are of working age will enter the workforce.

Thus, the U.S. workforce of the late 1990s and the early 21st century will be different from that of any previous decade of the 20th century in that the number of white men and traditional 16–24-year-old entrants will continue to decrease. Hence, the workforce will consist of more women, older workers, persons of color, immigrants. These demographic changes will continue to mandate the development of strategies to harness the resourcefulness and capacities of an increasingly diversified workforce to enhance the quality, value, and timely delivery of products and services for the global marketplace.

According to Johnston and Packer (1987), there will be a growth in professional, technical, and sales jobs throughout the 1990s that will require workers with the highest levels of education and skills. The increasing job requirements and the number of jobs available are more evident when jobs are ranked by the required skills (mathematics, language, and reasoning skills) than by educational levels. Job growth will require enhanced skills that can be acquired only from systematic educational programs, coupled with personal motivation and discipline (Johnston & Packer, 1987). Likewise, a report by the U.S. Department of Labor (1995) projected that from 1994 to 2005, jobs that require greater education and training will predominate in occupations that are growing the fastest and have the highest pay rates (computer and data processing services, business services, and home health care services). That educational opportunities without personal commitment are as inadequate as the latter without the former make it plain that both contextual and dispositional forces are essential for creating a strong, diversified workforce.

Morrison and Von Glinow (1990) argued that white women and people of color encounter the glass ceiling (a subtle, transparent, and intractable barrier to promotion to higher organizational levels of management and leadership), so even though they occupy an increasing number of managerial jobs, they are stuck in jobs with little authority and relatively low pay. For example, only 3.6% of board directorships and 1.7% of corporate officerships in Fortune 500 companies were held by women and only one African American headed a Fortune 1,000 company in 1988. The situation is as bleak in the public sector, where only 8.6% of the jobs in the upper management or senior executive service levels of the federal government were held by women, and, on average, there were only 1.1 women in senior administrative positions (deanships and above) in U.S. colleges and universities (Morrison & Von Glinow, 1990). As a consequence, women and African Americans have been fleeing corporate and midlevel governmental jobs when possible. Morrison, White, Van Elsor, and the Center for Creative Leadership (1987) concluded that the glass (or, in our view, cement) ceiling will continue to block the progress of women and persons of color to top managerial jobs in the next several decades unless barriers are systematically removed. These barriers have little or nothing to do with the quality and quantity of job performances and everything to do with the fear and uncertainty that separate organizational members from each other.

THE CHALLENGES OF DIVERSITY

There are two fundamental challenges of diversity that are strategic imperatives for the success of organizations in the global marketplace in the 1990s and beyond (Jackson & Associates, 1992). The first challenge is to adjust the availability of jobs and employment opportunities to obtain a better fit with the needs and expectations of a more diversified workforce than the standardized employment and job requirements of the past 40 years when the workforce was more monochromatic and monolithic.

The second challenge is for organizations to treat all employees and potential employees fairly and to be sensitive and responsive to employees, so they feel they are being treated fairly. The issue of fairness is bidirectional in that an employer's assertion that he or she treats employees fairly is not enough; the employer must also respond to and develop a partnership with current and potential employees to ensure their organizational experiences are fair and just. Organizations that are inclined to favor certain personal orientations and stifle others or that are insensitive to diversity issues of gender, race, cultural, and other legally protected attributes run the risk of low productivity as a consequence of the restricted pool of potential employees and employees' dissatisfaction, lack of commitment, turnover, or other dysfunctional activities.

These two challenges apply not only to the United States, but to almost any global organization, regardless of its geographic location in the global marketplace. Although the idea of a common culture of management that unifies organizational practices around the world is still an aspiration, rather than a reality, all organizations are experiencing an endless titration of changes, especially in the domain of workforce diversity (Kanter, 1991).

We now examine organizational developments and strategies for managing diversity. Although most of the material focuses on U.S. organizations, we believe it can be generalized with appropriate contextual modifications to global organizations anywhere in the world.

STAGES OF DIVERSITY

In a diverse workforce, competence counts more than ever before (R. R. Thomas, 1990). Harnessing diversity in the workforce requires a shift in paradigms such that every aspect of the business or organizational enterprise is affected—from monochromatic markets to organizational architectures and cultures—and the greater diversification of workforce profiles. Table 4–2 indicates the change in approaches to dealing with diversity from the industrial age (the first half of the 20th century) to the information-service age (the second half of the 20th century).

According to DeLuca and McDowell (1992), this shift in paradigms requires a change from managerial strategies that rewarded efficiency and uniformity to those that require creativity and the integration of diverse persons into responsive, teams learning to work with diverse members and customers. It involves double-loop learning (Argyris & Schon, 1978), discussed in

TABLE 4–2. Approaches to Diversity in the Workplace in Two Periods

Industrial Age	Information Age
Economies of scale and a stable environment made *efficiency* essential for success.	Market niches and rapidly changing environments make *effectiveness* essential for success.
Efficiency encouraged a focus on *costs*.	Effectiveness encourages a focus on *profits*.
Differences frequently meant exceptions that created inequity or inefficiency or both.	Differences frequently mean diversity that creates challenges or options or both.
The efficiency mind-set is geared to view differences as *problems* that need to be reduced.	The diversity mind-set is geared to view differences as *opportunities*.

Adapted from J. DeLuca, & R. McDowell, "Managing Diversity: A Strategic 'Grass-roots Approach,'" in S. E. Jackson & Associates, *Diversity in the Workplace*, p. 234. Copyright 1992 by Guilford Press, New York. Used with permission.

Chapter 3, which is much easier said then done. Progress has been made in managing diversity in many organizations around the world. However, much remains to be learned and implemented before the competitive and business advantages of diversity can be fully reaped. The following sections examine more closely some of the steps that have been taken in the attempt to manage diversity.

Affirmative Action

According to R. R. Thomas (1992), the three fundamental approaches to workforce diversity are affirmative action, valuing diversity, and managing diversity. Thomas defined managing diversity as creating an environment that works naturally for all people in a given workforce. The focus is on the broad mix, rather than the quick fix, and on empowering all persons so the capacities of the diverse workforce can be harnessed, cultivated, and deployed.

Affirmative action involves management processes to ensure that, on the basis of some specified dimension, such as race, gender, or ethnicity, selected persons receive equal opportunities to participate in a given organizational context. These management processes include such systematic activities as the sharply focused recruitment, development, promotion, and retention of members of a given targeted group like women or ALANAs. Affirmative action is designed to help individuals who are disadvantaged in some way, highlights the difference or differences among those who are subject to affirmative action, and is designed to promote equal opportunities but not equal outcomes for all participants.

In a series of important studies of the preferential selection or treatment of managers through affirmative action programs, Heilman, Simon, and Repper (1987) demonstrated that being selected for a leadership position on the basis of sex, rather than of merit, had detrimental effects on women's (but not men's) regard for their accomplishments, desire to remain in leadership roles, and views of their leadership skills. In a subsequent study, Heilman, Lucas, and Kaplow (1990) found that sex-based preferential selection gave rise to negative perceptions of competence only when individuals lacked confidence in their ability to perform effectively and that both men and women were adversely affected. The findings of these investigations indicate that preferential selection intensifies personal doubts and insecurities about one's ability to perform specific tasks or roles. Unlike merit-based selection, which affirms or disconfirms one's competence, preferential selection in a work-irrelevant dimension provides ambiguous information about one's competence, thus allowing such doubts and fears to go unchecked (Heilman, 1994). It is important to believe in oneself so others can believe in you and to insist on performance-based merit evaluations for all persons while you enhance the mix of persons in your organization and within different roles in your organization.

To demonstrate further that preferential selection and promotion, without the grounding of performance-based data about job-related skills and abilities, can give rise to a destructive cycle, Heilman, Kaplow, Amato, and Stathatos (1993) examined the effects of preferential selection on target persons and others who were seeking entry into or were current members of an organization. In two laboratory studies, they chose 145 men and women to serve as managers according to their demonstrated performance (merit) for the positions on or preferential selection for the positions on the basis of their sex. Heilman et al. found that women who were selected preferentially reacted more negatively than did those who were selected on merit to female but not to male applications for a neutral sex-role position (administrative assistant). Specifically, preferentially selected female managers gave significantly lower personnel evaluations and competence ratings and recommended female applicants for hire less frequently and less enthusiastically than they did male applicants.

No differences in personnel evaluations were found when performance and ability information was provided for either male or female applicants. In other words, preferential job assignments through affirmative action programs not only influence the target person or persons of such programs, but can have negative ripple effects on persons who are seeking entry to or are members of the organization.

As we indicated earlier, competency must be the centerpiece of managing diversity programs (R. R. Thomas, 1992). Individuals and organizations both benefit when the hiring and promotion processes provide salient information about individuals' job performance-related skills and abilities, rather than focus preferentially on job-irrelevant attributes. In the global workforce, organizational members who are competent, committed, and compassionate are key personnel for harnessing diversity and providing the competitive advantage. Thus, the rule is: Seek competence first, keep an open mind, pursue a mix of members, and rely on job performance-related data. No one group of persons has a monopoly on competence; rather, different persons have different competencies. You will not do your organization, yourself, or others any favor if you hire and promote individuals who lack competence unless they agree to participate in competence-enhancement education provided by the organization.

The Multicultural Organization

The combination of demographic trends in the workforces around the world or in any given nation and the increasing globalization of the marketplace and organizations highlights the centrality of harnessing diversity for competitive economic advantage. Despite some recent and isolated anti-affirmative action votes, such as in California, there are a number of U.S. laws, regulations, and executive orders that promote affirmative action that are fundamental for building a multicultural organization (see Table 4–3). However, the major impetus for doing so arises from the expected potential economic benefits from diversity of better decision making, greater creativity, innovation, and more successful marketing to different types of customers.

According to Cox (1991), the multicultural organization has specific cultural features that embrace the five fundamental dimensions presented in Table 4–4, which also includes suggested tools to enhance the robustness of each dimension of the multicultural organization. Thus, for example, pluralism involves socialization, whereby the marginalized group or person and the central group or person are educated about each other. Two other direct strategies for strengthening pluralism are to revise the mission statement so it explicitly mentions the importance of diversity to the organization and to give a specially composed diversity advisory group (a pluralism council) direct access to the senior levels of management.

In addition, Cox (1991) suggested that a potent intervention to promote pluralism and strengthen diversity in a multicultural organization is to develop flexible and highly tolerant organizational contexts, policies, and culture that encourage diverse approaches to solving problems among employees. For example, a multicultural organization could encourage, when appropriate, informality and unstructured work, devise flexible work schedules and loose supervision, set broad goals and encourage work teams to refine goals and achievement processes, and allow *all* organizational members to use at least 10% of their paid organizational time to explore and implement ideas for enhancing the status of their work teams and of the overall organization.

Diversity for Competitive Advantage

We believe that diversity in the workplace is a natural consequence of social systems, must be promoted legally and ethically, and will advance dramatically to the point where it can be demonstrated clearly that workforce diversity provides competitive advantage to an organization. This

TABLE 4–3. Laws, Executive orders, and Regulations to ensure Equal Opportunity for All Organizational Members

Equal Pay Act of 1963
Prohibits gender-based pay differentials for equal work.

Title VII, 1964 Civil Rights Act (as amended in 1972)
Prohibits job discrimination in employment based on race, religion, gender or national origin.

Executive Order 11246 (1965)
Requires contractors and subcontractors performing work on federal or federally-assisted projects to prepare and implement affirmative action plans for minorities and women, persons with disabilities, and veterans.

Age Discrimination in Employment Act (1967)—ADEA
Prohibits age discrimination in areas such as hiring, promotion, termination, leaves of absence, and compensation. Protects individuals age forty and over.

Rehabilitation Act of 1973
Prohibits contractors and subcontractors of federal projects from discriminating against applications and/or employees who are physically or mentally disabled, if qualified to perform the job. Requires the contractor to take affirmative action in the employment and advancement of individuals with disabilities.

The Vietnam Era Veterans Readjustment Assistance Act of 1972 and 1974
Requires government contractors and subcontractors to take affirmative action with respect to certain classes of veterans of the Vietnam Era and Special Disabled Veterans.

The Immigration Reform and Control Act of 1986 (IRCA)
Prohibits employers from discriminating against persons authorized to work in the United States with respect to hire or termination from employment because of national origin or citizenship status. All new hires must prove their identity and eligibility to work in the U.S.

The Americans with Disabilities Act of 1990, Title I
Prohibits employers from discriminating against qualified applicants and employees with disabilities in regard to any employment practices or terms, conditions, and privileges of employment.

Civil Rights Act of 1991
The Act grants to plaintiffs the right to a jury trial and makes available compensatory and punitive damages (capped at $300,000).

Reprinted with permission from John P. Fernandez with Mary Barr, *The Diversity Advantage: How American Business Can Out-Perform Japanese and European Companies in the Global Marketplace*, pp. 314–316. Copyright © 1993 by Jossey-Bass, Inc., Publishers. First published by Lexington Books. All rights reserved.

perspective is shared by many (Fernandez & Barr, 1993; Jackson & Associates, 1992; Kanter, 1993) and has been studied carefully by a number of experts on organizations, including Cox and Blake (1991) and Stuart (1992). Table 4–5 presents six organizational functions that can provide a competitive advantage by harnessing the resources of a diversified workforce and building a multicultural organization.

For example, with regard to costs, Cox and Blake (1991) noted that turnover and absenteeism are often higher among women and racial-ethnic minorities than among white men. The primary reasons they gave for the higher turnover were the lack of career growth (dead-end jobs or positions) and low rates of promotion and salary increases, especially for women. Stuart (1992) estimated that turnover among

TABLE 4–4. The Dimensions and Tools of a Multicultural Organization

Dimensions	Tools
1. Pluralism Create a two-way socialization process to ensure that minority-culture perspectives have an influence on the norms and values of the core organization.	1. Valuing diversity seminars 2. Orientation programs for new members 3. Language training 4. Diversity in key committees 5. Explicit treatment of diversity in mission statement 6. Advisory groups to senior management 7. Create flexibility in norm systems
2. Full Structural Integration There are no correlations between culture-group identity and job status.	1. Educational programs 2. Affirmative action programs 3. Targeted career development 4. Changes in managers' performance-appraisal and reward systems 5. Updates personnel policy and benefits
3. Integration in Informal Networks Eliminate barriers to entry and participation.	1. Mentoring programs 2. Company-sponsored social events
4. Cultural Bias Eliminate discrimination and prejudice.	1. Equal opportunity seminars 2. Focus groups 3. Bias-reduction training and task forces
5. Intergroup Conflict *Minimize* interpersonal conflict based on group identity and backlash by members of the dominant group.	1. Feedback on surveys 2. Conflict management training 3. Valuing diversity seminars 4. Focus groups

Adapted from T. Cox, "The multicultural organization," *Academy of Management Executive, 5,* p. 41. Copyright 1991 by Academy of Management.

managerial and nonmanagerial women caused by a glass ceiling can cost an organization as much as 1% of its total annual operating expenses. She reported that the failure to harness diversity cost one organization $22 million in a single year owing to the turnover of women and instances of sexual harassment in the organization. Any decent person realizes that such developments are unacceptable ethically and financially.

In a carefully reasoned and controlled investigation of costs associated with the failure to harness diversity in the workforce, Stroh, Brett, and Reilly (1992) examined the career progression of 1,029 female and male managers employed by 20 Fortune 500 corporations over a two-year period. They indicated that salary progression and job transfers were lower for women than for men. Even though the women had done all the right stuff, such as getting a similar education as men, maintaining similar levels of family power (earning more than their husbands), working in similar industries, not moving in and out of the workforce, and not removing their names from consideration for transfers, there were still significant disparities between the

TABLE 4–5. Organizational Functions that Can be Enhanced by Diversity

Function	Possible Outcomes
Costs	As organizations become more diverse, the costs of a poor job in integrating workers increase.
Resource acquisition	Organizations develop reputations as prospective employers for women and ethnic minorities. Those with the best reputations for managing diversity will win the competition for the best personnel.
Marketing	For multinational organizations, the insight and cultural knowledge that members from different countries bring to the marketing effort can improve these efforts. The same rationale applies to marketing to subpopulations within domestic markets.
Creativity	A diversity of perspectives and less emphasis on conformity to norms of the past may well improve the level of creativitiy.
Problem solving	Heterogeneity in decision-making and problem-solving groups may produce better decisions because of the wider range of perspectives and more thorough critical analysis of issues.
System flexibility	Organizations as systems will become less standardized and more fluid. The increased fluidity may well create greater flexibility to react to environmental changes, so that reactions should be faster and less costly.

Adapted from T. H. Cox & S. Blake, "Managing cultural diversity: Implications for organizational competitiveness," *Academy of Management Executive*, 5, p. 47. Copyright 1991 by Academy of Management.

salaries and career-advancement opportunities of the men and women. Stroh et al. concluded that in these circumstances, the only thing that women can do is to leave the organization. They also noted that organizational positions that attribute lower salary and promotion levels to women's behavior (the dispositional argument) are clearly inadequate and that situational forces (organizational discrimination) were responsible for the disparities between men and women in their study. We believe the handwriting is on the walls, and that all people must each look into themselves and come to grips, first at a personal

level and then at an organizational level, with the barriers that divide different groups. If they do not, they stand to lose both as individuals and members of an organization. What is the price one is willing to pay to avoid confronting her or his fear of others who are competent, capable, and motivated yet are different from one in some distinguishable way? This is a question all people must address if they want to be part of this diverse world.

Last, Watson, Kumar, and Michaelsen's (1993) longitudinal study of the problem-solving performances of homogeneous work groups

(groups with members from the same nationality and ethnic background) compared with diverse work groups (each with one African American, Hispanic, and white American and a foreign national) found that both types of groups performed equally well in terms of the range of perspectives they brought to the problem, their identification of the problem, the number of alternative solutions they proposed, and the quality of their solutions. During the first few weeks of the 15-week examination period, cultural diversity disrupted the culturally diverse group's processing, such as agreeing on what was an important, rather than a minor, problem of the task before the group more often than the homogenous group's. However, after 15 weeks, the diverse group performed higher than the homogeneous group (although not statistically or significantly higher) on identifying the problem and generating alternative solutions. Likewise, Cox, Lobel, and McLeod (1991) reported that problem-solving diverse groups (consisting of Asian, African American, Hispanic and white men or women) performed more cooperatively on a decision-making task (a two-party prisoners' dilemma; see Komorita, 1987) than did all-white groups, although both types of groups performed competitively when the demands of the task required competitive behaviors (Komorita, 1987).

In summary, it would be unwise to expect newly formed groups with a substantial degree of cultural diversity to perform initially as smoothly as more homogeneous groups. However, such groups are more likely to identify problems and generate alternative solutions as well as homogeneous groups do. Also, depending on the demands of the task, diverse groups can be as competitive or as cooperative as homogeneous groups.

REALITY CHECK

It is our firm belief that ignoring or denying diversity problems or not proactively solving them, regardless of their origins, will inevitably lead to dysfunctional conflict among organizational members and will put the organization at risk of losing its competitiveness in the global marketplace (Kanter, 1993).

Employment Opportunities

Until the Civil Rights Act of 1964, when white men applied for jobs or sought promotions, they competed with approximately 33 other persons (33% of a hypothetical pool of applicants or organizational colleagues). Today, they have to compete against 67 other persons (or 67% of a hypothetical pool now made up of women and ALANAs, as well as immigrants).

Fernandez and Barr (1993) reported that many white men believe they face reverse discrimination in the U.S. workforce and that qualified white men are losing out to unqualified women and minorities in hiring and promotion. In fact, 87% of the white men versus 40% and 20% of the white women and persons of color, respectively, in their survey thought that white men face reverse discrimination. Furthermore, Fernandez and Barr found that 44% of all employees (including white men) believed that white men got their jobs only because of their race and gender. However, only 27% of the white men compared to 83% of the black women concurred.

The facts are clear: Claims of reverse discrimination are more hype than real and are the result of inaccurate and incomplete reports issued by many U.S. organizations that are led by white men, as well as individuals (Dipboye, 1987; Hymowitz & Schellhardt, 1986; Olson & Frieze, 1987; Roman, 1990; U.S. Bureau of the Census, 1987). That it often takes longer to change a heart than a mind reflects the powerful role of affective as well as rational forces both in organizations and in individuals.

Salaries and Hiring

As we indicated earlier in this chapter, there is indisputable evidence of a gender gap in salaries, such that for some occupations (like engineering and financial services), women earn an average of 50%–75% of what men earn (National Committee on Pay Equity, 1986). Major, Vanderslice, and McFarlin (1984) found that job applicants who communicated lower pay expectations were offered less pay than identically qualified applicants with higher pay expectations. These differences resulted even though the prospective employers correctly perceived that applicants were similarly qualified. Accordingly, if a job applicant (female or male) expects less pay, then he or she is likely to be offered less pay than similarly qualified applicants.

Do women expect less entry and career-peak salaries than do men? Major and Konar (1984) reported that male management students expected to earn $2,600 more than did female students and almost $20,000 more at the peak of their careers. These findings were replicated by McFarlin, Frone, Major, and Konar (1989) and extended by Martin (1989), who found similar disparities in self-expected entry-level salaries of female and male college seniors who were studying business and economics, even though they had current salary information before them. In addition, Jackson and Associates (1992) noted that regardless of occupation, women had lower expectations than did men of their salaries at the peak of their careers and, except for social science majors, for their career-entry pay as well. Specifically, women in engineering and nursing and education expected to earn $35,000 and $20,000, respectively, less than men at the peak of the careers. Jackson et al. concluded that the disparity between men's and women's expectations for entry and career-peak pay were due to a variety of situational and dispositional forces. Most notably, organizations' publication and unswerving adherence to fair-pay standards (a situational force) reduced such disparities, while men's perceptions that they had higher business sophistication (and individuals' self-perceived knowledge of and comfort in the business world) and women's emphasis on jobs that facilitate family life and careers (dispositional forces) increased such disparities. In short, judge yourself as equally qualified as others of comparable education and experience, ask for a high (but not unreasonable) salary, believe in yourself, and demand fair pay standards.

In terms of specific strategies for negotiating higher starting salaries, Stevens, Banetta, and Gist (1993) used a two-phase program to train 36 male and 24 female MBA students. In Phase 1, the participants learned Fisher and Ury's (1981) philosophy of principled negotiations (discussed in greater detail in Chapter 9). They also learned five active-assertive negotiating tactics: (1) maintaining a confident, professional attitude; (2) coupling demands with opponents' interests; (3) framing demands favorably by use of contrasts; (4) stating options for contingent mutual gain (like a raise contingent on a six-month performance review); and (5) identifying noncontingent mutual gain (such as highlighting uncompensated benefits, such as language or computer skills). In addition, through lectures, discussions, and modeling, the participants learned the following strategies to counteract various attempts to intimidate them: (1) using prolonged silence to indicate an opponent's unreasonableness; (2) focusing on issues before seeking the premature resolution of problems, (3) persistently stating key points to an unyielding opponent; (4) identifying verbally an opponent's intimidating behavior; and (5) reframing weaknesses as potential strengths. In Phase 2, the participants learned the strategies of goal setting (for details, see Chapter 6) and self-management principles that included (1) identifying performance barriers; (2) planning to overcome barriers; (3) setting goals regarding barriers; (4) self-monitoring progress; and (5) self-administering rewards, such as a dinner, a movie, or a day off, on the achievement of a self-set important goal.

The results of Stevens et al.'s (1993) study indicated that content-oriented training programs (Phase 1 training) alone failed to prevent gender differences in negotiating salaries, since the negotiated salaries that were, on average, $1,350 less than those the men negotiated. However, after learning goal setting and self-management skills, the women negotiated significantly greater salary *gains* than did the similarly trained men, although the salaries for women were not significantly higher than the salaries for men. That is, parity, or win-win outcomes, rather than win-lose outcomes, resulted from learning these management strategies.

In summary, organizations must do their part by promoting fair-pay standards, and all job applicants or organizational members must do their part by demanding fairness and equity and learning effective negotiation, goal-setting, and self-management strategies for both private and public-sector organizations in the global marketplace (Ballard & Wright, 1993).

PROMOTIONS AND PERFORMANCE APPRAISALS

Once a person is hired by an organization, advancement and promotion usually are potential motivational incentives and represent avenues to higher compensation, greater organizational power, and enhanced decision-making authority (Burke & McKeen, 1992). Although promotions can be of great benefit to the individual and the organization, there are still fewer women and ALANAs in top positions, and those who are in these positions earn less than their white peers (Johnsrud, 1991).

Promotions and Competencies: United States and South Africa

Tshikororo (1993) investigated the key features of an organizational promotion process to determine which ones would increase the likelihood of equal treatment for black and white candidates on the basis of evaluations of their performances and potential merit for promotion.

Seventy female and male participants rated candidates for promotion according to fictitious personnel records in which the candidates' race (black or white) and level of job performance (high or low) were varied systematically. Additional control records were included to minimize socially desirable or politically correct responses.

Tshikororo (1993) found that black candidates whose job performance, education, and job tenure were comparable to the white candidates' were not discriminated against in the promotion process or in the number recommended for promotion. When black and white managers have information on subordinates' job performance, along with information on gender, race, or other attributes of group membership, both make fair and performance-based judgments about black and white subordinates. Hence, high performers, whether black or white, are generally promoted while low performers, whether black or white, are generally not promoted. Again, it is competence and information on job-related performance that are the keys to just and fair promotion decisions. Tshikororo (1994) reported similar findings in a study of the promotion decisions of black South African managers for similar fictitious personal records. That is, these managers recommended promotions for high performers, regardless of whether the candidates were black or white. Thus, in two different nations, the United States and South Africa, what counts, at least in simulated decision making on promotions, is job-related performance when such information is salient in the personnel records.

According to Tshikororo (1993, 1994), organizations around the world can take specific actions to enhance the equity of and reduce discrimination in their performance-appraisal and promotion processes when they

- include clear, specific, and realistic job-performance criteria as the bases of the decision-making task

- train managers for the evaluation-promotion task

- include only job-relevant information in personnel documents

- build accountability measures into the evaluation and promotion process

- implement a promotions committee for the entire organization.

Although these steps and strategies can improve the promotion process, it is still important to remember that both emotional (affective) and situational forces are also operative in the process (Eagly, Makhijani, & Klonsky, 1992; Goodale, 1993; Rosen, 1992; Sahl, 1990).

Performance Appraisals

We believe that organizations' evaluations of *all* members or those aspiring to be members is an inescapable fact of organizational life and can be most effective when implemented as a learning experience, rather than strictly as a reward or punishment experience (Bray & Associates, 1991; Campbell & Lea, 1988). Furthermore, having both supervisor-managers and employees do ratings allows for a comparison of the evaluations, so that discrepancies and correspondences can enhance the learning component of the evaluation process. We encourage you to use multiple raters in your performance-appraisal system, or a 360-degree system of ratings by peers, supervisors, subordinates, customers, and the individual, which has predictive validity and yields useful developmental feedback (Funder & Colvin, 1988; Mount, Barrick, & Strauss, 1994). It is important for each member of the diversified workforce to be evaluated individually, so that the rich descriptive feedback can be used to focus on major discrepancies among raters and collectively to provide a learning opportunity for the individual and the organization. Last, in our consulting practice, we have found that performance-appraisal in-

struments that concentrate on the domains of service to clients or customers; teamwork; empowerment of people; and the continuous improvement of services, products, and work processes have proved welcome and beneficial to our target organizations in both the private and public sectors. We usually tailor an instrument to a particular organization by working as a team with organizational members to develop an instrument and process that work for them. Accordingly, we model what the appraisal system is designed to promote, such as teamwork, empowerment, and continuous learning.

UNITY THROUGH DIVERSITY

As the global workforce becomes increasingly diverse, organizations are realizing from their experiences that diversity uniquely shapes the experiences of individuals and groups, relationships among groups in the organization, the organization as a whole, and even relationships among organizations (Jackson, Stone, & Alvarez, 1992). In other words, diversity has a wide influence on a variety of domains of human experience, including the psychological (self-esteem, self-concept) and the social (sense of belonging, relationships among persons from different groups). Furthermore, the issue of the organizational socialization of a diverse workforce is at center stage for competitive global organizations (Jackson, et al., 1992).

Socialization amid Diversity

An important issue for implementing diversity programs is whether people in general (a universal dispositional force) relate and form social relationships following similar fundamental rules or frameworks or whether each unique group (defined by gender, race, ethnicity, culture, age, sexual orientation, and so on) conducts social interactions within and outside organizations according to different rules for their social behaviors and self-referential constructs (self-esteem, self-conduct). If the former is the case, then similar socialization programs in organizations would be appropriate, whereas if the latter is the case, then a broad mix of such programs would be appropriate.

Universal Forms of Social Interaction

One model of human social relations (Fiske, 1992) suggests that people are fundamentally sociable (want to relate to each other, feel committed to four basic types of social relationships, consider themselves obligated to abide by these four types of relationships, and impose them on other people). In addition, they organize their social and organizational lives in terms of their relationships with other people according to four fundamental frameworks known to all persons, regardless of their cultural, racial, or ethnic origin.

According to Fiske (1992), people in all cultures use the following four frameworks when relating to each other, although the *expression* of these four schemata or paradigms varies from culture to culture or other salient defining features of a unique group:

- Communal sharing: relationships in which people treat each other as all the same, focusing on communalities and ignoring distinct individual identities—equivalence relationships as found within diverse subcultures in an organization.

- Authority ranking: relationships that are driven by asymmetry along some hierarchical social dimension, such as organizational authority relationships between managers and nonmanagers or experts and nonexperts or among the upper, middle, and lower levels of an organization.

- Equality matching: relationships that are based on an even balance and one-to-one correspondence among people, for example,

work teams or organizational groups in which each member has one vote; equal opportunity and affirmative action programs; and negotiations in which parties seek corresponding benefits, although the expression of the benefits may take different forms.

- Market pricing: relationships in which people focus on ratios and rates that are usually reduced to a single value or utility metric (like money) allowing them to compare many qualitatively and quantitatively diverse factors, for instance, cost-benefit: ratio calculations in organizations that include prices, wages, and commissions.

Thus, majority or minority persons in an organization do not have to learn these rules of social interaction in the four frameworks, since the rules unfold developmentally from early childhood to adulthood in the order just presented. In a given organization or context, a person needs only to learn how to implement the rules or, for example, who takes precedence over whom with regard to what things in what settings, whether it is an American working in a Chinese organization, or vice versa. All persons in social relationships experience sharing, ranking, matching, and pricing, and they all have to learn how these relationship categories are expressed or implemented in a given organization or context (Fiske, 1992).

According to Fiske (1992), all other social interactions outside the four universally shared relationship categories represent *asocial interactions* in which people either use other people purely as a means to some ulterior end (political guile or manipulation, often seen in organizations), ignore each other's goals and standards, or pursue an asocial orientation of sociopathy. The four modes of organizing social life are endogenous products of the human mind and determine how people transfer things, the foundations of social justice, organization of labor, and the formation of social identity and the relational self (Fiske, 1992). Accordingly, organizational diversity programs that embrace these four categories of social relationships may well speak to all members of a diverse workforce.

Strategies for Diversity

If organizations have diverse members who do not understand, appreciate, respect, and harness their differences from and similarities to other members, the workforce will not be committed to the organization, its products or services, and its customers or clients. This lack of commitment will eventually lead to decreased competitiveness and ultimately to organizational failure. We believe that the competitive and wholesome global organization will continue to experience a variety of problems. Therefore, we encourage you to consider carefully the suggested guidelines for harnessing diversity listed in Table 4–6, so your people—your most important organizational resource—can work effectively, efficiently, and positively to learn to solve the many problems in all people's organizational lives.

It is important to us that you plan and implement programs to harness diversity. We are confident that you have or will develop the ability to do so, so you can meet the needs and interests of all your organizational stakeholders. This important endeavor can bring out the best in all people by eliminating the walls within them that keep them apart.

SUMMARY

In this chapter, we examined global and local forces that shape workforce diversity in organizations around the world. We focused on workforce demographics in Asia, Europe, and the United States and examined the stages of harnessing diversity in organizations, from affirmative action through valuing diversity to man-

TABLE 4–6. Guidelines for Harnessing Workforce Diversity

- Organizations must invest continuously in the education and development of the competencies of diverse high performance quality oriented teams.

- Encourage awareness of diverse members strengths and educational strategies to address weaknesses and promote continuously interpersonal skills, self-management techniques, and problem solving.

- Implement organizational policies and practices that promote values, beliefs, and norms in support of diversity, teamwork, quality, and individual responsibility for the organization.

- Implement realistic and encouraging career planning and advancement programs centered upon team or unit rewards, a variety of pay incentive schemes, flexible benefits programs, and career tracks especially for those members who for organizational reasons must remain in their jobs for long periods of time.

Reprinted with permission from J. P. Fernandez with M. Barr, *The Diversity Advantage: How American Business Can Out-Perform Japanese and European Companies in the Global Marketplace*, p. 298. Copyright © 1993 by Jossey-Bass, Inc., Publishers. First published by Lexington Books. All rights reserved.

aging diversity. Diversity varies along many dimensions, such as race, ethnicity, gender, sexual orientation, and professional function in an organization.

We examined the positive and negative outcomes associated with affirmative action, which aims to enhance the organizational and psychological well-being of previously disadvantaged persons. Also, we reviewed the challenges and advantages of the multicultural organization and managing diversity as a strategic action to enhance organizational productivity and financial measures. In addition, we reviewed issues associated with promotion and performance-appraisal processes and indicated specific strategies to focus such processes on performance measures and to promote procedural justice for all members of a diverse workforce.

Workforce diversity is a challenge for all organizations in the world, and specific strategies can be applied in a variety of organizations to enhance harmony and productivity around the differences and similarities among people. People relate to each other within basic categories of interpersonal relationships, and the implementation of the guidelines for each category involves different cultural and contextual rules that all people are called on to learn when they work and live with diverse persons.

CHAPTER REFERENCES

Argyris, C., & Schon, D. (1978). *Organizational learning: A theory of action perspective.* Reading, MA: Addison-Wesley.

Ballard, A. M., & Wright, D. S. (1993). Circumventing the glass ceiling: Women executives in American state governments. *Public Administration Review, 53,* 189–202.

Bray D. W., & Associates. (1991). *Working with organizations and their people.* New York: Guilford Press.

Burke, R. J., & McKeen, C. A. (1992). Women in management. *International Review of Industrial and Organizational Psychology, 1,* 245–283.

Campbell, D. J., & Lee, C. (1988). Self-appraisal in performance evaluation: Development versus evaluation. *Academy of Management Review, 13,* 302–314.

Cox, T. (1991). The multicultural organization. *Academy of Management Executive, 5,* 34–47.

Cox, T. H., & Blake, S. (1991). Managing cultural diversity: Implications for organizational competitiveness. *Academy of Management Executive, 5,* 45–56.

Cox, T. H., Lobel, S. A., & McLeod, P. L. (1991). Effects of ethnic group cultural differences on cooperative and competitive behavior on a group task. *Academy of Management Journal, 34,* 827–847.

DeLuca, J. M., & McDowell, R. N. (1992). Managing diversity: A strategic "grass-roots" approach. In S. E. Jackson & Associates (Eds.), *Diversity in the workplace* (pp. 227–247). New York: Guilford Press.

Dipboye, R. L. (1987). Problems and progress of women in management. In K. S. Koziara, M. H. Moskow, & L. D. Tanner (Eds.), *Working women: Past, present, future* (pp. 118–153). Washington, DC: BNA Books.

Eagly, A. H., Makhijani, M. G., & Klonsky, B. G. (1992). Gender and evaluation of leaders: A meta-analysis. *Psychological Bulletin, 111,* 3–22.

Fernandez, J. P., & Barr, M. (1993). *The diversity advantage.* Lexington, MA: Lexington Books.

Fisher, R., & Ury, W. (1981). *Getting to yes.* Boston: Houghton Mifflin.

Fiske, A. P. (1992). The four elementary forms of sociality: Framework for a unified theory of social relations. *Psychological Review, 99,* 689–723.

Funder, D. C., & Colvin, C. R. (1988). Friends and acquaintanceship, agreement, and the accuracy of personality judgment. *Journal of Personality and Social Psychology, 55,* 149–158.

Goodale, J. G. (1993). Seven ways to improve performance appraisals. *HR Magazine, 38,* 77–80.

Heilman, M. E. (1994). Affirmative action: Some unintended consequences for working women. In B. M. Staw & L. L. Cummings (Eds.), *Research in organizational behavior* (Vol. 16, pp. 125–169). Greenwich, CT: JAI Press.

Heilman, M. E., Lucas, J. S., & Kaplow, S. R. (1990). Self-derogating consequences of preferential selection: The moderating role of initial self-confidence. *Organizational Behavior and Human Decision Processes, 46,* 202–216.

Heilman, M. E., Kaplow, S., Amato, M. A. G., & Stathatos, P. (1993). When similarity is a liability: Effects of sex-based preferential selection on relations to like-sex and different-sex others. *Journal of Applied Psychology, 18,* 917–927.

Heilman, M. E., Simon, M. C., & Repper, D. P. (1987). Intentionally favored, unintentionally harmed? The impact of gender-based preferential selection on self-perceptions and self-evaluations. *Journal of Applied Psychology, 76,* 99–105.

Henderson, G. (1994). *Cultural diversity in the workplace: Issues and strategies.* Westport, CT: Quorum Books.

Hymowitz, C., & Schellhardt, T. D. (1986, March 24). The glass ceiling. *Wall Street Journal*, pp. 1D, 4D–5D.

Jackson, S. E., & Associates (1992). *Diversity in the workplace*. New York: Guilford Press.

Jackson, S. E., Stone, V. K., & Alvarez, E. B. (1992). Socialization amidst diversity: The impact of demographics on work team old-timers and newcomers. In L. L. Cummings & B. M. Staw (Eds.), *Research in organizational behavior* (Vol. 15, pp. 45–109). Greenwich, CT: JAI Press.

Johnson, O. (1996). *Information please almanac*. Boston: Houghton Mifflin.

Johnsrud, L. K. (1991). Administrative promotion: The power of gender. *Journal of Higher Education, 62,* 119–149.

Johnston, W. B. (1991, Global work force 2,000: The new world labor market. *Harvard Business Review, 69,* 115–127.

Johnston, W. B., & Packer, A. E. (1987). *Workforce 2,000: Work and workers for the 21st century*. Indianapolis, IN: Hudson Institute.

Kanter, R. M. (1991). Transcending business boundaries: 12,000 world managers view change. *Harvard Business Review, 69,* 151–164.

Kanter, R. (1993). *Men and women of the corporation*. New York: Basic Books.

Komorita, S. S. (1987). Cooperative choice in decomposed social dilemmas. *Personality and Social Psychology Bulletin, 13,* 53–63.

Major, B., & Konar, E. (1984). An investigation of sex differences in pay expectations and their possible causes. *Academy of Management Journal, 27,* 777–791.

Major, B., Vanderslice, V., & McFarlin, D. B. (1984). Effects of pay expected on pay received: The confirmatory nature of expectations. *Journal of Applied Social Psychology, 14,* 399–412.

Martin, B. A. (1989). Gender differences in salary expectations when current salary information is provided. *Psychology of Women Quarterly, 13,* 87–96.

Mayer, R. C., Davis, J. H., & Schoorman, F. D. (1995). An integrative model of organizational trust. *Academy of Management Review, 20,* 709–734.

McFarlin, D. B., Frone, M., Major, B., & Konar, E. (1989). Predicting career-entry pay expectations: The role of gender-based comparisons. *Journal of Business and Psychology, 3,* 331–340.

Morrison, A. M., & von Glinow, M. A. (1990). Women and minorities in management. *American Psychologist, 45,* 200–208.

Morrison, A. M., White, R. P., Van Velsor, E., & the Center for Creative Leadership. (1987). *Breaking the glass ceiling: Can women reach the top of America's largest corporations?* Reading, MA: Addison-Wesley.

Mount, M. K., Barrick, M. R., & Strauss, J. P. (1994). Validity of observer ratings of the big five personality factors. *Journal of Applied Psychology, 79,* 272–280.

National Committee on Pay Equity. (1986, April). *Newsletter*. Washington, DC: Author.

Olson, J. E., & Frieze, I. H. (1987). Income determinants for women in business. In A. H. Stromberg, L. Larwood, & B. A. Cruted (Eds.), *Women and work: An annual review* (Vol. 2, pp. 173–191). Newbury Park, CA: Sage.

Roman, M. (1990, October 29). Women, beware: An MBA doesn't mean equal pay. *Business Week,* p. 57.

Rosen, D. I. (1992). Appraisals can make—or break—your court case. *Personnel Journal, 71,* 113–118.

Sahl, R. J. (1990). Design effective performance appraisals. *Personnel Journal, 69,* 53–60.

Shizhong, D., Zhang, D., & Larson, M. R. (1992). *Trade and investment opportunities in China*. Westport, CT: Quorum Books.

Smith, C. J. (1991). *China: People and place in the land of one billion*. Boulder, CO: Westview Press.

Stevens, C. K., Banetta, A. G., & Gist, M. E. (1993). Gender differences in the acquisition of salary negotiation skills: The role of goals, self-efficacy, and perceived control. *Journal of Applied Psychology, 78,* 723–735.

Stroh, L. K., Brett, J. M., & Reilly, A. H. (1992). All the right stuff: A comparison of female and male manager's career progression. *Journal of Applied Psychology, 77,* 251–260.

Stuart, P. (1992). What does the glass ceiling cost you? *Personnel Journal, 71,* 70–80.

Thomas, L. T., & Ganster, D. C. (1995). Impact of family-supportive work variables on work-family conflict and strain: A control perspective. *Journal of Applied Psychology, 80*, 6–15.

Thomas, R. R., Jr. (1990). From affirmative action to affirming diversity. *Harvard Business Review, 68*, 107–117.

Thomas, R. R., Jr. (1992). Managing diversity: A conceptual framework. In S. E. Jackson & Associates (Eds.), *Diversity in the workplace* (pp. 306–317). New York: Guilford Press.

Thomas, R. R., Jr. (1995). A diversity framework. In M. M. Chemers, S. Oskamp, & M. A. Costanza (Eds.), *Diversity in organizations* (pp. 245–263). New York: Guilford Press.

Tshikororo, L. (1993). *The effect of performance and race on employee promotion.* Unpublished master's thesis, University of Vermont, Burlington.

Tshikororo, L. (1994). *The promotion-advancement process and characteristics of Black managers in South Africa.* Unpublished doctoral dissertation, University of Vermont, Burlington.

U.S. Bureau of the Census. (1987). Household and family characteristics: March 1987. In *Current population reports* (Population Characteristics Series P-20, No. 424). pp. 1–127. Washington, DC: U.S. Government Printing Office.

U.S. Department of Labor. (1995). Charting the projections: 1994–2005. *Occupational Outlook Quarterly, 39*, 1–52.

Watson, W. E., Kumar, K., & Michaelsen, L. K. (1993). Cultural diversity's impact on interaction process and performance: Comparing homogeneous and diverse task groups. *Academy of Management Journal, 36*, 590–602.

SUGGESTED REFERENCES

We list here some suggested newsletters, videotapes, and organizations that may assist you in planning, implementing, or continuing to manage a diversity program in your organization. This is not an exhaustive list, so we welcome additional suggestions from readers. Thank you, and we hope to hear from you (R. B.

Lawson: -011-802-656-4032 (Voice) or 656-8783 (Fax) or R_Lawson@Dewey.uvm.edu; and Z. Shen 86-10-6275-4944 (Voice) or 6256-4095 (Fax) or shenz@pku.edu.cn).

Books and Awareness Instruments

Gardenswartz, L., & Rowe, A. (1994). *Managing diversity.*

Grote, K. (1994). *Diversity awareness profile (DAP)*

Kogod Kanu, S. (1994). *A workshop for managing diversity in the workplace*

All three books are available from
Pfeiffer & Company
8517 Production Avenue
San Diego, CA 92121-9984
(phone 011-1-800-274-4434)

Thomas, R. R., Jr. (1991). *Beyond race and gender: Unleashing the power of your total work force by managing diversity*

Available from
American Institute for Managing Diversity
PO Box 38
830 Westview Drive, S.W.
Atlanta, GA 30314
(phone 011-1-404-524-7316)

Leach, J., George, B., Jackson, T., & LaBella, A. (1995). *A practical guide to working with diversity: The process, the tools, and the resources.* New York: American Management Association.

Available from
American Management Association
135 West 50th Street
New York, NY 10020
011-1-800-262-9699

Newsletters

Cultural Diversity at Work (13751 Lake City Way N.E., Suite 106, Seattle, WA 98125-3615; phone 206-362-0336). Aimed at preparing readers for "managing, training, and conducting business in the global age." Six issues a year plus 11 bulletins listing training events.

Managing Diversity (PO Box 819, Jamestown, NY 14702-0819; phone 1-800-542-7869). For people managing diverse workforces.

Videotapes/Films

Valuing Diversity, a seven-part film-video tape series, aimed at such audiences as entry-level employees, supervisors, and senior managers. May be rented or purchased individually or as a group. Contact Griggs Productions, 302 23rd Avenue, San Francisco, CA 94121; phone 415-668-4200.

Bridging Cultural Barriers: Managing Ethnic Diversity in the Workplace, a 23 $^1/_2$-minute training videotape for managers and supervisors, based on Sondra Thiederman's book, *Bridging Cultural Barriers for Corporate*

Success. Contact Barr Films, 12801 Schabarum Avenue, Irwindale, CA 91706-7878; phone 1-800-234-7878.

Organizations

The American Institute for Managing Diversity (PO Box 38, 830 Westview Drive, S.W., Atlanta, GA 30314; phone 404-524-7316). An independent nonprofit affiliate of Morehouse College. Offers seminars, consultants, a speakers' bureau, and books and videotapes.

The International Society for Intercultural Education, Training, and Research (733 15th Street, N.W., Suite 900, Washington, DC 20005; phone 202-737-5000). An organization of professionals who share a common concern for intercultural understanding.

PART II

PROCESSES

5

Group Dynamics

CHAPTER OVERVIEW

Since groups are a fundamental feature of organizations around the world, it is imperative that their dynamics and effectiveness are understood. In this chapter, we define groups and indicate the similarities and differences between groups and teams, noting these relationships are more a matter of degree than of kind. The study of groups has pretty much been taken away from social psychology by organizational psychology; as a consequence, the focus of interest has tilted more to the study of teams, although knowledge of groups dynamics is important for managing both teams and groups in organizations.

Next, we identify formal and informal groups in organizations and clarify the fundamental differences between them and how knowledge of them is essential for the enhanced management of people in organizations. Thereafter, we examine the stages of group development, including forming, storming, norming, performing, and adjourning. Both the dynamics of each stage of group development and different strategies for dealing with group issues at each stage are discussed.

We then present the reasons for joining groups or teams, including downsizing, so that fewer people are left behind to do more work, as well as the fundamental psychological need to belong to a group or team. We define roles and norms and indicate how they provide stability and predictability to a group or team. We also review social facilitation or comparisons of performance when working alone or as a member of a group, including electronic or virtual groups or teams. We then define social loafing, free-rider effect, and the sucker effect and present strategies for managing these social or group dilemmas as well as cross-cultural studies of social loafing and social enhancement.

In our treatment of teams, we define their unique features, such as that they are designed around work processes (customer service), rather than organizational functions (like production and sales). We also delineate types of teams, including computer-assisted teams, quality circles, task forces, and autonomous or empowered teams, and offer specific tips for teams that have been clearly demonstrated to enhance team performances.

We conclude with a review of the factors that influence the performances of groups and teams, such as cohesiveness and familiarity, diversity of membership, and organizational context. The review of these factors indicates that, in general, when it comes to teams, be as specific as possible regarding design and process issues.

LEARNING OBJECTIVES

After studying this chapter, you will be prepared to

- describe the similarities and differences between groups and teams
- define formal and informal organizational groups and explain the stages of group development of forming, storming, norming, performing, and adjourning
- review the reasons for joining a group or team at work
- clearly define and present the implications of roles and norms for group dynamics
- describe the social dilemmas of social loafing, the free-rider effect, and the sucker effect

- discuss specific strategies to prevent or moderate these changes in the level of performance that arise when working in a group

- clearly define *team* and distinguish different types of teams, including, computer-assisted teams and empowered or autonomous teams

- present tips for teams

- review the influence of cohesiveness, membership diversity, and organizational context on the effectiveness of teams.

Groups are about belonging beyond oneself.

GROUPS AT WORK

Groups are everywhere at work, and membership in some of them may be mandated, for example, when a manager or supervisor asks you to join a certain group, team, or committee. Membership may be elected, such as when you choose to join one work group, rather than another, or an informal interest or friendship group. Obviously, groups at work and in other domains of life fulfill a variety of purposes and needs. We, like others (Baumeister & Leary, 1995; Buss, 1990, 1991; Coon 1946), believe that group membership is a response to a pervasive, powerful, universal, and fundamental need to belong or to form relationships with others. Patterns of group behaviors and close relationships at and away from work can be understood as serving the need to belong. In fact, the development and experience of shared emotions are an essential force for the formation of small groups, while the satisfaction of the need to belong and frequent and positive affective experiences in an ongoing relational bond contribute to the maintenance of groups (Clark & Watson, 1988; Moreland, 1987).

Groups at work can be more fully understood and yield enhanced satisfaction and productivity when their managers embrace a psychological framework that emphasizes sustained relationships and shared positive emotional experiences, rather than a cultural materialism framework that stresses economic needs and opportunities (Harris, 1979). In fact, people everywhere around the globe belong to a number of small primary groups in which they have face-to-face personal interactions (Mann, 1980). Thus, in the global marketplace, there are groups at work and social bonds that form easily. An important part of the bottom line with groups is belongingness—being regarded with concern by others. From these features flows enhanced productivity.

Group dynamics focuses on the nature of groups in terms of variables that influence their formation, development, operation or structure, membership, and relationships among groups primarily within a given organization.

Definition of Group

There are many definitions of the construct of group, and there is lack of agreement about the similarities and differences between the constructs of group and team (Guzzo & Dickson, 1996; Levine & Moreland, 1990; Sherman, 1996; Sundstrom, DeMeuse, & Futrell, 1990). The term *team* has replaced the term *group* in the argot of organizational psychology. Some organizational psychologists consider the two terms interchangeable constructs, while others consider them fundamentally different in that groups are transformed into teams when their members develop a sense of shared commitment and aspire to synergy (Guzzo & Dickson, 1996; Katzenbach & Smith, 1993). In general, groups and teams are similar constructs because they both embrace the idea of people in social interaction, people influencing each other, and people sharing some common purpose. Unlike groups, in which performance depends on the work of individual members, in teams, performance requires both individual contributions and collective work products—the joint outcome of team members working in concert. Likewise, members of a group or a team may share a common purpose or goal, but members of a team also share a common commitment to a purpose, such as being the best organization for producing a particular product or providing a particular service (Greenberg & Baron, 1995). Teams have been a major organizational adaptive response to increased global competition and customer service requirements in this age of downsizing, in which fewer members are left to do more work.

In this chapter, we first discuss the construct of group because it appears to be a broader construct than team, has been around longer in the psychological literature, and includes the organizational phenomena of committees, task forces, and teams. Thereafter, we discuss teams and the factors that influence their performance.

The many definitions of *group* usually include the following features: two or more individuals who are interdependent, interact with each other over time, share a common goal or purpose, and perceive themselves as being a group. We define a group as *two or more interdependent and interacting persons, sharing a common purpose or purposes, who perceive themselves as having an unique relationship link between members, as distinguished from interactions with nonmembers.* This definition implies that groups can vary in size, interact with each other, and share unique actions and experiences that give rise to boundaries that may be physical, psychological, social, or some combination of these boundary elements.

Types of Groups

Basically, there are two types of groups, formal and informal. Figure 5–1 presents the different types of groups that are found in an organization. A *formal group* is created by the organi-

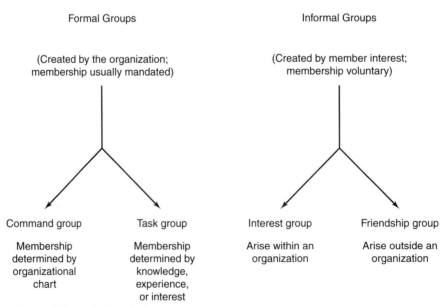

Figure 5–1   Types of Groups in Organizations.

zation and is designed to focus the resources of members on the attainment of some important organizational goal or goals. One type of formal group is the *command group*, which is determined or constructed by reference to the organizational chart in that members are subordinates who report directly to a given manager or supervisor. For example, a command group may be formed by a vice president, unit director, or department head for his or her subordinates to identify specific strategies to enhance organizational marketing, production, or the development of new products. Usually, command groups are formed by directors or heads of *line units* (units that are directly involved in delivering the product or service of the organization). However, they can also be formed by directors or heads of *staff units* (units that are not part of the direct product or service delivery command chain yet provide support to line units or personnel). Thus, for example, a large manufacturing organization that makes "goodies" (use your imagination) would include line units of marketing, production, and sales and would most likely include staff units or positions, such as human resources, payroll, and housekeeping. When a command group is formed, it is usually charged or given a specific mission or set of goals to attain, granted some manner of delegated authority, and held to some kind of accountability standards like providing a written or electronic report by a particular deadline.

The other kind of formal group, the *task group*, is usually constructed around some specific task, and unlike a command group, its members may be selected from various units or positions in the organization (line or staff), provided they have some knowledge, experience, or special interest that is relevant to the task group. Thus, for example, an organization that wants to diversify further the composition of the workforce or customer and client base may create a task group that includes persons from line units or positions (such as production), as well as staff units (such as human resources). Task

groups, like command groups, are also given a set of goals or objectives, empowered by means of delegated authority and resources (money, time, or whatever), and held accountable in some fashion. A task group may be a standing or permanent committee or an ad hoc (temporary) committee or task force that is formed to solve a specific problem, such as establishing policies for parking or access to parking spaces or the use of organizational electronic information systems and instruments.

The second major type of group that is frequently found in organizations around the globe is the *informal group*, which arises naturally without any direction from the organization and clearly reflects the fundamental need of people to belong to groups (Baumeister & Leary, 1995). One kind of informal group, *the interest group*, may arise from a particular interest, such as to bring employees of an organization together to demand or request modifications in employee benefits; enhance the organization's concern for environmental pollution and establish recycling projects and programs; seek support and arrange for an organizational party, picnic, or another kind of celebration; or unionize. Unlike formal groups, membership in informal groups is typically voluntary and largely independent of organizational line or staff units or positions. Generally, interest groups decide on (rather than have the organization mandate) some mission or goal, resources, and accountability feature.

The other type of informal group is the *friendship group*. This group usually extends outside the organization to bring people together around a common interest or activity, such as an athletic team or event or some type of entertainment, community action project, or interest in financial investments. Typically, friendship groups are less structured than are formal and informal interest groups. Taken together, both informal and formal groups are found in almost every organization around the world, are designed to promote interaction among people and to achieve specific objectives or goals, and are important to organizations and members alike. It is essential to be knowledgeable about both major types of groups in your organization so you manage and know your organization and people better.

Stages of Development

Groups, like individuals, go through stages of development that parallel to some extent the universal stages of infancy-childhood, adolescence, adulthood, and old age. According to Tuckman (1965) and Tuckman and Jensen (1977), groups move through five stages: *forming*, *storming*, *norming*, *performing*, and *adjourning*. Table 5–1 presents a brief list of members' behaviors and needs during these stages. In the first stage, *forming*, members seek information about the purpose or purposes of the group, begin to learn how the group will work or the rules of the road, and become acquainted with other team members. During this phase, it is usually important to reduce uncertainty, answer questions about the group as quickly and clearly as possible, and address the personal benefits and costs of being involved in the group. The forming stage is like the infancy-childhood stage of personal development in that members are inquisitive and seek information about the group and individual members. Although there is no time frame on this or the other stages, it should be noted that after the group passes from one stage to another it may (and probably will) go back to an earlier stage, especially during emotionally charged and critical experiences, such as when a member asks, "What is this group really supposed to be doing?" even though the group may be in the performing stage.

The second stage, *storming*, is somewhat like adolescence in that group members frequently conflict and, to some extent, compete with each other over the leadership role and group goals. Some members may withdraw emotionally or isolate themselves from any emotional conflict that arises. During this stage, it is critical to allow for the expression of conflict and feelings, ranging from uncertainty to frustration, and to encourage members to remain actively involved in the group.

During the third stage, *norming*, which is similar to the individual development stage of adulthood, informal and formal rules or guidelines about cohesiveness and teamwork are established. The members are more upbeat and positive about the group, their membership, and their work in the group. Work starts to get done, project reports begin to take shape, and a clear performance record emerges so the members begin to experience concretely some of their efforts to date. The norming stage ends when the members agree solidly about what to do and how to do it and engage in earnest in group projects.

The fourth stage, *performing*, (also similar to the individual development stage of adulthood), is characterized by a fully functional group in which projects are focused, the work is approaching completion, and intragroup interactions and relationships are harmonious. The members are fully focused on getting the work done.

Table 5–1. Stages of Group Development

Stage of Development	Members' Behaviors—Need
Forming	Seek information—direction
Storming	Conflict—emotional expression
Norming	Teamwork—task focus
Performing	Performance—protection from interruptions
Adjourning	Completion of task—recognition and gratitude

In the fifth stage, *adjourning* which is similar to the individual development stage of old age, the members prepare to dissolve the group. They focus on wrapping up activities and getting the group activities in order, rather than on the high performance of tasks. Some group members may be pleased that the group is breaking up, while others may be downhearted about the loss of camaraderie, friendship, and the structuring of their organizational time.

It is important to keep in mind that almost all groups evolve through these five stages and that in each stage the group can stay stuck, unravel, or move into the next stage. Studies (Bushe & Johnson, 1989; Gersick, 1988, 1989; Goodman, Ravlin, & Schminke, 1987) have found that although all groups do not evolve through a universal set of stages, the *timing* of when groups form and change the way they work seems to be highly consistent. Briefly, according to the so-called punctuated-equilibrium model of group development, in the first group meeting, the direction of the group is established, people size each other up, and a basic timetable of activities is established. This meeting initiates Phase 1, during which the group tends to remain locked into the initial direction established during the first meeting. Phase 2, a transition period, almost inevitably begins halfway between the group's first meeting and the official deadline. The first part of this phase involves open discussion, criticism, and a reassessment of the group's activities to date. In the remainder of Phase 2, necessary changes are made and the members focus on finishing their work within the readjustment direction of the group. At the last meeting, final issues are discussed, details are resolved, and decisions are finalized.

GROUP DYNAMICS

Because almost all of the work of the world is done by small groups, it is essential to know why people join groups; the influence of groups on individual members, and vice versa; and the forces that influence group performances.

Reasons for Joining

A fundamental reason for joining a group or team at work is that with downsizing, there are fewer persons in organizations who have a greater need to band together do more work (Sundstrom et al., 1990; Vaill, 1989). Even though an organizational member may not have much choice about joining a formal command group, he or she usually has some personal reason, such as the need for security or power and, most important, to belong or share a unique relationship or experiences with other members of the organization. An awareness of the various personal needs that draw members more deeply into their group or team is important so the team members and leaders can respond to each other's needs and, in return, have their own personal needs addressed—a psychic quid pro quo that does not show up in their paychecks.

Roles and Norms

A group has two structural features: *roles* (the pattern of interrelationships among the members based on the positions they hold in the group or team) and *norms* (the informal rules and expectations for behaviors that arise within a given group). A knowledge of roles and norms allows you to understand better the functioning of a group and to enhance the effectiveness of the group's performance.

Typical roles in a group or team include timekeeper, information seeker, recorder, facilitator, and devil's advocate (which involves questioning and making statements like "Well, on the other hand, there is some other explanation we need to consider") (Chen, Lawson, Gordon, & McIntosh, 1996). Many interactions among members of a group are role driven, and members are sometimes surprised and even unsettled when one member acts out of role and thus disrupts the structure of the group, as reflected in the expected behavioral patterns. To enhance a group's cohesiveness and members' appreciation of each other, we have found it useful to have different members play different roles, so each member can see for herself or himself that there is a structure and a sense of predictability of management that works clearly for groups and teams.

Most groups develop norms related to performance and associated processes, such as how hard, long, and smart to work and how to go about doing your work, especially in relation to other members (Goodman et al., 1987). Appearance norms, which are usually present in most groups and teams, include such issues as appropriate dress, appearance of loyalty to the team, and when and how to look busy or just to hang out. Two other types of norms that can be found in most groups are norms related to issues of informal social arrangements (who interacts with whom inside and outside the workplace) and allocation norms (who gets extra payments, equipment, or whatever and when, such as the norm that new members usually get the smallest space or office). Norms develop from explicit discussions by group members, may be absorbed from the larger organizational culture, or result from initial or primary reactions to poignant group situations or events.

Social Facilitation

Sometimes a person may perform a task better alone than in the presence of others, vice versa; both outcomes reflect the phenomenon of social facilitation (Zajonc, 1965). As we discuss shortly, the members of a group need not be physically present for social facilitation to take effect; rather, they may have an electronic presence (electronic performance monitoring) (Aiello & Kolb, 1995). Obviously, it is essential to know what factors or conditions in a group setting lead to enhanced performance in one case and to a decrement in performance in another case.

Weick (1984) and Zajonic (1965) found that when a person is to perform in a group, an initial reaction to the presence of others is emotional arousal (either tension or excitement). Furthermore, when they are tense or excited, people tend to perform the most dominant response associated with that group context. Thus, when a group member gets emotionally aroused in the presence of others and knows the task to be performed well as a result of extensive practice, her or his performance will be enhanced, but if the task is unfamiliar, the quality of her or his performance will decrease. Accordingly, to perform best in a group, you should practice the task in advance; visualize yourself performing in your group or team; and, if possible, perform in front of some other practice groups, especially if the task to be performed is important.

In 1990, electronic performance monitoring (EPM) monitored 10 million workers in the United States, and the number continues to grow. You may have experienced the presence of EPM when you called a financial service provider, a toll-free number of a mail order catalog, or some offices of the federal government and heard something like "This call is being monitored for quality-assessment purposes." Aiello and Kolb (1995) reported the results of a laboratory study of EPM whose participants were 202 undergraduate students. The participants entered a series of six-digit numbers from a worksheet into a computer for a five-minute practice period (to obtain baseline data for high- and low-skilled performances of this task) and then collected data for approximately 15 minutes. Some of the participants worked alone, others as members of a noninteracting group, and still others as members of a cohesive group that had interacted during an earlier brainstorming task. In addition, they were informed that individual- or group-level EPM would be used in all three conditions (solitary work and work in the noninteracting and cohesive groups).

The results of the study indicated an unequivocal social facilitation effect in that high-ability participants (with high baseline performances) worked faster when monitored, but low-ability participants (with low baseline performances) keyed fewer entries or exhibited a performance decrement. Furthermore, individually and work-group monitored participants performed almost identically. Thus, when monitored, faster workers get faster and slower workers get slower.

Aiello and Kolb (1995) also found that even for the 15 minutes of EPM, the monitored participants reported more stress than did the non-monitored participants, which is consistent with findings from field-based studies (DiTecco, Cwitco, Arsenault, Andre, 1992; M. J. Smith, Carayon, Sanders, Lim, & LeGrande, 1992). One conclusion that can be drawn from these findings is that organizations that plan to or already use EPM may enhance the productivity of members and members may experience less stress if they involve the members in the early design and implementation of EPM and allow the members to share in any increased net revenues that result from enhanced productivity with EPM. We believe that the important lesson is that high tech also requires high touch in that as the technological side of an organization is upgraded or reengineered the human and social dimensions require comparable nurturing and upgrading. Focusing on one side without the other will most likely create more problems than the intended enhancements are designed to address.

Social Loafing

If you have been a member of work groups or teams of various sizes, from small (3–7 persons) to large (9–15 or more persons), you may have noticed that size has an effect on a number of factors. One effect is on the performances of the group as a whole and of individual members (Guzzo & Dickson, 1996; Guzzo & Salas, 1995; Shaw, 1981; Thomas & Fink, 1963). In general, small groups are faster at completing tasks than are larger groups, but large groups are better at problem solving because of diverse inputs. Another, perhaps more noticeable, effect of group size is that as the group grows larger (beyond about 9 members), individual effort begins to fall off—a clear instance in which the sum of all the parts is less than the sum of the individual parts alone. *Social loafing* is the tendency of group members to do less, the more individuals there are contributing to the group task (Latané, Williams, & Harkins, 1979).

Shepperd (1993) suggested that low performance in work groups is an example of a social dilemma that includes two other effects in addition to social loafing. These effects are the *free-rider effect* (individuals reduce their contributions to the group because they believe they can reap the benefits of the group's success without having to contribute) and *the sucker effect* (the threat that others will free ride on one's efforts, which causes the member to withhold efforts in performance groups as a means of restoring equity and avoiding being a sucker to other members' free riding). Suggested remedies for the free-rider and sucker effects include providing incentives for contributing and decreasing the cost of contributing to the group task, respectively.

There are two specific strategies for dealing with social loafing in groups and teams at work. First, make each member identifiable and responsible for a specific task and publicly post this information, so that each member's performance record is available to all the members and it is impossible to hide or get lost in the group. Second, make individual and group tasks important and interesting by clearly stating the importance of each member's contribution to the overall group task and enrich tasks so they are sufficiently engaging to make the task as intrinsically appealing as possible (George, 1992; Shepperd, 1993).

In an interesting study of social loafing, Earley (1993) had managers from the United States, Israel, and China complete an "in-basket" exercise (see Chapter 2) either alone or as part of a group of 10 other managers. These other managers were not physically present, but were described to each participant in the group condition as being highly similar to them in terms of family, religion, and interests. The in-basket exercise required the participants to write memoranda, fill out forms, and perform other tasks much like the daily activities in the actual jobs. Earley found a social loafing effect for the American managers in that they performed better alone than in the group, but the opposite effect—no social loafing—for the Israeli and Chinese managers. In fact, the managers from Israel and China performed much better as part of a group than alone, a finding that suggests that the collective orientation of these cultures—shared responsibility for the good of all—may have been responsible for these managers' better performance in that group membership led to social enhancement rather than social loafing. Accordingly, one implication of Earley's results may be that for members of individualistic cultures, in which individual accomplishments and personal success are valued, social loafing may be attenuated or connected to social enhancement by making it plain that being socially responsible to the group and thus to other members is valuable and even by tying rewards for each group member to the group's, rather than to individual members' performance.

In working with groups or teams of any size, it is also important to have an odd number of members to avoid a deadlock owing to ties when votes are taken. When possible, choose a group of about five to seven members, a size that is small enough to get work done faster than in a large group yet large enough to allow for diverse inputs. If you have to work with a large group, perhaps you can configure it into a number of smaller and focused subgroups or task forces.

TEAMS IN ORGANIZATIONS

Teams are a valuable organizational resource that are being used increasingly in almost all organi-

zations around the world. Teams are generally successful, and the factors that influence their performance have been identified and applied in a wide variety of organizations (Guzzo & Dickson, 1996; Hackman, 1990; Manz & Sims, 1993). Although groups have been studied extensively by psychologists over the past 10 years (Levine & Moreland, 1990; Wilpert, 1995), the focus on teams has intensified because teams have been an excellent response to downsizing. Also, new organizational team strategies are needed to deal with wicked problems (complex, not easily identified problems for which guidelines to their solution are not readily available) compared to tame problems (problems for which there are established routine procedures and guidelines for solving less complex organizational problems) (Pacanowsky, 1995). For example, the response time of Hewlett-Packard (HP), rated one of the 10 best organizations in the United States in 1996, was 26 days (almost one month!) from the date of an order to the date on which a product reached a customer. A team of employees from HP and two other companies was assembled and led by two seasoned managers (Sherman, 1996). The team had no supervisors, no hierarchy, no titles, no job descriptions, and no plans. But it did have the goal of solving the wicked problem of reducing the time from order to delivery, which involved order information moving through 70 different computer systems. The team embraced the value of considering diverse points of view and looking at the entire system, rather than just the parts. The leaders simulated a kindergarten classroom to remind the members how they felt when learning was fun. The results were that the team was able to deliver consistently high-quality products in 8, not 26, days, and the team reached its goal in eight months, rather than the originally projected nine months. The team members experienced stress, but they noted that the nature of the stress had shifted from "fighting the same fires again and again" to realizing how little they knew until one day they realized they had enough knowledge and things started going more smoothly. Also, almost all the members reported that the team's work was enjoyable in that worrying about work was replaced by having fun around work. Hey, you never know!

Definition of Team

Teams have been defined as "interdependent collections of individuals who share responsibility for specific outcomes for their organizations (Sundstrom et al., 1990, p. 120) and as

> "individuals who see themselves and who are seen by others as a social entity . . . interdependent . . . embedded in one or more larger social systems (e.g., community, organization), and who perform tasks that affect others such as customers or coworkers." (Guzzo & Dickson, 1996, pp. 308–309)

Teams have a number of unique features, including being organized around work processes (such as speeding up cycle times or customers' orders, launching a new product, or devising new compensation plans), rather than specific functions like marketing, production, or sales (Wellins, Byham, & Dixon, 1994). Team members have cross-functional training and hence a variety of skills, so instead of doing the same thing over and over, they do many different things and can stand in for each other, which allows individuals to be more flexible but still to get the team's work done. Also, teams govern themselves, so they can roam freely throughout organizational hierarchies and structures and, in some instances, select their own leaders, whom they consider more like coaches than bosses. Last, teams are involved in organization-wide decisions; thus, decision making is not relegated primarily to managers who may be so removed from the product or service around which a decision is being made that they are clueless. The underlying notion here is that if you do it, you decide it. For a discussion of specific issues related to decision-making groups and teams, see Chapter 8.

Types of Teams

There are many schemes for categorizing different types of teams, most of which revolve around the teams' primary mission. Thus, the mission of the team determines the type of team. Another factor that determines the type of team is the life cycle. Some teams are created for a finite or fixed period (like a space team during a time of concentrated and extensive construction), whereas others are created for unlimited periods (such as a customer service, organizational justice, or climate team).

Most teams use computers to do their work for mediating meetings, generating ideas, or making choices (Guzzo & Dickson, 1996). Most of the research on *computer-assisted teams* has been driven by laboratory studies using ad hoc groups (constructed short-term groups mostly of college and university students) (Hollingshead & McGrath, 1995). In general, computer-mediated meetings generate more ideas than do face-to-face meetings, whereas face-to-face meetings yield better problem-solving and conflict-resolution outcomes. In addition, Dennis and Valacich (1993) and Gallupe, Cooper, Grise, and Bastianutti (1994) found that teams that interacted electronically (communicating via a computer) produced more ideas during a brainstorming task than did nominal groups (groups whose members did not interact). The topic of electronic brainstorming is treated in more detail in Chapter 8. Furthermore, Kiesler and Sproul (1992) found that groups that communicated solely or primarily by computer had greater equality of participation (even when members were of different status levels), made more extreme or risky decisions, and engaged in more hostile or extreme communications than did groups that interacted directly in face-to-face meetings.

Quality circles, like *task forces*, are created for the primary purpose of solving specific problems. Quality circles usually consist of 6–12 members who focus on raising the quality or productivity of their part of the organization. Usually, quality circles include training in group processes, such as brainstorming, and in quality management, such as using statistical indicators of quality. Quality circles appear to be the most effective early in the implementation phase of a new product or service (Guzzo & Dickson, 1996). Task forces solve specific problems, have a specific mandate, and are temporary groups that are disbanded once the task is completed.

Autonomous work groups, *self-managed teams*, or *empowered teams* perform highly interdependent jobs, are identified and identifiable as a social unit in the organization, are usually given significant authority and responsibility for many phases of their work, and make decisions that have economic consequences (Dobbelaere & Goeppinger, 1993). The effectiveness of self-managed teams appears to depend on the nature of the workforce (for example, shared dominant values) and the nature of the organization (such as a reward system that is inclined to reinforce the group's rather than only the individuals' work) (Guzzo & Dickson, 1996; C. Smith & Comer, 1994).

Team Building

Organizational support and sustained nurturing are prerequisites for effective teams, whether effectiveness is measured by group-produced outputs, the consequences the group has for its members, or the enhancement of the team's capacities to perform effectively in the future. Table 5–2 presents some guidelines for building a team and sustaining its successful performance that are based, in part, on our extensive experience working with and in groups in many different types of organizations.

We, as well as many others (see, for example, Katzenbach & Smith, 1993), have found that it is important for a team to have a clear and urgent mission even if the task or problem is not clearly definable in the beginning (for example, a problem in production, morale, or turnover; the organization's steady loss of its share, or the

Table 5–2. Tips for Teams

- Start with a clear mission.
- Select team members on the basis of their skills.
- Make the team's rules clear.
- Meet regularly for specified periods.
- Recognize the stages of the team's development.
- Encourage and reward individual and team accomplishments.
- Complete the final report, express gratitude to the team, and report the outcomes of the team's work later.

need to make work more enjoyable and productive). We encourage you to construct a team on the basis of the technical, interpersonal, and organization skills that are needed for the task at hand. We also suggest that you promote clear definitions of the team's rules of the road. These rules include issues of confidentiality; attendance; the use of only constructive criticism; equal airtime (time to speak) for all, with second or subsequent airtimes only after every member has had an opportunity to speak; keeping comments focused on the issue; guidelines for decision making (a majority or unanimous vote); and suggestions for how to make the work enjoyable.

It is also important to recognize and respond accordingly to the team's activities, depending on the stage of group development, discussed earlier in the chapter: forming, storming, norming, performing, and adjourning. Always recognize the individual members' and team's achievement of intermediate goals, process or talk out conflicts in the group, and meet regularly for a specified period (deadlines are wonderful levers for action whether a team meeting is 1 or 10 hours). Base your final report on the integration of reports from subgroups or task forces and label and date each draft. Finally, acknowledge the individual members' and team's contributions, wrap up appropriately, and report the outcomes arising from the team's final report to the members.

FACTORS INFLUENCING GROUPS AND TEAMS

A number of factors that influence the performance of groups or teams have been studied extensively: cohesiveness and familiarity, composition, and context. Unfortunately, most of these variables have been examined separately, rather than in combination, and the influence of each appears to depend, in good measure, on the situational specifics associated with each team, task, and organizational context or setting.

Cohesiveness and Familiarity

Specific group goals and feedback on performance increase a group's cohesiveness, which is positively linked to performance (Koch, 1979; O'Keefe, Kernaghan, & Rubenstein, 1975). K. A. Smith et al. (1994) reported a positive correlation between the cohesiveness of top management teams and an organization's financial performance. Cohesiveness can be a double-edged sword in that when it becomes the primary focus of the team, the opportunity for groupthink (see Chapter 8), leads to premature decisions without a full consideration of a variety of alternative solutions for the task or problem before the team (Aldag & Fuller, 1993; Chen et al., 1996; Guzzo & Shea, 1992).

Goodman and Leyden (1991) found that lower levels of familiarity among members were associated with lower levels of productivity, and Watson, Michaelsen, and Sharp (1991) reported a similar relationship between effective decision making and familiarity. It appears that teams that are composed of members who are familiar with each other are more effective than are teams composed of strangers (Guzzo & Dickson, 1996).

Composition

Diversity is a fundamental feature of organizations, and the effect of the diversity of membership on the performance of teams has been studied extensively. Sessa and Jackson (1995) suggested that there are two different perspectives and consequences of diversity for organizations, in general, and teams, in particular. According to the horizontal perspective of diversity, different types of diversity (such as age, gender, ethnicity, and race) yield about equal performance outcomes. Therefore, one type of diversity is as good as any other, and thus as long as a team is diversified, it is assumed that the factor of diversity will yield enhanced performances of decision-making and problem-solving teams. In contrast, the vertical-differentiation perspective assumes that diversity serves as the marker to assign members to positions in a hierarchy of asymmetrical power relationship (high- and low-status members). Hence, under vertical differentiation, team participation is moderated by the hierarchical relationships among members, so the members' voices are not equal and team outcomes are compromised. Accordingly, always keep your eye on the performance of individual members and the intent of each member to harvest the benefits of diversity. Furthermore, as a team leader, always promote the principles that team members are different yet similar in their commitment so as to focus on the team members' performance, positive intent, and regard for each other and the organization. In most organizations around the world, both the horizontal and vertical perspectives and consequences of diversity are in operation.

Watson, Kumar, and Michaelson (1993) constructed homogeneous teams of four members each of the same ethnic or racial identity and diverse teams of four different members each across the ethnic and racial markers. The decision-making teams worked on similar problems at four separate face-to-face meetings over a four-month period. The findings indicated that the homogeneous teams initially did better than the diverse teams, but in the third and fourth meetings, the teams' performances were just about identical, with the diverse team performing slightly better at the fourth meeting than the homogeneous team. In short, as the group members gained experience and familiarity in working with each other, the differences among them faded and no longer influenced the teams' performances.

Magjuka and Baldwin (1991) found that greater within-team heterogeneity in the types of jobs held by team members was positively associated with the effectiveness of teams. Similarly, after they examined a broad array of studies Jackson, May, and Whitney (1995) concluded that heterogeneity (defined as a mix of personalities, gender, and experiences) is positively related to creativity and effective decision making in teams. Furthermore, Bantel and Jackson (1989) found that innovations in the banking industry, for example, were positively related to heterogeneity of functional expertise among team members.

Thus, if you have a problem or task that requires different perspectives, construct a diverse team whose composition can be determined, for example, by the diversity mix of the customers or clients for a given product or service. Also, be patient and provide sustained support for diverse teams, especially during the early stages of their development (forming, storming, and norming). There is probably nothing more influential for shaping the performance of diverse teams than for the members to observe firsthand that they can work effectively and efficiently on a common task with clearly identifiable rules or norms and specific group goals.

Context

The effectiveness of teams is influenced substantially by the context, which includes such elements as organizational culture, mission, issues related to team autonomy, rewards and recognition, and physical environment (Guzzo & Dickson, 1996; Sundstrom et al., 1990). For example, an organizational culture that promotes innovations and shared expectations of success fosters effective teams (Shea & Guzzo, 1987). Also, issues involving autonomy, which are important for the effectiveness of the team, and revolve mainly around the level of power and responsibility associated with the team. Thus, for example, semiautonomous groups are led by supervisors, members of self-regulating or self-managing teams elect their leaders and control the division of labor within their teams, and members of self-designing teams define themselves and relations outside the group (Hackman, 1990; Sundstrom et al., 1990). In short, the clearer the organization context is about where the buck, lire, ruble, yen, or whatever stops relative to teams, the more likely the yield will be the teams' enhanced effectiveness.

The most robust influence on the effectiveness of a team will probably be an organizational context that provides appropriate support for the team's design (the specifics about membership, composition, roles, and goals) and process (the specifics about decision making, rules of operation, and conflict-management strategies). When it comes to teams, promote a context that is as specific as possible.

SUMMARY

This chapter began with a definition of a group and highlighted the differences and similarities between groups and teams, concluding that these relationships differed more by degree than by genre. When we examined formal and informal groups at work, we noted that the major difference is between groups with involuntary and voluntary members. Furthermore, we indicated that all groups, regardless of their type, seem to move through five stages of development: forming, storming, norming, performing, and adjourning.

In looking at the economic and psychological reasons for joining groups, we suggested that belonging to a work group or team is a robust and universal need of persons at work. We also examined group dynamics and the importance of roles and norms for promoting group stability and predictability.

We discussed social facilitation—a change in performance levels (either an increase or decrease) when moving from working alone to working as part of a group—as well as social loafing and specific strategies to prevent a reduction in individual performance levels when working in a group. We also noted that social loafing appears to be replaced by social enhancement (the increased performance of individuals in groups) when the groups are nested in collectivistic cultures, such as those found in China and Israel, rather than in the individualistic culture of the United States.

We presented definitions of teams and different types of teams, including computer-assisted teams and self-managing or autonomous teams, and seven specific steps to enhance the effectiveness of teams. Thereafter, we examined the influence of cohesiveness and familiarity, membership diversity, and organizational context on the performance of teams.

All organizations have to deal with teams, and we believe that the information and strategies presented here will be of value to a wide variety of organizations and members.

CHAPTER REFERENCES

Aiello, J. R., & Kolb, K. J. (1995). Electronic performance monitoring and social context: Impact on productivity and stress. *Journal of Applied Psychology, 80*, 339–353.

Aldag, R. J., & Fuller, S. R. (1993). Beyond fiasco: A reappraisal of the groupthink phenomenon and a new model of group decision processes. *Psychological Bulletin, 113*, 533–552.

Bantel, K. A., & Jackson, S. E. (1989). Top management and innovations in banking: Does composition of the top teams make a difference? *Strategic Management Journal, 10*, 107–124.

Baumeister, R. F., & Leary, M. R. (1995). The need to belong: Desire for interpersonal attachments as a fundamental human motivation. *Psychological Bulletin, 117*, 497–529.

Bushe, G. R., & Johnson, A. L. (1989). Contextual and internal variables affecting task group outcomes in organizations. *Group and Organization Studies, 14*, 462–482.

Buss, D. M. (1990). The evolution of anxiety and social exclusion. *Journal of Social and Clinical Psychology, 9*, 196–210.

Buss, D. M. (1991). Evolutionary personality psychology. *Annual Review of Psychology, 42*, 459–491.

Chen, Z., Lawson, R. B., Gordon, L. R., & McIntosh, B. (1996). Groupthink: Deciding with the leader and the devil. *Psychological Record, 46*, 311–321.

Clark, L. A., & Watson, D. (1988). Mood and the mundane: Relations between daily life events and self-reported mood. *Journal of Personality and Social Psychology, 54*, 296–308.

Coon, C. S. (1946). The universality of natural groupings in human societies. *Journal of Educational Sociology, 20*, 163–168.

Dennis, A. R., & Valacich, J. S. (1993). Computer brainstorms: More heads are better than one. *Journal of Applied Psychology, 78*, 531–537.

DiTecco, D., Cwitco, G., Arsenault, A., & Andre, M. (1992). Operator stress and monitoring practices. *Applied Ergonomics, 23*, 29–34.

Dobbelaere, A. G., & Goeppinger, K. H. (1993). The right way and the wrong way to set up a self-directed work team. *Human Resource Professional, 5*, 31–35.

Earley, P. C. (1993). East meets West meets Mideast: Further explorations of collectivistic and individualistic work groups. *Academy of Management Journal, 36*, 319–345.

Gallupe, R. B., Cooper, W. H., Grise, M. L., & Bostianutti, L. M. (1994). Blocking electronic brainstorms. *Journal of Applied Psychology, 79*, 77–86.

George, J. M. (1992). Extrinsic and intrinsic origins of perceived social loafing in organizations. *Academy of Management Journal, 35*, 191–202.

Gersick, C. J. G. (1988). Time and transition in work teams: Toward a new model of group development. *Academy of Management Journal, 31*, 9–41.

Gersick, C. J. G. (1989). Marking time: Predictable transitions in task groups. *Academy of Management Journal, 32*, 274–309.

Goodman, P. S., & Leyden, D. P. (1991). Familiarity and group productivity. *Journal of Applied Psychology, 76*, 578–586.

Goodman, P. S., Ravlin, E., & Schminke, M. (1987). Understanding groups in organizations. In L. L. Cummings & B. M. Staw (Eds.), *Research in organizational behavior* (pp. 124–128). Greenwich, CT: JAI Press.

Greenberg, J., & Baron, R. (1995). *Behavior in organizations: Understanding and managing the human side of work* (5th ed.). Englewood Cliffs, NJ: Prentice Hall.

Guzzo, R. A., & Dickson, M. W. (1996). Teams in organizations: Recent research on performance and effectiveness. *Annual Review of Psychology, 47*, 307–338.

Guzzo, R. A., & Salas, E. (Eds.). (1995). *Team effectiveness and decision making in organizations*. San Francisco: Jossey-Bass.

Guzzo, R. A., & Shea, G. P. (1992). Group performance and intergroup relations in organizations. In M. D. Dunnette & L. M. Hough (Eds.), *Handbook of industrial and organizational psychology* (pp. 269–313). Palo Alto, CA: Consulting Psychologists Press.

Hackman, J. R. (1990). *Groups that work (and those that don't)*. San Francisco: Jossey-Bass.

Harris, M. (1979). *Cultural materialism: The struggle for a science of culture*. New York: Random House.

Hollingshead, A. B., & McGrath, J. E. (1995). Computer-assisted groups: A critical review of the empirical research. In R. A. Guzzo & E. Salas (Eds.), *Team effectiveness and decision making in organizations* (pp. 46–78). San Francisco: Jossey-Bass.

Jackson, S. E., May, K. E., & Whitney, K. (1995). Understanding the dynamics of diversity in decision-making teams. In R. R. Guzzo & E. Salas (Eds.), *Team effectiveness and decision making in organizations* (pp. 204–261). San Francisco: Jossey-Bass.

Katzenbach, J. R., & Smith, D. K. (1993). The discipline of teams. *Harvard Business Review, 71*, 111–120.

Kiesler, S. & Sproul, L. (1992). Group decision making and communication technology. *Organizational Behavior and Human Decision Processes, 52*, 96–123.

Koch, J. L. (1979). Effects of goal specificity and performance feedback to work groups on peer leadership, performance, and attitudes. *Human Relations, 32*, 819–840.

Latané, B., Williams, K., & Harkins, S. (1979). Many hands make light the work: The causes and consequences of social loafing. *Journal of Personality and Social Psychology, 37*, 822–832.

Levine, J. M., & Moreland, R. L. (1990). Progress in small group research. *Annual Review of Psychology, 41*, 85–634.

Magjuka, R. J., & Baldwin, T. T. (1991). Team-based employee involvement programs: Effects of design and administration. *Personnel Psychology, 44*, 793–812.

Mann, L. (1980). Cross-cultural studies of small groups. In H. Triandis & R. Brislin (Eds.), *Handbook of cross-cultural psychology: Social psychology* (Vol. 5, pp. 155–209). Boston: Allyn & Bacon.

Manz, C. C., & Sims, H. P., Jr. (1993). *Business without bosses*. New York: John Wiley & Sons.

Moreland, R. L. (1987). The formation of small groups. In C. Hendick (Ed.), *Group processes: Review of personality and social psychology* (Vol. 8, pp. 80–110). Newbury Park, CA: Sage.

O'Keefe, R. D., Kernaghan, J. A., & Rubenstein, A. H. (1975). Group cohesiveness: A factor in the adoption of innovations among scientific work groups. *Small Group Behavior, 6*, 282–292.

Pacanowsky, M. (1995). Team tools for wicked problems. *Organizational Dynamics, 23*, 36–51.

Sessa, V. I., & Jackson, S. E. (1995). Diversity in decision-making teams: All differences are not created equal. In M. M. Champes, S. Oskamp, & M. A. Costanzo (Eds.), *Diversity in organizations: New perspectives for a changing workplace* (pp. 133–156). Thousand Oaks, CA: Sage.

Shaw, M. E. (1981). *Group dynamics: The psychology of small group behavior* (3rd. ed.). New York: McGraw-Hill.

Shea, G. P., & Guzzo, R. A. (1987). Group effectiveness: What really matters? *Sloan Management Review, 27,* 33–46.

Shepperd, J. A. (1993). Productivity loss in performance groups: A motivation analysis. *Psychological Bulletin, 113,* 67–81.

Sherman, S. (1996, March 18). Secrets of HP's muddled team. *Fortune,* pp. 116–118.

Smith, C., & Comer, D. (1994). Self-organization in small groups: A study of group effectiveness within non-equilibrium conditions. *Human Relations, 47,* 553–581.

Smith, K. A., Smith, K. G., Olian, J. D., Sims, H. P., O'Bannon, D. P., & Scully, J. (1994). Top management team demography and process: The role of social integration and communication. *Administrative Science Quarterly, 39,* 412–438.

Smith, M. J., Carayon, P., Sanders, K. J., Lim, S. Y., & LeGrande, D. (1992). Employee stress and health complaints in jobs with and without electronic performance monitoring. *Applied Ergonomics, 23,* 17–28.

Sundstrom, E., DeMeuse, K. P., & Futrell, D. (1990). Work teams: applications and effectiveness. *American Psychologist, 45,* 120–133.

Thomas, E. J., & Fink, C. F. (1963). Effects of group size. *Psychological Bulletin, 83,* 371–384.

Tuckman, B. W. (1965). Development sequence in small groups. *Psychological Bulletin, 63,* 384–399.

Tuckman, B. W., & Jensen, M. (1977). Stages of small group development revisited. *Group and Organization Studies, 2,* 419–427.

Vaill, P. B. (1989). *Managing as a performing art—New ideas for a world of chaotic change.* San Francisco: Jossey-Bass.

Watson, W. E., Kumar, K., & Michaelsen, K. K. (1993). Cultural diversity's impact on interaction process and performance: Comparing homogeneous and diverse task groups. *Academy of Management Journal, 36,* 590–602.

Watson, W. E., Michaelsen, L. K., & Sharp, W. (1991). Member competence, group interaction, and group decision making: A longitudinal study. *Journal of Applied Psychology, 77,* 682–693.

Weick, K. E. (1984). Small wins: Redefining the scale of social problems. *American Psychologist, 39,* 40–49.

Wellins, R. S., Byham, W. C., & Dixon, G. R. (1994). *Inside teams.* San Francisco: Jossey-Bass.

Wilpert, B. (1995). Organizational behavior. *Annual Review of Psychology, 46,* 59–90.

Zajonc, R. B. (1965). Social facilitation. *Science, 149,* 269–274.

SUGGESTED REFERENCES

We include here references for practical team issues, such as cross-functional teams, membership diversity, groupware (technological processes for enhancing communications and teamwork), pay, and techniques for building and maintaining effective teams. We especially recommend the *Team Handbook,* by P. R. Scholtes, for a detailed set of procedures and practices for team building and maintaining effective team performances.

Andrews, K. Z. (1995). Cross-functional teams: Are they always the right move? *Harvard Business Review, 73,* 12–19.

Caudron, S. (1994). Tie individual pay to team success. *Personnel Journal, 73,* 40–46.

Caudron, S. (1994). Diversity ignites effective work teams. *Personnel Journal, 73,* 54–62.

Gautschi, T. F. (1995). Groupware offers benefits and drawbacks. *Design News, 50,* 314–316.

Kazsbom, D. S. (1995). Making a team work: Techniques for building successful cross-functional teams. (Integrated planning process). *Industrial Engineering, 27,* 39–42.

Labich, K. (1996). Elite teams get the job done. *Fortune, 133,* 90–99.

Scholtes, P. R. (1988). *Team handbook: How to use teams to improve quality.* Madison, WI: Joiner Associates.

6

Individual and Organizational Motivation

CHAPTER OVERVIEW

Around the globe, all people are being asked or mandated to do more with less in almost every domain of their lives, most forcefully in their lives at work. In this chapter, we examine individual and organizational motivation, defined as a set of forces that initiates, directs, and sustains action toward a goal. We begin by recognizing the constraints and opportunities dealt all people, so as to appreciate contextual influences on motivational interventions and expected outcomes. Thereafter, we examine micromodels of motivation that focus exclusively on individual needs, beliefs, and expectations, such as Maslow's need hierarchy, McClelland's need achievement (nAch), and equity and expectancy models. Social loafing, a loss of productivity when one goes from working alone to working in a group, is presented as an example of important organizational behaviors that are predictable and manageable by an expectancy model of motivation.

We introduce total quality (TQ) programs as an important example of a macromodel of motivation that focuses on group-based and customer- or client-driven sources of motivation. In fact, client- or customer-driven imperatives (needs and demands) have moderated substantially the centrality of individual needs, expectancies, and concerns for equity as motivational levers that are used by organizational leaders and managers. Then we present the TQ philosophy, TQ tools, and TQ teamwork, which are the critical components of almost all TQ programs. TQ tools include easy-to-use yet powerful levers for enhancing quality and productivity, including the flowchart, check sheet, Pareto diagram, fishbone or Ishikawa diagram, scatter diagram, and control charts. We also look at different types of teams found in TQ programs, present guidelines for enhancing team meetings, and suggest a series of principles and a framework for implementing a TQ program. The TQ movement has led to a fundamental shift in how motivational strategies and programs are conceptualized and implemented that involves an unequivocal movement from an individual to a group and a process-level focus for enhancing individual and organizational productivity.

We treat specific motivational levers or strategies that are relatively easy to implement; can be combined into motivational packages; and usually require little, if any, financial resources to implement and maintain. One specific motivational lever is goal setting, which yields median improvements in performance of approximately 16% above the pre-goal-setting performance level. Another is self-fulfilling prophecies, which enhance performance by increasing expectations by others (the Pygmalion effect) or oneself (the Galatea effect), and still another is variation in perceived self-efficacy, which also moderates performance levels for individuals. In addition, the role of collective or organizational efficacy is suggested as a key source of group and organizational performance outcomes.

We then review intrinsic motivation, the relationship between work and play, mood and work, and organizational spontaneity (the tendency of an employee to perform or work involuntarily beyond the formal requirements of a role or job). Organizational spontaneity takes on more and more importance as organizations are deconstructed, flattened, or made nonhierarchical and teams in which members are trained or encouraged to become cross-functional are increasingly used.

We conclude with a discussion of the relationship between culture and motivation. We review findings that indicate unequivocally the importance of crafting motivational strategies relative to the larger cultural context in which an organization is nested, which also shapes the values that members carry with them into their organizations.

LEARNING OBJECTIVES

After studying this chapter, you will be able to

- define motivation, identify universal forces that influence motivational levels, and describe the components of the motivational cycle
- identify and explain five micromodels of motivation based on individual needs, beliefs, and expectations and define and discuss social loafing (or productivity loss) when an individual goes from working alone to working in a group
- identify and explain macromodels of motivation, including TQ programs
- explain the philosophical foundations of quality-improvement programs, define and use the six basic TQ tools for quality improvement, and apply fundamental guidelines for enhancing the process and outcomes of work meetings
- present and elaborate on the suggested guidelines and a framework for implementing quality-improvement programs in a variety of organizations and identify specific team tools to foster improvements in the quality of products and services
- define and explain the potent and valuable motivational levers, including goal setting, self-fulfilling prophecies, perceived self-efficacy, and organizational efficacy
- distinguish intrinsic from extrinsic motivation, appreciate the relationship between work and leisure, and identify factors that moderate some of the negative features of downsizing on productivity
- explain the relationship between positive mood (feelings of alertness and zestfulness) and negative mood (feelings of dullness and inactivity) and productivity and absence from work
- define and explain the motivational relationship between organizational spontaneity and the expanding presence of cross-functional teams in a wide variety of organizations
- demonstrate the moderating impact of culture on motivational strategies that requires that these strategies be crafted to align with the values of the larger culture.

Without passion, work is only a place; with passion, work is a part of us.

JUST DO IT

We believe that most people want to do a good job, enjoy challenging work, and must surmount barriers just to do it. The barriers to cognitive actions (thinking, creating, planning) and behavioral actions can be within the person (dispositional forces), imposed by the organizational or larger societal contexts (situational forces), and are usually a combination of both these forces.

Search for Levers

Accordingly, we search for levers to actions (cognitive, affective, and behavioral) that operate within the person (such as needs and expectations), as well as those that operate outside the individual within the organizational context (like goal setting and rewards). The search for the levers to the motivation to work is an important challenge because of enhanced global competitiveness, the shrinking pool of employees caused by downsizing (for example, freezes in hiring and voluntary and involuntary separations), and the need to match organizational motivational programs to the needs and values of an increasingly diversified workforce (Bowes & Goodnow, 1996; Katzell & Thompson, 1990; National Advisory Mental Health Council, 1995, Thompson & DiTomaso, 1988).

Definition of Motivation

The hundreds of definitions of motivation share some common properties that focus on the initiation, direction, and maintenance of behavioral, affective, or cognitive action (Steers & Porter, 1991). For our purposes, we define motivation as *forces within (dispositional or endogenous) or outside (situational or exogenous) the individual or group that initiate, direct, and sustain action toward a goal or set of goals.* We believe that dispositional and situational forces interact with each other to determine the level of motivation, that organizational members relentlessly pursue individual and organizational goals, and that motivation operates as a system in which outcomes provide feedback that influences subsequent motivational levels. We also believe that in some nations, organizations, and small groups, situational forces are so robust that they foster organizational systems that reinforce or promote a do-nothing strategy that leads to learned helplessness (a sense that one cannot achieve anything) despite one's endogenous effort or motivation, and that some individuals prefer to pursue this strategy even in highly supportive environments. In general, we believe that organizational members are motivated to do a good job, and when they have the appropriate abilities or skills, they can produce high-quality and competitive services and products. In fact, performance is a function of ability combined multiplicatively with motivation. Thus, abilities that are determined by natural or endowed capacities, as well as those acquired through learning and training programs, are only half the equation, just as motivation is only half of what is needed to get a job done. Education and the desire to work are keys to organizational performances and ultimately to competitiveness in the global marketplace.

The Dealt Hand

In general, each organizational member must confront common conditions that have an impact on all persons and moderate her or his motivational capacities. Although everyone may start from a common motivational platform, there is great variation in individual levels of motivation that, when coupled with feelings, serve to define each person as a unique individual in the workforce. Table 6–1 presents

Table 6–1. Common Conditions that Affect All Persons

- Everyone gets 24 hours per day.
- All people are terminal; they are just on different schedules.
- There are no more free lunches.
- Opportunity does not equal outcome.
- What you do with what you have can be as rewarding as what you have.
- Each person can be an active agent, rather than a passive victim.
- Things are easier said than done.
- All people need to be fit—disciplined, grounded, and aware—and, what is most important, must believe in themselves.

some of the shared forces that affect all persons and, in turn, their overall level of motivation. A firm understanding of motivation, levers for action, models of motivation, and strategies to enhance motivational levels can help managers get to know their colleagues fully and harness these motivational forces to enhance the effectiveness of individual members and the organization (Rafaeli & Sutton, 1989; Van Maanen & Kunda, 1989).

Figure 6–1 depicts the general pattern of motivational components that all persons experience, including endogenous and exogenous forces. These forces lead to an action, thought, or feeling (or a combination of the three) in pursuit of a goal in some future state, which affects the motivational forces that initiated the cycle. Just as sands shift, so do motivational levels and sources of motivation. Effective leaders must keep in touch with both their and their colleagues' motivational levels because motiva-

tional levels are subject to many forces and can change rapidly over time.

Models of Motivation

Today, motivation at work is a complex phenomenon. Therefore, simple rules or guidelines—such as higher pay for harder work, greater responsibilities, or higher positions in the organizational hierarchy (Taylor, 1911); the happy worker is automatically a good worker (Perrow, 1972); or what motivates employees in the United States may not be as effective in Asia or Europe (Erez, 1994; Erez & Earley, 1993)—may no longer be the sole or primary motivator. As a consequence, a number of micro- and macromodels of motivation to work have been developed and refined over the past 25 years. The micromodels focus primarily on internal forces that impel the individual to higher levels of motivation, and the macromodels focus on

Figure 6–1   The Pattern of Motivational Components for All Persons.

the entire organization, particularly organizational processes that are essential to the manufacture of a product or the delivery of a service. We first examine some illustrative micromodels, including those that deal with endogenous and exogenous forces, and then examine macromodels, represented primarily by quality-improvement programs.

MICROMODELS OF MOTIVATION

The micromodels of motivation include need and cognitive exemplars, are concerned with what the individual brings to the workplace, and stress the centrality of endogenous forces for motivation at work. These models assume that a highly motivated member alone can bring about enhanced productivity at the individual level and, perhaps, at the organizational level. However, although motivation is important and necessary, it is not a sufficient condition for enhanced productivity and competitiveness at the organizational level (Human Capital Initiative,

1993). Rarely can one motivated person alone make a substantial difference at the organizational level, whereas a small group of motivated persons often can.

Maslow's Need Hierarchy

Maslow (1943, 1954), a clinical psychologist, believed that human needs could be divided into five levels and arranged in order of importance and that higher-level needs (self-esteem and self-actualization) are not expressed until the basic, lower-level needs are satisfied (see Table 6–2). Although Maslow's theory is the foundation of many organizational development programs, such as participative management and quality-of-work life projects, there is little empirical evidence to support the fundamental features of the model. Perhaps the most important point to bear in mind is that different organizational members may be operating at different levels of the need hierarchy; therefore, the manager must be aware of the diversity of needs and

Table 6–2. Maslow's Hierarchy of Needs

Levels of Needs	General Rewards	Organizational Rewards
Physiological	Food, water, sex, rest	Pay and fringe benefits
Safety	Safety, security stability, protection	Safe working conditions, job security
Social	Love, affection, belongingness	Cohesive work group, friendly supervision, membership
Self-esteem	Self-esteem, self-respect, prestige, status	Social recognition, job title, feedback from customers
Self-actualization	Growth, advancement, creativity	A challenging job, opportunities for creativity, achievement in work, advancement in the organization

have access to appropriate rewards to address them.

Alderfer (1969) refined Maslow's theory and reduced the five levels of needs to three: existence (subsistence needs), relatedness (social and self-esteem needs), and growth (self-actualization) needs (the ERG model). He suggested that unlike Maslow's view, the three levels are not linked serially and hence that the satisfaction of needs at one level is not necessary before the next level becomes activated. Again, there is little empirical evidence to support either of these models, although there is little doubt that organizational members have these needs (Maddi, 1972; National Advisory Mental Health Council, 1995; Wahba & Bridwell, 1976).

McClelland's nAch

According to McClelland, Atkinson, Clark, and Lowell (1953), human needs are learned, and the three most important ones for work motivation are the needs for achievement (nAch), affiliation (nAff), and power (nPow). The presence and intensity of these three needs for a person are determined in a variety of ways, including brief written narratives in response to pictures of persons in a workplace situation and simulated decision-making tasks.

Persons who have high nAch assume personal responsibility for the solution of tasks or problems, set moderately difficult goals, take calculated risks, and have a strong desire for feedback on their performance, as indexed, for example, by compensation (Atkinson & Reitman, 1965). According to McClelland et al. (1953), nAch is critical for national economic development and organizational competitiveness; thus, they developed a four-step management program to increase nAch that included (1) setting goals and keeping records of goal-related performances, (2) cognitive intervention to promote the dispositions to think, talk, and act like people with high nAch, (3) focused education on the positive relationship between high nAch and success, and (4) the provision of group sup-

port from colleagues. McClelland (1976) and McClelland & Boyatzis (1982) reported that this brief training program doubled the rate of managers' entrepreneurial activities.

Persons who have high nAff prefer to work with others, have low absenteeism rates, and tend to perform better in situations in which personal support and approval are linked to performance. Finally, McClelland (1976) argued that nPow is the most important determinant of managerial success and that it includes the desire to influence and exercise control over others and to maintain specific leader-follower relations. McClelland also stated that there are two faces to power: the need for personal power (striving for dominance for the sake of dominance) and the need for social power (having a greater interest in the problems of the organization and strategies to achieve organizational goals).

Need-based models of motivation highlight the importance of establishing a good match between the motives of organizations and of members that is leveraged by the selection of personnel and motivational training to promote members' acceptance of the organization's motives. In a 20-year follow-up of organizational members, Howard and Bray (1989) found that the motivation to achieve and involvement in work were the strongest predictors of career advancement. Thus, the selection of new members with high nAch and a commitment to work may well yield many dividends for both an organization and the individuals involved.

In summary, it is important to be aware of and as responsive as possible to the different needs of your organizational members. These needs include the need for achievement, affiliation, power, and such other organizationally shaped needs as flexible work schedules, benefit plans, and job assignments (Loden & Rosener, 1991).

Equity and Expectancy

The micromodels just considered focused on individual need and are known as "push" models of motivation because they propel the individual into the organizational context or situation. In contrast, equity and expectancy models of motivation, or "pull" models, are cognitive models of motivation that emphasize the cognitive processes of motivation that people undergo in deciding to work or remain in a particular organization.

The most prominent equity model of motivation, by Adams (1963), focuses primarily on the ratio of inputs (*I*—what the member brings and puts into the job, such as specific skills, talents, or extra work effort) to outputs (*O*—what the member gets out of the job like pay, advancement opportunities, and fringe benefits). The critical ratio is of the individual (target, or *t*) outcomes to inputs compared to the ratio of outcomes to inputs of another individual or group (other, or *o*). Thus, equity exists when

$$O_t \backslash I_t = O_o \backslash I_o \qquad (1)$$

and inequity exists when

$$O_t \backslash I_t < O_o \backslash I_o \text{ or } O_t \backslash I_t > O_o \backslash I_o \qquad (2)$$

In Equation 1, the target individual and an other (a colleague or another referent person, group, or standard) generate equal input and, in turn, receive equal output, whereas in Equation 2, the target's ratio is less than or more than, respectively, the other's, which creates tension in the individual and leads to actions to dissipate the tension. According to Adams (1965), the target can choose one of the following actions to restore equity: altering inputs or outputs, cognitively distorting inputs or outcomes, leaving the position or organization, changing the inputs or outcomes of the other, or changing the other.

Empirical evaluations of equity models of motivation have been mixed. Nevertheless, it is clear that organizational members observe actions and associated consequences of other members and compare themselves to others and that the perception of equity, especially regarding compensation, is much more important than actual equitable conditions (Mowday, 1991). As a manager or leader, always remember that your treatment of an individual member in your or-

ganization is never done in isolation and that other members may consider that treatment a standard of equitable treatment when they are the subjects of managerial actions.

An organizational member not only compares herself or himself with other members but makes choices and considers alternative courses of action on the basis of expected or future outcomes (Pinder, 1991). Vroom's (1964) valance-instrumentality-expectancy (VIE) model of motivation assumes that people make choices that, in general, maximize pleasure and minimize pain. *Valance* refers to a person's *expected* level of satisfaction from a work-related outcome, rather than the real value the person actually derives from the outcome; for example, a promotion reflected by a change in title that may be coupled with more responsibility but the same salary or a marginal salary increase. *Instrumentality* is the member's belief that certain actions will lead to other outcomes (second-level outcomes) that are desirable or will avoid undesirable outcomes. Thus, it is important for employees to understand and internalize the connection between specific actions and specific outcomes and for the organization to deliver on the connection (keep its promises). *Expectancy* is the strength of a member's belief that a particular outcome will materialize, ranging from zero (the person's subjective probability of attaining an outcome is psychologically zero, or "I can't do it") to 1.0 (indicating "I can do it, no problem").

To apply the VIE model of motivation in the workplace, managers need to be certain that positively valent rewards are associated with good job performance and that their employees perceive the connection between the two conditions. Linking rewards to performances, of course, is easier said than done, so a motto for managers should be, Don't promise what you can't deliver, and always deliver what you promise. As was noted in Chapter 2, promise keeping is an important, and, we believe, a nearly universal human value.

Shepperd (1993) used the expectancy model of motivation to explain productivity loss, which often arises when an individual goes from working alone to working as a member of a group or team. In general, productivity losses in groups are due to one of three factors that lead to lower motivation: *social loafing* (individuals exert less effort when they work in a group than when they work alone because each person in a group expects other members to exert extra effort to pick up any slack), *free riding* (the members think their efforts are dispensable and thus reduce their contributions, expecting that they can enjoy the benefits of the work group without having to contribute), and the *sucker effect* (the members judge their partners or other members to be competent and hardworking and hence reduce their contributions, expecting the other members to contribute at higher levels and thus become suckers by contributing to the collective good when others in the group do not). Shepperd presented specific strategies for counteracting these three factors: provide specific job assignments and incentives for contributing (social loafing), make contributions indispensable (free riding), and decrease the cost of contributing to the group (sucker effect).

We turn now to consider macromodels of motivation that we believe are extremely important for the practicing manager because they are designed to have an impact on the motivational levels of all organizational members and involve relatively simple processes for initiating, directing, and sustaining actions.

HERZBERG'S TWO-FACTOR MACROMODEL OF MOTIVATION

This is a macromodel because it focuses on both the individual member and the organizational context (Herzberg, 1966; Herzberg, Mausner, & Synderman, 1959). Herzberg surveyed 200 accountants and engineers in the mid-1950s and concluded that the features that gave rise to job satisfaction (motivator factors) and job dissatisfaction (hygiene factors) were different. He found that motivators (like opportunities for achievement, recognition, responsibility, advancement, and growth) were intrinsic to a particular job, and when they were strengthened, the level of motivation would increase. The hygiene factors were extrinsic to the job, yet included features of the organizational context, such as organizational policies, salaries, members' relationships, and supervisory or management styles. Herzberg (1966) and Herzberg et al. (1959) argued that inadequate policies, salaries, and other "hygiene factors" yielded dissatisfaction and adequate policies eliminated dissatisfaction (negativity or whining), but only the motivator factors directly influenced motivation beyond the psychological neutral level (the absence of whining). An organizational member's motivational level is influenced by the design of the job (what the person does), and the organizational context predisposes the member to be motivated.

Although there have been numerous criticisms of Herzberg's model, it is important because it included the role of the organizational context, rather than just the individual, as a variable for understanding and manipulating motivational levels in the workplace (King, 1970). It is also interesting to note that the model was generated directly from data derived from organizational members, unlike the individual-based need, equity, and expectancy models that were derived from laboratory-based studies and clinical case histories of psychotherapy clients (Steers & Porter, 1991).

THE TQ MACROMODEL OF MOTIVATION

All the models presented so far were devised primarily during the 1950s, focus on the individual (micro) level of analysis, and are culturally bound (Erez, 1994; Erez & Earley, 1993). In contrast, TQ programs (also called quality-improvement, QI, programs) recognize the importance of the context or system and its role in determining motivation in the workplace (Dean & Evans, 1994). They are easy to understand and implement, are applicable in a variety of cross-cultural and organizational contexts in both the public and private sectors, have been used successfully in global organizations, and can serve as a catalyst for enhancing the motivational levels of all members. In TQ programs, the customer or client is the primary focus for organizational motivation, and this focus, in turn, has an impact on all members of an organization. In the global organization, the management of motivation shifts from a primary focus on just the organizational member to include the customer or client and the management of organizational processes that are essential for delivering the best net value in the global marketplace.

Although there are many TQ or QI programs, we present Deming's model because it is a coherent program that includes a management philosophy, a set of tools for data collection and analyses, and a sound grounding in group dynamics and teamwork (Aguayo, 1990; Crosby, 1979; Dean & Evans, 1994; Deming, 1982, 1986; Gabor, 1990; Gitlow & Gitlow, 1987; Juran, 1992; Walton, 1986).

Deming, trained as a physicist, was influenced by Shewhart's (1924) techniques for bringing industrial manufacturing processes into what he called "statistical control" when he worked for the U.S. Department of Agriculture. He introduced statistical sampling in the 1940 U.S. census and first conducted seminars on quality management and process-control techniques in the United States and Japan in the early 1950s (Walton, 1986). Unlike American businesspersons and management specialists of the 1950s, the Japanese not only listened to Deming's TQ presentations, but also (reluctantly, at first) internalized and then implemented his management strategies. It was not until 1979 that some American firms (notably the Nashua Corporation in Nashua, New Hampshire) were willing to take a chance on TQ. However, after a television news documentary on TQ was aired

on NBC on June 24, 1980, many other firms sought Deming out. Today, TQ programs of one variety or another are used by almost all successful organizations throughout the world. In the following sections, we describe the management philosophy and strategy of TQ, briefly discuss the statistical tools or measures to ground the philosophy in data, and examine some strategies to enhance teamwork.

TQ Management Philosophy

The fundamental force of TQ programs is to deliver products or services that are of a quality that meets or exceeds customers' or clients' expectations. Think for a moment of a product or service that you need or would like to purchase in the next day or two and the attributes of that product or service that you want. TQ programs begin with you as the client or customer, a perspective that energizes all subsequent organizational actions. This is a fundamental shift from the employee, manager, or organizational leader to the customer or client as the primary initiator of action, which is the first component in the motivational pattern (see Figure 6–1).

Deming's TQ management philosophy:

- focuses on systems that manufacture a product or deliver a service, rather than on an individual or a single group of individuals

- involves data-based problem solving

- requires constant contact with the customer or client

- pursues relentlessly the continuous improvement of processes, products, and services

- involves the adoption of TQ principles by organizational members

- works only if the philosophy and principles are internalized and modeled, not just verbalized by the leadership team (Dean & Evans, 1994; Deming, 1982, 1986; Gitlow & Gitlow, 1987; Walton, 1986).

Approximately 80% to 90% of the instances of defects in a given product or service are attributable to the system of manufacturing the product or the delivery of the service, rather than to a given individual. Only management has the authority and power to change a system, and a system always exhibits common variation and periodically exhibits special variation. Therefore, in the beginning, the leadership of an organization must commit fully to a TQ program. The first commitment is to Deming's 14 points for quality, which are presented in Table 6–3. Since most of these points are self-evident, we describe only a few of them here.

We discussed the first point listed in Table 6–3—constancy of purpose or mission issue—in Chapter 3, so here, we add only that it is im-

Table 6–3. Deming's 14 Points for TQ

1. Create a constancy of purpose for improving a product or service.

2. Adopt the new philosophy because this is a new economic age.

3. Cease the dependence on inspection as a way to achieve quality.

4. End the practice of awarding business on the basis of a price tag.

5. Constantly improve the system of production and service; the system includes people.

6. Provide training on the job.

7. Improve supervision.

8. Drive out fear.

9. Break down barriers among departments or units.

10. Eliminate slogans and targets that ask for increased productivity but do not provide methods and resources to increase productivity.

11. Eliminate numerical quotas or piecework.

12. Remove barriers between the worker and her or his right to pride in work.

13. Institute a vigorous program of education and retraining.

14. Put everybody in the organization to work to accomplish the transformation.

portant for the leader or leadership team to remain in place for at least five years to provide some continuity of leadership and commitment to TQ (Gitlow & Gitlow, 1987). From our consulting practices, we have observed that a frequent turnover in leaders usually generates ambiguity and turbulence throughout the organization. Regarding the second point, the new philosophy embraces concepts, such as a focus on the customer and system and an openness to the competitive global economy. For the third point, instead of inspecting the quality of a product or service just before it goes to the customer or client, the TQ philosophy emphasizes making quality activities part of the manufacturing or delivery process. With respect to the eighth point, we have found that driving out fear is critical because many employees believe that the implementation of TQ programs will cause some to lose their jobs. Thus, to the extent possible, the management should assure organizational members that even if they lose their current positions, there will always be jobs for them in the organization. This point is essential because TQ came on the American scene as the United States and the global economy were going downhill, causing job losses from layoffs that, in the minds of many members of the workforce, were attributed primarily to TQ, rather than to the downturn in the global economy. Even in Japan, where TQ programs led, in large part, to Japan's role as a key player in the global economy, unemployment in the late 1980s and early 1990s was due primarily to the global economic recession, not to these programs. We now turn to TQ tools for collecting and analyzing data about organizational systems.

TQ Tools

The second commitment that the leadership team must make to a TQ program is to use the seven TQ tools for the collecting and analyzing data about the system. These tools are relatively easy to apply and can yield a wealth of data about the system that can be used to direct or guide changes that will continuously improve the quality of products and services.

The first tool is the *flowchart*, which is simply a picture of the process under study. It allows organizational members to see how they fit into a process, and simply by participating in the description of the process, the members often develop a sense of ownership of it. Figure 6–2 is an example of a flowchart for training a team leader for a nine-person work team. Once constructed, the flowchart can serve as the guide for identifying problems or defects in quality, as well as areas that require continuous improvement. With it, you can question whether a component of the process can be improved further or even eliminated. The flowchart focuses at-

tention on the process, rather than on a given individual or individuals who are responsible for implementing the process. The *check sheet* is a tool for data collection about a process, and it can be used to interpret initial data about a process. If you inspect the check sheet presented in Figure 6–3, you can readily see some of the areas or components of a process that can be targets for improvement.

The *Pareto diagram* allows you to separate the "vital few" from the "trivial many" defects in quality and to focus on the most promising component of a process that can benefit from TQ interventions (see Figure 6–4). The Pareto diagram shows the relative magnitude of problems or defects, and when it is constructed over time, it can help you visualize the results of improvement projects.

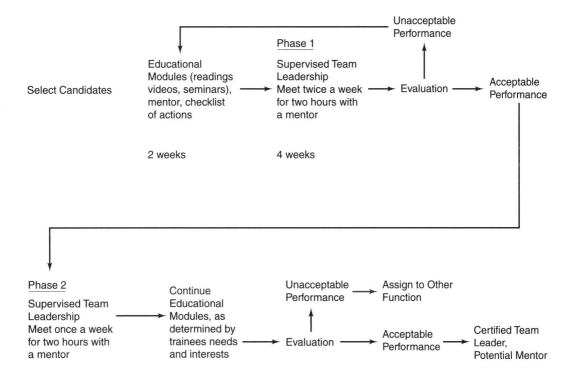

Figure 6–2 Flowchart for Training New Team Leaders.

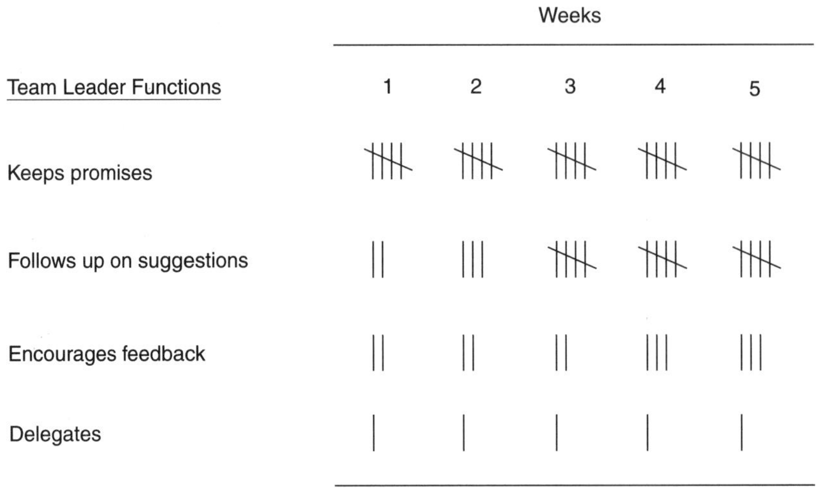

Team Leader Functions	Weeks				
	1	2	3	4	5
Keeps promises	卌	卌	卌	卌	卌
Follows up on suggestions	‖	‖‖	卌	卌	卌
Encourages feedback	‖	‖	‖	‖‖	‖‖
Delegates	│	│	│	│	│

Figure 6–3 Check Sheet for Specific Functions of a Leader of a Team Training Program.

Figure 6–5 presents a *fishbone diagram*, (also called a cause-and-effect or Ishikawa diagram, after Kaoru Ishikawa, the Japanese TQ expert who introduced the tool). In general, fishbone diagrams are constructed in a group brainstorming session, contain four categories of possible causes of an effect (materials, methods, machines, and people), and are designed to represent the chain of possible causes of a given effect. According to Ishikawa (1976), the construction of the fishbone diagram achieves a number of objectives for the group, including these:

- the promotion of discussion and learning through analyses of the causes and effects of a given process

- the reduction of complaints and irrelevant discussion by focusing the discussion on the process

- the promotion of an active search for the causes of a given effect that leads to data collection

- the promotion of a greater understanding of cause-and-effect relationships by generating a detailed diagram

- the use of the process for almost any problem.

Again, the fishbone diagram, in conjunction with the other tools, promotes data-based problem solving and keeps attention focused on problems.

Scatter diagrams indicate the correlation between (but not the cause and effect of) any two variables or conditions. Usually, the variables chosen represent possible causes and effects that were identified by the construction of a fishbone diagram (as in Figure 6–6, which indicates that the higher the quality of a team leader training program, the higher effectiveness of a leader). For example, if the number of your requests for customers to repeat what they just said goes up and their patience goes down, and this relationship is observed consistently over time, it is obviously important to pay more attention to customers, so you can correctly enter their telephone orders into the system.

Last, *control charts* are used to study variation over time, so one can distinguish between common and special variations. In general, common causes of variation account for about 80% to 90% of the observed variation in a process, and special causes account for the remainder. Usually, special causes arise from external sources that are not inherent in the process, such as a poorly trained team leader, flimsy or inadequate materials, or worn-out equipment or

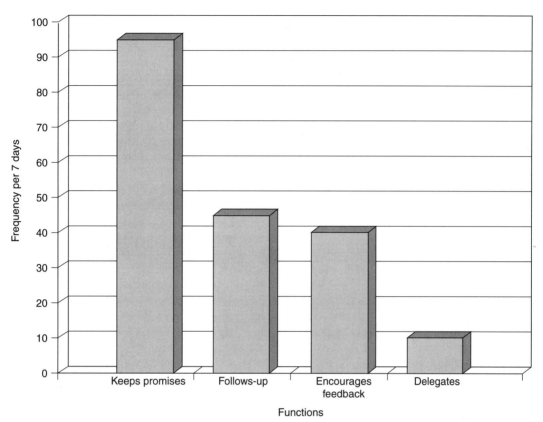

Figure 6–4   Pareto Diagram of the Strengths and Weaknesses of a Team Leader Observed over Four Weeks.

tools. Thus, special causes yield unnatural variations in a system and disrupt the random pattern of common causes; are fairly easy to detect; and if removed, lower the costs of the product or service. It should be noted, however, that variations can be minimized but not eliminated unless the process is terminated.

Shewhart (1924) developed the statistical process-control tool to identify the effects of special causes of variation. A control chart displays the state of control of a process. It presents the average value of a process output, with 50% of the values or data points above the average and the other 50% below the average, along with upper and lower control values, which usually embrace all the common variations in the process, and special variations that fall outside these limits. The control chart presented in Figure 6–7 represents the number of complaints by team members of a team leader for a six-week period following the completion of a team leader training program. The point outside the upper-control (UCL) and lower-control (LCL) limits represent an example of a special variation in Week 2 (such as a broken personal computer that prevented the leader from making timely responses to requests), whereas those within the upper and lower control limits represent common variations.

Control charts clearly illustrate that every process contains variation, and the more refined the process, the less deviation or common variation there is from the average. According to Deming (1986), a system can best be improved when special causes of variation are eliminated and the system is under statistical control. When

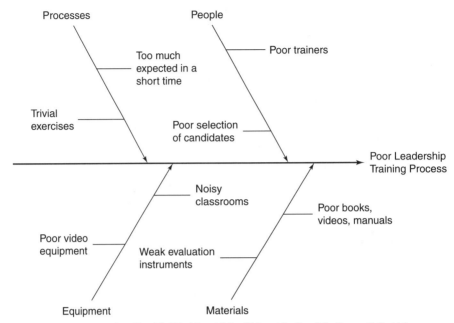

Figure 6–5   Fishbone Diagram of an Identified Problem (right side) and Its Possible Causes (left side).

a system is under control, there are no large variations that would require additional resources and energy to get it back into control, so the management can focus resources on further refining or continuously improving the process.

TQ tools are often used in conjunction with *benchmarking*—a search for the best practices that yield superior performance. Benchmarking can be either competitive or generic. In competitive benchmarking, an organization observes how a competitor implements a particular process, especially one through which customers' or clients' needs are addressed. In generic benchmarking, the organization examines the best practices for a given function or process, regardless of the industry or organization; compares its processes with the best-in-class processes; and, if appropriate, takes the necessary actions to modify its processes to meet or exceed the best ones.

Many global organizations pursue the philosophy of *continuous improvement* (*kaizen*), using the TQ tools just described, with the underlying

expectation that a great number of small improvements over time will lead inevitably to substantial improvements in organizational performance. Just as a focus on customers stimulates the motivation of members of a TQ program and the TQ tools direct it, teamwork sustains it, thus completing the pattern of organizational motivation shown in Figure 6–1.

TQ Teamwork

Almost all organizations hold scheduled and unscheduled meetings, and a growing number use teams to implement organizational projects. In TQ programs, there are generally three kinds of teams, all of which hold meetings: *quality councils*, *problem-solving teams*, and *self-managed teams*. Table 6–4 presents some guidelines for conducting organizational meetings in general, many of which are applicable to the three most common types of meetings of TQ teams. TQ teams usually spend most of their meeting times defining problems, identifying solutions, and

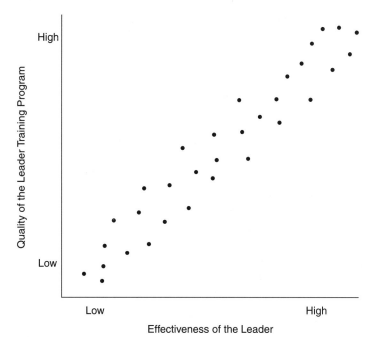

Figure 6–6   A Scatter Diagram Showing the Correlational Relationship between Two Variables.

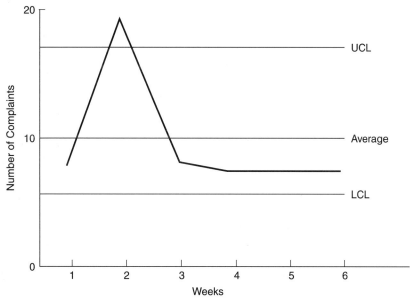

Figure 6–7   Control Chart.

Table 6–4. Guidelines for Conducting Meetings at Work

In many organizations many members spend approximately 25%–50% of their workdays in scheduled and unscheduled meetings. The following guidelines for meetings are grounded in some important findings about groups.

- Typically, the preferred size for an action group is five to seven members.

- As the size of a group increases, the members become more tolerant of directive and authoritarian leadership, rules are formalized, productivity eventually decreases because of problems of coordination, and social loafing increases. Assign specific tasks to specific members to minimize social loafing.

- Since it is difficult to alter the dispositional traits of members of a group, in forming a work group, it is important to select members based, in part, on their problem-solving strategies (for example, members who seek facts and action, rather than those who pursue ideas and possibilities).

- In general, as the size of a group increases, decrease the length of meetings and do not exceed meeting times of two hours at most. When appropriate, prepare and distribute the agenda *before* the meeting.

- For sequential, ongoing meetings, keep minutes of the meetings because they represent the group's and institution's memory.

- Keep members focused on the agenda item, limit each member's initial airtime to three to five minutes, and allow less time for subsequent input.

- A strategy that promotes effective group decision making includes defining the problem, separating the generation from the evaluation of ideas, connecting ideas with actions, and assessing outcomes.

- When appropriate, end a meeting with a decision or a series of decisions, including the decision to meet again, if necessary, to discuss further the major agenda items for subsequent decision making.

examining feedback on improving a process in statistical control (pursuit of kaizen) or one that needs to be brought under control.

The *quality council* (also called the steering committee or QI team) is usually responsible for establishing policies and guiding the overall implementation of a TQ program throughout the organization. Its members generally include the president or chief executive officer, the vice president for quality, and other persons from the organization who have organization-wide authority and responsibility. Thus, the quality council may identify the quality principles for the program (noted in Table 6–5) and provide an initial framework for implementing the TQ program (presented in Table 6–6).

Problem-solving teams (configured as departmental or cross-functional teams) concentrate on solving focused problems (usually within a given department or unit) and cross-functional problems. Hence, their members are from a number of appropriate functional units in which a problem is expressed or that are the loci for the potential remediation of the problem.

Self-managed teams (also called self-directed, autonomous work groups or simply teams) generally have no supervisor, although a facilitator, coordinator, spokesperson, or leader may be elected or duties may be rotated among members, with the team assuming responsibility for budgeting, work schedules, goal setting,

Table 6–5. Suggested Quality Principles for a TQ Program

We suggest the following quality principles only as a point of departure and encourage you to select others in relation to Deming's 14 points for improving quality. These principles can serve as a set of algorithms for all phases, processes, and decision making.

- Promote constancy of purpose—mission and sustained leadership
- Always be customer or client focused
- Invest continuously in processes and people
- Empower all organizational associates
- Do teamwork
- Plan-do-check-act
- Continuously improve

hiring and discharging members, and any other functions that are essential for getting the job done (Dean & Evans, 1994). These teams frequently use all or some of the TQ tools for their work and generate their own, specifically tailored, tools (see Table 6–7).

We conclude this brief description of some of the essential components of a TQ program by presenting the centrality of the *Shewhart or Deming cycle*, which consists of four components—plan, do, check and act and is designed to address three questions:

- What are our objectives?
- What changes can we institute that will yield improvement?
- How will we know if a manipulated change is an improvement?

Essentially, in the *plan* component, the current situation or process is observed, the data are assembled, and a plan for improvement is devised. In the *do* component, the plan is implemented as a trial experiment or with a focused group of customers or clients. In the *check* component, the implemented plan is assessed on the basis of customer, client, or process measures to determine what further changes can be instituted to

enhance quality. In the *act* component, implementation of the earlier and more focused plan is broadened with an emphasis on standardization. The Shewhart or Deming cycle is a continuous process that leads to continuous improvement. Here, as in other aspects of life, the journey is all and the destinations are many.

TQ programs are here to stay in global organizations, and the best ones are awarded national prizes, whether in Japan (the Deming Prize), the United States (the Malcolm Balridge National Quality Award), or the ISO9000 program of the European Community (EC). The ISO9000 program is not an award, but a verification process administered by the International Organization of Standardization (ISO), with members from 91 nations, that determines if products meet the quality standards of the EC and those of adopting nations. The ISO standards focus on the design and manufacturing of products, process, and service, whereas the Deming and Balridge awards are for organizational dimensions, such as leadership, strategic planning, or management of customer relations. If products are verified by an independent ISO9000 auditor, they are ISO registered, and whether they are purchased in Beijing, Boston, Burlington, or wherever, they will be the same, regardless of the point of contact with the customer or client. It

Table 6.6. Framework for Implementing a TQ Program

The following is a basic framework for implementing a TQ program in a relatively small organization (approximately 50 or fewer members) or for a department or unit (25–50 members). We encourage you to modify this framework to accommodate your specific situational requirements.

Identify a Core Quality Team in Your Unit

Choose five to seven members.

Keep the rest of the unit informed and seek their input by a "draft mechanism" (running important action documents by other members before implementing planned action).

Acknowledge and use, when appropriate, the ideas of a larger contextual work group.

Build alliances and quality advisory teams outside your immediate work unit.

Use Gap Analysis for each Quality Principle

Identify areas in your work unit that most indicate that change has occurred or is taking place toward the achievement of any or all the quality principles.

Identify obvious needs for change to achieve any or all the quality principles and examples of why the needs are real.

Indicate Present Tensions

Identify indices of dissatisfaction with the way things are and the sources of dissatisfaction that may arise from the realization that things could be better if any or all the quality principles were implemented systematically.

Provide a Reality Check

Identify any quality principle that, if implemented, would not give rise to a change for the better.

Identify any quality principle that, no matter what is done, cannot be implemented in your organization and explain why on the basis of your experiences in the organization.

Implement only those quality principles that would give rise to a fairly immediate change and would meet with minimal resistance to implementation. Thereafter, build on your small wins and implement those quality principles that were ruled out initially by the foregoing two considerations.

Determine the Sources of Social Support

What engines of social, group, or team support do you see for changes in your work unit or division in the organization? Harness the power of such engines to implement your TQ program.

What additional sources of support are needed to implement any or all the quality principles?

Alternative Pathways

What specifically would you change in the way you carry out your own work that would be a better way of implementing any or all the quality principles? Model the implementation of the TQ program on what you do, not just by what you say.

Table 6–7. Tools for Teamwork

Tool	Objective
Brainstorming	Get everyone's input, generate creative ideas, and separate the generation of ideas from the evaluation of ideas.
Posting on the board or wall	Display and then allow the members to organize ideas and information generated by the team.
Round-and-round voting	Identify priorities from a long list of items by ranking alternatives from the highest to the lowest.
Seek closure and consensus	Develop a limited plan of action, do it, check, and act.
Repeat these tools again and again	Engage in continuous improvement.

is these types of TQ-related programs, as well as the application of TQ in public-sector organizations and governmental agencies, that will further strengthen the infrastructure of the global marketplace (Swiss, 1992; Wagenheim & Reurink, 1991).

We next consider some specific applied strategies (motivational levers) that can be used in a wide variety of organizations to enhance motivation at the individual and organizational levels and, in turn, the real value of the product or service delivered to the customer. These strategies include goal setting, self-fulfilling prophecy, efficacy, equity, flow, and individual and group mood.

MOTIVATIONAL LEVERS

You or your organization may find that, at times, you have an unending list of tasks or projects—that the phone mail and E-mail messages, letters, memoranda, and reports keep streaming in at such a pace that you feel up to your eyebrows in turbulence. If this description does not apply to you or your organization, you get almost everything done, or you do not know what turbulence feels like, skip this section. If, however, work comes at you from all directions and piles up and it is difficult to organize your activities at the individual team, or organizational level, then perhaps some of the following motivational levers or applied strategies to enhance productivity that work for us and for many of our organizational clients may be helpful to you.

Goal Setting

In general, a goal is a desired state or object that a person seeks at some point in the future. According to Locke and Latham (1984, 1990), goals are immediate regulators of or, in other words, determine, in large measure, the performance of tasks. It has been shown that across a variety of organizations and managerial levels, goal setting yields median improvements in the quantity and/or quality of tasks performed of 16%, with a range of 2% to 57.5% above the pre-goal-setting performance level (Locke & Latham, 1984, 1990). Two consistent findings of the many hundreds of field-based and laboratory studies of goal setting (Locke & Latham, 1990) are as follows:

- Increasing the difficulty of the goal is translated almost directly into higher performance levels. Assuming that goals are accepted, the difficult ones result in greater effort, persistence, and satisfaction arising from higher levels of performance.

- Goals that are specific and difficult yield higher levels of performance than do vague, nonquantitative goals, such as do your best, or no assigned goal. In general, people welcome challenging, realistic, and specific goals, compared to easy, impossible, or unspecified goals.

To demonstrate the efficacy of goal setting, we ask you to look around the room you are in for about 20 seconds. Now write down the number of circles or circular objects you observed during the 20-second period and keep looking at your paper or computer screen. Then look around your environment again for about 20 seconds and count the number of circles or circular objects you now observe. After 20 seconds, write down your count. You will find that just by setting a specific and realistic goal, the second number is much higher than the first number, which was generated in the absence of a specific goal.

Table 6–8 presents a brief outline of the components and steps of goal setting and some reasons for the pitfalls and effectiveness of goal setting and enhanced persistence. When we have applied goal setting in our consulting practices, it has been extremely successful. In fact, this book was written on the basis of specific and challenging goals, measured by specific deadlines for the completion of each chapter. In addition, a variety of studies have demonstrated, and we have confirmed in our consulting practices, that public commitment to a goal or set of goals induces a stronger commitment to goals than does private commitment (Hallenbeck, Williams, & Klein, 1989; Locke & Latham, 1990).

Just as goal setting by an individual directly influences the person's goal-related performances, group goal setting improves a group's performances (Pritchard, Jones, Roth, Stuebring, & Ekeberg, 1988; Weingart & Weldon, 1991; Weldon, Jehn, & Pradhan, 1991). For example, in a laboratory study, Weingart (1992) showed that increasing the difficulty of a group's goals, and hence the complexity of the tasks, led to a higher level of performance because of more and higher-quality planning (for example, consideration of a wide range of alternatives strategies for completing tasks) and greater effort. Also, Pritchard et al.'s (1988) field-based study of work teams found that goal setting, feedback on the group's goal-related performance of complex tasks, and incentives to achieve goals increased productivity 75%, 50%, and 76%, respectively, above the eight-month baseline observation period and that these changes were not associated with any increases in the size or number of work teams.

Furthermore, Gilliland and Landis (1992) noted that goal setting by both individuals and groups results in different strategies for simple tasks (usually greater effort) than for complex tasks (generally increased search strategies, such as gathering more information and considering alternative strategies). When persons are assigned difficult goals, they produce more, experience a stronger sense of self-efficacy (confidence), and have a higher heart rate than when they are given simple goals (Gellatly & Meyer, 1992).

Table 6–8. Goal Setting

Components of Goal Setting

specific and challenging goals
standards for measuring goal-related performance
specific and systematic feedback on goal-related performance
incentives and rewards for achieving goals
recalibrating goals or setting new goals on the basis of feedback

Steps to Setting Goals

specify the goals
specify how performance will be measured using
   temporal units (the amount of time to achieve the goal)
   physical units (like the number of items to be made)
   resource outcomes (such as cost-cutting measures)
   behavioral observation scales, (for instance, responding
   to customers' requests within some specified time)
specify the target to be achieved
specify the time to achieve the target
establish priorities among goals
determine the requirements for coordination—important for
interdependent tasks
trust and believe in yourself and others

Goal Setting is Effective Because

specific goals (rather than the goal of do your best)
direct action or behavior
specific goals yield clear expectations
more challenging goals lead to higher performance
within limits, people prefer challenging goals.

Goal Setting Enhances Persistence by

directing attention and action
mobilizing energy and effort
developing appropriate strategies to achieve tasks.

The Potential Pitfalls of Goal Setting and Moderator Effects Include

excessive risk taking
stress
failure
ignoring nongoal areas
short-range thinking
dishonesty and cheating.

Goal setting is an effective and sound motivational tool because it activates both cognitive and emotional processes in the person or group. Thus, people first judge the reasonableness of a goal, and if they conclude that the goal is realistic and challenging, they focus their cognitive and affective resources and "go for it," thus adding passion to the task. In turbulent times, goal setting may be an invaluable tool to keep you or your organization focused as well as energized.

Self-fulfilling Prophecies

One of the earliest definitions of the self-fulfilling prophecy in the psychological literature was by Merton (1948, p. 195), who wrote that "in the beginning, a false definition of the situation [evokes] a new behavior which makes the originally false conception come true." Self-fulfilling prophecies for interpersonal relationships have been studied in a variety of contexts, including the educational system (Jussim, 1986; Rosenthal, 1974; Rosenthal & Jacobson, 1986) and the military (Eden, 1984, 1988, 1990; Eden & Kinnar, 1991; Eden & Ravid, 1982; Eden & Shani, 1982; Livingston, 1969).

The *Pygmalion effect* is one form of self-fulfilling prophecy in which the performance of one person (such as a subordinate) is enhanced when another person (such as a manager) expects her or him to perform better. In short, if you expect a lot or a little of others at work, that is usually what you will get. Thus, the Pygmalion effect is like goal setting except that it is more suggestive than directive because goals are not imposed on a person. Eden (1990) showed that Pygmalion effect occurs in groups as well as in individuals. However, Sutton and Woodman (1989) did not observe it among sales personnel in a retail setting perhaps because retail sales is an interactive task between a salesperson and a customer (a type of task that none of the reports of a positive Pygmalion effect included). Therefore, it is probably best to use the Pygmalion effect as a motivational tool when the target person is involved in a noninteractive task, such as learning a new skill.

The *Galatea effect*, another form of the self-fulfilling prophecy, involves raising a person's self-expectations for the performance of specific tasks, rather than relying on an authority figure, such as a manager (Eden, 1984) or a teacher (Jussim, 1986), to heighten the person's expectations. Thus, for example, an organizational member other than a manager (such as a mentor) may inform her or his colleagues that they have a high potential to succeed in the tasks they are about to undertake. In fact, Eden and Kinnar (1991) found evidence for the Galatea effect in relation to increased volunteering.

When others expect more of you (the Pygmalion effect) or you expect more of yourself (the Galatea effect), your performance can be enhanced without an increase in salary or other external resources. Obviously, there are limits to the effects of heightened expectations on performance levels, whether imposed (the Pygmalion effect) or chosen (the Galatea effect). Nevertheless, within boundaries determined on a situational basis, it is worthwhile for individuals and the organization to expect more of each other and for individuals to expect more of themselves.

Perceived Self-efficacy

The motivational construct of perceived self-efficacy (PSE), introduced by Bandura (1982, 1986), is probably the central psychological mechanism that mediates both goal setting and the self-fulfilling prophecy. According to Bandura (1986, p. 391), PSE is "people's judgments of their capabilities to organize and execute courses of action required to attain designated types of performances." PSE is a robust motivational force in that it focuses on what a person judges can be done with whatever skills or talents he or she possesses, is task specific, and largely determines what an individual chooses to do or not to do. For example, a manager who considers herself to be an efficacious engineer and negotiator is likely to initiate and pursue such activities, rather than those in which she believes she is less efficacious.

PSE is a cognitive judgmental process representing one form of self-referential thought that includes thinking about and talking to oneself. Most people spend a fair amount of time thinking about and reacting to themselves. it has been estimated that if self-ideation was transposed into words and scripts, it would be found that individuals talk to themselves at a rate of about 1,000 words per minute. Much self-talk involves people's judgments about what they can or cannot do (efficacy) or what they feel or do not feel like doing (mood). Therefore, if you set a goal to complete a work project or report by a given time and you did so, you are likely to judge yourself highly capable of accomplishing this kind of task again. If, you did not achieve your goal in the specified time because of factors that were within your control, then you would probably judge yourself less efficacious to perform this kind of task in the future and, hence would probably revise your goals related to this task in the future. It is likely that this chain of psychological events would be similar for self-fulfilling prophecies in that both the Pygmalion and the Galatea effects also involve goal setting.

It is important to note that persons who consider themselves to be highly efficacious are more persistent than are those who judge themselves to be less efficacious and thus are more likely to see tasks through to completion by interpreting setbacks as temporary and changing strategies to reach their goal, rather than blaming themselves (Bandura, 1982, 1986, 1989; Gist, 1987; Gist & Mitchell, 1992; Wood & Bandura, 1989). Therefore, managers or associates who know their subordinates' levels of PSE can assign or work with these individuals on tasks or projects that are most likely to yield positive outcomes. In general, a person's level of PSE is shaped by the following sources of robust information, beginning with the most robust:

Enactive attainment: a sense of mastery gained from successfully completing a task and reaching a goal. The person then knows that he or she can do so again.

Modeling: working with a mentor (an experienced person) who is similar to oneself or observing videotapes of a person executing a simple target task or a complex target task divided into manageable incremental levels of learning.

Verbal persuasion: a form of coaching in which the trainee or learner is given specific, realistic praise that includes suggestions for attaining the goal.

Arousal: increased heart and respiration rates and tightening of muscles experienced when facing challenging and personally important tasks or projects. People who interpret these arousal cues as a harnessing of intellectual and physical resources, rather than a signal of uncertainty or pressure, are more likely to have an enhanced sense of efficacy.

According to Bandura (1986, 1989), optimism is necessary for a sense of well-being and accomplishment because most social situations are strewn with problems and tasks. Thus, it is valuable to have a robust sense of personal efficacy so as to persevere in order to succeed. Since it is natural for setbacks or failure to arouse self-doubts at first, a person needs to make speedy recovery from these self-doubts to regain his or her PSE. As the Reverend Martin Luther King, Jr., once said, "The future belongs to the fit." He meant that what counts is not so much success, but resilience in the belief that one can deal with the failures, setbacks, and frustrations that people experience in all domains of life, including work.

Lawson and his associates (Chen, Lawson, Gordon, McIntosh, 1996; Danielski, 1993; Lawson & Ventriss, 1992), recognizing that almost all organizational work is done in some kind of group, interdependent, or collective context, examined the relationship between perceived individual efficacy (IE, or PSE) and collective efficacy (CE) in laboratory- and field-based organizational settings (health care and computer firms). We measured IE and CE with the instrument presented in Table 6–9 and found, in both settings, that IE was significantly higher than CE and that the higher the IE and CE, the higher the individual and group performances. Furthermore, at the end of an extremely turbu-

Table 6–9. Instrument for Measuring Individual and Organizational Efficacies

On two separate instruments, organizational members complete the IE and CE items displayed together here using a five-point scale from 1 (incapable) to 3 (likely) to 5 (extremely capable). Thereafter, a mean score across all items for all respondents is computed, and comparisons are made between the IC and CE scores. Also, item-by-item or item clusters can be examined to identify domain of personal and organizational capabilities.

I [This organization] can

    meet deadlines on time
    resolve conflicts between employees
    treat employees fairly
    reward employees based solely on their performance
    treat employees in a friendly manner
    respond to customers' or clients' needs
    be a leader in my [its] field
    make effective decisions
    motivate employees to do their best
    set specific goals for employees
    communicate effectively with employees
    achieve specific goals
    operate effectively under pressure
    achieve challenging goals
    share decision-making responsibilities
    correct my [its] mistakes
    respond to employees' needs
    manage personnel problems
    provide a sense of purpose to work

Individual [Collective] Performance Items
    During the past six months, I would rate my overall performance [the overall performance of the organization] for the above items as

poor   ___ ___ ___ ___ ___ excellent
        1   2   3   4   5

lent 16-month period of unheard-of layoffs, voluntary separation packages, and erosion of the firm's market share, employees' and managers' IEs and CEs were significantly higher than they were at the beginning of the period (Danielski, 1993). The employees and managers indicated that working with their organization and specific work teams to achieve extremely challenging goals (enactive attainment), watching colleagues find ways to complete subprojects (modeling), and organizational stories of gallant efforts by diverse teams (verbal persuasion) boosted their sense of CE.

Many questions remain regarding IE and CE, but we believe that organizational members make judgments not only about their own levels of efficacy but about their colleagues' and organization's levels, so that the higher the levels of IE and CE, the higher the performance enhancements at the individual (micro) and organizational (macro) levels. We are now studying IEs and CEs in Chinese organizations and expect to find that unlike the situation in some U.S. organizations, CE will be judged higher than IE in Chinese organizations, given that country's emphasis on collectivism.

Intrinsic Motivation

The construct of intrinsic motivation is related to the work of Woodworth (1918), who focused on "the need for competence," and Hebb (1955), who posited the "optimal arousal hypothesis," both of which suggest that there is something intrinsically positive about performing a task, seeking information, or just doing something without any immediate external reward or payoff. In a test of Hebb's hypothesis, Deci (1971, 1972, 1975) found that when people were given money (extrinsic motivation) for doing things they enjoyed (intrinsic motivation), they lost interest faster than when they were not rewarded. According to Deci (1975) and Deci and Ryan (1985), when people are paid for doing something they enjoy, they perceive that their involvement is under the control of external forces, rather than freely chosen, which suggests that intrinsic motivation is based on the need for self-determination (choice) and competence (personal efficacy). Deci and Ryan's (1985) concept of intrinsic motivation has been criticized on a number of accounts. The main criticisms are that it does not distinguish clearly between liking an activity for its own sake and liking it because it makes one feel competent, and, perhaps what is more important, if intrinsic motivation is wiped out by such factors as incentives and rewards, competition, imposed goals, deadlines, and pressure, then it probably does not have much application to real organizational life. As Deci and Ryan (1986) stated, intrinsic motivation arises primarily from choice and, to a lesser extent, controllability, which are also important for understanding Bandura's concept of PSE. Thus, choice appears to be an important moderator of flow, which is the affective or experiential side, compared to the behavioral or performance side of the motivational coin.

Work and Leisure

Do people prefer to engage in leisure activities or to work? Csikszentmihalyi and Csikszentmihalyi (1988) and Csikszentmihalyi and LeFevre (1989) observed, across a widely diversified set of activities, persons working hard and appearing to enjoy the experience, which they called the autoletic (or flow) experience. People experience flow when the challenges of a task and their skills for performing that task are equally high and therefore congruent. On the other hand, they feel anxious when the challenges are greater than their skills; bored, when the challenges are low and their skills are high; and apathetic, when both the challenges and their skills are low (Csikszentmihalyi & LeFevre, 1989).

In tracking 78 adult workers, these investigators used their experience sampling method in which the participants were required to indicate, on the sound of a beeper, what they were doing at the time, to assign their activity to one of four categories (flow, anxiety, boredom, or apathy), and to assess their level of motivation for performing the activity from low to high (Csikszentmihalyi & LeFevre, 1989). The participants experienced more flow at work than during leisure activities, although their motivation was higher for leisure than for work activities. In other words, they seemed to enjoy work activities more than leisure activities, although they were more highly motivated to perform the latter than the former. Perhaps, the fact that people have a greater choice of leisure activities makes these activities more appealing, even though they enjoy the experience of work more than that of playing. These findings suggest that the behavioral and affective aspects of motivation can be high at work if people have an enhanced sense of choice or autonomy, when possible and within the constraints of their work assignments.

Eisenberger's (1992) model of learned industriousness rests on the proposition that variations in industriousness from one person to another may be learned as a result of the secondary reinforcing properties of working hard, achieving challenging goals, and enjoying the experience. Thus, flow and learned industriousness may well be enhanced if members are afforded autonomy, which is a central feature of many self-managed teams associated with TQ programs (Eisenberger & Cameron, 1996).

Equity and Hard Times

All organizations, like individuals, enjoy good times and have to deal with hard times. For individuals, hard times, represented most poignantly by pay cuts or the loss of jobs (organizational downsizing), are often painful and stressful experiences. Thus, it can be extremely difficult to maintain a motivated workforce under difficult economic conditions.

Greenberg (1990) studied employees' theft rates in manufacturing plants when employees pay was cut 15% to keep all current members employed rather than to lay off some workers. In line with equity theory (Adams, 1965), Greenberg anticipated that pay cuts would be perceived as unfair and that theft by employees might increase to restore equity. That was what Greenberg found in one manufacturing plant when no explanation for the basis, duration, or extent of the pay cut was offered. However, in a comparable plant of the same national organization, when the basis of the pay cut was made plain (loss of contracts), all personnel experienced the same 15% pay cut, and it was indicated that the cuts would be in place for about 10 weeks, employee theft was significantly lower. Thus, procedural justice (an open and systematic explanation of critical organizational events) moderates, in part, distributive justice (the fair and equitable distribution of resources across organizational units and individuals). This finding is in agreement with the model that the procedures and outcomes of decision making are better accepted and motivation is generally not reduced when (1) organizational members are assured that a higher authority (management) is sensitive to their viewpoints, (2) a decision is made without bias and is applied consistently, (3) decision makers communicate fully and honestly on the basis of available information, and (4) members are treated in a courteous and civil manner (Greenberg, 1990).

In summary, motivation at work can be enhanced by setting specific and challenging goals, promoting high but realistic expectations; assigning efficacious people and teams to appropriate tasks or projects; increasing opportunities to make choices, when possible and feasible; and, when hard times strike, explaining the basis, extent, and duration of cost-saving actions. These specific levers of motivation match fairly closely the consensual values presented in Chapter 2 and indicate that people expect to be treated equitably and respectfully, want promises kept, and respect honesty. The application of these levers and the supporting values in an organization is a dignified and worthy challenge that can enhance the flow experiences of organizational members.

MOOD AT WORK

Some days you may not feel like going to work (mood), although you know you have to be at work for any of a variety of reasons (cognition). The question then arises, How does a person's mood and overall disposition influence a variety of work activities, including absenteeism? In a series of field-based organizational studies, George (1989, 1990) and George and Brief (1992) examined the impact of mood (a pervasive generalized affective state) on a variety of work behaviors.

Mood and Absence

Positive mood is a general feeling of being alert, active, and zestful, whereas negative mood is a general feeling of being drowsy, dull, inactive, and sleepy (Watson & Tellegen, 1985). George (1989) assessed the positive and negative moods of 210 salespeople at work using the 20-item (10 positive and 10 negative mood items) Job Affect Scale (Brief, Burke, George, Robinson, &

Webster, 1988) and the personality traits of positive and negative affectivity using the Multidimensional Personality Questionnaire (Tellegen, 1982). She found that positive mood at work was significantly and negatively related to absenteeism while negative mood at work was not significantly associated with absenteeism. In other words, whether people experienced upbeat feelings or dull, flat feelings at work, they came to work. In addition, George found that employees whose personalities she characterized as expressing positive affectivity (upbeat and optimistic) were significantly predisposed to experience a positive mood at work, while the reverse was true for employees with personalities she described as expressing negative affectivity. George concluded that situational (contextual) forces exert a greater impact on positive moods, whereas internal (dispositional) factors have a greater affect on negative moods. Thus, moods at work and their personality antecedents (positive and negativity affectivity) appear to have substantial influences on a variety of thought processes and behaviors at work.

In an extension of her study of the moods of individuals, George (1990) examined the influence of the positive and negative affectivity of groups or teams on prosocial behaviors at work and on absenteeism. George's basic hypothesis was that teams (salespeople) whose members generally score high on positive affectivity will be absent from work less often than will teams whose members score high on negative affectivity. However, George found the same relationship between the moods of teams and absenteeism as she did for individuals. In addition, she found that prosocial behavior, defined as improved service to customers, was significantly influenced by negative affectivity but not by positive affectivity. Thus, teams whose members scored high on negative affectivity were not absent significantly more than were teams whose members scored high on positive affectivity. But they did exhibit significantly less customer service behaviors, which suggests that if an employee is experiencing a negative mood at work, then he or she is less likely to assist customers or clients.

Organizational Spontaneity

George and Brief (1992) proposed that positive mood at work is directly related to organizational spontaneity, which they defined as work-related behaviors that go beyond a person's role, job description, and job requirements; are performed voluntarily; and contribute to the organization's effectiveness. Specific examples of organizational spontaneity include activities like helping co-workers, protecting the organization (such as reporting a potential fire or safety hazard), making constructive suggestions, developing oneself (for instance, taking a course after work to improve one's job-related performance), and spreading goodwill (like telling friends about the high-quality products or services that one's organization provides). No empirical studies have directly tested the relationship between positive mood at work and organizational spontaneity. However, the topic is timely, given the rapidly changing requirements of a wide variety of jobs, which suggests that organizations may benefit by seeking members who are likely to exhibit a high degree of organizational spontaneity.

In summary, motivation can be influenced directly by a variety of applied strategies, such as goal setting, and when coupled with the selection of members who exhibit positive moods at work or who can be socialized to exhibit such moods, the organization is likely to be competitive and an enjoyable place to work. Thus, no whining unless you are prepared to do something about it, and, if so, welcome!

CULTURE AND MOTIVATION

As globalization—"the crystallization of the entire world as a single place" (Robertson, 1987, p. 38)—proceeds, the need to understand the relationship between culture and motivation assumes greater importance to determine how motivation is moderated or influenced by the larger culture that embraces a particular organization.

In many instances, the role of work reflects salient dimensions of a society's values. For example, the Meaning of Working International Team (1987) found, on the basis of surveys in the United States, Japan, and six West European countries, that "work centrality" (the devotion to work) was the highest in Japan (Bond & Smith, 1996). Ralston, Gustafson, Elass, Cheung, and Terpstra (1992), using the Chinese Value Survey (CVS, Chinese Culture Connection, 1987) of managers in Hong Kong, the United States, and the People's Republic of China reported that the Chinese managers scored significantly higher than did the managers in Hong Kong and the United States on Confucian-work dynamism (CVS-II), which emphasizes social hierarchy and protection of the status quo. The U.S. managers scored significantly higher than did the Hong Kong managers, who scored higher than the Chinese managers on the Human Heartedness scale for which a higher score indicates a higher value on a task than of relationship orientation. Thus, the Chinese managers highly value maintaining an harmonious environment, whereas managers in the United States and Hong Kong highly value getting the job done. Schwalb, Schwalb, Harnisch, Maehr, and Akabane (1992) stated that in their study, the Japanese employees were motivated by the task itself, self-improvement, and financial reward, whereas the U.S. employees were motivated by opportunities for affiliation, social concern, and recognition.

According to Hofstede (1991) and Triandis (1995), individualism is characteristic of societies in which there are loose ties among individuals, individual goals are pursued, and the independent self is valued. On the other hand, collectivism flourishes in societies in which members are integrated into strong, cohesive in-groups that protect members throughout life in exchange for unquestioning loyalty. Hofstede (1991) concluded that Japan and India, followed by Israel, Scandinavia, and West Germany, are highly collectivistic countries, and the United States is the most individualistic of the 40 countries that participated in the Hofstede (1980) study. In general, managerial techniques, such as goal setting, incentives, and job design, that focus on the individual are more effective in individualistic than in collectivistic cultures (Earley, 1989; Erez, 1986; Erez & Earley, 1987). By the same token, collectivistic management strategies, such as quality circles, autonomous work groups, and participation in goal setting and decision making, are better fits in collectivistic than in individualistic cultures (Erez & Earley, 1987; Matsui, Kakuyama, & Onglatco, 1987). Also, Earley (1994) reported that efficacy training was more effective for Chinese than for American managers when the focus was on group-level rather than individual-level, information.

In Japan, group and individual goals are more effective than are individual goals alone (Matsui et al., 1987), but in individualistic cultures, group goals usually give rise to social loafing (see Chapter 5) because group members usually do not share responsibility to the same extent as do group members in collectivistic cultures (Earley, 1989). Clearly, the performance of groups can be enhanced in individualistic cultures by assigning specific goals to each member of the groups (Weldon & Gargano, 1988). In a laboratory study of goal setting Erez and Earley (1987) found that Israeli college students performed significantly lower on the target task than did American college students when the goals were assigned, but that there was no difference between the Israelis and Americans when the goals were set participatively.

Different models of job design to enhance motivation and productivity have evolved in the United States than in Norway, Sweden, and Japan. For example, the job-enhancement model, developed by Hackman and Oldham (1980), emphasizes a variety of tasks, the individual worker's identification with outcomes, autonomy, and individual feedback. The critical psychological states that mediate between the dimensions of a job and the motivation to work stress the independent self, including the meaningfulness of the work, a sense of responsibility, and knowledge of the results. On the other hand, the sociotechnical systems model of job enrichment in autonomous work groups in Sweden, Japan, England, and Israel almost always involves the design of jobs on the group level. The key features of group job enhancement—like those of individual job enrichment—are team autonomy, team responsibility, feedback on performance, and meaningfulness of the task. The development of the individual job-enrichment model in the United States and the sociotechnical systems model in Scandinavian countries indicates that the potential of a task to motivate workers takes different forms in different cultures.

The relationship between culture and motivation is also clearly visible in participative management techniques in Japan. Respect for seniority, collectivism, and group orientation are important values of the Japanese culture (Erez, 1994; Triandis, Bontempo, Vilareal, Masaaki, & Lucca, 1988). Quality control circles are small-group activities, recognize that workers understand their work better than almost anyone else, can significantly contribute to the improvement of quality and productivity, and have flourished in Japan (there were 6,000 in 1975 and almost 230,000 in 1985), but have been less successful in the United States (Lawler, 1986; Onglatco, 1988).

Last, the relationship between culture and motivation is also apparent when one examines reward-allocation systems across different cultures. Rewards can be distributed by the principle of equity—to each according to her or his contribution; the principle of equality—to each equally; or by the principle of need—to each according to her or his need. In the United States, motivational theories have centered on the equity principle, stressing rewards distributed differentially on the basis of performance, as reflected in the equity and expectancy models of motivation and merit-based compensation plans. The Chinese, guided by collectivistic values, have applied the equality principle in allocating rewards to in-group members more than have Americans, who are guided by individualistic values (Bond, Leung, & Wan, 1982; Leung & Bond, 1984). The equality principle is also significantly stronger among Swedes than Americans or Indians (Berman & Singh, 1985; Tornblom, Jonsson, & Foa, 1985).

We concur with Erez and Earley (1993) that although there are universal human needs, such as the need to belong and to do a good job, the salience of various needs and the means for satisfying them vary across cultures. The motivation sequence is universal (see Figure 6–1), whereas the meaning of specific goals may change, depending on cultural values. The fundamental features of goal setting (a focus on establishing challenging goals, accompanied by feedback and a commitment to goals) appear to work soundly as a robust motivational strategy across cultures. However, it is clear that the nature of the goals, whether individual or group and whether mandated, participatively set, or self-set, have a differential motivational impact across cultures. In light of these differences, it is essential to apply these strategies in relation to the larger cultural context in which your organization is nested, which also shapes the values that the organization's members bring to the organization.

SUMMARY

Clearly, one of the fundamental organizational mantras of the 1990s—Do more with less—has been recited around the world by almost all organizations and their members. As a consequence, the topic of individual and organizational motivation has been on many agendas, first to establish a definition of motivation and then to understand the fairly universal forces that moderate levels of motivation.

In this chapter, we examined micro- and macromodels of motivation and described the shift from models of individual motivation to a model of group or organizational motivation, as reflected in TQ programs. TQ programs have three basic components—a management philosophy; six fundamental TQ tools, such as flowcharts, fishbone diagrams, and control charts; and tools for teamwork emphasizing improvements in the quality of products or services. In general, TQ programs are organization-wide, although they are initially implemented in selected departments or units. The major change in recent years has been the shift from motivational strategies focused on the individual to the robust motivational influence of customers' and clients' demands for higher-quality products and services at the lowest possible prices.

We then described specific motivational tactics that are used in a wide variety of organizations (goal setting, self-fulfilling prophecies, and variations of perceived self-efficacy and organizational efficacy). We also described intrinsic motivation that arises from a person being intensely involved and committed to a particular task or job independent of contingent access to extrinsic or external reinforcements like money and other resources.

Organizational spontaneity is the motivation to perform tasks outside or beyond the specific responsibilities and duties of a particular job. It is an important source of motivation as organizations continue to downsize and those who are still employed have to do many different jobs, and participate in cross-functional training programs, or learn many different skills beyond those of their jobs.

Finally, we discussed the moderating effect of culture upon motivational systems and concluded that the motivational sequence is universal, but motivational interventions need to be aligned with the values of the larger culture to enhance their effectiveness as motivational levers.

CHAPTER REFERENCES

Adams, J. S. (1963). Wage inequities, productivity and work quality. *Industrial Relations, 3,* 9–16.

Adams, J. S. (1965). Inequity in social exchange. In L. Berkowitz (Ed.), *Advances in experimental social psychology,* (pp. 267–299). New York: Academic Press.

Aguayo, R. (1990). *Dr. Deming: The American who taught the Japanese about quality.* New York: Simon & Schuster.

Alderfer, C. P. (1969). An empirical test of a new theory of human needs. *Organizational Behavior and Human Performance, 4,* 142–175.

Atkinson, J. W., & Reitman, W. R. (1965). Toward a theory of motive acquisition. *American Psychologist, 20,* 321–333.

Bandura, A. (1982). Self-efficacy mechanism in human agency. *American Psychologist, 37,* 122–147.

Bandura, A. (1986). *Social foundations of thought and action: A social cognitive theory.* Englewood Cliffs, NJ: Prentice Hall.

Bandura, A. (1989). Human agency in social cognitive theory. *American Psychologist, 44,* 1175–1184.

Berman, J. J., & Singh, P. (1985). Cross-cultural similarities and differences in perceptions of fairness. *Journal of Cross-Cultural Psychology, 16,* 55–67.

Bond, M. H., & Smith, P. B. (1996). Cross-cultural social and organizational psychology. *Annual Review of Psychology, 47,* 205–235.

Bond, M. H., Leung, K., & Wan, K. C. (1982). How does cultural collectivism operate? The impact of task and maintenance contributions on reward distribution. *Journal of Cross-Cultural Psychology, 13,* 186–200.

Bowes, J. M., & Goodnow, J. J. (1996). Work for home, school, or labor force: The nature and sources of changes in understanding. *Psychological Bulletin, 119,* 300–321.

Brief, A. P., Burke, M. J., George, J. M., Robinson, B., & Webster, J. (1988). Should negative affectivity remain an unmeasured variable in the study of job stress? *Journal of Applied Psychology, 73,* 193–198.

Chen, Z., Lawson, R. B., Gordon, L., & McIntosh, B. (1996). Groupthink: Deciding with the leader and the devil. *Psychological Record, 46,* 581–590.

Chinese Culture Connection. (1987). Chinese values and the search for culture-free dimensions of culture. *Journal of Cross-Cultural Psychology, 18,* 143–164.

Crosby, P. B. (1979). *Quality is free.* New York: McGraw-Hill.

Csikszentmihalyi, M., & Csikszentmihalyi, I. S. (1988). *Optimal experience: Psychological studies of flow in consciousness.* New York: Cambridge University Press.

Csikszentmihalyi, M., & LeFevre, J. (1989). Optimal experience in work and leisure. *Journal of Personality and Social Psychology, 56,* 815–822.

Danielski, C. (1993). *Efficacy, job satisfaction, and adaptation in an environment of organizational change.* Unpublished master's thesis, University of Vermont, Burlington.

Dean, J. W., Jr., & Evans, J. R. (1994). *Total quality.* Minneapolis: West.

Deci, E. L. (1971). Effects of externally mediated rewards on intrinsic motivation. *Journal of Personality and Social Psychology, 18,* 105–115.

Deci, E. L. (1972). Intrinsic motivation, extrinsic reinforcement, and inequity. *Journal of Personality and Social Psychology, 22,* 113–120.

Deci, E. L. (1975). *Intrinsic motivation.* New York: Plenum Press.

Deci, E. L., & Ryan, R. M. (1985). *Intrinsic motivation and self-determination in human behavior.* New York: Plenum Press.

Deming, W. E. (1982). *Quality, productivity, and competitive position.* Cambridge, MA: MIT Center for Advanced Engineering Study.

Deming, W. E. (1986). *Out of the crisis.* Cambridge, MA: MIT Center for Advanced Engineering Study.

Earley, P. C. (1989). Social loafing and collectivism: A comparison of the United States and the People's Republic of China. *Administrative Science Quarterly, 34,* 565–581.

Earley, P. C. (1994). Self or group? Cultural effects of training on self-efficacy and performance. *Administrative Science Quarterly, 39,* 89–117.

Eden, D. (1984). Self-fulfilling prophecy as a management tool: Harnessing Pygmalion. *Academy of Management Review, 9,* 64–73.

Eden, D. (1988). Pygmalion, goal setting, and expectancy: Compatible ways to boost productivity. *Academy of Management Review, 13,* 639–652.

Eden, D. (1990). *Pygmalion in management: Productivity as a self-fulfilling prophecy.* Lexington, MA: Lexington Books.

Eden, D., & Kinnar, J. (1991). Modeling Galatea: Boosting self-efficacy to increase volunteering. *Journal of Applied Psychology, 76,* 770–780.

Eden, D., & Ravid, G. (1982). Pygmalion vs. self-expectancy: Effects of instructor- and self-expectancy on trainee performance. *Organizational Behavior and Human Performance, 30,* 351–364.

Eden, D., & Shani, A. B. (1982). Pygmalion goes to boot camp: Expectancy, leadership, and trainee performance. *Journal of Applied Psychology, 67,* 194–199.

Eisenberger, R. (1992). Learned industriousness. *Psychological Review, 99,* 248–267.

Eisenberger, R. & Cameron, J. (1996). Detrimental effects of reward: Reality or myth? *American Psychologist, 51,* 1153–1166.

Erez, M. (1986). The congruence of goal setting strategies with socio-cultural values, and its effect on performance. *Journal of Management, 12,* 588–592.

Erez, M. (1994). Toward a model of cross-cultural industrial and organizational psychology. In H. C. Triandis, M. D. Dunnette, & L. M. Hough (Eds.), *Handbook of industrial and organizational psychology* (2nd ed., Vol. 4, pp. 559–607). Palo Alto, CA: Consulting Psychologists Press.

Erez, M., & Earley, P. C. (1987). Comparative analysis of goal-setting strategies across cultures. *Journal of Applied Psychology, 72,* 658–665.

Erez, M., & Earley, P. C. (1993). *Culture, self-identity, and work.* New York: Oxford University Press.

Gabor, A. (1990). *The man who discovered quality: How W. Edwards Deming brought the quality revolution to America—The stories of Ford, Xerox, and G. M.* New York: Times Books.

Gellatly, I. R., & Meyer, J. P. (1992). The effects of goal difficulty on physiological arousal, cognition, and task performance. *Journal of Applied Psychology, 77*, 694–704.

George, J. M. (1989). Mood and absence. *Journal of Applied Psychology, 74*, 317–324.

George, J. M. (1990). Personality, affect, and behavior in groups. *Journal of Applied Psychology, 75*, 107–116.

George, J. M., & Brief, A. P. (1992). Feeling good—doing good: A conceptual analysis of the mood at work-organizational spontaneity relationship. *Psychological Bulletin, 112*, 310–329.

Gilliland, S. W., & Landis, R. S. (1992). Quality and quantity goals in complex decision task: Strategies and outcomes. *Journal of Applied Psychology, 77*, 672–681.

Gist, M. (1987). Self-efficacy. Implications for organizational behavior and human resource management. *Academy of Management Review, 12*, 472–485.

Gist, M. E., & Mitchell, T. R. (1992). Self-efficacy: A theoretical analysis of its determinants and malleability. *Academy of Management Review, 17*, 183–211.

Gitlow, H. S., & Gitlow, S. J. (1987). *The Deming guide to quality and competitive position.* Englewood Cliffs, NJ: Prentice Hall.

Greenberg, J. (1990). Employee theft as a reaction to underpayment inequity: The hidden cost of pay cuts. *Journal of Applied Psychology, 75*, 561–568.

Hackman, J. R., & Oldham, G. R. (1980). *Work redesign.* Reading, MA: Addison-Wesley.

Hallenbeck, J. R., Williams, C. R., & Klein, H. J. (1989). An empirical examination of the antecedents of commitment to difficult goals. *Journal of Applied Psychology, 74*, 18–23.

Hebb, D. O. (1955). Drives and the C.N.S. (conceptual nervous system). *Psychological Review, 62*, 243–254.

Herzberg, F. (1966). *Work and the nature of man.* Cleveland: World.

Herzberg, F., Mausner, B., & Synderman, B. (1959). *The motivation to work.* New York: John Wiley & Sons.

Hofstede, G. (1980). *Culture's consequences: International differences in work related values.* Newbury Park, CA: Sage.

Hofstede, G. (1991). *Culture and organizations: Software of the mind.* London: McGraw-Hill.

Howard, A., & Bray, D. W. (1989). *Managerial lives in transition.* New York: Guilford Press.

Human Capital Initiative. (1993). *Report of the committee on the changing nature of work.* Washington, DC: American Psychological Society.

Ishikawa, K. (1976). *Guide to quality control.* Tokyo: Asian Productivity Organization.

Juran, J. M. (1992). *Juran on quality by design.* New York: Free Press.

Jussim, L. (1986). Self-fulfilling prophecies: A theoretical and integrative review. *Psychological Review, 93*, 429–445.

Katzell, R. A., & Thompson, D. E. (1990). Work motivation: Theory and practice. *American Psychologist, 45*, 144–153.

King, N. (1970). Clarification and evaluation of the two-factor theory of job satisfaction. *Psychological Bulletin, 74*, 18–31.

Lawler, E. E., III. (1986). *High involvement management.* San Francisco: Jossey-Bass.

Lawson, R. B., & Ventriss, C. L. (1992). Organizational change: The role of organizational culture and organizational learning. *Psychological Record, 42*, 205–219.

Leung, K., & Bond, M. (1984). The impact of cultural collectivism on reward allocation. *Journal of Personality and Social Psychology, 47*, 793–804.

Livingston, J. S. (1969). Pygmalion in management. *Harvard Business Review, 47*, 81–89.

Locke, E. A., & Latham, G. (1984). *Goal setting: A motivational technique that works.* Englewood Cliffs, NJ: Prentice Hall.

Locke, E. A., & Latham, G. (1990). *A theory of goal setting and task performance.* Englewood Cliffs, NJ: Prentice Hall.

Loden, M., & Rosener, J. (1991). *Workforce America!* Homewood IL: Richard D. Irwin.

Maddi, S. (1972). *Theories of personality, a comparative analysis.* Homewood, IL: Dorsey Press.

Maslow, A. H. (1943). A theory of human motivation. *Psychological Review, 1*, 370–396.

Maslow, A. H. (1954). *Motivation and personality.* New York: Harper & Row.

Matsui, T., Kakuyama, T., & Onglatco, M. L. (1987). Effects of goals and feedback on performance in groups. *Journal of Applied Psychology, 38,* 299–337.

McClelland, D. (1976). Power is a great motivator. *Harvard Business Review, 54,* 100–110.

McClelland, D. C., Atkinson, J. W., Clark, R. W., & Lowell, E. L. (1953). *The achievement motive.* New York: Appleton-Century-Crofts.

McClelland, D. C., & Boyatzis, R. E. (1982). Leadership motive pattern and long-term success in management. *Journal of Applied Psychology, 67,* 744–751.

Merton, R. K. (1948). The self-fulfilling prophecy. *Antioch Review, 8,* 193–210.

MOW International Research Team. (1986). *The meaning of working: An international perspective.* New York: Academic Press.

Mowday, R. T. (1991). Equity theory predictions of behavior in organization. In R. M. Steers & L. W. Porter (Eds.), *Motivation and work behavior* (pp. 111–131). New York: McGraw-Hill.

National Advisory Mental Health Council. (1995). Basic behavioral science research for mental health: A national investment—emotion and motivation. *American Psychologist, 50,* 838–845.

Onglatco, D. W. (1988). *Japanese quality control circles: Features, effects, and problems.* Tokyo: Asian Productivity Center.

Perrow, C. (1972). *Complex organizations.* Glenview, IL: Scott, Foresman.

Pinder, C. C. (1991). Valence-instrumentality-expectancy theory. In R. M. Steers & L. W. Porter (Eds.), *Motivation and work behavior* (pp. 144–164). New York: McGraw-Hill.

Pritchard, R. D., Jones, S. D., Roth, P. L., Stuebring, K. K., & Ekeberg, S. E. (1988). Effects of group feedback, goal setting, and incentives on organizational productivity. *Journal of Applied Psychology, 73,* 337–358.

Rafaeli, A., & Sutton, R. I. (1989). The expression of emotion in organizational life. In L. L. Cummings & B. M. Staw (Eds.), *Research in Organizational Behavior* (Vol. 11, pp. 1–42). Greenwich, CT: JAI Press.

Ralston, D. A., Gustafson, D. J., Elsass, P. M., Cheung, F., & Terpstra, R. H. (1992). Eastern values: A comparison of managers in the United States, Hong Kong, and the People's Republic of China. *Journal of Applied Psychology, 77,* 664–671.

Robertson, R. (1987). Globalization and societal modernization: A note on Japan and Japanese religion. *Sociological Analysis, 47,* 35–43.

Rosenthal, R. (1974). *On the social psychology of the self-fulfilling prophecy: Further evidence for Pygmalion effects and their mediating mechanisms* (Module 53). New York: MSS Modular Publications.

Rosenthal, R., & Jacobson, L. (1986). *Pygmalion in the classroom: Teacher expectation and student intellectual development.* New York: Holt, Rinehart & Winston.

Schwalb, D. W., Schwalb, B. J., Harnisch, D. L., Maehr, M. L., Akabane, K. (1992). Personal investment in Japan and the USA: A study of worker motivation. *International Journal of Intercultural Relations, 16,* 107–124.

Shepperd, J. A. (1993). Productivity loss in performance groups: A motivation analysis. *Psychological Bulletin, 113,* 67–81.

Shewhart, W. (1924). Some applications of statistical methods. *Bell Systems Technical Journal, 3,* 1–45.

Steers, R. M., & Porter, L. W. (1991). *Motivation and work behavior.* New York: McGraw-Hill.

Sutton, C. D., & Woodman, R. W. (1989). Pygmalion goes to work: The effects of supervisor expectations in a retail setting. *Journal of Applied Psychology, 74,* 943–950.

Swiss, J. E. (1992). Adapting total quality management (TQM) to government. *Public Administration Review, 52,* 356–361.

Taylor, F. W. (1911). *The principles of scientific management.* New York: Harper & Bros.

Tellegen, A. (1982). *Brief manual of the differential personality questionnaire.* Minneapolis: University of Minnesota Press.

Thompson, D. E., & DiTomaso, N. (Eds.). (1988). *Ensuring minority success in corporate management.* New York: Plenum Press.

Tornblom, K. Y., Jonsson, D., & Foa, U. G. (1985). Nationality resource class and preferences among three allocation rules: Sweden vs. USA. *International Journal of Intercultural Relations, 9,* 51–77.

Triandis, H. C. (1995). *Individualism and collectivism.* Boulder, CO: Westview Press.

Triandis, H. C., Bontempo, R., Vilareal, M. J., Masaaki, A., & Lucca, N. (1988). Individualism and collectivism: Cross-cultural perspectives on self-ingroup relationships. *Journal of Personality and Social Psychology, 54,* 328–338.

Van Maanen, J., & Kunda, G. (1989). Real feelings: Emotional expression and organizational culture. In L. L. Cummings & B. M. Staw (Eds.), *Research in organizational behavior* (Vol. 11, pp. 43–103). Greenwich, CT: JAI Press.

Vroom, V. H. (1964). *Work and motivation.* New York: John Wiley & Sons.

Wagenheim, G. D., & Reurink, J. H. (1991). Customer service in public administration. *Public Administration Review, 51,* 263–270.

Wahba, M. A., & Bridwell, L. G. (1976). Maslow reconsidered: A review of research on the need hierarchy theory. *Organizational Behavior and Human Performance, 151,* 212–240.

Walton, M. (1986). *The Deming management method.* New York: Putnam.

Watson, D., & Tellegen, A. (1985). Toward a consensual structure of mood. *Psychological Bulletin, 98,* 219–235.

Weingart, L. R. (1992). Impact of group goals, task component complexity, effort, and planning on group performance. *Journal of Applied Psychology, 77,* 682–693.

Weingart, L. R., & Weldon, E. (1991). Processes that mediate the relationship between a group goal and group member performance. *Human Performance, 4,* 33–54.

Weldon, E., & Gargano, G. M. (1988). Cognitive loafing: The effects of accountability and shared responsibility on cognitive effort. *Personality and Social Psychology Bulletin, 14,* 159–171.

Weldon, E., Jehn, K., & Pradhan, P. (1991). Processes that mediate the relationship between a group goal and improved group performance. *Journal of Personality and Social Psychology, 61,* 555–569.

Wood, R., & Bandura, A. (1989). Social cognitive theory of organizational management. *Academy of Management Review, 14,* 361–384.

Woodworth, R. S. (1918). *Dynamic psychology.* New York: Columbia University Press.

7

Leadership, Power, and Politics

CHAPTER OVERVIEW

Effective leaders are a renewable resource, and the conditions that yield good leaders have been of interest to a wide variety of organizations for thousands of years. Studies of leadership have focused on three fundamental features that are critical to leadership: traits or personal characteristics, behaviors, and situations that are featured in three major models of leadership. In this chapter, we first present definitions of leadership and then examine this construct in relation to power, politics, and the relationship between leaders and managers. We believe that leadership is a relational mix, and can be learned by almost anyone anywhere.

We discuss recent models and practices of charismatic and transformational leadership, especially as they may function in global and diverse organizations. Thereafter, we explore sources of power, power and organizational politics, influence tactics, and the value of empowering members of an organization by emphasizing individual and collective efficacies.

We conclude by examining leadership issues that all organizations around the world are facing: differences and similarities between female and male leaders, leadership in different cultures, leading and managing with diverse leaders and a diverse workforce, and dysfunctional leadership. Effective leadership requires competence, emotional maturity, and a commitment to learn continuously throughout life.

LEARNING OBJECTIVES

When you finish studying this chapter, you will be prepared to

- define leadership as a relational process and a mix of forces of traits, behaviors, and situations
- differentiate between leaders and managers
- describe the trait, behavior, and situational or contingency models of leadership and discuss clearly empirical findings associated with each model
- define and distinguish between charismatic and transformational leaders and learn the strategies used by each type of leader
- define and identify sources of power in organizations
- learn the organizational political strategies of coalition building, control over important decision processes, and co-optation
- define Machiavellianism and a variety of influence tactics for effective leadership in dynamic environments
- define empowerment and identify the role of individual and collective efficacies for empowering followers
- understand the issues, dynamics, and strategies arising from issues of leadership and gender, cross-cultural leadership, leadership of a diverse workforce, and the symptoms of dysfunctional leadership.

*It will be said of the best leader when gone—
we did it ourselves.*

—Chinese proverb

THE MIX

There can be no leader without followers and no followers without a leader, which makes leadership a relational process. For example, when you encounter heavy turbulence at 30,000 feet in the air, the pilot is considered the leader by the passengers, but when all the passengers are safely at the terminal gate and the airplane is empty, the pilot, although still a pilot, is no longer the leader. In addition, since leaders and followers influence each other, leadership is a reciprocal or bidirectional influence process. Leadership is not the result of some kind of secret talent, personal quality, or knowledge that you either have or do not have; rather, it appears to arise from a mix of dispositional features (traits), behaviors, and contextual settings. In this chapter, we examine the leadership mix to clarify the capacities of leaders and followers in organizations.

We invite you to reflect for a moment on what it takes to be a leader in general and especially in your organization. Did you envision a person who

- has some special traits, skills, or tactics
- acts in a special way
- quickly reads situations and then takes action
- speaks clearly to both the head (ideas) and heart (emotions)
- knows how to get and use power
- considers people as pawns to be moved to achieve specific goals or satisfactions
- is driven by endless activities and agendas
- has some other features not listed?

Obviously, the list can get lengthy because leadership is expressed and perceived in many different ways and leaders usually influence multiple outcomes. We believe that the capacity to influence, shape, and capture the thoughts, actions, and emotions of others and organizations involves the mix of leadership, power, and politics. Accordingly, if you want to advance your personal and selected organizational goals and your career, derive satisfaction from influencing and directing others, and give something of value to others, then you will need to know how to exercise leadership and power and behave as an organizational politician.

Leaders must always be aware of and responsive to their followers. Once a leader turns away consistently from what he or she judges may be best for her or his followers and organization then the leader has to resign. Leadership is about stewardship—the cultivation and enhancement of people, ideas, technology, the organization, and the environment, all of which the leader is a part of as well. We turn now to definitions of leadership, power, and politics—the ingredients of the mix.

Leadership

In general, a leader defines and communicates an organizational situation to her or his many followers and directs and maintains collective activity. Inasmuch as the leader cannot do everything alone, he or she must share power and engage followers' skills by empowering the followers to pursue appropriate goals to address the situation confronting the organization. As Pfeffer (1977) and Stewart (1982) pointed out, leadership is a system of relationships with constraints as well as opportunities.

There are literally hundreds of definitions of leadership that focus on one or a combination of the following definitional elements: individual traits, the leader's behavior, interactional patterns, role-making processes, followers' perceptions, influence over followers, influence on group goals, and influence to shape and change the organizational culture (Bass, 1990; Hogan, Curphy, & Hogan, 1994; Pfeffer, 1977; Stogdill, 1974). The definition of leadership serves to direct an investigation and the type of model of leadership that is generated from the findings. Thus, for example, Graen (1976, 1990) considered leadership a role-making process involving leader-member exchanges (LMX). Thus, effective leaders develop mature leadership relationships with their followers (high LMX), reflected by leaders and members experiencing reciprocal influence, mutual trust, respect, and internalization of shared goals (Duchon, Green, & Taber, 1986; Zalesney & Graen, 1986). Ineffective leaders (low LMX) have not established mature relationships with their followers, reflected by a primarily downward influence from leaders to followers, contractual and formalized exchanges, limiting role-defined relationships, and loosely coupled goals (Graen, 1976).

Some other definitions of leadership include

- "interpersonal influence, exercised in a situation, and directed through the communication process, toward the attainment of a specific goal or goals" (Tannenbaum, Weschler, & Massarik, 1961, p. 24)

- "the influential increment over and above mechanical compliance with the routine directives of the organization" (Katz & Kahn, 1978, p. 528)

- "the process of influencing the activities of an organized group toward goal achievement" (Rauch & Behling, 1984, p. 46)

- "a process of giving purpose (meaningful direction) to collective effort, and causing willing effort to be expended to achieve purpose" (Jacobs & Jaques, 1990, p. 281).

Our definitional list of leadership could go on almost endlessly, so we end with a definition of leadership that is broad, includes many of the definitional elements just mentioned, and captures the essence of leadership:

> a process that includes influencing the task objectives and strategies of a group or organization, influencing people in the organization to implement the strategies and achieve the objectives, influencing group maintenance and identification and influencing the culture of the organization. (Yukl & Van Fleet, 1992, p. 149)

Power

In most cases, one cannot lead unless one has power, which makes power a necessary but not sufficient condition for leadership. All organizational members are concerned with power and use it in the pursuit of a variety of personal and organizational goals (Gioia & Sims, 1983). Many times, those with the most power in an organization exercise their power in subtle and even shielded ways that preclude direct observation, let alone systematic study (Kipnis, 1976). We refer to the powerful few who can influence many persons in an organization yet who are almost hidden from view in the penumbra or partial shadow of power.

In general, power is a relational construct between parties that is the perceived control that an individual actor or actress or organizational unit has over others (Bacharach & Lawler, 1980; Hollander & Offermann, 1990; Pfeffer, 1981; Zaleznik & Kets de Vries, 1975). Yukl (1994, p. 195) defined power "as an agent's potential influence over the attitudes and behavior of one or more designated target persons." The influence is not only over people but over decisions, events, and resources. Accordingly, the consequences of exercised power can be highly focused or dispersed within an organization, and, at times, an agent must decide when and when not to exercise power, depending upon the organizational situation (the calculus of power). Later in this chapter, we examine the different types of power, how leaders acquire and lose power, and influence tactics that leaders and followers use when they interact with each other.

Politics

Our focus here is on organizational politics, which Pfeffer (1981, p. 7) defined as "those activities taken within organizations to acquire, develop, and use power and other resources to obtain one's preferred outcomes in a situation in which there is uncertainty or dissensus about choices." According to Pfeffer (1981, 1992a, 1992b), organizational politics is the use of power to get things done in an organization. There are many sources of power arising from, for example, one's talents and skills; position in the organization; access and ability to deploy scarce yet unencumbered resources (slack resources), such as money, physical space, or equipment; access to coveted organizational information; and knowledge of influence tactics like how to develop coalitions of influential persons to sway a critical decision.

As Pfeffer (1981) noted, power is a force or set of forces at rest, whereas politics is the use of power to get things done. In our view, power in the pursuit of personal ambitions and goals with little, if any, regard for or benefit to other organizational members or the organization will inevitably lead to isolation, not leadership. On the other hand, power in the pursuit of primarily organizational goals, developed openly, and arising from some form of agreement with and potential benefits to organizational members or the organization inevitably leads to or reflects leadership.

Power, the potential capacity to influence events, others, or outcomes, and politics, the use of power, are neither intrinsically good nor evil. Both organizational leaders and ambitious opportunists deploy power by means of political tactics, while ignorance of organizational power and politics puts organizational members at risk

for dysfunctional organizational activities, ineffective leadership, or both. In fact, Bennis and Nanus (1985) suggested that too few organizational members exercise power and that power is conspicuous by its absence, which give rise to powerlessness in the face of crises and complexities in organizations. They stated that "power is at once the most necessary and the most distrusted element exigent to human progress . . . the capacity to translate intention into reality and sustain it" (Bennis & Nanus, 1985, pp. 15–17).

Similarly, Henry Kissinger, reflecting on his experiential education in politics, observed that he, like most academics, had believed that decision making was largely an intellectual process. But he learned quickly, as a consultant to U.S. presidents, that this perspective "is as dangerously immature as it is widely held" (Kissinger, 1979, p. 39). Good politicians, like good leaders, do not like surprises, especially big surprises, and are pleasantly surprised when there are no surprises. Later, we examine strategies for diagnosing power relationships in an organization so as to enhance political strategies that are essential to organizational leadership.

Leaders and Managers

The relationship between leaders and managers has been the subject of extensive consideration (Kotter, 1982; Luthans, Rosenkrantz, & Hennessey, 1985; Mintzberg, 1973; Zaleznik, 1992). Mintzberg identified 10 management roles that are found in all managerial jobs—figurehead, leader, liaison, monitor, disseminator, spokesperson, entrepreneur, disturbance handler, resource allocator, and negotiator—although not all these roles have been verified by other investigators (Morse & Wagner, 1978). In an insightful article, Pfeffer (1977) raised some of the difficulties of clearly defining leadership and its relationship to organizational performances and of distinguishing leadership from other socially constructed roles, such as manager. He suggested that leadership is concerned with the management of a set of myths that reinforce and legitimate socially constructed meanings. One such myth is the belief that a leader causes organizational performances to occur, rather than that a leader anticipates and accurately reads situational forces that influence organizational performances, such as changing economic cycles or the demand for products. In general, managers have limited authority or power over a limited number of persons, are focused on dealing with the present ("what is happening now"), and tend to fix, rather than explore, organizational problems and situations.

The issue of the relationship between leaders and managers is important, in part, because some have suggested that leadership is primarily at the upper levels of an organization and that influence by leaders yields enthusiastic commitment by followers, in contrast to the alleged indifferent compliance or reluctant obedience arising from managerial influence. Likewise, as Yukl and Van Fleet (1992) pointed out, a person can be a leader without being a manager and a person can be a manager without leading, as in the case of a "manager" of financial accounts who has no followers.

Bennis and Nanus (1985, p. 21) proposed that "managers are people who do things right and leaders are people who do the right thing." Zaleznik (1992) observed that managers are concerned about how things get done, while leaders focus on what organizational and other related events mean to members. In essence, leaders seem to influence members' commitment or cognitive and affective experiences and managers carry out the responsibilities of their positions and exercise authority that is confined to their group or unit (Yukl & Van Fleet, 1992). We believe there is overlap between the functions of leaders and managers and that the former are primarily concerned with discovering new opportunities, while the latter concentrate on controlling current opportunities and getting things done. We now consider briefly three models of leadership: the *traits*, *behaviors*, and *situations* models.

MODELS OF LEADERSHIP

Just as there are many definitions of leadership, there are numerous models of leadership. It is important to realize that there is some overlap among the different models of leadership, reflecting the complex pattern of attributes, behaviors, and situations out of which leadership arises. The trait model focuses on what a person brings to leadership activities, the behavioral model examines the actions or behaviors of a leader, and the situational model identifies the contextual forces that shape and determine leadership.

Traits

The trait, or dispositional, model of leadership rests on the premise that leaders have some unique attributes as a result of inherited capacities, learning experiences, or a combination of the two. Accordingly, if you have all the right stuff, then you are a leader, and organizations seek persons with the right stuff. Basically, the search for personal attributes that are essential for leadership has focused on individual traits, motives, and skills. Although studies of leadership traits have been dismissed as too simplistic (Mann, 1959; Stogdil, 1948; 1974), recently they have found that a certain pattern or profile of traits, motives, and skills increases the likelihood that leadership will be effective, especially when these attributes are balanced or deployed in moderation.

In general, look for the person with the following attributes if you are looking for a leader:

Individual traits. The trait profile includes a high energy level, tolerance of stress, integrity, emotional maturity, and self-confidence, all of which appear to be related to effective leadership and managerial activities (Bass, 1990; Kirkpatrick & Locke, 1991; Yukl, 1994). A leader with integrity is honest, ethical, and trustworthy, while one who is emotionally mature knows and respects herself or himself and others, maintains a sense of balance between personal and organizational goals, and is calm in turbulent contexts or situations.

Motives. The motivational pattern for an effective leader includes a strong social, rather than personal, power orientation (seeking power to address the concerns of others, not personal goals), relatively strong motivation to achieve (to complete programs and projects successfully), and a relatively modest need for affiliation (McClelland & Boyatzis, 1982; McClelland & Burnham, 1976; Yukl & Van Fleet, 1992).

Skills. The basic taxonomy of skills for effective leaders encompasses technical, conceptual, and interpersonal skills (Yukl, 1994; Yukl & Van Fleet, 1992). Technical skills include knowledge about processes and methods of performing specific activities (e.g., finance); conceptual skills involve the abilities to develop ideas, reason, and interpret meaningfully ambiguous events or data; and interpersonal skills focus on understanding interpersonal and group processes, sensitivity to ideas and feeling of others, and articulateness. In general, the higher the level of authority, the greater the need for conceptual skills in that leaders must deal with complex problems that involve multiple units or functional areas of an organization (Boyatzis, 1982; Jacobs & Jaques, 1987).

Assessment centers use standardized procedures (such as interviews, written personality and aptitude tests, and situational exercises like in-basket and leaderless group discussions) to evaluate a person's leadership potential over a two- or three-day period. For the in-basket exercise, the candidate must respond in writing to a set of hypothetical problems represented by memos, reports, charts, and printouts found on the desk of a typical manager or leader. With the leaderless group exercise, the candidate is inserted into a simulated group and must deal with a hypothetical decision scenario or conflict issue. In a 20-year follow-up of candidates at an assessment center, Howard and Bray (1988) found that personal attributes, such as the desire for advancement, need for power, and interpersonal and cognitive skills, were good predictors of successful leadership. Likewise, investigations by the Center for Creative Leadership (Lombardo & McCauley, 1988; McCall & Lombardo, 1983) of managers who derailed (were not promoted to top-level executive positions) and successful managers who were promoted found that derailed managers were less able to handle pressure, were defensive about their failures, and had marginal interpersonal skills and narrow technical and cognitive skills; in contrast, successful leaders were stronger in all of these areas and had high integrity.

The foregoing pattern of traits, motives, and skills provides a fairly valid snapshot of the dispositional features that promote but do not guarantee successful leadership. Zaccaro, Foti, and Kenny (1991) reported that social perceptiveness (the capacity to recognize the requirements of different groups) and behavioral flexibility (the ability to respond appropriately to a particular situation) are important personal attributes for effective leadership. Thus, multiple traits, rather than a single trait or domain of traits, best describe effective leaders, and the balancing of the expression of these traits, coupled with the capacity to read people and situations, can serve to promote effective leadership.

Behaviors

The focus of behavioral models of leadership is on what the leader or manager *does* with whatever personal traits, skills, or motivational capacities he or she has been endowed with or acquired as a result of organizational experience and education. The primary concern of behavioral models is actions and the impact of those actions on effectiveness. In general, behavioral models have included descriptions of managerial activities, taxonomies of leadership behavior, and the nature of the relationship between behaviors and indices of effective leadership.

Leaders operate in dynamic and turbulent environments in which conflicts, people, productivity issues, outcome reports, events, and unanticipated developments converge on them daily if not hourly. Accordingly, they are continuously involved in work that is hectic, varied, fragmented, reactive, and disorderly (Kanter, 1983). Leaders must make decisions on the basis of incomplete and ambiguous information and must rely heavily on others to implement their decisions. In many instances, decision-making processes are highly political, rather than rational, and little time is devoted to planning and proactive or anticipatory behaviors (Cohen & March, 1986; Schweiger, Anderson, & Locke, 1985; Simon 1987). Decisions by leaders almost inevitably affect a variety of persons and units in an organization, and given this high dispersion of decisions, leaders must develop coalitions of support so their decisions can be implemented (Gioffre, Lawson, & Gordon, 1992). Thus, the descriptive behavioral profile of a leader includes maintaining a relentless pace; making multiple, minimally reflective decisions; building coalitions and networks; and searching for clarity and meaning in ambiguous situations.

The list of effective leadership behaviors, like the list of leadership traits, can be long, detailed, and complex and thus of limited applied value. Accordingly, beginning in the 1950s, the Ohio State University (OSU) leadership studies developed a more tightly focused taxonomy of leadership behaviors based on the Leadership Behavior Description Questionnaire (LBDQ), which consisted of 150 items whittled down from an initial list of 1,800 examples of leadership behavior (Fleishman, 1953; Halpin & Winer, 1957). From a factor analysis of the LBDQ responses, reflecting how subordinates perceived their managers' behaviors, came two behavioral categories: consideration and initiating-structure behaviors. In general, *consideration (or people-oriented) behaviors* reflect the extent to which a leader behaves in a warm and supportive manner, exhibits concern for subordinates, and looks out for the well-being of the members of her or his group or unit. *Initiating-structure (or task-oriented) behaviors* reflect the degree to which a leader defines a task and the roles of a task, assigns subordinates to different task roles, monitors subordinates' performance, and provides feedback on task-related performances. The two-factor taxonomy of the LBDQ represented a solid point of departure for identifying effective leadership behaviors. However, the behavioral categories are too broadly defined to allow for a clear understanding of how leaders behave or need to behave in various situations that confront them. Accordingly, a search for a more finely grained set of leadership behavior categories was undertaken, beginning with Stogdill's (1974) revision of the OSU questionnaire—the LBDQ-XII, which includes 12 categories of leadership behaviors, two of which are consideration and initiating structure.

Another major research project to identify leadership behaviors was conducted at the University of Michigan at about the same time as the OSU studies. Likert (1961, 1967) summarized the results of this project, which found three categories of effective leadership behaviors:

Task-oriented behaviors. Effective leaders did not do the same kind of work as their subordinates but focused on planning and coordinating activities.

Relationship-oriented behaviors. Effective leaders were considerate, supportive, and appreciative of the efforts and accomplishments of their subordinates. Two other important behaviors were coaching and mentoring.

Participative-leadership behaviors. Effective leaders used group meetings to engage subordinates' participation in decision making, promote communication, and resolve conflicts.

The Survey of Organizations is a questionnaire that assesses the prevalence of these leadership behaviors, as well as peer leadership behaviors, in a given organization (Taylor & Bowers, 1972).

Table 7–1 presents a more refined taxonomy of most of the leadership behaviors that are measured by the Managerial Practices Survey (Yukl,

1994). In general, this taxonomy was derived from the earlier leadership behavior studies begun in the 1950s and involves a wide variety of laboratory and field-based data. The categories are sufficiently generic to encompass the behaviors of a wide variety of managers yet specific enough to relate to specific situations and the demands of managerial tasks (Yukl, 1994).

The behavioral models, like the trait models, focus on the acquired behaviors and personal attributes that the person brings to the situation, and provide a framework for identifying and cultivating leaders in organizations. Likewise, both models recognize the importance of the situa-

---

Table 7–1. Taxonomy of Leadership Behaviors

Planning and Organizing: Determining long-term objectives and strategies, allocating resources according to priorities, and determining how to improve coordination, productivity, and the effectiveness of the organization or unit.

Problem Solving: Identifying work-related problems, analyzing problems in a timely but systematic manner to find solutions, and acting decisively to implement solutions.

Clarifying Roles and Objectives: Assigning tasks and communicating a clear understanding of job responsibilities, deadlines, and performance expectations.

Informing: Disseminating relevant information about decisions, plans, and activities to people who need it to do their work.

Motivating and Inspiring: Using influence that appeals to emotion or logic to generate enthusiasm for work; commitment to task objectives; and compliance with requests for cooperation, assistance, support, or resources.

Consulting: Checking with people before making changes that affect them and inviting them to participate in decision making.

Delegating: Allowing subordinates to have substantial responsibility and discretion in handling problems and making important decisions.

Supporting: Acting friendly and considerate, being patient and helpful, showing sympathy and support when someone is upset or anxious, and listening to complaints and problems.

Developing and Mentoring: Providing coaching and doing things to facilitate a person's professional development and career advancement.

Managing Conflict and Team Building: Facilitating the constructive resolution of conflict and encouraging cooperation, teamwork, and identification with the work unit.

Networking: Socializing informally, developing contacts with people who are a source of information and support, and maintaining contacts through periodic interaction and attendance at meetings and social events.

Recognizing: Providing praise and recognition for effective performance, significant achievements, and special contributions.

Rewarding: Providing or recommending tangible rewards such as a pay increase or promotion for effective performance, significant achievements, and demonstrated competence.

Leadership in Organizations (3rd ed.), by G. Yukl, © 1994. Adapted by permission of Prentice Hall, Upper Saddle River, NJ.

tion or context that can shape, and in some cases, determine the effectiveness of leadership.

Situations

In situational models of leadership, the focus is on how the organizational situation shapes the leader's thoughts, feelings, and actions or how situational variables moderate the relationship between the leader's attributes and behaviors and her or his effectiveness. The former approach considers situational forces the primary determinant of leadership, while in the latter approach, leadership actions are contingent and moderated by certain factors that may or may not emerge from a given situation (Davis-Blake & Pfeffer, 1989). In either approach, what is important is that the leader must focus her or his energies on interpreting the situation to determine what can be done and how and then to implement an action or get out of the situation.

Fielder (1964, 1967) introduced the first systematic situational or contingency model of leadership with his measure of the least-preferred co-worker (LPC) that arose from his research begun in 1953 at the University of Illinois. A leader completes the LPC instrument by thinking of the person he or she could work least well with and then rates this person on a list of 16 contrasting adjectives displayed across eight-point scales for each pair of adjectives (such as pleasant-unpleasant and efficient-inefficient). These ratings yield two global scores for two types of leadership styles. A respondent who scores high on the LPC instrument (describes the least-preferred co-worker in relatively positive terms) has a relationship-oriented leadership style, whereas one who scores low on the LPC score has a task-oriented leadership style. Fielder (1967) suggested that the effectiveness of both leadership styles, which he considered fixed or immutable dispositional traits, is contingent on or moderated by three situational variables that he identified as leader-member relations (for instance, the degree of confidence or trust that subordinates have in their leader), task structure, and position power (control over discretionary resources, such as money or space). Thus, in selecting leaders, it is important, according to Fielder's model, to match a person's leadership style with the situations; for example, it would be preferable to assign a task-oriented leader, rather than a relationship-oriented leader, to a group or situation in which the leader is respected, the task is highly structured, and position power is high. The empirical support for Fielder's model has been mixed, so the model was revised by Fielder and Garcia (1987); the revised model is discussed briefly later in this chapter as the cognitive resources theory. An important point here is that Fielder's original model was the first to point out that situational or contextual variables are critical determinants of effective leadership.

On the basis of extensive observations and interviews with leaders, Stewart (1982) found that their interactive patterns with subordinates, colleagues, and persons outside the organization was determined mainly by whether their task demands (what they had to do in a given time frame) were proactive or reactive, repetitive or variable, fragmented or sustained, and hurried or unhurried. Basically, leadership was constructed from situational demands, constraints, and choices. The *multiple influence model* emphasizes that both macro- and microlevel situational variables, such as the global-national economies and task interdependence-complexity, respectively, shape leaders' actions (Hunt & Osborn, 1982).

The issue of what a leader does with information gleaned from a situation was addressed, in part, by Green and Mitchell (1979), who described a two-stage process involving the leader's attribution of causality and response to the poor performance of subordinates or colleagues. In the first stage, the manager attempts to determine if the poor performance arises from internal (such as lack of effort) or external (such as inadequate resources and poor timing) barriers. If the manager makes an internal attribution of insufficient effort, then she or he will monitor the person or group more closely, find new incentives, or issue a warning of potential sanctions. On the other hand, if the manager makes an external attribution, he or she is likely to provide more resources or better information; remove obstacles; or change the assignment or task, if possible.

There is a wide variety of situational models of leadership, all of which focus on explaining how aspects of the situation moderate the relationship between leaders' traits, behaviors, or both and the outcomes arising from a particular situation. We now examine a representative sample of these remaining theories.

According to the *path-goal model* of leadership (House, 1977; House & Mitchell, 1974), the primary job of the leader is to enhance employees' satisfaction with their jobs and to increase employees' productivity. To achieve these objectives, the leader must identify two critical situational variables—employee needs and task demands—and then choose one of the following four possible categories of leadership. The four categories are supportive (similar to the OSU consideration style), directive (similar to the OSU initiating-structure style), participative (shared decision making), or achievement-oriented (setting high goals and expressing confidence that employees can achieve them). Thus, employees with strong needs for encouragement and affiliation would be most responsive to a supportive leadership style, whereas a mix of participative and achievement-oriented leadership would be most appropriate for employees with strong needs for autonomy and responsibility. Also, leaders must assess the tasks or job demands confronting their employees and would be most effective as leaders if they adopt a supportive style when the task is tedious and routine, such as collecting tolls or tickets, and a directive style when the job is unstructured, complex, and nonroutine, at least until the employees gain appropriate experiences with their job-related activities. Obviously, no one leadership style fits the needs of all employees and the job characteristics of all situations, so it is likely that some mix or blend of the four styles, with perhaps one or two of the most prominent, would be the most appropriate. Although all the research findings are not positive (see Indvik, 1986), many of them have confirmed that employees who perform highly routine or tedious tasks prefer leaders who use a supportive leadership style, whereas employees who do unstructured tasks prefer and are more productive with leaders who adopt a more directive leadership style (Keller, 1989; Yukl, 1989).

The *situational leadership model* (SLM) (Hersey & Blanchard, 1969, 1988), depicted in Figure 7–1, grew out of the earlier leadership studies conducted at OSU and the University of Michigan, as did Reddin's (1967) theory of the three-dimensional management style. Hersey and Blanchard (1988) identified four leadership styles—*telling*, *selling*, *participating*, and *delegating*—each of which can be chosen by a leader, contingent on the leader's judgment of the readiness of the subordinates to handle the specific task facing the group or organization. Each of these four leadership styles is basically a mix of task behaviors (similar to the OSU initiating-structure style) or relationship behaviors (similar to the OSU consideration style). Thus, in Figure 7–1, if the followers' readiness is low, as is often the case with new employees, then the telling leadership style, which is relatively high on task behaviors and low on relationship behaviors would be most appropriate. It is possible to be both task oriented and supportive at the same time. The SLM model has been extremely popular in leader training programs, rather than personnel selection programs, partly because it makes plain what a leader *does*, rather than what her or his personal characteristics need to be. In general, the SLM model is much more widely used by organizations than it is supported by empirical research (Blank, Weitzel, & Green, 1990; Vecchio, 1987).

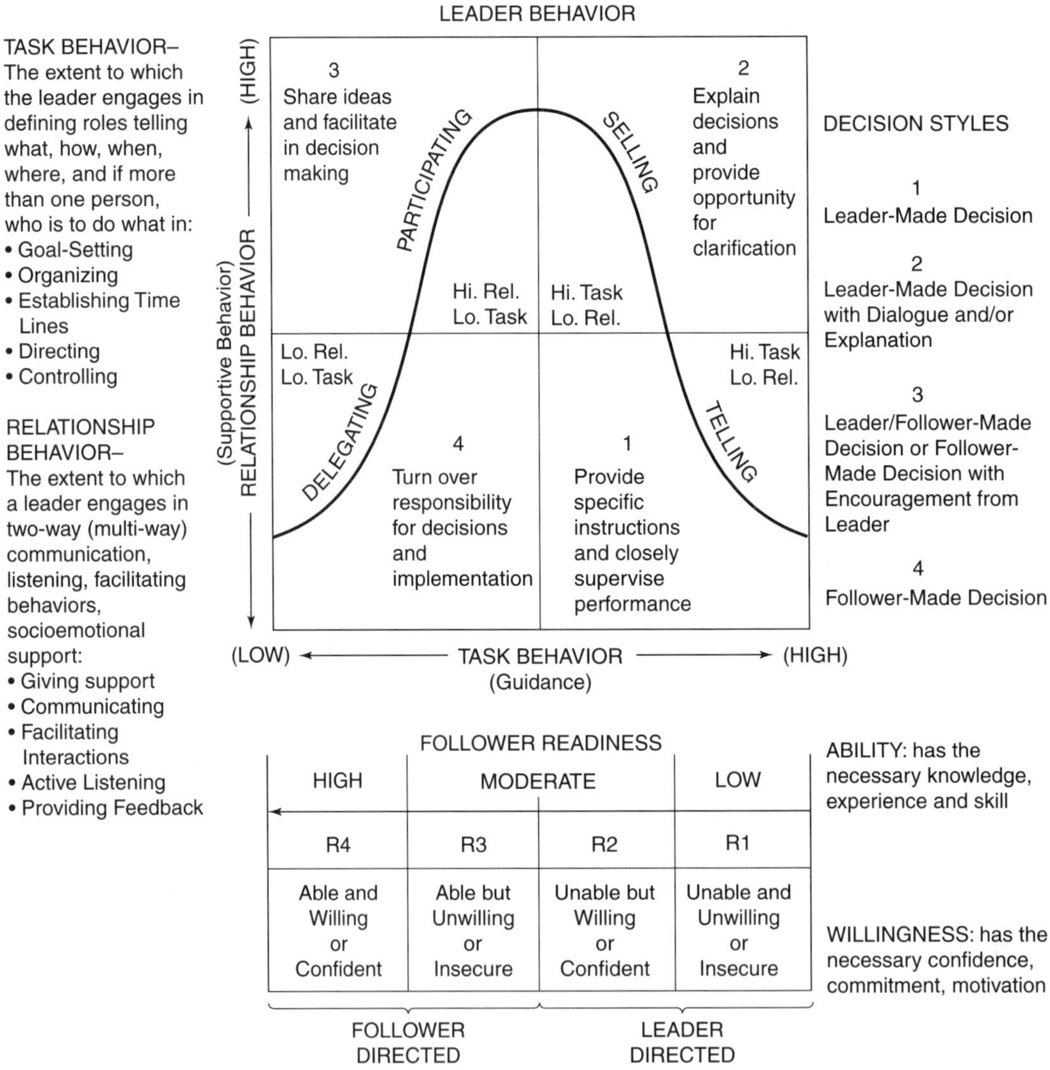

LEADER BEHAVIOR

TASK BEHAVIOR–
The extent to which
the leader engages in
defining roles telling
what, how, when,
where, and if more
than one person,
who is to do what in:
• Goal-Setting
• Organizing
• Establishing Time
  Lines
• Directing
• Controlling

RELATIONSHIP
BEHAVIOR–
The extent to which
a leader engages in
two-way (multi-way)
communication,
listening, facilitating
behaviors,
socioemotional
support:
• Giving support
• Communicating
• Facilitating
  Interactions
• Active Listening
• Providing Feedback

(HIGH)
(Supportive Behavior)
RELATIONSHIP BEHAVIOR

3
Share ideas
and facilitate
in decision
making

PARTICIPATING

2
Explain
decisions
and
provide
opportunity
for
clarification

SELLING

Hi. Rel.
Lo. Task

Hi. Task
Lo. Rel.

Lo. Rel.
Lo. Task

Hi. Task
Lo. Rel.

DELEGATING

TELLING

4
Turn over
responsibility
for decisions
and
implementation

1
Provide
specific
instructions
and closely
supervise
performance

(LOW) ◄─── TASK BEHAVIOR ───► (HIGH)
(Guidance)

DECISION STYLES

1
Leader-Made Decision

2
Leader-Made Decision
with Dialogue and/or
Explanation

3
Leader/Follower-Made
Decision or Follower-
Made Decision with
Encouragement from
Leader

4
Follower-Made Decision

FOLLOWER READINESS

HIGH	MODERATE		LOW
R4	R3	R2	R1
Able and Willing or Confident	Able but Unwilling or Insecure	Unable but Willing or Confident	Unable and Unwilling or Insecure

ABILITY: has the
necessary knowledge,
experience and skill

WILLINGNESS: has the
necessary confidence,
commitment, motivation

FOLLOWER
DIRECTED

LEADER
DIRECTED

When a Leader Behavior is used appropriately with its corresponding level of readiness, it is
termed a High Probability Match. The following are descriptors that can be useful when using
Situational Leadership for specific applications:

S1	S2	S3	S4
Telling	Selling	Participating	Delegating
Guiding	Explaining	Encouraging	Observing
Directing	Clarifying	Collaborating	Monitoring
Establishing	Persuading	Committing	Fulfilling

Figure 7–1 Situational Leadership Model.
Situational Leadership® is a registered trademark of the Center for Leadership Studies, Escondido, CA. All rights reserved. Reprinted with permission.

160

The *Vroom-Jago normative-decision* model of leadership (Vroom & Jago, 1988; Vroom & Yetton, 1973) stresses that decision making is the critical leadership activity with groups, identifies seven key situational variables that influence a leader's decision-making style, and identifies three decision-making or leadership styles: *autocratic (A)*, *consultative (C)*, and *group decision making (G)*. Essentially, leadership is primarily decision making and a leader's effectiveness is high when both the quality and the acceptance of the decision by parties who are influenced or involved in the decision are high, and the decision is made in a timely fashion and is of benefit to the further development of employees. Table 7–2 presents a summary of the major decision-making styles for leading a group decision: making the decision alone, requesting information from the group and then making the decision, consulting one to one with relevant parties to the decision, and group decision making on the basis of a consensus.

The Vroom-Jago normative-decision model considers decision-making processes to be discrete singular organizational events, whereas many major organizational decisions involve reciprocal influence processes with a number of parties interacting repeatedly for extended periods. The model is cumbersome and, therefore, difficult to apply readily in fast-paced organizational settings. However, on the basis of six studies involving 1,545 decisions, Vroom and Jago (1988) reported that when a leader's behavior conformed to the normative model, 62% of the reported decisions were successful, but when the leader's behavior did not, only 37% of the reported decisions were successful.

The final situational model of leadership considered here is the cognitive resources theory (CRT) (Fielder, 1986; Fielder & Garcia, 1987), which focuses on (1) the cognitive resources of the leader (intelligence and experience, (2) the directive leadership style, and (3) the two situational variables—interpersonal stress and the nature of the group's task. Basically, when subordinates require guidance or direction to perform effectively and perceived stress is low, superior intelligence yields good plans and decisions; however, high perceived stress prevents intelligent leaders from making good decisions because of the effects of emotional interference and turbulence on information gathering, processing, and decision making. Last, in high-stress situations, experience is positively related to high-quality decisions in that leaders with extensive experience can rely on their experience, but less experienced leaders cannot; in low-stress situations, what counts is intelli-

Table 7–2. Leadership Styles for Group Decision Making

AI	Solve the problem or make the decision yourself using available information.
AII	Obtain any necessary information from employees, then decide on the solution to the problem yourself.
CI	Share the problem with relevant team members individually, getting their ideas and suggestions without bringing them together as a group. Then make the decision.
GII	Share the problem with your subordinates as a group. Together, you generate and evaluate alternatives and attempt to reach a consensus on a solution. You do not try to influence the group to adopt "your" solution, and you are willing to accept and implement any solution that has the support of the entire group.

The New Leadership: Managing Participation in Organizations, by V. H. Vroom and A. G. Jago, Eds., © 1988. Adapted by permission of Prentice Hall, Upper Saddle River, NJ.

gence, rather than experience. The CRT model is important, given the emphasis that organizations place on intelligence and experience in recruiting and selecting persons for key leadership positions, and the research findings to date have generally, but not conclusively, supported this model (Murphy, Blyth, & Fielder, 1992; Vecchio, 1990).

In general, situational models of leadership are fairly complex and have received moderate support from empirical studies. However, given the hectic pace of managerial work and leaders' relative lack of control over the flow of work, some of the detailed prescriptions of these models are difficult to apply (Yukl, 1994). Nevertheless, the situational models are important because they emphasize the need to interpret situations and to bring specific traits to the situation to be an effective leader.

CHARISMATIC LEADERSHIP

Charisma, a Greek word meaning special or divine gift, was, until the early 1980s considered descriptive only of some religious or political leaders (Conger & Kanungo, 1987). Such charismatic leaders usually presented a radical vision of a new world so as to lead followers out of a crisis, were perceived by followers as having extraordinary talents, were trusted, and seldom found a voice in business organizations around the world.

However, as global competition has stiffened, the global economy continues to wobble, and levels of trust in organizations and various nations seesaw, charismatic leadership has become of great interest and value to business firms and governments around the world. Charisma is a process by which leaders influence followers by arousing strong emotions in them and causing them to identify with the leaders. Charismatic leaders move followers emotionally; they do not overwhelm followers with detailed information.

The Gifts of Charisma

According to House (1977), charismatic leaders in organizations have certain traits and exhibit certain behaviors, and their impact is moderated by certain situational forces. Charismatic leaders have a strong need for power, high self-confidence, and strong beliefs. In addition, they

1. articulate a compelling vision in which organizational goals are expressed in ideological, not functional, language (for example, "We can provide a safe and secure world for people by challenging ourselves continuously to be better in every way in what we do," rather than "We will sell 1 million seatbelts over the next two years")

2. communicate high yet realistic expectations of their followers (see Chapter 6, the Pygmalion effect)

3. model or set examples by their own behaviors for followers to imitate

4. express confidence in the followers' capacities to achieve the challenging goals articulated in the vision for the organization.

Charismatic leadership is likely to be most effective when there is a profound sense of organizational discouragement or retreat from proactive organizational actions and when the tasks of the group or unit are fairly complex and non-routine.

The Consequence of Charisma

The findings of a variety of studies of charismatic leadership have indicated that the followers experienced greater self-confidence and found their work meaningful (Smith, 1982). In addition, when the leader used the three charismatic behaviors—articulating a vision, modeling desirable behavior, and communicating high performance expectations—the followers were more trusting of the leader, loyal, and exhibited more organizational spontaneity (Podsakoff, MacKenzie, Morrman, & Fetter, 1990). Kirkpatrick and Locke's (1996) laboratory study of charismatic leadership reported that articulation of a high-quality vision significantly influenced followers' attitudes, such as trust and inspiration of the leader, while implementation of the vision by task cues, such as providing individualized support and recognizing accomplishments, influenced the quality and quantity of followers' performances. Thus, if you wish to pursue a course of charismatic leadership, develop a bold yet believable vision; communicate confidence in yourself and others to achieve goals that you present inspirationally, rather than functionally; model desired behaviors; and keep a careful eye on the organizational context and members' reactions.

Conger and Kanungo (1987) and Conger (1989) stated that charismatic leadership arises primarily from the attributions of followers who perceive leaders as charismatic when the leader:

- advocates a vision that is highly discrepant with the status quo but still believable

- implements innovative actions to achieve goals that are embedded in the vision

- harnesses the followers' trust by taking personal risks to advance the vision, such as being consistent or risking rejection by a particular constituency

- appears confident and enthusiastic about the vision but not overbearing

- uses personal power and persuasive appeals, rather than authority and participative decision making

Conger (1989) asserted that personal identification is the primary mechanism by which charismatic leadership is translated into followers' commitment and extraordinary attachment and productivity because the followers internalize the beliefs and values of the leader to be-

come more like the leader and bolster their own self-esteem. Also, charismatic leaders are most likely to emerge when there is an organizational crisis or followers are disenchanted with the current organizational state of affairs. Charismatic leaders lift members above the plateau of daily routines and endless hassles by presenting a bold vision and making plain that they believe in the followers' ability to deal with the problems before the organization. Shamir, House, and Arthur (1993) presented a revised model of House's (1977) charismatic leadership theory that stresses the important role of motivation and self-efficacy in increasing effective charismatic leadership.

TRANSFORMATIONAL LEADERSHIP

Unlike charismatic leadership, which stresses the role of the individual leader, transformational leadership emphasizes the process of building and strengthening followers' commitment to organizational goals and empowering them to achieve those goals. Charisma is a necessary but not sufficient condition for transformational leadership. In addition, the transformational leader

- focuses on long-term goals (three to five years)

- inspires followers to pursue an articulated vision

- changes or reconfigures organizational systems to advance the vision, rather than working within existing systems

- coaches followers to assume greater responsibility for their own development

- at the appropriate time, develops a leader-succession plan, so the transformational activities continue within the organizational systems, rather than within particular individuals.

In short, transformational leaders act to empower followers and pursue organizational changes that institutionalize new systems, processes, and values.

Bass (1985) and Bass and Avolio (1990) built on the earlier work of Burns (1978), who distinguished between transactional and transformational leadership. The leadership models presented so far in this chapter are examples of transactional leadership in that the leader guides or motivates followers to achieve established goals by clarifying the requirements of roles and tasks. Transactional leaders appeal to the self-interests of followers and promote exchange processes, such as merit-based salary and performance systems or organizational recognition by promotion or ceremonial activities in exchange for high and sustained performances and the attainment of goals. Transformational leaders, on the other hand, inspire followers to transcend their self-interests and focus their efforts on the advancement of the organization, offer a bold yet believable vision, introduce intellectual challenge by examining old problems in new ways, and pay particular attention to the developmental needs of individual members. Although transactional and transformational leadership are different, a leader may use both processes, depending on organizational situations and the requirements of tasks.

What Transformational Leaders Do

Bass (1990, p. 23) suggested that "the real movers and shakers of the world are transformational leaders." According to Bass (1985) and Bass and Avolio (1990), transformational leaders do three things. They make followers aware of the importance of task outcomes, continuously encourage followers to transcend their own personal interests for the sake of the organization or team, and fulfill the higher-order needs or inspirational motivation of followers by communicating an appealing vision and modeling appropriate behaviors. Transformational leaders, like charismatic leaders, influence followers by arousing strong emotions and promoting identification with them. However, unlike charismatic leaders, who may be inclined to keep followers dependent on and loyal to them, they transform followers by serving as coaches, teachers, and mentors to empower followers to enhance their personal competencies and commitment to ideals. In short, charismatic leaders are more likely to provide fish for followers, whereas transformational leaders are more likely to teach followers how to fish and in so doing, promote their independence yet commitment to the ideal of education as a great liberator of organizational members and humankind in general.

The Consequences of Transformational Leadership

Tichy and Devanna (1986) extensively interviewed 12 chief executive officers (CEOs) and their followers in a variety of large organizations and found that transformational leaders used almost all the three primary actions presented earlier. In general, they found that the transformational process began with the organizational member's recognition of the need for change, construction of a new, shared vision for the organization, and incorporation of change into the organizational systems and processes, which inevitably changed the organizational culture (see Chapter 3). They developed the shared visions in a variety of ways. For example, they listened to the aspirational statements and suggestions of a variety of organizational members and, in some instances, invited members of the leadership team to write a brief article about what they would like their organization to be like in three or five years.

Bennis and Nanus (1985) interviewed 60 top-level corporate leaders and 30 leaders of public-sector organizations. They found that transformational leaders develop a vision of a desirable yet reasonable future for their organization and then harness the collective energies of the organizational members in pursuit of the common vision. The vision is usually a clear, appealing, and concise statement of the future goals of the organization, developed by listening to the aspirations of organizational members and stakeholders and then synthesizing the various statements into a unifying vision. The following is an example of a vision statement:

> Each of us is deeply committed to providing world-class products [or services], working together while allowing sufficient space for different perspectives, and embracing opportunities to enjoy and learn from each other.

A vision statement, or "This is what we aspire to do," gives meaning to work, identifies a worthwhile enterprise, and serves as a guideline or internal compass for all members to shape decision making and choose courses of action. It is enriched by constructing or revising the mission statement, or "This is what we do," and then making the statement more specific and operational by a patterned series of tactical plans to operationalize it or indicate "This is how we do it" to realize the vision.

Bennis and Nanus (1985), Senge (1990), and Deming (1986) all stressed that individual and organizational learning (see Chapter 3) are essential for effective leadership and the creation of competitive world-class organizations, whether business or public service organizations.

Leaders are learners, teachers, and stewards whose primary responsibility is to promote individual and organizational learning, with the former a prerequisite for the latter. Thus, if a member learns a new idea, technology, or practice as a result of experimenting or attending a conference, shares it with other members who internalize it, and it is ultimately incorporated into organizational handbooks and policy and procedural manuals, then organizational learning has taken place (see Chapter 3). A leader, in cooperation with followers, generates a creative tension by accurately describing the current state of the organization (see Chapter 3, Table 3–8)

and then develops a compelling vision of what "we can be."

The recent models of charismatic and transformational leadership clearly recognize the importance of both the affective and cognitive capacities of followers and emphasize that the integration of and respect for these capacities will create more competitive and wholesome organizations. A leader as a steward understands and accepts herself or himself as well as others and is grounded in an authentic sense of what is and an aspirational sense of what can be. From our consulting practice, we have observed that the alternative appears to be cynicism, which is a short-term adaptive response to protect oneself from pain and thwarted hope.

POWER AND INFLUENCE

Regardless of what model of leadership you subscribe to or what type of leader you choose to be, power is essential to leadership and the processes of influencing members of an organization. We now examine sources of power, power and politics, influence tactics, and empowerment.

Sources of Power

Power arises from a number of sources, some of which are based in the organizational position the member holds and some of which the individual brings to the organization.

Table 7–3 presents French and Raven's (1959) taxonomy of sources of power, the first three of which are coupled with the organizational position and, in general, are more abundant as one ascends the hierarchy of an organization. *Reward power* and *coercive power* usually involve positive and negative consequences, respectively, associated with an organizational position that an "agent" (the boss or supervisor) can use to influence the behaviors, thoughts, and feelings of a "target" person or

Table 7–3. French and Raven's Taxonomy of Sources of Power

Reward	The target person complies to obtain rewards he or she believes are controlled by the agent.
Coercive power	The target person complies to avoid punishments he or she believes are controlled by the agent.
Legitimate power	The target person complies because he or she believes the agent has the right to make the request and the target person has the obligation to comply.
Expert power	The target person complies because he or she believes the agent has special knowledge about the best way to do something.
Referent power	The target person complies because he or she admires or identifies with the agent and wants to gain the agent's approval.

Leadership in Organizations (3rd ed.), by G. Yukl, © 1994. Adapted by permission of Prentice Hall, Upper Saddle River, NJ.

group in the organization. Examples of reward power include compensation, promotion, larger or private office space, flexible work schedules, or whatever the "target" deems desirable and the "agent" can deliver. The denial of pay increases or promotion, warnings, and exclusion from the flow of information or appropriate decision-making situations (putting the target out of the loop) are examples of coercive power.

Legitimate power (formal authority) represents the institutionalized or contractual power between the agent and target that the target thinks the agent has as a result of her or his position in the organizational hierarchy; the target believes that he or she must comply with what the agent wants because the agent is the boss. An agent may have a great deal of legitimate power because of her or his position, but may have little, if any, *expert power*, which leads the target to think, "The boss doesn't have a clue or understand the problem we have to deal with, but we have got to do it his way because he is the boss." *Referent power* arises from the attraction of followers to some behavioral or personality attribute that a particular person has, as in the target's belief, "I am going to comply or go along with what she has asked me to do because she works very hard and has thought out clearly what needs to be done."

Sources of expert and referent power are grounded in the individual. French and Raven's (1959) taxonomy clearly indicates that the sources of power are from the position and the person, and some believe that most power that is wielded in organizations is primarily position-based, rather than person-based, power. In fact, Bass (1960) proposed that there are two fundamental sources of power: position power, arising from attributes of the organizational position, and personal power, arising from attributes of the person. Yukl and Falbe (1991) proposed two other sources of power beyond French and Raven's (1959) five—persuasiveness and control of information.

Despite some methodological limitations with these studies, such as that they have measured primarily subordinates' levels of satisfaction, not changes in subordinates' attitudes and behaviors, their findings indicate that, overall, effective leaders appear to rely more on expert and referent power than on the other sources to influence subordinates (Hinkin & Schriesheim, 1989; Rahim, 1989; Yukl, 1994; Yukl & Falbe, 1991; Yukl & Van Fleet, 1992). Yukl and Falbe reported that for daily routine types of tasks, legitimate power was the primary reason why a subordinate complied with requests from the boss even though the subordinate may have been committed not to getting the task finished but just to doing what the boss wanted.

According to the leader-member exchange theory of the acquisition and use of power, leaders develop special relationships with a small group of subordinate advisers or lieutenants and use mainly reward power with them and legitimate power with all other subordinates to gain their compliance with the demands of tasks (Dansereau, Graen, & Haga, 1975; Graen & Cashman, 1975). In general, a mix of power sources is the most effective. As the complexity of tasks increases, the importance of expert power rises among the mix, but for routine tasks, legitimate power, coupled with a dose of reward or coercive power, is the most appropriate. Table 7–4 presents a summary of how to acquire, maintain, and use the five primary types of power (Yukl, 1994). We wish you and your colleagues well in the power enterprise.

Power and Politics

As we indicated earlier in this chapter, organizational politics includes actions to acquire, cultivate, and deploy power and related resources

Table 7–4. Guidelines for Acquiring, Maintaining, and Using Power

Acquiring and Maintaining Power	Using Power
Legitimate Power Gain more formal authority. Exercise authority regularly. Back up authority with reward and coercive power.	*Legitimate Power* Explain the reasons for a request. Do not exceed your scope of authority. Follow up to verify compliance.
Reward Power Discover what people need and want. Do not promise more than you can deliver. Do not use rewards for personal benefit.	*Reward Power* Offer fair and ethical rewards. Explain your criteria for giving rewards. Provide rewards as promised
Expert Power Gain more relevant knowledge. Demonstrate your competence by solving difficult problems. Don't lie or misrepresent the facts.	*Expert Power* Explain the reasons for a request or proposal. Listen seriously to concerns. Act confident and decisive in a crisis.
Referent Power Show acceptance and positive regard Act supportive and helpful. Keep promises.	*Referent Power* Use personal appeals when necessary. Indicate that a request is important to you. Provide an example of proper behavior (role-modeling).
Coercive Power Identify credible penalties to deter unacceptable behavior. Do not make rash threats. Do not use coercion for personal benefit.	*Coercive Power* Inform colleagues of rules and penalties. Understand a situation before use of discipline. Administer discipline in private.

Leadership in Organizations (3rd ed.), by G. Yukl, © 1994. Adapted by permission of Prentice Hall, Upper Saddle River, NJ.

to obtain one's preferred outcomes (personal, organizational, or a mix of such goals), particularly in ambiguous or uncertain contexts in which there is a dissensus about choices (Pfeffer, 1981, 1992a, 1992b).

Political power is grounded in authority, control over resources, and access to information, although there are political processes to amplify and secure these power bases. These political processes are *coalition building*, *gaining control over important decision processes*, and *co-optation*.

Coalitions are alliances of persons to support or oppose a particular policy, program, or decision. The parties to the coalition assist each other in getting what they want; for instance, if one manager wants X while another wants Y, they may form a coalition of their departmental members, all of whom will be directed or encouraged to support both X and Y, even though any given department may have no interest in or gain no benefit from the other desired outcomes. The currency of coalitions is usually called a chit; chits are exchanged symbolically as in, "If you help me on this project, I will then help you on that project" and thus repay the chit.

Gaining control over important decision-making processes is done by shaping the agenda of an important meeting (influencing or determining what items are placed on the agenda for the meeting and where on the agenda they will appear), controlling what data and other information are available and sanctioned for decision making or are related to specific agenda items, determining criteria for making decisions, and influencing or selecting who attends critical decision-making meetings. This is a robust political process that many organizational members use to strengthen their power base.

Co-optation is a frequently employed political tool that is designed to undermine opposition to a particular policy, project, or decision by a group or key persons whose support is needed to obtain one's desired outcomes. Usually, a vocal critic of a particular policy or upcoming important decision is co-opted by appointing her or him to a task force or committee to study and then offer recommendations regarding the issue at hand. As a result of being surrounded by other committee members who are inclined to support the pending decision and by helping to make decisions and develop recommendations, the co-opted person loses her or his salience and no longer stands out in the crowd. Also, the co-opted person is usually rewarded for publicly supporting the pending decision that earlier had been a major source of contention and controversy (Pfeffer, 1981; 1992a, 1992b).

Another important political process to enhance power involves the politics of budgets to create a dependence on resources by deploying slack (extra), discretionary, or flexible resources (usually money but also equipment, space, or any other desirable item). In almost all organizations, as well as units or departments of organizations, approximately 75% to 90% of the annual total budget is encumbered or designated for specific expenses, *mainly salaries*, wages, and fringe benefits. Thus, the remaining 10% to 25% of the budget is a slack resource (one that is not committed for a particular expense). Pfeffer (1981), recognizing the potency of slack resources, suggested what he called the 10% rule by which an organization could be taken over by discretionary control of no more than 10% of the total annual organizational budget. Hence, for a total organizational budget of $1 million, only $50,000 to $100,000 would be needed to gain power over the organization. In our consulting practices, we have observed how potent the selective deployment of a modest amount of slack resources can be in influencing particular organizational members and decisions. In short, as we stated in Chapter 6, it is not only what you have that is important, but what you do with whatever resources are available to you.

With the proper mix and nimble use of these political processes, it is possible to institutionalize your power base by forming a dominant coalition that determines who gets what information, resources, and assignments to committees or task forces and even who is separated or expelled from the organization. Powerful coalitions get things done, but if they are out of touch with substantive changes in the external or internal organizational environments, a power "meltdown" usually occurs, either gradually or abruptly.

The pursuit of power without listening carefully first to oneself and then to others inside and outside the organization frequently leads to the loss of what was most pursued—power. It is likely that there is a Niccolò Machiavelli in each of us. Machiavelli (1469–1527) was a Florentine diplomat who wrote *The Prince* (1513/1966) to ingratiate himself with his new superior. *The Prince* is a book on how to acquire and use power that is based entirely on expediency and silent on virtues like trust, honor, and decency. Machiavelli wrote other books, such as *Discourses* (1513/1950), which focuses on non-manipulative influence strategies employed by diplomats and leaders who were perhaps not as high on Machiavellianism—a strategy of social conduct designed to manipulate others for personal gain—as were others whom Machiavelli observed in various courts of Europe in the 16th century (Christie & Geis, 1970; Wilson, Near, & Miller, 1996). In the final analysis, power is a relational process that can be moderated by a variety of influence tactics.

Influence Tactics

Influence is the impact of one party (the agent, who can be one person or a group of persons) on another party (the target, who can also be one person or a group of persons) and usually involves a bidirectional interaction between the parties. In general, the outcomes of an influence tactic, whether the exercise of power, political processes, or a mix of them, can be *commitment* (the target internalizes a request from the agent and vigorously pursues the requested goal or objective), *compliance* (unenthusiastic acceptance

of the request, with only minimal effort expended to achieve the requested goal or objective), or *resistance* (active avoidance of doing the requested task or assignment). Table 7–5 lists influence tactics that leaders and other members of a wide variety of organizations can use.

On the basis of the results of surveys and analyses of critical incidents (crises or major problems) that some organizations face, Yukl and Van Fleet (1992) found that the influence tactics of rational persuasion, consultation, and inspirational appeals were the most effective for gaining a sustained commitment from the target, while pressure, coalition tactics, and legitimating tactics were least effective. In general, effective leaders use a mix of political and influence tactics, and they select such tactics according to their judgment of what would be most appropriate for a given situation (Howell & Higgins, 1990; Kotter, 1985; Yukl & Van Fleet, 1992).

Empowerment

Leaders and managers often delegate or share power with subordinates to accomplish a variety of organizational tasks and objectives. The scope and duration of activities for which power is delegated are usually limited, and the decision to delegate rests almost exclusively with the leader or manager. Conger and Kanungo (1988) proposed that empowerment is different from delegation, since the former is a motivational process whose intent is to enable subordinates to act without consultation with superiors across situations and time, whereas delegation focuses on delimited power sharing. They defined empowerment as

> a process of enhancing feelings of self-efficacy among organizational members through the identification of conditions that foster powerlessness and through their removal by both formal organizational practices and informal techniques of providing efficacy information. (Conger & Kanungo, 1988, p. 474)

Table 7–5. Influence Tactics

Legitimating tactics: The person seeks to establish the legitimacy of a request by claiming the authority or right to make it or by verifying that it is consistent with organizational policies, practices, or traditions.

Rational persuasion: The person uses logical arguments and factual evidence to persuade you that a proposal is practical and likely to result in the attainment of task objectives.

Inspirational appeals: The person makes a request by appealing to your values, ideas, and aspirations or by increasing your confidence that you can do it.

Consultation: The person seeks your participation in planning a strategy, activity, or change or is willing to modify a proposal to deal with your concerns and suggestions.

Exchange: The person offers an exchange of factors, indicates a willingness to reciprocate at a later time, or promises you a share of the benefits if you help accomplish a task.

Pressure: The person uses demands, threats, or persistent reminders to influence you to do what he or she wants.

Ingratiation: The person seeks to get you in a good mood or to think favorably of him or her before asking you to do something.

Coalition tactics: The person seeks the aid of others to persuade you to do something or uses the support of others as a reason for you to agree.

From G. Yukl & D. Van Fleet, "Theory and Research on Leadership in Organizations," in M. D. Dunnette & L. M. Hough (Eds.), *Handbook of Industrial and Organizational Psychology.* Copyright 1992 by Gary Yukl, Clifton Park, NY. Used with permission.

In a series of subsequent works, Conger (1989, 1990, 1993) further developed the empowerment process by grounding the construct in perceived self-efficacy (see Chapter 6) and by identifying contexts and leadership styles (especially charismatic and transformational styles) that are the most conducive to empowerment. The empowerment process has also been referred to as distributed leadership; at the micro (individual) level, it involves strengthening individual efficacy, while at the team or organizational level, it involves strengthening collective efficacy. As Huey (1994) stated, the aim of empowerment, or distributed leadership, is to enable organizational members to solve organizational problems, from the most routine and focused hassles to the development of a shared vision for their organization.

In many respects, empowerment, or the enhancement of individual and collective efficacies, is a timely leadership development, given the turbulent pace of change, global competition, and diversification of the workforce, for it is likely that an organization can accomplish more than the sum of the delegated accomplishments of each member. Inasmuch as no single person has a monopoly on good ideas, strategies, or tactics, empowerment enables all members to contribute and increases the probability that the needed organizational strategy will emerge from a diverse yet competent, committed, and compassionate mix of members.

LEADERSHIP ISSUES

Much of the accumulated and systematic knowledge about leadership has been derived from field and laboratory-based studies primarily of white male leaders. These leaders were in organizations with nondiversified workforces in which the forces of global competition were just beginning to have a substantial and dramatic impact on organizational performances (Eagly & Karau, 1991; Eagly, Karau, & Makhijani, 1995; Eagly, Makhijani, & Klonsky, 1992; Heilman, Block, Martell, & Simon, 1989; Hollander & Offermann, 1990; Morrison & Von Glinow, 1990; Offerman & Gowing, 1990; Powell, 1988, 1990; Ragnis & Sundstrom, 1989). Obviously, there are many as yet unanswered questions about leadership and gender, leadership in different cultures, the impact of workforce diversification on leadership style, and the role of leadership in learning organizations that promote empowerment and shared power.

Leadership and Gender

The paucity of women in higher-level leadership and managerial positions in organizations raises the issue of why women have limited access to leadership roles (Eagly et al., 1992, 1995; Powell, 1988, 1990). According to Eagly's (1987) gender-role theory, people develop expectations for their own behavior and the behavior of others that are grounded in beliefs about what behavior is appropriate for men and women. Eagly et al. (1992) reported on a meta-analysis of 60 studies of gender and leadership from 1966 to 1988 that examined the evaluation of the leadership of men and women who were as similar to each other as possible in years of experience and management and educational levels. They found a modest overall tendency for female leaders to be devalued compared to male leaders and substantial evidence of the selective devaluation of female leaders. A follow-up meta analysis by Eagly et al. (1995) of gender differences in leadership performance found that the overall differences between men and women were minimal. A moderator variable that influenced leadership performance was the organizational culture, such as the military, which disadvantaged women leaders; in general, women performed better in settings that were more congenial to female leaders. Thus, organizational

culture can differentially influence the performance of leaders, depending on their gender. Therefore, we encourage you to seek or cultivate a culture that is conducive to both female and male leaders.

In accordance with gender-role theory, the devaluation of women was high when women occupied male-dominated roles (such as managerial positions in engineering or financial firms) and when the evaluators were men. Inasmuch as people's expectations about leaders' behaviors match their expectations of men more closely than of women (Heilman et al., 1989), women may be disadvantaged by incompatible expectations for their leader and gender roles. In other words, women who behave like men in leadership roles pay a price in terms of negative evaluation if they adopt stereotypically male leadership styles (autocratic and task oriented). An important preventive strategy to moderate the potential devaluation of women leaders is to include as much specific and individualized information about their performance, especially outcome measures related to subordinates' ratings and group- or organizational-level performances (Eagly et al., 1992).

Murphy's (1994) self-report survey of 60 women leaders in business firms (CEOs, presidents, and vice presidents) found that they chose a more task-oriented leadership style than did their male counterparts. In addition, both male and female leaders reported higher levels of perceived self-efficacy than did middle-level managers, but there were no differences in the efficacy levels of female and male leaders.

Cross-cultural Leadership

Almost all the studies of leadership reported in the psychological and management literatures have been of leaders in the United States, Canada, and Western Europe, which raises the issue of how much of the current knowledge about leadership is generalizable and universal and how much is moderated by cultural and situational forces (Graen & Wakabayashi, 1994; Triandis, 1994). The *performance maintenance (PM)* theory of leadership is one theory that was developed and tested in Japan and some other countries (Misumi, 1985; Misumi & Peterson, 1985; Smith, Peterson, Misumi, & Bond, 1992). It proposes that effective leaders are high on both the performance-oriented approach (with a focus on planning, executing, and enhancing subordinates' performance of tasks) and the maintenance-oriented approach (with a focus on supporting, encouraging, developing, and responding to subordinates' needs) to leadership. Likewise, Xu (1989a, 1989b) found that effective Chinese and Japanese managers were both high on the performance and maintenance orientations, according to their subordinates' evaluations. In a field-based study of PM theory in the northern Chinese port city of Da Lian, Xu (1989b, pp. 56–57) reported that effective managers practiced the following basic management principles:

- They esteemed the needs and working activities of the employees.

- They encouraged and supported the employees' active participation in decision making in management.

- They widened their communication with the employees by exchanging information, sharing feelings and interests, engaging in joint recreational activities, and coordinating employees before decision making.

On the basis of over twenty years of leadership studies in Japan and the United States, Graen and Wakabayashi (1994) suggested that a productive approach to cross-cultural studies of leadership is to consider a culture not as a set of predispositions acquired over an extended period of enculturation, but as a set of conceptual tools to be used to solve different types of problems. As Swidler (1986) suggested, a person from a different culture can learn such tools during a cross-cultural leadership training program. Obviously, the increasing expansion of the global economy and the emergence of open economies in a number of strategic sectors of the world, including China and the countries of the former Soviet Union, will necessitate further research on cross-cultural leadership strategies (Wang, 1994).

Leadership and Diversity

What types of leadership are most effective for harnessing the talents and energies of a diverse workforce? Chemers and Murphy (1995) suggested that leading a diverse group or organization requires leaders who must be sensitive to real differences when they exist and at the same time reduce the negative impact of stereotypes. Effective leadership is grounded in authentic and open relationships between leaders and followers that require leaders to be sensitive to the needs, expectations, and perceptions of followers, whatever the followers' origins. Leaders have many different followers, and when they are held accountable for the development of all their followers, their leadership can be firmly grounded in diversity.

Chemers (1993) stated that effective leaders systematically engage in the management of their image, the development of relationships, and the coordination and deployment of teams. A recognizable stream of research on leadership has confirmed that leaders who demonstrate and project competence and trustworthiness are perceived as legitimate by their followers (Hollander, 1964; Scott, 1983). Jeanquart-Barone (1993) reported that trust is moderated by gender and race; that is, the highest level of trust was for female subordinates reporting to male supervisors, but there were no significant differences in trust between men reporting to men and women reporting to men. In terms of race, blacks reporting to blacks exhibited a higher level of trust than did blacks reporting to whites, whites reporting to blacks, or whites reporting to other whites.

With regard to the development of relationships, a leader as a mentor or coach must be sensitive and responsive to the work-related values of followers; thus, a follower who is high in power distance (strong adherence to *hierarchy* and power differentials between roles) would be more comfortable with authoritarian and directive leadership than would a follower of a more egalitarian culture who is low in power distance (Chemers & Murphy, 1995; Hofstede, 1983). For example, Triandis, Marin, Lisansky, and Betancourt (1984) found that Hispanics are more likely than are non-Hispanics to expect high frequencies of positive social behaviors and low frequencies of negative social behaviors in their interactions with others in an organization or social context. Hence, an effective leader of a diverse workforce has to be responsive to pervasive subcultural differences in work-related values and open to learning about the unique and shared features of her or his followers. Furthermore, individual members of homogeneous teams of Asians, Africans, or Hispanic Americans have a more collectivist and cooperative orientation to a task than do members of a team of Euro-Americans and even of ethnically diverse teams (Cox, Lobel, & McLeod, 1991).

In summary, stereotypical beliefs and expectations based on categorical membership (gender, race, and ethnicity) limit opportunities to achieve and distort evaluations of such persons in leadership positions. Accordingly, leaders need to focus on the similarities of needs, values, and abilities of different people and minimize their differences (Chemers & Murphy, 1995; Fiske, Bersoff, Borgida, Deaux, & Heilman, 1991). Leaders also must be responsible for the development of all members and must continuously and systematically attempt to find and harness the shared "one" out of the many different ones on a team or in an organization.

Dysfunctional Leadership

Leaders can have a substantial negative impact on the performance of organizational members and of the overall organization. In a series of studies of leaders with narcissistic personalities (with an extreme need for attention, admiration, and power and weak self-control and who are indifferent to the needs and welfare of others), Kets de Vries (1993) and Kets de Vries and Miller (1984, 1985) found that such persons seek subordinates who are loyal and uncritical, ignore or dismiss objective and impartial advice, monopolize decision making, and launch grandiose organizational projects, primarily for their own glorification, that they seldom monitor or follow up on. Unlike emotionally mature leaders, narcissistic leaders cling to power and rarely step aside gracefully in the face of mounting negative evidence and the organization's clear sense that new leaders are required to meet dynamic challenges from within and outside the organization.

Leadership requires competence, emotional maturity, authentic knowledge of one's strengths and weaknesses, the valuing of partnership with followers, and a commitment to learn continuously throughout life.

SUMMARY

We began our discussion of leadership by making plain that it is a relational process between the leader and her or his followers. Leadership involves a mix of three clear features: a leader's traits (or personal characteristics), leadership behaviors, and situations that moderate leadership. Key traits include high energy; a tolerance of stress; integrity and emotional maturity, coupled with a strong social power orientation; and sound technical, conceptual, and interpersonal skills. The behavioral models of leadership focus on two broad domains of consideration that were identified by studies at OSU and the University of Michigan: people-oriented behaviors and task-oriented behaviors. The situational models of leadership include the LPC models, the multiple influence model, the path-goal model, the situational leadership model, the Vroom-Jago normative decision model, and cognitive resources theory, each of which emphasizes different situational features that moderate leadership behaviors. The empirical findings on leadership that we reviewed clarified that leadership is a mix of traits, behaviors, and the ability to interpret distinctive environmental features that moderate leadership behaviors.

We then examined the models and strategies of charismatic and transformational leadership and evaluated their effects on the performance of followers and the organization. That both leadership styles can be acquired indicates that leadership is a renewable resource.

Power arises from the organizational position held by a member, as well as from the member's unique features, including expert and referent (personal traits) sources of power. We examined the relationship between authority and power and power and organizational politics and described a variety of influence tactics, some of which were identified by Machiavelli in the 16th century but are still applicable in contemporary organizations around the world. In addition, we briefly discussed the relationship between empowering followers and the centrality of individual and collective efficacies to empowerment.

Finally, we examined a variety of leadership issues, including strategies to minimize the influence of categorical membership (gender, race, and ethnicity) on access to leadership positions and the evaluation of leaders' performances, leadership in different cultures, leadership of a diverse workforce, and the indices of dysfunctional leadership.

Leadership is about giving yourself to others. If you do it well, you grow as a person and as a leader and earn the respect and support of your followers.

CHAPTER REFERENCES

Bacharach, S. B., & Lawler, E. J. (1980). *Power and politics in organizations.* San Francisco: Jossey-Bass.

Bass, B. M. (1960). *Leadership, psychology, and organizational behavior.* New York: Harper & Row.

Bass, B. M. (1985). *Leadership and performance beyond expectations.* New York: Free Press.

Bass, B. M. (1990). *Bass and Stogdill's handbook of leadership: Theory, research, and managerial applications* (3rd ed.). New York: Free Press.

Bass, B. M., & Avolio, B. J. (1990). Developing transformational leadership: 1992 and beyond. *Journal of European Industrial Training, 14,* 21–27.

Bennis, W. G., & Nanus, B. (1985). *Leaders: The strategies for taking charge.* New York: Harper & Row.

Blank, W., Weitzel, J. R., & Green, S. G. (1990). Test of situational leadership theory. *Personnel Psychology, 43,* 579–597.

Boyatzis, R. E. (1982). *The Competent manager.* New York: John Wiley & Sons.

Burns, J. M. (1978). *Leadership.* New York: Harper & Row.

Chemers, M. M. (1993). An integrative theory of leadership. In M. M. Chemers & R. Ayman (Eds.), *Leadership theory and research: Perspectives and directions* (pp. 293–319). San Diego, CA: Academic Press.

Chemers, M. M., & Murphy, S. E. (1995). Leadership and diversity in groups and organizations. In M. M. Chemers, S. Oskamp, & M. A. Costanzo (Eds.), *Diversity in organizations: New perspectives for a changing workplace* (pp. 157–188). Thousand Oaks, CA: Sage.

Christie, R., & Geis, F. (1970). *Studies in Machiavellianism.* New York: Academic Press.

Cohen, M. D., & March, J. G. (1986). *Leadership and ambiguity: The American college president* (2nd ed.). Cambridge, MA: Harvard Business School Press.

Conger, J. A. (1989). *The charismatic leader: Behind the mystique of exceptional leadership.* San Francisco: Jossey-Bass.

Conger, J. A. (1990). The dark side of leadership. *Organizational Dynamics, 18,* 44–55.

Conger, J. A. (1993). The brave new world of leadership training. *Organizational Dynamics, 21,* 46–58.

Conger, J. A., & Kanungo, R. (1987). Toward a behavioral theory of charismatic leadership in organizational settings. *Academy of Management Review, 12,* 637–647.

Conger, J. A., & Kanungo, R. N. (1988). The empowerment process: Integrating theory and practice. *Academy of Management Review, 13,* 471–482.

Cox, T. H., Lobel, S. A., & McLeod, P. L. (1991). Effects of ethnic group cultural differences on cooperative and competitive behavior on a group task. *Academy of Management Journal, 34,* 827–847.

Dansereau, F., Jr., Graen, G., & Haga, W. J. (1975). A vertical dyad linkages approach to leadership within formal organizations: A longitudinal investigation of the role making process. *Organizational Behavior and Human Performance, 13,* 46–78.

Deming, W. E. (1986). *Out of the crisis.* Cambridge, MA: MIT Center for Advanced Engineering Study.

Davis-Blake, A., & Pfeffer, J. (1989). Just a mirage: The search for dispositional effects in organizational research. *Academy of Management Review, 14,* 385–400.

Duchon, D., Green, S., & Taber, T. (1986). Vertical dyad linkage: A longitudinal assessment of antecedents, measures, and consequences. *Journal of Applied Psychology, 71,* 56–60.

Eagly, A. H. (1987). *Sex differences in social behavior: A social-role interpretation.* Hillsdale, NJ: Lawrence Erlbaum.

Eagly, A. H., & Karau, S. J. (1991). Gender and emergence of leaders: A meta-analysis. *Journal of Personality and Social Psychology, 60,* 685–710.

Eagly, A. H., Karau, S. J., & Makhijani, M. G. (1995). Gender and the evaluation of leaders: A meta-analysis. *Psychological Bulletin, 117,* 125–145.

Eagly, A. H., Makhijani, M. G., & Klonsky, B. G. (1992). Gender and the evaluation of leaders: A meta-analysis. *Psychological Bulletin, 111,* 3–22.

Fielder, F. E. (1964). A contingency model of leadership effectiveness. In L. Berkowitz (Ed.),

Advances in experimental social psychology (pp. 149–190). New York: Academic Press.

Fielder, F. E. (1967). *A theory of leadership effectiveness.* New York: McGraw-Hill.

Fielder, F. E. (1986). The contribution of cognitive resources to leadership performance. *Journal of Applied Social Psychology, 16,* 532–548.

Fielder, F. E., & Garcia, J. E. (1987). *New approaches to leadership: Cognitive resources and organizational performance.* New York: John Wiley & Sons.

Fiske, S. T., Bersoff, D. N., Borgida, E., Deaux, K., & Heilman, M. E. (1991). Social science research on trial. Use of sex stereotyping research in Price Waterhouse v. Hopkins. *American Psychologist, 46,* 1049–1060.

Fleishman, E. A. (1953). The description of supervisory behavior. *Personnel Psychology, 37,* 1–6.

French, J. R. P., & Raven, B. H. (1959). The bases of social power. In D. Cartwright (Ed.), *Studies of social power* (pp. 150–167). Ann Arbor: Institute for Social Research, University of Michigan.

Gioffre, K. R., Lawson, R. B., & Gordon, L. R. (1992). The effects of decision outcome dispersion upon organizational decision making. *Psychological Record, 42,* 427–436.

Gioia, A. J., & Sims, H. P. (1983). Perceptions of managerial power as a consequence of managerial behavior and reputation. *Journal of Management, 9,* 7–26.

Graen, G. B. (1976). Role making processes within complex organizations. In M. D. Dunnette (Ed.), *Handbook of industrial and organizational psychology* (pp. 1201–1245). Chicago: Rand McNally.

Graen, G. B. (1990). Designing productive leadership systems to improve both work motivation and organizational effectiveness. In E. Fleishman (Ed.), *International work motivation* (pp. 200–233). Hillsdale, NJ: Lawrence Erlbaum.

Graen, G., & Cashman, J. F. (1975). A role making model of leadership in formal organizations: A developmental approach. In J. G. Hunt & L. L. Larson (Eds.), *Leadership frontiers* (pp. 46–62). Kent, OH: Kent State University Press.

Graen, G. B., & Wakabayashi, M. (1994). Cross-cultural leadership making: Bridging American and Japanese diversity for team advantage. In H. C. Triandis, M. D. Dunnette, & L. M. Hough (Eds.), *Handbook of industrial and organizational psychology* (pp. 415–446). Palo Alto, CA: Consulting Psychologists Press.

Green, S. G., & Mitchell, T. R. (1979). Attributional processes of leaders in leader-member exchanges. *Organizational Behavior and Human Performance, 23,* 429–458.

Halpin, A. W., & Winer, B. J. (1957). A factorial study of the leader behavior descriptions. In R. M. Stogdill & A. E. Coons (Eds.), *Leader behavior: Its description and measurement* (pp. 39–51). Columbus: Bureau of Business Research, Ohio State University.

Heilman, M. E., Block, C. J., Martell, R. F., & Simon, M. C. (1989). Has anything changed? Current characterizations of men, women, and managers. *Journal of Applied Psychology, 74,* 935–942.

Hersey, P., & Blanchard, K. H. (1969). Life cycle theory of leadership. *Training and Development Journal, 23,* 26–41.

Hersey, P., & Blanchard, K. H. (1988). *Management of organizational behavior* (5th ed.). Englewood Cliffs, NJ: Prentice Hall.

Hinkin, T. R., & Schriesheim, C. A. (1989). Development and application of new scales to measure the French and Raven bases of social power. *Journal of Applied Psychology, 74,* 561–567.

Hofstede, G. (1983). Motivation, leadership, organization: Do American theories apply abroad? *Organizational Dynamics, 11,* 42–63.

Hogan, R., Curphy, G. J., & Hogan, J. (1994). What we know about leadership: Effectiveness and personality. *American Psychologist, 49,* 493–504.

Hollander, E. P. (1964). *Leaders, groups and influence.* New York: Oxford University Press.

Hollander, E. P., & Offermann, L. R. (1990). Power and leadership in organizations. *American Psychologist, 45,* 179–189.

House, R. J. (1977). A 1976 theory of charismatic leadership. In J. G. Hunt & L. L. Larson (Eds.), *Leadership: The cutting edge* (pp. 189–207). Carbondale: Southern Illinois Press.

House, R. J., & Mitchell, T. R. (1974). Path-goal theory of leadership. *Contemporary Business, 3,* 81–98.

Howell, J. M., & Higgins, C. A. (1990). Leadership behaviors, influence tactics, and career experiences of champions of technological innovation. *Leadership Quarterly, 1,* 249–264.

Huey, J. (1994, February 21). The new post-heroic leadership. *Fortune,* pp. 42–50.

Hunt, J. G., & Osborn, R. N. (1982). Toward a macro-oriented model of leadership: An odyssey. In J. G. Hunt, U. Sekaran, & C. Schriesheim (Eds.), *Leadership: Beyond establishment views* (pp. 196–221). Carbondale: Southern University Press.

Indvik, J. (1986). Path-goal theory of leadership: A meta-analysis. In *Academy of Management, Best paper proceedings* (pp. 189–192). Chicago: Academy of Management.

Jacobs, T. O., & Jaques, E. (1987). Leadership in complex systems. In J. Zeidner (Ed.), *Human productivity enhancement* (pp. 7–65). New York: Praeger.

Jacobs, T. O., & Jaques, E. (1990). Military executive leadership. In K. E. Clark & M. B. Clark (Eds.), *Measures of leadership* (pp. 281–295). West Orange, NJ: Leadership Library of America.

Jeanquart-Barone, S. (1993). Trust differences between supervisors and subordinates: Examining the role of race and gender. *Sex Roles, 29,* 1–11.

Kanter, R. M. (1983). *The change masters.* New York: Simon & Schuster.

Katz, D., & Kahn, R. L. (1978). *The social psychology of organizations* (2nd ed.). New York: John Wiley & Sons.

Keller, R. T. (1989). A test of path-goal theory of leadership with need for clarity as a moderator. *Journal of Applied Psychology, 74,* 208–212.

Kets de Vries, M. F. R. (1993). *Leaders, goals, and impostors.* San Francisco: Jossey-Bass.

Kets de Vries, M., & Miller, D. (1984). *The neurotic organization: Diagnosing and changing counterproductive styles of management.* San Francisco: Jossey-Bass.

Kets de Vries, M. F. R., & Miller, D. (1985). Narcissism and leadership: An object relations perspective. *Human Relations, 38,* 583–601.

Kipnis, D. (1976). *The powerholders.* Chicago: University of Chicago Press.

Kirkpatrick, S. A., & Locke, E. A. (1991). Leadership: Do traits matter? *Academy of Management Executive, 5,* 48–60.

Kirkpatrick, S. A., & Locke, E. A. (1996). Direct and indirect effects of three core charismatic leadership components on performance and attitudes. *Journal of Applied Psychology, 81,* 36–51.

Kissinger, H. (1979). *The White House years.* Boston: Little, Brown.

Kotter, J. P. (1982). *The general managers.* New York: Free Press.

Kotter, J. P. (1985). *Power and influence. Beyond formal authority.* New York: Free Press.

Likert, R. (1961). *New patterns of management.* New York: McGraw-Hill.

Likert, R. (1967). *The human organization: Its management and value.* New York: McGraw-Hill.

Lombardo, M. M., & McCauley, C. D. (1988). *The dynamics of management derailment* (Technical Report No. 34). Greensboro, NC: Center for Creative Leadership.

Luthans, F., Rosenkrantz, S. A., & Hennessey, H. W. (1985). What do successful managers really do? An observation study of managerial activities. *Journal of Applied Behavioral Science, 21,* 255–270.

Machiavelli, N. (1950). *Discourses.* London: Routledge & Kegan Paul. (Original work published 1513)

Machiavelli, N. (1966). *The Prince.* New York: Bantam Books. (Original work published 1513)

Mann, R. D. (1959). A review of the relationships between personality and performance in small groups. *Psychological Bulletin, 56,* 241–270.

McCall, M. W., Jr., & Lombardo, M. M. (1983). *Off the track: Why and how successful executives get derailed* (Technical Report No. 21). Greensboro, NC: Center for Creative Leadership.

McClelland, D. C., & Boyatzis, R. E. (1982). Leadership motive pattern and long term success in management. *Journal of Applied Psychology, 67,* 737–743.

McClelland, D. C., & Burnham, D. H. (1976,

March–April). Power is a great motivator. *Harvard Business Review, 98,* 100–110.

Mintzberg, H. (1973). *The nature of managerial work.* New York: Harper & Row.

Misumi, J. (1985). *The behavioral science of leadership: An interdisciplinary Japanese research program.* Ann Arbor: University of Michigan Press.

Misumi, J., & Peterson, M. (1985). The performance-maintenance (PM) theory of leadership: Review of a Japanese research program. *Administrative Science Quarterly, 30,* 198–223.

Morrison, A. M., & Von Glinow, M. A. (1990). Women and minorities in management. *American Psychologist, 45,* 200–208.

Morse, J. J., & Wagner, F. R. (1978). Measuring the process of managerial effectiveness. *Academy of Management Journal, 21,* 23–35.

Murphy, D. (1994). *A multi-dimensional theory of the glass ceiling.* Unpublished master's degree thesis, University of Vermont, Burlington.

Murphy, S. E., Blyth, D. E., & Fielder, F. E. (1992). Cognitive resources theory and the utilization of the leader's and group member's technical competence. *Leadership Quarterly, 3,* 237–255.

Offerman, L. R., & Gowing, M. K. (1990). Organizations of the future: Changes and challenges. *American Psychologist, 45,* 95–108.

Pfeffer, J. (1977). The ambiguity of leadership. *Academy of Management Review, 2,* 104–112.

Pfeffer, J. (1981). *Power in organizations.* Boston: Pitman.

Pfeffer, J. (1992a). *Managing with power.* Cambridge, MA: Harvard Business School Press.

Pfeffer, J. (1992b). Understanding power in organizations. *California Management Review, 34,* 29–50.

Podsakoff, P. M., MacKenzie, S. B., Morrman, R. H., & Fetter, R. (1990). Transformational leader behaviors and their effects on follower's trust in leader, satisfaction, and organizational citizenship behaviors. *Leadership Quarterly, 1,* 107–142.

Powell, G. N. (1988). *Women and men in management.* Newbury Park, CA: Sage.

Powell, G. N. (1990). One more time: Do female and male managers differ? *Academy of Management Executive, 4,* 68–75.

Ragnis, B. R., & Sundstrom, E. (1989). Gender and power in organizations: A longitudinal perspective. *Psychological Bulletin, 105,* 51–88.

Rahim, M. A. (1989). Relationships of leader power to compliance and satisfaction: Evidence from a national sample of managers. *Journal of Management, 15,* 545–556.

Rauch, C. F., & Behling, O. (1984). Functionalism: Basis for an alternative approach to the study of leadership. In J. G. Hunt, D. M. Hosking, C. A. Schriesheim, & R. Stewart (Eds.), *Leaders and managers: International perspectives on managerial behavior and leadership* (pp. 46–62). Elmsford, NY: Pergamon Press.

Reddin, W. J. (1967). The 3-D management style theory. *Training and Development Journal, 21,* 8–17.

Schweiger, D. M., Anderson, C. R., & Locke, E. A. (1985). Complex decision making: A longitudinal study of process and performance. *Organizational Behavior and Human Decision Processes, 36,* 245–272.

Scott, W. (1983). Trust differences between men and women in superior-subordinate relationships. *Group and Organization Studies, 8,* 319–336.

Senge, P. M. (1990). *The fifth discipline: The art and practice of the learning organization.* New York: Doubleday/Currency.

Shamir, B., House, R. J., & Arthur, M. B. (1993). The motivational effects of charismatic leadership: A self-concept based theory. *Organization Science, 4,* 1–17.

Simon, H. (1987). Making managerial decision: The role of intuition and emotion. *Academy of Management Executive, 1,* 57–64.

Smith, B. J. (1982). *An initial test of a theory of charismatic leadership based on the response of subordinates.* Unpublished doctoral dissertation, University of Toronto, Canada.

Smith, P. B., Peterson, M., Misumi, J., & Bond, M. (1992). A cross-cultural test of Japanese PM leadership theory. *Applied Psychology: An International Review, 41,* 5–19.

Stewart, R. (1982). *Choices for the manager.* Englewood Cliffs, NJ: Prentice Hall.

Stogdill, R. M. (1948). Personal factors associated with leadership: A survey of the literature. *Journal of Psychology, 25,* 35–71.

Stogdill, R. M. (1974). *Handbook of leadership: A survey of the literature.* New York: Free Press.

Swidler, A. (1986). Culture in action. *American Sociological Review, 51,* 273–286.

Tannenbaum, R., Weschler, I. R., & Massarik, F. (1961). *Leadership and organization.* New York: McGraw-Hill.

Taylor, J., & Bowers, D. (1972). *The survey of organizations: A machine-scored standardized questionnaire instrument.* Ann Arbor: Institute for Social Research, University of Michigan.

Tichy, N. M., & Devanna, M. A. (1986). *The transformational leader.* New York: John Wiley & Sons.

Triandis, H. C. (1994). Cross-cultural industrial and organizational psychology. In H. C. Triandis, M. D. Dunnette, & L. M. Hough (Eds.), *Handbook of industrial and organizational psychology* (pp. 103–172). Palo Alto, CA: Consulting Psychologists Press.

Triandis, H. C., Marin, G., Lisansky, J., & Betancourt, H. (1984). Simpatía as a cultural script of Hispanics. *Journal of Personality and Social Psychology, 47,* 1363–1375.

Vecchio, R. P. (1987). Situational leadership theory: An examination of a prescriptive theory. *Journal of Applied Psychology, 72,* 444–451.

Vecchio, R. P. (1990). Theoretical and empirical examination of cognitive resource theory. *Journal of Applied Psychology, 75,* 141–147.

Vroom, V. H., & Jago, A. G. (1988). *The new leadership.* Englewood Cliffs, NJ: Prentice Hall.

Vroom, V. H., & Yetton, P. W. (1973). *Leadership and decision making.* Pittsburgh, PA: University of Pittsburgh Press.

Wang, Z. M. (1994). Culture, economic reform, and the role of industrial and organizational psychology in China. In M. D. Dunnette & L. M. Hough (Eds.), *Handbook of industrial and organizational psychology* (pp. 689–725). Palo Alto, CA: Consulting Psychologists Press.

Wilson, D. S., Near, D., & Miller, R. R. (1996). Machiavellianism: A synthesis of the evolutionary and psychological literatures. *Psychological Bulletin, 119,* 285–299.

Xu, L. (1989a). Chinese management style. In B. J.

Fallon, H. P. Pfister, & J. Brebner (Eds.), *Advances in industrial organizational psychology* (pp. 13–17). Amsterdam, NY: North-Holland U.S. distributors for Elsevier Science.

Xu, L. (1989b). Comparative study of leadership between Chinese and Japanese managers based upon PM theory. In B. J. Fallon, H. P. Pfister, & J. Brebner (Eds.), *Advances in industrial organizational psychology* (pp. 53–57). Amsterdam, NY: North-Holland U.S. distributors for Elsevier Science.

Yukl, G. A. (1989). Managerial leadership: A review of theory and research. *Journal of Management, 15*, 251–290.

Yukl, G. (1994). *Leadership in organizations* (3rd ed.). Englewood Cliffs, NJ: Prentice Hall.

Yukl, G., & Falbe, C. M. (1991). The importance of different power sources in downward and lateral relations. *Journal of Applied Psychology, 76*, 416–423.

Yukl, G., & Van Fleet, D. (1992). Theory and research on leadership in organizations. In M. D. Dunnette & L. M. Hough (Eds.), *Handbook of industrial and organizational psychology* (pp. 147–197). Palo Alto, CA: Consulting Psychologists Press.

Zaccaro, S., Foti, R. J., & Kenny, D. (1991). Self-monitoring and trait-based variance in leadership: An investigation of leader flexibility across multiple group situations. *Journal of Applied Psychology, 76*, 308–315.

Zalesny, M. D., & Graen, G. (1986). Exchange theory in leadership research. In A. Kieser, G. Reber, & R. Wunderer (Eds.), *Encyclopedia of leadership* (pp. 714–727). Stuttgart, Germany: C. E. Poeschel Verberg.

Zaleznik, A. (1992). Managers and leaders: Are they different? *Harvard Business Review, 114*, 126–135.

Zaleznik, A., & Kets de Vries, M. F. R. (1975). *Power and the corporate mind.* Boston: Houghton Mifflin.

SUGGESTED REFERENCES

There is an endless list of materials on leadership and, accordingly, our three suggested references focus primarily on fundamental assumptions about the nature of humans and organizations. We are confident that you will find them informative, and we hope they are useful and enjoyable as well.

Senge, P. M. (1990). *The fifth discipline: The art and practice of the learning organization.* New York: Doubleday/Currency.

Weisbord, M. R. (1987). *Productive workplaces: Organizing and managing for dignity, meaning, and community:* San Francisco: Jossey-Bass.

Williams, M., & Nicholson, W. (1922). *The velveteen rabbit.* New York: Doubleday.

8

Decision Making

CHAPTER OVERVIEW

Organizations make decisions continuously, and it is therefore critical to have a sound grasp of the process and outcomes of decision making. The flattening of organizations, the growing use of autonomous (self-directed) teams, and the rapidity of technological developments have accelerated the frequency and speed at which organizational members must make decisions. Most investigations of decision making have focused on the process (the how-to-do-it) component because outcomes of decisions are highly contextualized and subject to a wide variety of situational influences.

We define decision making as the process of choosing among alternatives, implementing the decision, and using outcome data to refine or reshape the initial decision. Thereafter, we present a model of decision making, distinguish between programmed and nonprogrammed decisions, and examine individual and organizational decision making. Investigations make plain that decisions are influenced by nonrational forces, as reflected in confirmatory bias (the search for decision-relevant information that conforms to existing beliefs) and the false consensus bias (the overestimation of the number of persons who agree with the decision makers' attitudes and beliefs). Thereafter, we briefly describe risk preferences and make plain that decision making is influenced by emotions and self-esteem, which moderate the decision maker's proneness to take risks.

In discussing organizational decision making as primarily a social process, we explore the rational, bounded-rational, and political models of decisions made by organizations. Groupthink (premature consensus) and the Abilene Paradox (disagreement from agreement) are common problems in organizational decision making, so we present specific strategies to prevent or minimize these forces that can yield defective and harmful organizational decisions.

We then turn to strategies for obtaining good ideas or alternatives that are critical for effective decision making, including recent developments in electronic brainstorming, the nominal group technique, the delphi technique, and the stepladder technique, each of which can be implemented readily. We also look at high-velocity decision making, a characteristic of rapidly changing, dynamic, and turbulent organizational events and contexts. We conclude with information avalanches that can arise from the failure to manage properly gossip, rumor, and ethical decision making. Gossip is considered a form of idle talk through which organizational members who do not frequently interact with each other on specific decision situations maintain communication. We outline specific rumor-management strategies and the personal and situational forces that enhance ethical decision making in the global marketplace.

LEARNING OBJECTIVES

When you finish studying this chapter, you will be prepared to

- define decision making; describe a model of decision making that includes process and outcome; and identify types of decisions and nonrational forces, such as the confirmatory and false-consensus biases that moderate decision making

- describe risk preferences and explain how emotions and self-esteem influence the decision maker's risk preferences, making plain that decision making is not strictly a rational process

- explain the basic features of three models of decision making—the rational, bounded-rational, and political models—each of which addresses decision making as a social process

- define Groupthink and the Abilene Paradox and identify strategies to prevent or minimize these forces that can yield defective organizational decisions

- discuss a variety of strategies to generate good ideas and alternatives that are essential for effective decision making, including electronic brainstorming, the nominal group technique, the stepladder technique, and high-velocity decision making

- define gossip and rumor and describe strategies to harness the positive contributions of gossip in organizations and to manage rumors.

- explain ethical decision making and identify the dispositional and situational forces that enhance it in organizations in different regions of the global marketplace.

If you don't choose, you lose.

DECISION MAKING

Decision making consists of process and outcome components, either or both of which can be used as a measure of the effectiveness of decision making. The process component includes identifying the problem ("Do we have a problem here and, if so, what is it?"), a judgment about the importance of the problem for the individual or the group (if the problem is not important, the process is terminated at this stage), a search for and evaluation of alternatives if the problem is judged important, and the selection of an alternative to prevent or respond to the problem. The outcome component includes implementing or initiating the actions of the selected alternative and evaluating the results by some type of performance measure. In general, most organizational members are much more willing to make decisions than to implement them, for implementation can be time consuming, extensive, and labor intensive.

Most models of organizational decision making focus on the process, rather than the outcome, component of decision making for the latter is shaped primarily by situational forces that are highly variable and thus difficult to include in a normative or prescriptive model. Furthermore, many models of organizational decision making assume that unstructured or complex problems, in which the outcomes of a decision are not clearly predictable, are usually made by upper-level managers and that it is the responsibility of lower-level managers and operational members to implement the decision and eventually to give feedback on the outcomes to the decision makers. However, as organizations become flatter or less hierarchical and decision making is nested more and more in self-directed work teams, there is a growing emphasis on both the process and outcome components of decision making. Also, as both the internal and external environments of organizations become more turbulent, it becomes necessary to attend more to real-time ("what is happening now") data than to historical data, which may be many months old by the time it is reviewed by upper-level decision makers, or forecasts of future environmental conditions, which are subject to rapidly changing conditions in the high-velocity environments that are characteristic of many global organizations (Eisenhardt, 1989, 1990).

Furthermore, every person and organization has to deal almost daily with uncertainty about the future. This exposure to uncertainty can create a sense of risk or exposure to the chance of loss or injury. In general, individuals and organizations frequently decide to minimize risk in important areas, which usually makes for less uncertainty. Thus, in both your organizational and personal lives, if you do not choose when you can, others will choose for you—you can count on it. And if others choose for you, you lose some stewardship over your journey and risk increased uncertainty.

In this chapter we first define decision making and provide a brief model of decision making. Then we examine the process and outcome components of decision making to develop a set of strategies for decision making in a variety of organizations in the global marketplace. It is important to remember that the process and outcome components of decision making influence and interact with each other and that both contribute to the effectiveness or adaptability of organizational decision making.

Definition of Decision Making

We define *decision making* as the process of choosing among alternatives, implementing a decision, and using the subsequent outcome data to shape any further decisions associated with the earlier one. The process of choosing among alternatives almost always involves some combination of evaluation of data on the alternatives, one's values or preferences about what is important, one's expectations or predictions about what is likely to happen at some future time, and some emotional signals about the alternatives.

We have frequently observed that in many organizations, most members (if given a choice) want to participate in making a decision, but few want to be involved in implementing a decision or closely monitoring the real-time, actual out-

comes of a decision. However, the more closely decision making, implementing, and outcome monitoring are joined, the more quickly and effectively subsequent decisions can be made on the basis of real-time or modestly aged data.

Model of Decision Making

Organizational members must make a variety of decisions each day that will affect a limited or wide range of organizational members in the near future (a few seconds to a few days) or the remote future (from a few weeks to many months to many years). Furthermore, almost all organizational decision making is made by a group, rather than by an individual, so decision making is primarily a social process whose outcomes are usually dispersed among an array of organizational members (Chen, Lawson, Gordon, & McIntosh, 1996; Gioffre, Lawson, & Gordon, 1992; Offermand & Gowing, 1991; Sniezek & Henry, 1990).

Table 8–1 presents a six-step model of organizational decision making that includes both process (Steps 1–4) and outcome (Steps 5 and 6) components. It is important to appreciate that organizational decision making usually arises within turbulent, cacophonous, or high-velocity environments in which change is ever present, there is a lot of noise or interruptions of any given decision activity, and opportunities and

Table 8–1. A Model of Decision Making

Process Component
Identification of an opportunity or problem
Determination of the importance of the opportunity or problem
A search for and evaluation of alternatives
The selection of an alternative or alternatives

Outcome Component
Implementation of the decision
Provision of feedback on and evaluation of the decision outcome or outcomes

problems keep streaming into or arising from within the organization.

We have observed in our work with many different kinds of organizations that decision making usually begins with the identification of an opportunity (anticipatory decision making) or a problem (reactive decision making). In general, the more closely the decision-making group is to real-time data, the more likely they can spot opportunities (such as new markets, organizational processes, or technology) rather than focus on problems defined by historical or forecast data sets. Thereafter, the organizational member or decision-making group needs to determine if the focal situation is an important opportunity or problem that requires attention and action. Steps 3 and 4 can be completed quickly or slowly, depending on the decision maker's level of tolerance for risk; a high tolerance allows for more speedy decision making. In considering different alternatives, decision makers focus on implementation issues, so there is a clear linkage between the process and outcome components. In Steps 5 and 6, there is a shift to what may be called right-to-left thinking in that the goal or anticipated outcome of the decision is now clearly stated and attention is given to plans of action that outline what specifically needs to be done, working from the goal backward to the present. This right-to-left thinking increases the anticipation of barriers and the development of strategies to deal with them. Once a decision is implemented, it is important to monitor the outcome measures (improved quality, reduced expenses, and shorter delivery time) carefully, for without systematic feedback it is impossible to determine the overall effectiveness of decision making. In actual organizational situations, the six steps do not necessarily occur as discretely as is presented in Table 8–1 because some steps are taken simultaneously or are executed by individuals or groups that support the actual decision-making group.

Types of Decisions

In general, decisions can be classified as either *programmed* or *nonprogrammed* (Simon, 1977). Programmed decisions usually involve highly repetitive and routine problems in which the procedures for decision making are well established, applied frequently, and triggered by structured or clearly defined problems that require immediate action. In programmed decision making, the focus is on the implementation of the decision, with the first four steps highly standardized, as represented in operating manuals and standard operating procedures.

Nonprogrammed decisions are rare, infrequently encountered, or unique opportunities or problems that cannot be accommodated by standard operating procedures. This type of decision making is usually made by upper-level managers or self-directed work teams who go through all six steps. There is typically much more uncertainty involved with nonprogrammed than programmed decisions, and the focus is on cognitive processes, such as creativity, simulation, and perhaps the implementation of trial-balloon or limited-action outcome projects.

We now examine why some people prefer a sure outcome of a decision while others are more inclined to a risky outcome. According to Larrick (1993), preferences for risk or certainty arise not only from the perceived value of the outcomes of different courses of action and the probability that each of the outcomes will occur, but, more important, from the belief that making a choice can enhance or erode one's self-esteem and efficacy as a decision maker when the outcomes turn out well or poorly, respectively.

DECISION MAKING: INDIVIDUALS

In general, most people believe that they reason clearly, exercise sound judgment, and make decisions rationally and logically. However, many investigators have identified a number of systematic errors and fallacies that people tend to commit when thinking and making decisions (Basic Behavioral Science Task Force, 1996). For example, people are influenced by whether a choice is framed in terms of gains or losses. Similarly, people often take risks because they do not assume that they will have to suffer the consequences. Thus, people's choices are often unduly tilted in the direction of what they want to believe—the confirmatory bias effect. Last, in making decisions, people tend to overestimate how many other persons agree with their attitudes and beliefs—a judgmental bias known as the false-consensus bias. It is important to be aware of these forces that moderate decision making so you can appreciate the value of both the rational, objective forces and the cognitive and affective forces that shape the decisions that individuals and organizations make.

Risk Preferences

People tend to avoid taking risks when the potential for gain is involved, preferring the known and predictable to the unknown (Kahneman & Tversky, 1979, 1982; Schoemaker, 1980). In general, they do not like surprises because they assume the surprises will be negative. However, people prefer to take risks when the choice is between an inevitable loss and an uncertain loss (Fishburn & Kochenberger, 1979; Hershey & Schoemaker, 1980; Kahneman & Tversky, 1979). For example, when persons had to choose between losing $3,000 for certain or losing $4,000 with an 80% probability, 92% selected the latter and 8% selected the former, exhibiting a proneness to take risks (Kahneman & Tversky, 1979). When people seek to improve what they already have and must choose between a lower-level sure improvement versus a higher-level improvement with a greater risk, they tend to select the former, reflecting an aversion to risk. However, if they are faced with los-

ing a lower amount for certain, compared to losing a greater amount with a remote chance of not losing anything, then they will take the risk and select the latter alternative. In general, if you already have something of value to you, you will be conservative in your risk taking, whereas if you have nothing or are bound to lose, then you are more likely to take a risk. In other words, in most organizational situations, the haves are more likely to be risk averse, while the have-nots are more likely to be risk prone.

Emotions, Self-esteem, and Risk

People usually respond to the emotional consequences of decision making, as reflected in their feelings of success or failure, enhanced or lowered self-esteem and self-efficacy, and elation or disappointment (Larrick, 1993). Decision making is more than a cold cognitive experience; it also includes hot emotional components. According to Josephs, Larrick, Steele, and Nisbett (1992), when feedback about a decision is poor, people often feel regret, which can tarnish their self-image by leading to self-doubts about the wisdom of the original decision. In this regard, risk preferences are considered to be shaped by the motivation to protect their self-image. Josephs et al. and Larrick both reported that when faced with risky decisions, persons with low self-esteem were more risk averse when they expected feedback on their decisions, whereas persons with high self-esteem never made regret-minimizing choices. It appears, then, that the ability to maintain a good self-image in the face of regret is an important determinant of a person's preference for taking risks.

Larrick (1993) suggested that risk preferences are determined primarily by cognitive forces when a given decision poses little or no threat to self-esteem. However, as the potential of a threat to self-esteem increases (for example, when one regrets an earlier, publicly made, decision), risk preferences are determined mainly by the motivation to protect and enhance one's self-image and self-esteem.

MODELS OF DECISION MAKING

In most instances, decision making involves perceived, rather than objective, measures of risk. Of the many models of how organizations make decisions, three—the *rationality*, *bounded-rationality*, and *political models* are briefly discussed in this section (Browne, 1993; Harrison, 1987). Organizational decision making usually involves processes described in each of the three models, so the adoption of a blended approach will lead you closer to what actually transpires than will strict adherence to one model.

Rationality

This model is a cold, cognitive model in that it is based on the assumptions that decision makers are entirely rational and seek the best or most effective alternative for a given problem (Browne, 1993). The model further assumes that decision makers

- have complete information about the opportunity or problem.
- have complete information about all alternatives and the consequences of selecting one alternative over any other.
- make a decision solely on the basis of expectations about future outcomes, rather than on power or political considerations.

In using a rational approach to decision making, organizational members would follow all the steps presented in Table 8–1 and examine logically and analytically all the information they had before they made a decision. In general, individuals and organizations aspire to make as many decisions as possible on the basis of rational considerations. However, there are many obstacles to doing so because of the nature of organizations, such as constraints on resources that limit the amount of information that can be assembled and processed by the decision-making group within a given time.

Bounded Rationality

This model has been put forth as a more accurate description of how decisions are actually made in a variety of organizations (Cyert & March, 1963; March & Simon, 1958; Simon, 1955, 1976). A fundamental assumption of this model is that decision makers behave rationally within the constraints of their cognitive capabilities to attend to and define the problem and gain information about alternatives. In other words, decision makers aspire to make optimal choices but are hampered by the following two boundaries to rationality:

- All possible information about the problem and alternatives cannot be known within a given period.
- A decision may be based on criteria other than the rational and logical evaluation of information, such as consideration of members' preferences and coalitions in the organization.

As a consequence of the cognitive constraints of not being able to gather and process all the possible information about a problem and all the alternatives, decision makers "satisfice," rather than "optimize," by selecting the alternative that appears good enough to solve the problem.

Since alternatives are often ambiguously defined, decision making is primarily a process of deciding what to pay attention to and searching for information about alternatives. According to Cyert and March (1963), decision making is shaped by four basic forces that operate in all organizations:

- Conflict arising from the choice of an alternative is seldom totally resolved or confronted; rather it is only partially resolved through satisficing.

- Decision makers limit their search for alternatives to a problem by staying within the boundaries of prior or existing alternatives that they know about and thus that do not add further ambiguity to the situation.

- As a result of observing the consequences of their decisions, organizations learn to modify their aspirations or goals on the basis of their own experiences and those of other organizations with whom they compare themselves.

According to the bounded-rationality model of decision making, most decisions are made using relatively stable, routine organizational processes that operate incrementally in response to problems and serve to maintain the stability of an organization over time.

Politics

The political model proposes that decisions result from bargaining by individuals or coalitions, rather than from the operation of routine organizational information-gathering and processing processes. Accordingly, decision making is a matter of seeking a solution that is acceptable to all parties and following a strategy of incrementalism in search of what is possible, rather than what is optimal or satisficing (Lindblom, 1959; Wildavsky, 1975). An incremental approach to decision making, or inching along a step at a time, limits the definition of the problem, the information-search processes, the number of alternatives, and the number of participants only to those who have a stake in the outcome and power either to block or implement the decision. According to Harrison (1987) and Browne (1993), political decision making also usually includes

- considering only alternatives that differ slightly, marginally, or incrementally from existing policies or practices

- considering a small number of alternatives and only those with limited consequences

- continually massaging or redefining the problem and alternatives to make the decision acceptable to all parties

- focusing on short-term problems.

Organizations are considered contexts for decision making in which various coalitions of individuals and subunits are nested, all of which have goals and aspirations that evolve over time and make decisions based on successive and limited comparisons of alternatives. As Cohen, March, and Olson (1972) suggested in their *garbage-can model of decision making*, organizational contexts are defined by disorderly streams of decision makers, problems, solutions, and opportunities for making choices that are loosely coupled or linked only by their arrival and departure times in the organization. Critics of the garbage-can model (see Bass, 1983; Perrow, 1977) consider it to be too descriptive; applicable primarily to public service and nonhierarchical organizations; and focused mainly on reactive, rather than proactive, decision making.

Central to each of the three models is the fact that decision making is primarily a group or social process. Accordingly, we now consider empirical studies of group decision making.

GROUP DECISION MAKING

Most decisions in organizations are made by groups because it is assumed that group decision making can promote and sustain the competitive position of the organizations (Heil, 1991; Sundstrom, Demeuse, & Futrell, 1990). However, the growing reliance on group decision making is not risk free because this process can be influenced markedly by an "agreement norm" that may restrict or suppress disagreements that may be necessary for making effective decisions (Gero, 1985; Harvey, 1974). Levine and Moreland (1990) reported that generic group norms (such as norms to prevent or minimize conflict and to regulate contact between group members and outsiders with different perspectives on particular issue) emerge in almost every group.

Groupthink and the *Abilene Paradox* are examples of problematic group decision making.

Groupthink

Groupthink is the tendency of a group to pursue and attain a premature consensus for a given decision. Janis (1972, p. 9) defined Groupthink as

> a mode of thinking that people engage in when they are deeply involved in a cohesive in-group . . . members' striving for unanimity override their motivation to realistically appraise alternative courses of action . . . a deterioration of mental efficiency, reality testing, and moral judgment that results from ingroup pressures.

The construct of Groupthink grew out of Janis's analytical case studies of major decision-making fiascoes, including the Bay of Pigs invasion, the escalation of the Vietnam conflict, the Watergate cover-up, the explosion of the space shuttle Challenger, and flawed group problem solving in business organizations (Aldag & Fuller, 1993; Janis, 1982, 1989).

According to Janis and Mann (1977), Groupthink is most likely to arise under certain conditions, to be reflected in specific symptoms exhibited by the decision-making groups, and to result in specific defects in decision making that lead inevitably to a poor decision outcome. Janis (1982) stressed that the primary antecedent of Groupthink is a moderate to high level of cohesiveness in the decision making group and that structural faults in the group and a provocative situational context are secondary antecedents. Structural faults include a group's insulation from external, especially contradictory information or expert testimony; biased leadership; lack

of clear-cut guidelines for the process; and members whose social and ideological backgrounds are similar. The provocative situational context consists of stressors outside the group, such as pressure to make a decision or the threat of the potential loss of power, and internal stressors, including the group members' perceptions of the difficulty of the task and that there is no morally correct alternative, as well as the group's recent history of decision-making failures.

According to Janis (1982) and Janis and Mann (1977), Groupthink is reflected in its symptoms, such as an illusion of invulnerability, belief in the inherent morality of the group, self-censorship (ignoring contradictory thoughts or self-doubts about the emerging decision), and self-appointed "mind guards" that shield the group from adverse decision-related information. As Groupthink grows and the decision-making group continues the journey to consensus, defects in decision making begin to surface. These defects include the avoidance of new information about the consensual decision and the failure to re-examine the preferred choice or rejected alternatives and to develop contingency plans.

Almost all the empirical studies of Groupthink have focused primarily on the two antecedent conditions: the group's cohesiveness and directive leadership (Aldag & Fuller, 1993; Chen, 1993; Chen et al., 1996; McCauley, 1989; Montanari & Moorehead, 1989; Park, 1990; Tetlock, Peterson, McGuire, Chang, & Feld, 1992). The effect of leadership style on Groupthink is much more consistent than the effect of cohesiveness alone or their interaction effect on Groupthink. Groups with directive leadership styles generally produce more symptoms of Groupthink and more observable defects in their decision-making processes than do groups with participative leadership styles (Flowers, 1977; Fodor & Smith, 1982; Leana, 1985; McCauley, 1989; Moorhead & Montanari, 1986).

According to Janis (1982), cohesiveness is a necessary but not a sufficient condition for producing Groupthink. The results of research on the antecedents of group cohesiveness have been mixed; however, most of the studies have failed to find a significant influence of cohesiveness alone on Groupthink symptoms, defective decision processes, or final decision outcomes (Callaway, Marriott, & Esser, 1985; Courtright, 1978; Esser & Lindoerfer, 1989; Flowers, 1977; Fodor & Smith, 1982; McCauley, 1989). Leana (1985) and Moorhead and Montanari (1986) reported negative relationships between cohesiveness and the symptoms of Groupthink or observable defects in the decision-making process. Turner, Pratkanis, Probasco, and Leve (1992) revealed that the relationship between cohesion and Groupthink symptoms is mixed. For example, they claimed that cohesion apparently contributed to the illusion of invulnerability, as Janis (1982) predicted, but it also decreased self-censorship. Nevertheless, three studies have found an effect of high cohesiveness on the presence of Groupthink in different degrees, which supports Janis's (1982) analysis (Callaway & Esser, 1984; Moorhead & Montanari, 1986; Park, 1990).

Groupthink occurs when cohesiveness interacts with other antecedent conditions. For example, Courtright (1978) and Callaway and Esser (1984) reported an interaction effect between high cohesiveness and the lack of decision-making procedures or guidelines to avoid defective decision-making processes. High cohesiveness, coupled with the lack of such procedures or guidelines, discouraged disagreement and produced fewer alternative solutions to problems.

Preventing Groupthink

Janis (1982, 1989) suggested a number of preventive measures to avoid or minimize Groupthink, including participative, rather than directive leadership, and the appointment of a group member to play devil's advocate. Another preventive measure is to invite experts to the group's meetings to moderate any Groupthink tendencies and to encourage the members to explore possible alternatives. Janis (1989) also suggested that the decision-making group could be divided into subgroups to develop different decision alternatives and that a "second-chance" meeting could be held after initial consensus is reached on the preferred alternative.

The appointment of a *devil's advocate* is designed to promote an open discussion of suggested solutions, rather than to rely on a one group member to criticize the dominant alternative (Cosier & Schwenk, 1990). To achieve this goal, the role of devil's advocate should be rotated among group members, so no single member is perceived as the critic on all issues or as a whiner, and the members should be helped to understand that criticism of the dominant alternative is not to be taken personally but should be perceived as being part of the decision-making process. Studies of groups that have used this strategy have found that the groups produced significantly higher-quality decisions (that led to higher profits) on a hypothetical financial problem than did the groups who did not use it (Chanin & Shapiro, 1984; Schweiger, Sandberg, & Ragan, 1986; Schweiger, Sandberg, & Rechner, 1989). Table 8–2 presents a devil's advocate strategy that can be employed in a wide variety of organizational decision making (Cosier & Schwenk, 1990).

Table 8–2. Devil's Advocate Strategy

- A proposed course of action is identified.
- A devil's advocate (individual or group) criticizes the proposal.
- The critique is presented to key decision makers.
- Additional information relevant to the decision is gathered.
- The decision to adopt, modify, or discontinue the proposed course of action is made.
- The decision is monitored.

Adapted from R. A. Cosier & R. Schwenk, "Agreement and Thinking Alike: Ingredients for Poor Decisions," *Academy of Management Executive, 4*, p. 72. Copyright 1990 by Academy of Management.

Another strategy to deal with Groupthink is the *dialectical method*. This strategy for organizational decision making, introduced by Mason (1969), consists of a structured debate on markedly different plans during which the advocates present the assumptions of their plans and as much of the details of the plans as possible. After the debate, the group comes to a decision by voting on the basis of an examination of the assumptions and features of two alternatives. Table 8–3 presents a dialectical-method strategy that can be used to prevent or minimize Groupthink.

The devil's advocate and dialectical-method strategies are examples of programmed or infused conflict, on the assumption that the careful exploration of alternatives is more likely to yield a higher-quality decision than is the absence of such exploration (Janis & Mann, 1977; Schwenk, 1990). Schwenk's meta-analysis of the literature on decision making reported that the devil's advocate resulted in better-quality decisions than did the dialectical method or the expert-based approach (in which there is no conflict because the expert makes the decision), but that both the devil's advocate and dialectical-method strategies were equally effective for in-

troducing programmed conflict into the decision-making context. Finally, Chen (1993) and Chen et al. (1996) found, after an extensive study of group decision making, that the quality of decisions (indexed by an objective comparative measure with actual experts' decisions) was significantly higher for groups with participative leaders and devil's advocates than for groups with directive leaders and no devil's advocates.

In sum, the quality of decisions is higher when groups have participative leaders who encourage members to contribute actively and incorporate devil's advocates (infused conflict) into the group decision-making process. Thinking alike and only agreeing can be a superhighway to hell!

Abilene Paradox

The Abilene Paradox refers to the fact that organizations frequently make decisions that are the opposite of what they actually want to do, thus setting out on a journey that takes them away from their desired goals (Harvey, 1974). The paradox arises from the failure to manage agreement (for example, when all or most of the decision makers agree publicly on one alternative during the decision meeting but state privately after the meeting that they actually preferred other alternatives). Perhaps you can remember attending decision meetings in which no one criticized or suggested alternatives to the dominant proposal. However, after the participants voted unanimously or by a large majority to accept the proposal, people gathered in small clusters in the hallway, where they indicated that they preferred some other alternative than the one they just voted on. Welcome to Abilene!

The Abilene Paradox is an example of compliant groupthink (public agreement, coupled with private individual disagreement that is expressed outside the decision-making group) as contrasted with internalized Groupthink (in

---

Table 8–3. Dialectical-Method Strategy

- A proposed course of action is devised.

- Assumptions underlying the proposal are identified.

- A conflicting counterproposal based on different assumptions is generated.

- Advocates of each position present and debate the merits of their proposals before key decision makers.

- The decision to adopt either position or some other position (a compromise) is made.
- The decision is monitored.

Adapted from R. A. Cosier & C. R. Schwenk, "Agreement and Thinking Alike: Ingredients for Poor Decisions," *Academy of Management Executive, 4*, p. 73. Copyright 1990 by Academy of Management.

which the group members come to a consensus both publicly and privately, so there are no intrapersonal experiences of conflict or regret) (McCauley, 1989).

The inability to manage agreement is the defining feature of the Abilene Paradox (Harvey, 1974). That no one goes to Abilene alone indicates that decision makers collude with each other to agree, rather than risk being outcasts or separated from the group. The strategies for programmed or infused conflict discussed earlier—the devil's advocate and dialectical-method strategies—are also appropriate for preventing or detouring from the Abilene Paradox. Other possibilities are to take a straw vote, call a brief recess, and circulate around the meeting room or in the hallways to solicit individual members' opinion about the straw-vote decision. Thereafter, reconvene the meeting, and if you sense a lot of private disagreement with the straw vote, then take the risk of raising the potential for disagreement and perhaps appoint someone to play the role of devil's advocate. For costly, emotionally charged, or politically loaded issues, some extra time spent during the decision-making process may yield many positive dividends in the long run for all parties to the decision.

Last, it is important to keep in mind that group discussions usually result in more extremes—more risky or conservative decisions or more positive or negative attitudes than each member had before the discussions. This phenomenon is known as *group polarization* (Isenberg, 1986; Meyers & Lamm, 1976). Thus, it is essential to assess, when possible, individual members' inclinations before important group decisions on a particular issue. If such an assessment yields a sense of alignment with the direction that is important to you or the organization, then you can expect greater support after the group discussion; if not, you have your work cut out if you wish to realign the members' inclinations in accord with the organization's objectives.

GOOD IDEAS: HOW TO GET THEM

The generation of ideas or alternatives is a critical component of decision making (see Table 8–1). Since the influential work of Osborn (1957), it had been assumed that *brainstorming* (the generation of ideas by a group) is better than the generation of ideas by individuals working alone (Dennis & Valacich, 1993; Gallupe, Bastianutti, & Cooper, 1991). The general guidelines for brainstorming or idea-generating groups include (1) no criticism of any suggested idea until all the ideas have been generated, (2) freewheeling (the wilder the idea, the better—anything goes), (3) encouraging the expression of as many ideas as possible, (4) building on an already expressed idea. There are many strategies for brainstorming that are extensions of these basic guidelines (De Bono, 1985; Parnes, 1992).

According to Osborn (1957), during brainstorming, members of a group hear other ideas that trigger ideas they would not have thought of if they had been working alone. This, of course, would be good news, especially given the emphasis on self-managed teams in organizations, and would further reinforce the value of employing teamwork in the workplace. However, the evidence indicates that individuals who work separately generate many more ideas—and more creative ones—than do groups (Diehl & Stroebe, 1987; McGrath, 1984; Taylor, Berry, & Block, 1958). It is unequivocally clear that verbal brainstorming groups of four or more individuals produce significantly fewer ideas than do nominal groups (ideas generated by individuals on their own that are then combined with the ideas of other persons also working alone). Verbal brainstorming groups have never outperformed nominal groups (Diehl & Stroebe, 1987).

Electronic Brainstorming

There are three reasons why verbal brainstorming groups are not as productive as nominal groups (Gallupe et al., 1991). First, social loafing arises in verbally interacting groups in which the members do not work as hard as when they work alone. Second, production blocking occurs because only one person can speak at a time and some persons may be more verbal than others. Third, group members may feel apprehensive about how other members will react to their verbally expressed ideas.

Gallupe et al. (1991) and Gallupe et al. (1992) used electronic brainstorming to determine if group members interacting electronically (via computer), would be as effective or more effective than members working alone electronically and then combining their ideas, as in nominal groups. In the Gallupe et al. (1991) study electronic and nonelectronic groups and nominal and interacting groups were compared in a 2×2 factorial design. Electronically interacting groups of four members were constructed in which each member entered ideas as they arose and could, with a single keystroke, see on the computer screen a random set of ideas generated by the other members. When the researchers compared the work of these groups with that of constructed groups of four members each who worked independently and then pooled their ideas electronically, they found that both types of groups produced about an equal number of ideas and produced significantly more ideas than the usual verbal interacting and nominal groups. Also, the interacting electronic groups found brainstorming easier, participated more, and experienced little apprehension compared to the verbal interacting group. Dennis and Valacich (1993) reported that electronic brainstorming was superior to conventional brainstorming in which group members interact verbally, especially for large groups (12 members). They concluded that electronic brainstorming reduces production blocking, members' apprehension about how other members will judge their ideas, and social loafing and avoids the production of redundant ideas by timely electronic exposure to the ideas of other members of the group.

Furthermore, Nunamaker, Dennis, Valacich, Vogel, and George (1991) found that electronic brainstorming can be used with large groups (30 or more members) and that it would be extremely difficult to manage verbally interacting groups of this size that were responsible for generating alternative ideas for decision making.

Nominal Group Technique

Many strategies have been developed to enhance the creative problem solving of conventional verbally interacting groups. The nominal group technique (NGT) uncouples the generation of ideas from the evaluation of ideas while incorporating both activities into this group decision-making process (Bartunek & Murningham, 1984; Delbecq, Vande Ven, & Gustafson, 1975; Fox, 1987). There are four steps to the NGT process:

1. *Generation of ideas.* Group members are usually presented with a written question, such as "What should be our three major goals, products, or services for the upcoming fiscal year?" They write down their ideas in response to the question.

2. *Recording of ideas.* Each member, in turn, reads her or his idea and a designated person writes down each idea, which is displayed on a big screen or board that all members can view. During the recording stage, there is no discussion or evaluation of the presented ideas. Once each group member has presented the first round of ideas the process is repeated until all members have had the opportunity to express all their written ideas. The posted public ideas are now ideas in the name of the group and do not belong to any particular member.

3. *Clarification of ideas.* Each posted idea is discussed, so the members can better understand the rationale of all the ideas. The primary aim is to clarify the ideas, rather than

to debate the merits of one idea versus another.

4. *Voting on ideas.* Each member privately votes on the top 3, 5, or whatever desired number of rankings; these rankings are summarized; and the top ideas emerge in the name of the group. If there are no clear-cut preferences in the first round of voting, the process is repeated until the top ideas emerge from the group. The results of the final vote represent the group's decision.

The NGT is an easy and effective group decision-making procedure, can be used with groups of 8–25 persons, and is best used for exploring new ideas and possible courses of action (like criteria for promotion or features of a reward system), rather than for routine or highly personal decision making, such as promotion or pay adjustments for specific individuals.

The *delphi technique* is a group decision-making process that can be employed with large groups (25 or more persons) and when members are unable to meet face to face, as they do in the NGT (Delbecq et al., 1975). Basically, it is a process of systematically soliciting and collating ideas on a particular topic (for example, "What should be our three major organization-wide goals for the next one to three years?") by means of sequentially presented questionnaires interspersed with feedback from the responses to earlier questionnaires.

The Stepladder Technique

In organizations, groups make decisions about new products and services; create new policy statements or revise old ones (to incorporate policies on valuing diversity, harassment in the workplace, and violence and emergency processes in the workplace); develop marketing proposals; and, in fact, decide on almost every issue or problem that requires attention and a solution. In general, over a wide range of tasks,

the score for group decision making is higher than the average of individual members' scores (Bottger & Yetton, 1987), but not as good as the performance of the best member of a group (Burleson, Levine, & Samter, 1984; Libby, Trotman, & Zimmer, 1987). Inasmuch as most decision making by organizational groups involves face-to-face interactions, communication may be dominated by one or two highly vocal members who appear "to thrive on air time" (Johnson & Johnson, 1987). Likewise, conformity norms (groupthink) may be quite high, or some members might be inclined to let the other members do the work (social loafing), since none has personal responsibility or accountability (Latané, Williams, & Haskins, 1979).

The *stepladder technique*, introduced by Rogelberg, Barnes-Farrell, and Lowe (1992), is designed to enhance group decision making by regulating the entry of group members into the core decision-making group. For example, with a four-member decision group, two members (the initial core group) work together on the problem for some period, after which the third member enters the group and presents her or his suggestions, and there is a three-person group discussion. Then the fourth member joins the three-member group, presents her or his suggestions, and there is a four-member discussion, followed by a group decision. In effect, the staggering of members' entry into the decision-making group addresses some of the problems of members' dominance, conformity, and social loafing that usually arise in conventional groups (fully constituted groups in which all members interact and work on the problem at the same time).

Rogelberg et al. (1992) found that stepladder groups produced significantly higher-quality decisions than did conventional groups and about the same-quality decisions as the best decisions by individuals, as determined by an objective measure of quality. This objective measure was used in Johnson and Johnson's (1987) winter survival exercise in which survivors of an imagined plane crash had to rank 12 items remaining from the crash in terms of their importance to survival. To be effective, the stepladder technique requires that each group member gets the problem at the same time and is allowed to think about it before he or she enters the core decision-making group, the entering member must present her or his decision before learning the decision of the core group or the subsequent enlarged group, and there is time for discussion after each suggested alternative is presented and before the fully constituted group makes a final decision.

Electronic brainstorming (if computers and software are available), the NGT, the stepladder technique, or some combination of these strategies can be of great value to group-based decision making, especially if the members have time to make decisions, which may not always be the case with turbulent organizations and high-velocity contexts.

High-Velocity Decision Making

Many times, organizational events change so rapidly that important decisions on such issues as new products or services or new alliances with other organizations have to be made in a few weeks or months, rather than a year or more (Eisenhardt, 1989, 1990). Eisenhardt (1990) examined decision making in the high-velocity environments of 12 microprocessor firms by means of extensive interviews with members of the top management team and observations of group meetings. In general, she found that fast decision makers maintained constant vigilance over real-time operating information, simultaneously compared three to five multiple alternatives, and promoted the quick resolution of conflicts. In addition, they used consensus with qualification in which group members were encouraged to express their alternatives and if the group could not reach a consensus, the responsible officer or manager made the decision. Finally, fast decision makers integrated a focal decision with

other decisions and tactical plans. Table 8–4 presents specific steps for fast decision making that can be applied in a variety of organizations.

AVALANCHES OF INFORMATION

In almost every organization, more information usually floats around the organization, is stored in information banks (computer center databases, or libraries), or is packaged for release to the public by the public relations office or official organizational spokesperson than any decision-making group can use. In short, most organizational members are struck by an avalanche of information each day—in the form of stacks of letters and memorandums and endless streams of E-mail and phone-mail messages, notes scribbled on scraps of paper, gossip, and rumors.

Gossip

A lot of the information that organizational members exchange is *gossip*—idle talk or information that is not relevant for decision making. March and Sevón (1984) suggested that

Table 8–4. Specific Steps for Making Fast High-Quality Decisions

- Before decisions arise track real time information to develop a deep and intuitive grasp of the business.
- During the decision process, immediately begin to build multiple alternatives using your intuitive grasp of the business.
- Ask everyone for advice, but depend on one or two key counselors. Look for savvy, trustworthy, and discreet colleagues.
- When it's time to decide try for consensus, but if it doesn't emerge then don't delay. Delaying won't make you popular and won't make you fast.
- Ensure that you have integrated your choice with other decisions194   194 and tactical moves.

gossip is valuable to an organization and serves the following purposes:

- Information is exchanged between persons to maintain the informational systems of the organization.

- Human action is more a matter of imitating the actions of others than a matter of choice.

- Organizational decisions are usually loosely coupled to available decision-relevant information.

- Information is used mainly to interpret and understand organizational events, rather than to make specific choices.

For example, gossip maintains connections among organizational members who may not communicate frequently with each other on specific decisions or between formal decision-making situations. It keeps the informational links open, so when decision-relevant information is needed, the decision maker knows whom to turn to for it. The idea that human action arises primarily from imitation suggests that learning about the experiences of others through idle talk emphasizes the importance of history or past experiences.

Organizations, like individuals, collect a great deal of information, from published reports, books, and periodicals and various forms of mail, that is not necessarily linked tightly to a specific decision context or deadline. This kind of idle talk or decision-irrelevant information may become decision relevant at a later time, in which case members access it through an organizational library or another information center. Finally, the notion that organizations have control over their fate by means of their decisions is illusory, according to March and Sevón (1984); thus, decision-relevant and decision-irrelevant information are gathered not so much to prepare for the future as to interpret organizational and members' events.

Gossip is not necessarily pejorative or negative. Rather, it can serve important organizational purposes, such as keeping in touch with people, having a sense of what is going on around one, learning from the experiences of others, and dealing with the future, all of which are important parts of organizational life.

Rumor

The management of rumors is a necessary organizational process, especially in contexts in which members experience high levels of uncertainty and anxiety (Mishra, 1990; Rosnow, 1991).

Rumor is "a specific (or topical) proposition for belief, passed along from person to person, usually by word of mouth, without secure standards of evidence being present" (Allport & Postman, 1947, p. ix). Rosnow (1991) suggested the following three guidelines for managing rumors:

- Anticipate organizational events that are likely to generate high levels of uncertainty and anxiety and open up lines of communication that are honest and direct so as not to foster further suspicions or mistrust.

- Once a strong, malicious rumor is identified, the most appropriate response is to get the facts out promptly and circulate them widely throughout the organization and the external organizational environment if appropriate.

- If the rumor persists, is malicious and unfounded, and the source can be identified, then it is appropriate to take legal action against the rumor mongers to focus attention on their behavior.

Rumor treads a fine line between reality and illusion, and a preventive or remedial strategy requires sound judgment, logical thought, and a dose of compassion.

Ethical Decision Making

According to the "bad-apples" (dispositional) theory, unethical decisions are made by a few sleazy individuals in an organization who lack some personal attribute, such as a mature moral cognitive framework for making ethical decisions, or are highly Machiavellian (Hegarty & Sim, 1978, 1979; Simpson, 1987). On the other hand, the "bad-barrels" (situational) theory attributes unethical decisions to a poisonous organizational environmental influence, such as competition, the management's results orientation, the lack of reinforcement of ethical behavior (Baumhart, 1961; Brenner & Molander, 1977), and requests from authority figures to behave unethically (Rickles, 1983). Furthermore, it has been found that extrinsic rewards for unethical behavior and increased pressure for competition significantly increased unethical decision making (Hegarty & Sims, 1978), whereas the existence of an organizational ethics policy, the threat of dismissal, and the direct punishment of unethical behavior significantly reduced it (Hegarty & Sims, 1979; Laczniak & Inderrieden, 1986; Trevino & Youngblood, 1990).

In an informative laboratory-based study of ethical decision making in organizations, Trevino and Youngblood (1990) tested the bad-apples and bad-barrels theories. They found that ethical decision making is enhanced by the cognitive moral development of organizational members and a strong internal locus of control (members are more likely to do what they think is right and are prepared to bear the consequences of their position) but that vicarious or expected rewards or punishment had no direct influence on it. Thus, organizations would be well served if they recruited and retained individuals with high integrity by emphasizing the importance of integrity and ethical behaviors in their recruiting materials and company policies. Trevino and Youngblood's (1990) study clearly indicates that ethical decision making can be studied empirically, that the findings of such studies yield important insights into applied strategies, and that ethical behavior in organizations is influenced by dispositional forces (cognitive moral development) and situational forces (severe sanctions).

Finally, in some regions of the global marketplace, there are no systems of business law, clear governmental policies on ethics, and established business relationships. Hence, it is necessary to establish a common ethical framework with organizations in these areas before joint organizational opportunities can be pursued. For example, Pfuffer and McCarthy (1995) reported that American and Russian businesspersons had both common and disparate ethical standards. On the basis of interviews with Americans and Russians involved in joint ventures in Russia, they found that both parties thought that keeping promises, maintaining trust, promoting fair competition, and giving rewards for good performance were important shapers of ethical decision making. These ethical standards are similar to the globally shared or consensual values held by all persons, discussed in Chapter 2 (see Table 2–3). It was interesting that the Russians considered maximizing profits and layoffs to be unethical, but not price fixing and ignoring senseless laws, whereas both the Americans and Russians believed that gangsterism, extortion, and refusing to pay debts are unethical. Pfuffer and McCarthy concluded that it is important to be firm about ethical standards and to delineate clearly the common from the uncommon ground between parties when new learning opportunities and cultural constraints are present.

SUMMARY

Decision making in organizations is a social process that is influenced by rational and nonrational forces and consists of process and outcome components. It involves choosing among alternatives, implementing the decision, and examining outcome data that shape later decisions associated with the earlier decision. Most organizational decisions are programmed (routine) or nonprogrammed (unique and infrequent); the former require increasingly refined decision processes, while the latter require strategies that contribute to the generation of new and creative alternatives. Decision making is influenced by the risk preferences, emotions, and self-esteem of the decision makers, which are influenced by the potential gains and losses of a decision.

There are three models of decision making: the rationality, bounded-rationality, and political models, each of which makes plain that decisions arise primarily from social or group processes. We reviewed Groupthink and the Abilene Paradox as examples of defective group decision making and identified specific strategies to prevent or minimize these widespread and frequently occurring organizational phenomena.

Among the many ways to generate good ideas or alternatives, we described electronic brainstorming and the nominal group, delphi, and stepladder techniques. We also examined a strategy for dealing with decisions in highly dynamic or turbulent organizational contexts. Gossip or idle talk affords the exchange of information with no relevance to decisions among organizational members who do not communicate frequently with each other and thus keeps informational links open within organizations. Finally, we identified strategies to manage rumors within organizations, as well as dispositional and situational forces that shape ethical decision making in the global marketplace.

CHAPTER REFERENCES

Aldag, R. J., & Fuller, S. R. (1993). Beyond fiasco: A reappraisal of the groupthink phenomenon and a new model of group decision processes. *Psychological Bulletin, 113,* 533–552.

Allport, G. W., & Postman, L. (1947). *The psychology of rumor.* New York: Holt, Rinehart & Winston.

Bartunek, J. M., & Murningham, J. K. (1984). The nominal group technique: Expanding the basic procedure and underlying assumptions. *Group and Organization Studies, 9,* 417–432.

Basic Behavioral Science Task Force, National Advisory Mental Health Council. (1996). Basic behavioral science research for mental health: Thought and communication. *American Psychologist, 51,* 181–189.

Bass, B. M. (1983). *Organizational decision making.* Homewood, IL: Irwin.

Baumhart, R. C. (1961). How ethical are businessmen? *Harvard Business Review, 39,* 6–8.

Bottger, P. C., & Yetton, P. W. (1987). Improving group performance by training in individual problem solving. *Journal of Applied Psychology, 72,* 651–657.

Brenner, S. N., & Molander, E. A. (1977). Is the ethics of business changing? *Harvard Business Review, 55,* 57–71.

Browne, M. (1993). *Organizational decision making and information.* Norwood, NJ: Ablex.

Burleson, B. R., Levine, B. J., & Samter, W. (1984). Decision-making procedure and decision quality. *Human Communication Research, 10,* 557–574.

Callaway, M. R., & Esser, J. K. (1984). Groupthink: Effects of cohesiveness and problem-solving procedures on group decision making. *Social Behavior and Personality, 12,* 157–164.

Callaway, M. R., Marriott, R. G., & Esser, J. K. (1985). Effects of dominance on group decision making toward a stress-reduction explanation of groupthink. *Journal of Personality and Social Psychology, 49,* 949–952.

Chanin, M. N., & Shapiro, H. J. (1984). Dialectical and devil's advocate problem-solving. *Asia Pacific Journal of Management, 1,* 159–170.

Chen, Z. (1993). *The effects of leadership style and preventive strategy of devil's advocacy upon groupthink—A diagnosed problem in collective decision-making process.* Unpublished doctoral dissertation, University of Vermont, Burlington.

Chen, Z., Lawson, R. B., Gordon, L., & McIntosh, B. (1996). Groupthink: Deciding with the leader and the devil. *Psychological Record, 46,* 581–590.

Cohen, M. D., March, J. G., & Olsen, J. P. (1972). A garbage can model of organizational choice. *Administrative Science Quarterly, 17,* 1–25.

Courtright, J. A. (1978). A laboratory of group-think. *Communication Monographs, 5,* 229–246.

Cosier, R. A., & Schwenk, C. R. (1990). Agreement and thinking alike: Ingredients for poor decisions. *Academy of Management Executive, 4,* 69–74.

Cyert, R. M., & March, J. G. (1963). *Behavioral theory of the firm.* Englewood Cliffs, NJ: Prentice Hall.

De Bono, E. (1985). *Six thinking hats.* Boston: Little, Brown.

Delbecq, A. L., Vande Ven, A. H., & Gustafson, D. H. (1975). *Group techniques for program planning: A guide to nominal and delphi processes.* Glenview, IL: Scott, Foresman.

Dennis, A. R., & Valacich, J. S. (1993). Computer brainstorms: More heads are better than one. *Journal of Applied Psychology, 78,* 531–537.

Diehl, M., & Stroebe, W. (1987). Productivity loss in brainstorming groups: Toward the solution of a riddle. *Journal of Personality and Social Psychology, 53,* 497–509.

Eisenhardt, K. (1989). Making fast strategic decisions in high velocity environments. *Academy of Management Journal, 28,* 73–85.

Eisenhardt, K. M. (1990). Speed and strategic choice: How managers accelerate decision making. *California Management Review, 29,* 39–54.

Esser, J. K., & Lindoerfer, J. S. (1989). Groupthink and the space shuttle Challenger accident: Toward a quantitative case analysis. *Journal of Behavioral Decision Making, 2,* 167–177.

Fishburn, P. C., & Kochenberger, G. A. (1979). Two-piece von Neurmann-Noigenstern utility functions. *Decision Sciences, 10,* 503–518.

Flowers, M. L. (1977). A laboratory test of some implications of Janis's groupthink hypothesis. *Journal of Personality and Social Psychology, 33,* 888–895.

Fodor, E. M., & Smith, T. (1982). The power motive as an influence on group decision making. *Journal of Personality and Social Psychology, 42,* 178–185.

Fox, W. M. (1987). *Effective group problem solving.* San Francisco: Jossey-Bass.

Gallupe, R. B., Bastianutti, L. M., & Cooper, W. H. (1991). Unblocking brainstorms. *Journal of Applied Psychology, 76,* 137–142.

Gallupe, R. B., Dennis, A. R., Cooper, W. H., Valacich, J. S., Nunamaker, J. F. Jr., & Bastianutti, L. (1992). Electronic brainstorming and group size. *Academy of Management Journal, 35,* 350–369.

Gero, A. (1985). Conflict avoidance in consensual decision processes. *Small Group Behavior, 16,* 487–499.

Gioffre, K., Lawson, R. B., & Gordon, L. R. (1992). The effects of decision outcome dispersion upon organizational decision making. *Psychological Record, 42,* 427–436.

Harrison, E. F. (1987). *The managerial decision-making process* (3rd ed.). Boston: Houghton Mifflin.

Harvey, J. B. (1974). The Abilene Paradox: The management of agreement. *Organizational Dynamics, 3,* 63–80.

Hegarty, W. H., & Sims, H. P. Jr. (1978). Some determinants of unethical decision behavior: An experiment. *Journal of Applied Psychology, 63,* 451–457.

Hegarty, W. H., & Sims, H. P., Jr. (1979). Organizational philosophy, policies and objectives related to unethical decision behavior: A laboratory experiment. *Journal of Applied Psychology, 64,* 331–338.

Heil, W. B. (1991, August). *Reviewing participation in decision making: Toward a multidimensional model.* Paper presented at the 99th annual convention of the American Psychological Association, San Francisco.

Hershey, J. C., & Schoemaker, P. J. H. (1980). Prospect theory's reflection hypothesis: A critical examination. *Organizational Behavior and Human Performance, 25,* 395–418.

Janis, I. L. (1972). *Victims of groupthink.* Boston: Houghton Mifflin.

Janis, I. L. (1982). *Groupthink* (2nd ed.). Boston: Houghton Mifflin.

Janis, I. L. (1989). *Crucial decisions: Leadership in policy making and crisis management.* New York: Free Press.

Janis, I. L., & Mann, L. (1977). Decision making: A psychological analysis of conflict, choice, and commitment. New York: Free Press.

Johnson, D., & Johnson, F. (1987). *Joining together: Group theory and group skills.* Englewood Cliffs, NJ: Prentice Hall.

Josephs, R. A., Larrick, R. P., Steele, C. M., & Nisbett, R. E. (1992). Protecting the self from the negative consequences of risky decisions. *Journal of Personality and Social Psychology*, *62*, 26–37.

Isenberg, D. J. (1986). Group polarization: A critical review and meta-analysis. *Journal of Personality and Social Psychology*, *50*, 1141–1151.

Kahneman, D., & Tversky, A. (1979). Prospect theory: An analysis of decision under risk. *Econometrica*, *47*, 263–291.

Kahenman, D., & Tversky, A. (1982). The psychology of preferences. *Scientific American*, *246*, 160–173.

Laczniak, G. R., & Inderrieden, E. J. (1986). The influence of stated organizational concern upon ethical decision-making. *Journal of Business Ethics*, *6*, 297–307.

Larrick, R. P. (1993). Motivational factors in decision theories: The role of self-protection. *Psychological Bulletin*, *113*, 440–450.

Latané, B., Williams, K., & Haskins, S. (1979). Many hands make light the work: The causes and consequences of social loafing. *Journal of Personality and Social Psychology*, *37*, 822–832.

Leana, C. R. (1985). A partial test of Janis' groupthink model: Effects of group cohesiveness and leader behavior on defective decision making. *Journal of Management*, *11*, 5–17.

Levine, J. M., & Moreland, R. L. (1990). Progress in small group research. *Annual Review of Psychology*, *41*, 585–634.

Libby, R., Trotman, K. T., & Zimmer, I. (1987). Member variation, recognition of expertise, and group performance. *Journal of Applied Psychology*, 81–87.

Lindblom, C. E. (1959). The science of muddling through. *Public Administration Review*, *19*, 79–88.

March, J. G., & Sevón, G. (1984). Gossip, information, and decision making. *Advances in Information Processing in Organizations*, *1*, 95–107.

March, J. G., & Simon, H. A. (1958). *Organizations*. New York: John Wiley & Sons.

Mason, R. (1969). A dialectical approach to strategic planning. *Management Science*, *15*, 403–414.

McCauley, C. (1989). The nature of social influence in groupthink: Compliance and internalization. *Journal of Personality and Social Psychology*, *57*, 250–260.

McGrath, J. E. (1984). *Groups: Interaction and performance*. Englewood Cliffs, NJ: Prentice Hall.

Meyers, D. G., & Lamm, H. (1976). The group polarization phenomenon. *Psychological Bulletin*, *83*, 602–627.

Mishra, J. (1990). Managing the grapevine. *Public Personnel Management*, *19*, 213–228.

Montanari, J., & Moorhead, G. (1989). Development of the groupthink assessment inventory. *Educational and Psychological Measurement*, *49*, 209–219.

Moorhead, G., & Montanari, J. R. (1986). An empirical investigation of the groupthink phenomenon. *Human Relations*, *39*, 399–410.

Nunamaker, J. F., Dennis, A. R., Valacich, J. S., Vogel, D. R., & George, J. F. (1991). Electronic meeting systems to support group work. *Communications of the ACM*, *34*, 40–61.

Offermand, L. R., & Gowing, M. K. (1990). Organizations of the future: Changes and challenges. *American Psychologist*, *45*, 95–108.

Osborn, A. F. (1957). *Applied imagination* (rev. ed.). New York: Scribner's.

Park, W. (1990). A review of research on groupthink. *Journal of Behavioral Decision Making*, *3*, 229–245.

Parnes, S. J. (1992). *Source book for creative problem-solving: A fifty year digest of proven innovation processes*. Buffalo, NY: Creative Education Foundation Press.

Perrow, C. (1977). Review of ambiguity and choice in organizations. *Contemporary Sociology*, *6*, 294–298.

Pfuffer, S. M., & McCarthy, D. J. (1995). Finding the common ground in Russian and American business ethics. *California Management Review*, *37*, 29–46.

Ricklees, R. (1983, October 31–November 3), Ethics in America series. *Wall Street Journal*.

Rogelberg, S. G., Barnes-Farrell, J. L., & Lowe, C. A. (1992). Stepladder technique: An alternative group structure facilitating effective group decision making. *Journal of Applied Psychology, 77*, 730–737.

Rosnow, R. L. (1991). Inside rumor. *American Psychologist, 46*, 484–496.

Schoemaker, P. J. H. (1980). *Experiments on decisions under risk: The expected utility hypothesis*. Dordrecht, the Netherlands: Martinus Nijhoff.

Schweiger, D. M., Sandberg, W. R., & Ragan, J. W. (1986). Group approaches for improving strategic decision making: A comparative analysis of dialectical inquiry, devil's advocacy, and consensus. *Academy of Management Journal, 29*, 51–71.

Schweiger, D. M., Sandberg, W. R., & Rechner, P. L. (1989). Experiential effects of dialectical inquiry, devil's advocacy, and consensus approaches to strategic decision making. *Academy of Management Journal, 32*, 745–772.

Schwenk, C. R. (1990). Effects of devil's advocacy, and dialectical inquiry on decision making: A meta-analysis. *Organizational Behavior and Human Decision Processes, 47*, 161–176.

Simon, H. A. (1955). A behavioral model of rational choice. *Quarterly Journal of Economics, 69*, 129–138.

Simon, H. A. (1976). *Administrative behavior* (3rd ed.). New York: Free Press.

Simon, H. A. (1977). *The new science of management*. Englewood Cliffs, NJ: Prentice Hall.

Simpson, J. C. (1987, January 28). Wall Street's courting of MBAs proceeds apace despite scandals. *Wall Street Journal*, Sec. 2, p. 1.

Sniezek, J. A., & Henry, R. A. (1990). Revision, weighting, and commitment in consensus group judgment. *Organizational Behavior and Human Decision Processes, 45*, 66–84.

Sundstrom, E., Demeuse, K. P., & Futrell, D. (1990). Work teams. Applications and effectiveness. *American Psychologist, 45*, 120–133.

Taylor, D. W., Berry, P. C., & Block, C. H. (1958). Does group participation when using brainstorming facilitate or inhibit creative think-ing? *Administrative Sciences Quarterly, 3*, 23–47.

Tetlock, P., Peterson, R., McGuire, C., Chang, S., & Feld, P. (1992). Assessing political group dynamics: A test of the groupthink model. *Journal of Personality and Social Psychology, 63*, 403–425.

Trevino, L. K., & Youngblood, S. A. (1990). Bad apples in bad barrels: A causal analyses of ethical decision-making behavior. *Journal of Applied Psychology, 75*, 378–385.

Turner, M. E., Pratkanis, A. R., Probasco, P., & Leve, C. (1992). Threat, cohesion, and group effectiveness: Testing a social maintenance perspective on groupthink. *Journal of Personality and Social Psychology, 63*, 781–796.

Wildavsky, A. (1975). *Budgeting: A comparative theory of budgetary processes*. Boston: Little, Brown.

SUGGESTED REFERENCES

Ethics, or determining right from wrong, is, of course, a difficult, complex, and lifelong issue for individuals as well as organizations. Ethics focuses on obedience to the unenforceable and requires that the individual and the organization develop and sustain the capacities of authentic observation of oneself while considering the perspective or position of the other person, group, or organization on a given decision situation. We list below suggested sources that address ethical and justice issues, principles, and strategies that can be applied in a wide variety of organizations.

Brady, F. N. (1990). *Ethical managing: Rules and results*. New York: Macmillan.

Cropanzano, R. (1993). *Justice in the workplace*. Hillsdale, NJ: Lawrence Erlbaum.

Freeman, E. E. (1991). *Business ethics: The state of the art*. New York: Oxford University Press.

Nash, L. L. (1990). *Good intentions aside: A manager's guide to resolving ethical problems*. Cambridge, MA: Harvard Business School Press.

9

Conflict and Negotiation

CHAPTER OVERVIEW

Conflict is global, immune to cultural and other boundaries, and can be a source of constructive energy or wrenching angst and even violent death. Thus, it is neither intrinsically good nor bad; it is what you do about it that really counts. Conflict arises from a relationship between two or more parties (individuals, groups, or organizations) in a situation defined by finite resources in which there are perceived or real incompatibilities or disagreements between the parties and hence is multidimensional and frequent in organizations.

Conflict consists of three stages: escalation, in which one party attempts to prevail; stalemate, in which the parties exhaust their energies or resources; and deescalation, in which the parties reach some kind of agreement to cooperate with each other. The various behavioral styles in response to conflict—integrating, obliging, dominating, avoiding, and compromising—are driven by the extent of your concern for yourself and others and the context. Thus, if issues are complex, there is time for problem solving, and you have a high concern for yourself and others, then the integrating approach may be preferable.

Negotiations involve the costs of transactions (the time and money spent on the negotiation process), satisfaction with outcomes, effect on relationships, and the recurrence of disputes. They are formal systematic processes for resolving conflicts and, in many ways, are one of the finest and most distinguished features of human and organizational activities. We provide a number of guidelines for negotiations, including be prepared, be prepared to say no, and make your word your bond (keep promises). A central feature of successful negotiations is to know yourself, so you can know others' latitudes and limits. Also, always focus on relationship issues because once the negotiations are finished, the parties will most likely interact in some way in the future.

Before you negotiate, make sure you know your best alternative to a negotiated agreement (BATNA) and, when possible, pursue principled, rather than soft or hard, bargaining, as outlined in the foundational work of Fisher and Ury (1981). In this chapter, we briefly examine whistle-blowing as an example of the lack of a BATNA.

We then discuss the impact of gender, context, and dispositional forces on negotiating processes and outcomes. Kolb (1993) found that women bring an inclination for dialogue, rather than persuasion, argument, or debate, to negotiations. She also suggested that such an inclination may prove extremely valuable in complex and ambiguous organizational situations in that alternatives emerge more readily from the interaction between the parties than when the parties are inclined to persuade each other to adopt the respective views. A variety of contextual forces shape negotiations, including the power relationship between the parties, such that "things go better" when the parties have equal amounts of power. The dispositional forces of planning (conscientiousness) and humor are also important and usually result in positive outcomes. The failure to plan can well be a plan to fail, and humor, along with giving small gifts can set a positive tone for subsequent negotiations.

Last, we examine negotiations between small groups, rather than between dyadic groups (two-party negotiations), because such negotiations occur frequently in organizations. For small-group negotiations, it is important to focus on setting an agenda (what is on and off), decision rule (majority or unanimity rule), and the balance of power in the group.

We conclude with negotiations in various areas of the world and provide a list of excellent sources for negotiating in many different countries in the suggested readings.

LEARNING OBJECTIVES

When you finish studying this chapter, you will be able to

- define conflict and appreciate the potential of conflict to shape organizational events
- identify the phases and many sources of conflict
- describe and, what is more important, know when and how to apply the behavioral styles of integrating, obliging, dominating, avoiding, and compromising in response to conflict.
- apply the components of negotiations that represent formal systematic processes of conflict resolution
- define and internalize as a lifelong set of skills the guidelines for negotiating, such as the centrality of self-knowledge for appreciating your own limits, as well as those of the other party to the negotiations
- learn about your BATNA and the features and benefits of principled strategies
- define whistle-blowing and identify the conditions that give rise to this organizational phenomenon
- identify the impact of gender, context, and dispositional forces on negotiating processes and outcomes
- identify the features of group negotiations that occur frequently within and between organizations, including the need for a clear agenda, a decision rule, and knowledge of the power relationship between the parties
- identify some of the factors that influence negotiating strategies around the world, including countries in Asia and the United States.

Wisdom is knowing when and how to get from me to we.

CONFLICT

Most people spend much of their daily lives interacting with others; remembering others; or making decisions about themselves, such as between what they feel like doing and what must be done. That they often must choose between what they and others need or want, the founda-

tion is laid for conflict, harmony, or indifference. This chapter focuses on conflict, which is a fundamental part of organizational life, and presents a variety of strategies for responding to and dealing with it.

In our view, conflict can be both a cold (cognitive) and a hot (emotional and cognitive) experience. Cold conflict mainly involves the cognitive experiences of seeking information, examining alternatives, evaluating options, and then deciding between two or more alternatives; in cold conflict, the experience is primarily adult, computational, and without emotion. On the other hand, hot conflict involves a mix of cognitive and emotional experiences within and between conflicting persons that can erupt into hurtful or extremely harmful behaviors by either party. In cold conflict, people are usually considerate, calculating, and well intentioned when they attempt to resolve the conflict and to optimize their outcomes. In hot conflict, people are usually angry, frustrated, and sad and may be malicious or even murderous if the dynamics of the conflict go beyond acceptable rational and social constraints.

There are different kinds of conflict, all people have to deal with conflict, most of the conflict they encounter in their organizational and personal lives is a mix of cold and hot components, and if they do not learn how to deal with conflict by either preventive or remedial strategies, a great deal of organizational and personal resources can be wasted.

Definitions of Conflict

Conflict is neither intrinsically good nor bad; rather how one attempts to prevent or respond to it can result in positive or negative experiences and outcomes. Conflict can be a positive force in an organization when members openly acknowledge its existence and then pursue problem-solving and change strategies to deal with it. However, conflict can be bad and even horrorific when people respond by excluding, insulting, hurting, maiming, or murdering members of their or other organizations. Rigdon (1994) reported that a quarter of the 311 organizations surveyed by the American Management Association had at least one of their employees attacked or killed on the job between 1990 and 1994. In 1992, 1,004 Americans were murdered on the job, and homicide was the number one cause of death in the workplace. Clearly, conflict at work can be as catastrophic as that waged on streets and battlefields around the world.

Conflict has been defined as

- "a situation in which the conditions, practices or goals for the different participants, are inherently incompatible" (Smith, 1966, p. 511).

- "a situation or state between at least two interdependent parties, which is characterized by perceived differences that the parties evaluate as negative. This often results in negative emotional states and behaviors intended to overcome the opposition" (Katz & Lawyer, 1993, p. 7).

- "a feature of normal and frequently collaborative and creative relationships, endemic in all social relationships, and an integral part of competitive systems. . . . Conflicts . . . are deeply-rooted in human needs, and . . . frequently require major environmental and policy restructuring for their resolution" (Burton, 1990, p. 1).

- "the process that begins when one party perceives that the other has negatively affected something that he or she cares about" (Thomas, 1992, p. 653).

- "an interactive process manifested in incompatibility, disagreement, or dissonance within or between social entities (i.e., individual, group, organization, etc.) (Rahim, 1992, p. 16).

These definitions indicate that both situational and dispositional forces give rise to conflict. Thus, parties (two or more persons, groups, organizations, or nations) may find themselves in a situation defined by finite resources that must be dispersed among a variety of alternatives, (for example, choosing between two equally promising organizational projects, applicants for a job, or divergent goals for the next fiscal year). Conflict may also arise from dispositional forces, such as when one party has been mistreated or perceives that he or she has been mistreated by another party, one party believes the other is acting unfairly on an issue of importance to both parties, or one party or both parties are cantankerous, greedy, or hostile persons who must interact with each other regarding resources or other issues of importance to each.

Baron (1990) suggested that the following are common elements in most definitions of conflict:

- Conflict involves *opposing interests* between parties in a zero-sum or negative-sum situation (positive outcomes to one party are directly and equally matched by negative outcomes to the other as a result of their joint choices during their interactions).

- The parties must be *aware* of the opposing interests between them.

- Each party must *believe* that the other will thwart or has already thwarted his or her interests.

- Conflict is a *process* arising from past and current interactions and the context in which they took place.

- Each party *acts* to thwart the other's goals.

Thus, if you find yourself in a situation or dealing with a party (person, group, organization, or nation) featuring these elements, you are probably up to your eyebrows in conflict, especially if it is a zero-sum or purely competitive situation. Most of these elements of conflict are also likely to operate in a non-zero-sum or positive-sum situation in which the parties mutually profit by cooperating with each other, as well as in a mixed-motive situation or context in which the parties must give and take, cooperate and compete, and share portions of a divided outcome or set of goals (the most frequently encountered form of conflict).

It is possible to compete with another party but not necessarily be in conflict with that party, for example, when departments or members of an organization seek some outcome that does not preclude the attainment of each other's goals, the outcomes for each party are positive sum, or there are specific rules and norms that regulate the interactions between the parties. Likewise, it is possible to cooperate with another party while being in conflict with that party, for instance, when you cooperate on one issue or domain of interaction but are in conflict over another. The experiential and behavioral boundaries among competition, conflict, and cooperation are not always clearly delineated. The big three Cs—competition, conflict, and cooperation—are on a continuum of interactions between parties, each can give rise to the other, and most organizational interactions carry the potential for each type of relationship.

Experiences of Conflict

In considering the kinds of experiences that most people have in most conflict situations, one learns that the *perceptions of the parties*, rather than the *reality of the situation*, are usually the currency of the exchanges between the parties and that there appear to be specific stages of conflict (Rubin, 1993).

The stages of conflict, according to Rubin (1993), are *escalation*, in which one party attempts to prevail and get the other to submit; *stalemate*, in which the parties are stuck or have run out of energy or resources to prevail, although each party may still be determined to prevail; and *deescalation*, in which the parties reach some kind of agreement or relationship pattern to cooperate with each other.

During escalation, issues tend to proliferate, there is a shift from criticism of a specific behavior to a focus on the personalities of the parties, from positive to negative or coercive tactics, and from wanting to do as well as possible together to an interest in prevailing or doing better than the other. At some point during the escalation stage, which may range from a few minutes to many years, the parties run out of energy and lose hope of prevailing or beating each other and are now in a stalemate. According to Rubin (1993), when the parties reach a stalemate, the opportunity arises to deescalate the conflict by bringing the parties into contact and allowing them to experience the uniqueness and the similarities between them or the conflicting members of the group they represent. During deescalation, the parties listen to and communicate with each other, building on a momentum of small wins, identify superordinate or shared goals, are firm about their goals but flexible about the means of attaining their goals, and just do something different when all else has proved unsuccessful.

An awareness of the stages of conflict can facilitate the resolution of conflict, and sharing this information with the conflicting parties can at least begin to establish some common ground between them.

Sources of Conflict

Sources of conflict can be classified into four broad domains: *intrapersonal, interpersonal, intergroup*, and *interorganizational*.

Intrapersonal conflict arises within an individual and usually involves three basic dynamics in relation to real or perceived oppositional alternatives, for example,

1. having to choose between two positive and equally attractive alternatives, such as accepting a promotion or leaving the organization for a promising career opportunity (approach-approach conflict)

2. having to choose between two negative and equally unattractive alternatives, such as taking a major cut in pay or moving to another workplace that is far from one's home (avoidance-avoidance conflict)

3. having to choose one action that has both negative and positive features, such as accepting a promotion and pay raise that will lead to substantially more time at work.

Generally, for intrapersonal conflict, responsive strategies are focused on the individual and may involve exploring options with one's manager or team members, seeking advice from family members and friends, or obtaining professional career or personal counseling, depending on the severity of the conflict.

Interpersonal conflict arises most frequently between two persons (dyadic conflict), although more persons can be involved, such as all members of a team or members of other departments. Most of the conflict-management strategies focus on dyadic interpersonal conflict, and their basic thrust is to get the parties to address the conflict without having it spill over to other group members. Thus, a manager, team leader, or supervisor may separate two members of a given work unit who do not get along with each other if they fail to work out their interpersonal conflict or other members of the work unit are getting drawn into the conflict.

Intergroup conflict can be damaging to an organization and occurs frequently; a manager should address it immediately by bringing together the members or representatives of each department or unit and then move quickly to resolve the conflict by serving as a third-party observer of mandated meetings between the parties. Intergroup conflict is usually limited to one organization, whereas interorganizational conflict arises mostly between organizations that operate in the same market. Conflict among a business firm, a governmental agency, and an advocacy organization or between a labor union and a business firm are other examples of interorganizational conflict. In general, as one moves from interpersonal to interorganizational conflict, more persons are usually involved and influenced by the conflict, the conflict is likely to be driven more by economic, technological, or ideological issues than by direct and sustained contact between the same persons, and the management of the conflict usually involves more formal, mediated, or legalistic responses by the parties.

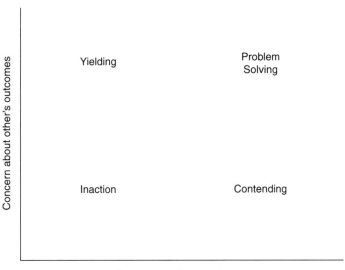

Figure 9–1 The Dual-Concern Model.
Adapted from J. Z. Rubin, D. G. Pruitt, & S. H. Kim, *Social Conflict: Escalation, Stalemate, and Settlement* (2nd ed.).
Copyright © 1994. Reproduced with permission of the McGraw-Hill Companies.

Managers and leaders in organizations will have to deal on an almost daily basis with some of or all these sources of conflict, as well as with potential conflict between hierarchical levels in the organization (vertical conflict), from units at the same level of the organization (horizontal conflict), between line units and personnel (that conduct the major operations of the organization, such as production) and staff units and personnel (that assist line units by providing specialized expertise or services like accounting functions), and role conflict caused by ambiguities in, the overload of, or incompatible expectations for a given organizational role. There appears to be no shortage of opportunities for conflict in organizations (Pondy, 1992), and there are different styles for dealing with a wide variety of conflicts, regardless of their source.

Styles

In general, people respond to conflict according to various styles of behavior. Blake and Mouton (1964) discussed five styles for handling in-terpersonal conflict, depending on a manager's level of concern for production and for people: forcing, withdrawing, smoothing, compromising, and problem solving. Thomas (1976) extended this taxonomy of conflict-handling styles to include the intentions of a party (cooperativeness, or attempting to satisfy the other party's concerns, or assertiveness, or seeking satisfaction only of one's own concerns).

Pruitt and Rubin (1986) introduced the dual-concern model to indicate that responses to conflict yield different behaviors, depending on the level of concern—low to high—for one's own outcomes and for the outcomes of the other party (see Figure 9–1). In a series of studies, Pruitt and Carnevale (1993) reported that manipulation of the level of concern for self or other outcomes leads to the styles presented in Figure 9–1; that is, a high concern for self and others results in problem-solving or integrative approaches to addressing conflict, whereas a low concern for self and a high concern for the other party results in yielding, reflected in many concessions.

Rahim and Bonoma (1979) and Rahim (1992) suggested that there are five styles for handling conflict that arise from two basic dimensions: concern for self and concern for others (see Figure 9–2). Thus, as shown in Figure 9–2, if a person's concern for self and others is high, then the person is likely to respond to the conflict with integrative behaviors, such as openness, an exchange of information, and an examination of differences between the parties, to reach a solution that is satisfactory to both sides. However, if the person's concern for self is high and concern for others is low, then the person will use a dominating or competing style, consisting of a cluster of behaviors in which winning is the primary objective. The compromising style involves give and take in that each party gives up something to arrive at an acceptable solution, but it involves giving up less than in the obliging style and more than in the domineering style.

It is important to remember that a person can choose different styles, depending on the conflict situation. Table 9–1 presents a summary of situations in which it would be appropriate or inappropriate to adopt each of the five styles. Ting-Toomey et al. (1991) reported that Americans used the dominating style more frequently than did Japanese or Koreans, whereas Chinese and Taiwanese used the obliging or avoiding styles more often than did Americans. Ting-Toomey et al. concluded that national culture influences the styles of responding to interpersonal conflict and that in global organizations, managers and members need to learn when to use the five styles, as indicated in Table 9–1.

NEGOTIATION

In general, organizational members want to win, but although the most successful members are highly motivated, they are not willing to win at the expense of their colleagues, clients, or other persons. In effect, such people have the wisdom to know when and how to get from me to we; they understand that if you always win, you end up isolated from other members of your organization or in other domains of your life.

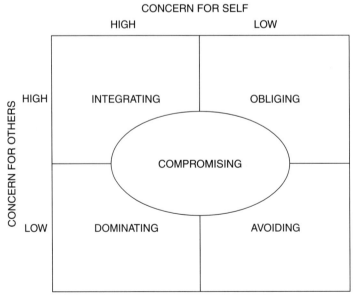

Figure 9–2   Styles of Handling Conflict.
Managing Conflict in Organizations (2nd ed.), M. A. Rahim. Copyright © 1992 by Praeger, Westport, CT. Reproduced with permission of Greenwood Publishing Group, Inc., Westport, CT.

Table 9-1. Guidelines for Using Five Conflict-Response Styles

Conflict Style	Situations When Appropriate	Situations When Inappropriate
Integrating	The issues are complex. A synthesis of ideas is needed for better solutions. Time is available for problem solving. One party alone cannot solve the problem. Resources possessed by different parties are needed to solve common problems.	The task or problem is simple. An immediate decision is required. The other parties do not have problem-solving skills.
Obliging	You believe that you may be wrong. The issue is more important to the other party. You are dealing from a position of weakness. Preserving the relationship is important.	The issue is important to you. You believe that you are right. The other party is wrong or unethical.
Dominating	A speedy decision is needed. An unpopular course of action is implemented. An unfavorable decision by the other party may be costly to you. Your subordinates lack expertise to make technical decisions.	The issue is complex. The issue is not important to you. Both parties are equally powerful. Your subordinates are highly competent.
Avoiding	The potential dysfunctional effect of confronting the other party outweighs the benefits of resolution. A cooling-off period is needed.	The issue is important to you. It is your responsibility to make a decision. Prompt attention is needed.
Compromising	The goals of the parties are mutually exclusive. The parties are equally powerful. A consensus cannot be reached.	One party is more powerful than the others. The problem is complex enough to need a problem-solving approach.

Managing Conflict in Organizations (2nd ed.), M. A. Rahim. Copyright © 1992 by Praeger, Westport, CT. Reproduced with permission of Greenwood Publishing Group, Inc., Westport, CT.

Negotiations involve transaction costs, satisfaction with outcomes, effect on the relationship, and recurrence of disputes. If the negotiations are not performed correctly, the transaction costs (including the time, money, and emotional energy expended in the dispute, resources consumed and destroyed, and lost opportunities) may be high. Satisfaction with outcomes depends on the extent to which the outcomes address the interests and needs of the parties; furthermore, negotiations in which the disputing parties are allowed to vent their emotions, voice their concerns, and influence the final decision are perceived as yielding fairer outcomes than those that do not or that allow only a minimal expression of opinions and feelings (Brett, 1986; Lind & Tyler, 1988). The impact of the negotiation is extremely important, for many times the conflicting parties must continue to have a relationship of some sort; as we will discuss, different negotiation strategies yield different consequences for the relationship between the parties.

Negotiation involves two or more parties with both common and conflicting goals who decide to come together to discuss and bargain with each other to reach an agreement. There are two approaches to negotiation: distributive and integrative. In *distributive negotiations*, the focus is mainly on self-interest, exchanges between the parties are highly guarded, and the primary motive is to win or get as much of the desired outcome as possible for oneself. In *integrative negotiation*, the parties are concerned with themselves as well as the others and openly state their preferences and desires, and the primary motive is to reach a mutually acceptable solution to the conflict (Thomas, 1992).

Definitions

There are a number of definitions of negotiation including these:

- "the process by which two or more interdependent parties who do not have identical preferences across decision alternatives make joint decisions" (Bazerman & Carroll, 1987, p. 248).

- "a joint interdependent process that entails coordinated action of parties with non-identical preference structures" (Neale & Northcraft, 1991, p. 148).

- "the deliberate interaction of two or more complex social units which are attempting to define or redefine the terms of their interdependence" (Walton & McKersie, 1965, p. 35).

These definitions make plain that the central issues of negotiation are the interdependence of the parties, the parties' different preferences, and the allocation of resources. Table 9–2 presents some general guidelines to use in negotiating in a variety of organizational situations that are, of course, influenced by the amount of time the parties have available before and during the sessions (Economy, 1994).

Common Features

Almost all negotiations have common features, which Johnson summarized (1993, p. 3) as follows:

- At least two parties must be involved: two individuals, members of a group or unit in an organization, or two or more organizations or nations.

Table 9–2. Seven Guidelines for Negotiating

- Be prepared.
- Maximize your alternatives.
- Negotiate with the right person.
- Give yourself room to maneuver.
- Don't give away too much too soon.
- Be prepared to say no.
- Make your word your bond.

Adapted from P. Economy, *Business Negotiating Basics*, pp. 16 & 17. Copyright 1994 by Irwin, New York, NY. Used with permission.

- Each party must have a sense of its own interests and purposes and what it expects to accomplish with the assistance or compliance of the other party.

- Each party must understand the role and needs of the other party and be willing to exchange and examine proposals in an attempt to reach an agreement.

- Each party must be convinced that the negotiations will offer some relief, opportunity, or profit.

At the outset of negotiations, it is important to assess whether the other party is open to negotiating a joint settlement; otherwise, you will waste time, energy, and resources and may end up with an agreement that is worse than no agreement (Sondak & Bazerman, 1989). Some obstacles to negotiation that can be addressed early on in the process include a sense that agreement is not the goal of the parties, one of the negotiators lacks the power to represent her or his party, the parties are unwilling to submit to reason, and one of the parties is relatively powerless. However, if you sense that the goal of both parties is to reach an agreement or that one party can be convinced that an agreement will benefit both parties, that the parties are open to reason, and that both parties are on the same power plane, then negotiation may be realistic and beneficial. Trust your judgment.

Focusing and Sense of Self

Once you have decided that there is an opportunity to negotiate, follow Saunders's (1985) five steps to focus the process and context of negotiation:

- Identify and define the issues that generate the conflict.

- Secure a commitment from all appropriate parties to negotiate a settlement.

- Arrange the location and proceedings for negotiations.

- Create an environment for visible negotiations.

- Seek methods for implementing the negotiations and the agreement by the parties.

From our experience, we have found that it is essential to make a list of issues, so everybody knows the main points of the negotiation. You can agree to add issues after the original issues have been addressed. Setting the issues helps to keep the negotiations focused, avoids the untimely or deflective intrusion of other issues that can be addressed after the original issues are dealt with, and serves as a referent to measure or make visible the progress (or lack of progress) of the negotiations.

In making a commitment to negotiate, a sense of self or self-knowledge is important because it demonstrates that you can effectively evaluate information about yourself, which requires that you can recognize your strengths and weaknesses. If you have self-knowledge, it is likely that you can see the merits and shortcomings of alternatives suggested during the negotiations, have realistic self-confidence (and hence will be more flexible and concessionary than a negotiator who has either excessively high or low self-confidence), and have a clear sense of what you want and do not want (Neale & Bazerman, 1985). In short, if you can deal with yourself, you can deal with others.

BATNAs and Listening

The sooner you know your BATNA, the better. Your BATNA is your best alternative to a negotiated agreement (Fisher & Ury, 1981), and it serves as your referent for evaluating the negotiating process and the potential agreement. It is best to know your BATNA before or shortly after you begin negotiating because it will give you a contingency plan and thus afford you greater independence from the other party; in addition, you can evaluate the potential alternatives before an agreement is reached and evaluate a potential agreement against some standard. In effect, your BATNA gives you a yardstick, recognizes that a negotiated agreement is not always possible, and can keep you alert to new information the other party may give about specific proposals and your BATNA (Johnson, 1993).

Listening to yourself—knowing your strengths, weaknesses, BATNA, and thoughts and feelings during the negotiations is as important as listening to the other party. Some useful tips for listening, whether to yourself or the other party, include these:

- Actively listen. Stay focused and summarize quickly in your mind what you hear and see (nonverbal behaviors) in the interaction.

- Suspend judgements until you get the information. Judging tends to distort the information, not the speaker.

- Search and summarize ideas, rather than facts and figures; seek the thematic idea of the speaker.

- Engage the speaker by asking questions and probing for ideas.

Active listening, together with warmth, affability, and questioning, communicates to the speaker that you, the other party, are interested in the speaker and what he or she is saying and allows you to detect any subtle shifts in the other party's perspective (Johnson, 1993).

Whistle-blowing (when an organizational member goes public about an organization's harmful or illegal actions) is an example of not having a BATNA. In most instances, it is usually damaging to the individual, as well as to the organization. According to De George (1994), whistle-blowing is clearly justified and not an extreme example of disloyalty when an organization's actions cause serious harm to the public, the member immediately reported the harmful or questionable practice to an immediate superior, and nothing was done to address the problem. On the other hand, others (see, for example Westin, 1992) have argued that whistle-blowing charges are frequently inaccurate and the whistle-blower may be protesting not unlawful or unsafe actions but disliked policies. When possible, an organization should focus on conditions to make whistle-blowing unnecessary, such as having an ombudsperson (a person who helps employees solve problems) to assist in identifying a BATNA.

Soft or Hard Bargaining

There are many strategies to follow when negotiating, including soft or hard bargaining. Ideally, it is best to use different approaches to negotiating, depending on the situation (Johnson, 1993).

A soft approach usually works in everyday transactions (for example, "Do you mind if we meet this time in my office and next time in your office or wherever you want for coffee, which will be my treat?") because almost everyone responds positively to warmth and kindness and because the approach minimizes or avoids the issues and the conflict.

A hard approach to negotiating gets right to the issues, but reduces the regard for and value of the parties' current or any future relationship (Johnson, 1993). Hard bargaining is generally effective with short-term relationships, especially when the other party is ill prepared, lacks confidence, and appears confused.

Table 9–3 summarizes the core features, advantages, and disadvantages of the soft and hard approaches (Johnson, 1993).

Hilty and Carnevale (1993) studied the black (hard) hat/white (soft) hat negotiating strategy, a sequential shifting process involving two people working as a team. The first person, the black hat, takes a competitive and tough stance while the second person, the white hat, assumes a more

Table 9–3. Core Features, Advantages, and Disadvantages of Hard and Soft Bargaining

Core Features	
Soft	**Hard**
Be agreeable and flexible.	Be tough, rigid, and adversarial.
Use your relationship with the other party to extract concessions.	Use the power of your position or personality.
Use words like *family, friends, community, partners*, and *common purpose*.	Make trades or concessions only on your own terms.
	Use persuasion to convince the other party that negative consequences will follow noncompliance.

Advantages	
Advances the parties' relationship.	Promotes power.
Is useful for breaking deadlocks.	Is effective if the party is also credible ("she knows what she is talking about").
Avoids short-term hassles.	Clear and focused intentions.

Disadvantages	
Crumbles against aggressive opponents.	Risks damaging the parties' relationship.
Gives up more than is usually necessary.	May be costly to enforce.
Erodes long-term credibility because the other party is not sure what the person stands for.	Misses good bargains by driving away the other party who does not tolerate aggressive tactics.

Adapted from R. A. Johnson, *Negotiation Basics*, pp. 73–80, copyright © 1993 by Sage Publications. Reprinted by permission of Sage Publications.

cooperative and softer stance. Hilty and Carnevale found that this sequence led to greater concessions, less distance between offers during negotiations, and the other party's greater sense of cooperation than did the reverse situation. This shift in the negotiation strategy from competitive to more cooperative behaviors seems beneficial and can be pursued as a general principle.

Principled Negotiations

Principled negotiation is a sound alternative to the soft and hard approaches (Barrett, 1990; Fisher & Ury, 1981; Johnson 1993; Nierenberg, 1971; Ury, Brett, & Goldberg, 1988). We have used this approach extensively in our consulting practices and other domains of our lives and have found it to be beneficial. The following basic components of principled negotiations were presented by Fisher and Ury (1981):

- Separate the person from the problem.
- Focus on interests, not positions.
- Generate options for mutual gain.
- Use objective standards.

When negotiating in organizations, we have found it helpful to give the other party a copy of Fisher and Ury's (1981) book, to indicate that we plan to follow the four principles in the current negotiation, and to ask for comparable material from the other party. This simple gesture, even if no negotiated agreement results (which has been seldom the case) represents an educational opportunity that can benefit at least one and usually both parties.

Separate the problem from the person. When negotiating with a stranger, a business colleague, or a person or group with whom you have had limited personal or emotional involvement, it is usually easier to separate the problem from the person. The basic idea is to depersonalize the issue as much as possible; to search for facts, rather than personal flaws; to be rational, not emotional; and to appreciate that the issue is not necessarily the other person (although it could be), but the interaction between the parties, the context, or yourself. If the issue is yourself or the other party, you will have to exert great discipline to separate the issue from the person and doing so usually leads to a negotiated settlement involving some kind of behavioral change by you, the other party, or both parties. At best, as a negotiator, you can only change yourself and put your needs on the table, listen carefully to the other person or party, and focus your attention on the problem, rather than the person.

Most negotiations of personal meaning and impact involve proximal (at the time of the negotiation) or distal emotional experiences. It is best to be aware of your feelings; to keep them as separate as possible from the issues; and, when necessary, to take a break from the negotiating session if it gets emotionally charged. During the break, you and the parties can let out emotions by taking a walk, hollering, spending some time alone, or in any other appropriate ways. It is best if the parties can see themselves as working side by side as partners to attack the problem, rather than each other. Being firm about the problem and nurturing the relationship between the parties are difficult but not mutually exclusive activities.

Focus on interests, not positions. Interests—the need or desire for safety, security, affiliation, and recognition—transcend any specific negotiating situation, whereas positions (demands) are usually specific to a given negotiation. Take the case of an employee who, after several coaching sessions followed by specific warnings, must now be fired; you do not want a lot of publicity about the firing, whereas the employee wants to keep her or his job and has threatened to go public with the firing. Your position is to fire the employee, whereas the employee's position is to publicize the issue if he or she is fired. The interests are being viewed positively by others, getting the job done, and having enough money to maintain a stable standard of living. The alternative solutions for dealing with both parties' interests may be to retain the employee as a consultant, contingent on his or her satisfactory performance until the employee finds a new job within or outside the organization; to help the employee search for a new job; to fire the employee; or to issue a joint publicity release.

Generate options for mutual gain. To generate options, you may want to apply some of the brainstorming strategies presented in Chapter 8. Basically, the parties want to create an atmosphere in which ideas can be generated; to work as a team to identify options; and if appropriate, to obtain suggestions from other persons. In general, it is best to foster an atmosphere of enjoyment, relaxation, and humor so the parties can disengage their internal censors.

Use objective standards. Use some objective standards that both parties can support for evaluating the suggested options for a negotiated settlement. Objective standards may be published or publicly accessible information, testimony by credible individuals, or a survey of other persons who have no stake in the negotiations or outcomes.

Settlements arising from principled negotiations generally increase the parties' respect for each other, yield wise outcomes because the issues have been evaluated from at least two perspectives, and are amicable and efficient because the emphasis has been on gathering and evaluating data, working as a team on the identified and shared problem, and crafting a settlement that embraces interests, rather than capitulates to the parties' positions.

Table 9–4 presents a summary of Fisher and Ury's (1981), soft, hard, and principled bargaining strategies. Sometimes it may not be possible to pursue a principled negotiating strategy because of time limits or because the problem is one of the parties to the negotiations. Inasmuch as the goal of principled negotiation is to go beyond the quid pro quo to seek a mutually optimal gain for both parties, we encourage you to persevere in your efforts to initiate principled negotiations and if you fail, to choose your BATNA and walk away from the situation. In the long run, relationships, as reflected in self-acceptance and appreciation of yourself and others, that may be tarnished by being too soft or hard are much more important than a particular

Table 9–4. Features of Soft, Hard, and Principled Negotiations

Problem		Solution
Positional Bargaining: Which Game Should You Play?		Change the Game—Negotiate on the Merits
Soft	**Hard**	**Principled**
Participants are friends.	Participants are adversaries.	Participants are problem-solvers.
The goal is agreement.	The goal is victory.	The goal is a wise outcome reached efficiently and amicably.
Make concessions to cultivate the relationship.	Demand concessions as a condition of the relationship.	Separate the people from the problem.
Be soft on the people and the problem.	Be hard on the problem and the people.	Be soft on the people, hard on the problem.
Trust others.	Distrust others.	Proceed independent of trust.
Change your position easily.	Dig in to your position.	Focus on interests, not positions.
Make offers.	Make threats.	Explore interests.
Disclose your bottom line.	Mislead as to your bottom line.	Avoid having a bottom line.
Accept one-sided losses to reach agreement.	Demand one-sided gains as the price of agreement.	Invent options for mutual gain.
Search for the single answer: the one *they* will accept.	Search for the single answer: the one *you* will accept.	Develop multiple options to choose from; decide later.
Insist on agreement.	Insist on your position.	Insist on using objective criteria.
Try to avoid a contest of will.	Try to win a contest of will.	Try to reach a result based on standards independent of will.
Yield to pressure.	Apply pressure.	Reason and be open to reasons; yield to principle, not pressure.

position, power or status issue, or thing. This, of course, is the challenge of negotiation.

Gender

As more women enter the workforce and assume leadership positions, it is inevitable and encouraging that more women will participate in the negotiations of global organizations. Kolb (1993) summarized the alternative voice or perspective that women bring to negotiations that includes the following:

- a relational view of others
- an embedded view of agency
- a focus on empowerment

According to Kolb, women view life in terms of relationships and expect their interactions to provide grounding for emotional connection, empathy, shared experiences, mutual sensitivity, and responsibility. Thus, to understand is as important as to be understood and to be empowered is as important as being empowered. Women, Kolb found, understand events contextually whereas men stereotypically focus on individual achievement and activities defined by task and structure. In addition, mutual versus individual empowerment and power *with* or power *from* emerging interactions, rather than dominion, mastery, or power over, may represent more accurately the female than the male perspective, which is the preferred perspective in conflict situations involving valued relationships. Furthermore, Kolb noted that dialogue is central to women's model of problem solving, compared to persuasion, argument, and debate, which are central to men's model. With problem solving through dialogue, the process is less structured, goals emerge from mutual inquiry, and the parties must be flexible and adaptive in response to uncertainty.

Kolb (1993) suggested that this alternative voice needs to be documented more fully in ne-

gotiating situations (in both female or female-dominated organizations, as well as in female-male organizations). She also pointed out that this voice is not *the* women's voice but only an alternative that individual women (or men) can articulate, depending on variations in class, race, culture, and the negotiating context. In most cases, there is more variation within than between groups (such as men and women) for almost any behavior or set of behaviors.

The voicing of alternative perspectives at the negotiating table provides the opportunity for airing a number of proposed solutions that may go unheard, especially if the other party is a hard bargainer.

The truly round bargaining table is defined by alternative voices or perspectives, all of which are connected by the conflict issue that requires some kind of response and from which an integrated or connected solution can emerge. Regardless of whether one addresses conflict by power over (domineering) or power with (integrative) strategies, personal energy will be expended. However, it is more likely that the latter strategy will allow the parties to emerge from the negotiation as a single team with shared energies, rather than as two teams with oppositional energies that will serve to keep the parties apart.

FORCES SHAPING NEGOTIATION

In this section we examine the two major forces—contextual and dispositional variables—that influence a wide array of organizational behaviors and experiences, including the negotiation process and outcomes (Neale & Northcraft, 1991).

Contextual Forces

Three major contextual variables that influence negotiation include the *power relationship between parties*, *deadlines*, and *integrative potential*.

In terms of power, Rekosh and Feigenbaum (1966) and Baranowiski and Summers (1972) found more cooperation between the two parties in a dyadic negotiation when the parties were of equal status than when one party had a higher status than the other. Negotiations within, rather than across, levels of an organization may yield more cooperative behaviors, especially if there is a salient power differential between the different levels in the organization. Similarly, Pinkley, Neale, and Beggs (1989) reported that the negotiated outcomes of parties with equal BATNAs (and hence equal power) were superior to those of parties with unequal power, reflected in unequal BATNAs. Thus, equal power between parties (a level playing field) is more likely to result in cooperation and better negotiated outcomes than unequal power relationships in which the higher-power party usually acts exploitatively and the lower-power party acts submissively (Thibaut & Gruder, 1969).

The use of deadlines may serve as an incentive for completing organizational projects and can expedite the negotiation process, although they have been shown to have no effect or a negative effect on outcomes because they lead to larger or more frequent concessions (Komorita & Barnes, 1969; Pruitt & Drews, 1969). Also, Yukl, Malone, Hayslip, and Pamin (1976) reported that working under time pressures yielded quicker agreements, but both parties reached agreements that were of lower joint benefit. Thus, it is best to leave sufficient time for negotiations and use deadlines only when necessary to speed up the process; however, it is essential not to reduce the time allocated for exchanging information because you can reduce the possibility of achieving higher mutual gains.

An *integrative* agreement reconciles the interests of the parties, whereas a *distributive* agreement divides the available resources between the parties without coordinating the parties, differential needs (for an excellent example of integrative versus distributive agreements, see the "Ulgi Orange" case in Lewicki, Bowen, Hall, & Hall, 1988). Pruitt (1983) reported that high aspirations and a strong problem-solving orientation, geared to fulfilling the parties' differential needs, make integrative trade-offs possible. Thus, a contextual variable in achieving a higher negotiated outcome is the joint orientation the parties bring to the table to negotiate for example, the allocation of a fixed resource, which takes into account the fact that the parties need different parts of the resource. In short, for integrative settlements, it is better to consider trading off differentially valued elements of a resource than simply splitting the resource.

Finally, organizational negotiations are influenced by the other organizational members who surround or provide the context for the negotiating parties. For example, when agents (managers or representatives of owners or stakeholders), rather than principals (owners or stakeholders), are involved in negotiations, the outcomes are usually not as positive as when the principals do their own negotiation (Neale & Northcraft, 1991). Also, as a negotiator's commitment to the positions endorsed by her or his membership group increases (for example, a manager representing her or his department in a negotiating situation, salary negotiations with the vice president), that person's ability to evaluate alternative proposals (especially those suggested by the other party) and to act by reciprocal concession or acceptance is significantly decreased (Lamm & Kogan, 1970; Roby, 1960). Thus, it is best, when possible, to do your own bidding or negotiating and to pay careful attention to the positions and needs not only of the other party but of the group that you represent, especially if you are a member of that group.

Dispositional Forces

Three important dispositional forces that influence negotiations are *planning*, *information processing*, and *affect*.

According to Lewicki and Litterer (1985), planning and preparation are the fundamental infrastructure of negotiation and include such activities as developing arguments for advocacy, building a relationship between the parties, logrolling (deciding up front what elements of a resource or component you may be likely to trade off in a concession), and constructing a BATNA. In general, bargaining outcomes are enhanced by planning (Carroll, Bazerman, & Maury, 1988).

The information-processing influences that negotiators bring to the situation include framing, anchoring, and reactive devaluation (Neale & Northcraft, 1991). As was discussed in Chapter 8, decision makers are risk averse when they evaluate potential gains, but seek risks when they assess potential losses. Framing determines one's attitude toward taking risks. Thus, negotiators with positive frames close more deals by accepting offered settlements they assume are the best deals with the least potential losses, whereas negotiators with negative frames achieve greater individual outcomes by holding out for potential concessions in the future (Bazerman, Magliozzi, & Neale, 1985; Neale & Bazerman, 1985; Neale, Huber, & Northcraft, 1987). Bottom and Studt (1993) reported that two positively framed bargainers are more likely to reach integrative settlements than are two negatively framed bargainers and, contrary to earlier findings, that negative framing results in better outcomes than does positive framing.

In terms of anchoring, or defining the boundaries of acceptable agreements, early moves (hard, soft, or principled bargaining behaviors) or offers in negotiation play a critical role in determining the psychological context in which negotiation occurs (Rubin & Brown, 1975). Also, final agreements are more strongly influenced by initial offers than by subsequent concessionary behaviors (Liebert, Smith, Hill, & Keiffer, 1968). Reactive devaluation reflects the tendency of parties to devalue or downgrade each other's offers simply because they were presented by the other side (Neale & Northcraft,

1991). Thus, in negotiating, it is important to keep in mind the impact of framing (if you seek many agreements, then frame positively); make clear and up-front moves and offers to set the anchor for the subsequent negotiations; and do not be surprised or disappointed by the other party's devaluative responses to your proposals.

The influence of affect on the negotiation process and outcomes has been studied the least, even though almost all negotiations involve emotional experiences that vary from mild to intense. Carnevale and Isen (1986) found that good humor facilitates creative problem solving and integrative agreements, and Tidd and Lockard (1978) reported that smiling significantly enhanced the amount of earned outcomes. Also, events surrounded by positive emotions are more likely to be remembered than are those surrounded by negative emotions (Teasdale & Fogarty, 1979). Furthermore, persons who score high on a Machiavellianism scale tend to have a cynical view of people, express their feelings of hostility and distrust more openly, influence the emotional tone of the negotiations, tend to initiate and make more offers, and are highly valued as partners in a coalition. Expressing positive and upbeat emotions seems to enhance the negotiating process and outcomes, and it is important to keep an eye out for a party who may be a high Machiavellian.

Last, Kramer, Newton, and Pommerenke (1993) reported that a positive mood and high self-esteem generate overconfidence and an overly positive self-evaluation in some negotiators. Such a disposition explains why these negotiators are reluctant to concede points or reach agreements even when the agreements appear to be in their best interests (Pruitt & Lewis, 1975). Kramer et al. suggested that unrealistic optimistic beliefs about their abilities and outcomes may dispose negotiators to reject agreements that they perceive as falling short of their aspirations. Furthermore, these findings seem to explain why negotiators tend to be overconfident and unrealistically optimistic, a tendency found among both laboratory (Neale & Bazerman, 1985) and real-world negotiators (Bach, 1985).

Small Groups

Most of the studies of negotiation have focused on dyadic negotiation despite the fact that small-group negotiations (of three to five persons) are also frequent in organizations (Lewicki & Litterer, 1985).

Mannix, Thompson, and Bazerman (1989) studied three-person negotiating teams who were engaged in a mixed-motive negotiating task that included both cooperative and competitive components (such as cooperating to get interdependent jobs done but competing for scarce resources). Regardless of whether the negotiations are between two persons or two small groups, the challenge is the simultaneous search for an agreement that increases the available resources (an integrative task) and allocates the highest possible percentage of the increased resources to oneself (Bazerman, 1986; Lax & Sebenius, 1986). Groups who are involved in negotiations have to pay more careful attention than do dyads to such features as agenda setting (the use of a sequential agenda, in which issues are discussed and voted on one at a time versus a bundled or packaged agenda, in which all the items are discussed and then reviewed and voted on later), decision rule (usually either a majority or unanimous vote), and the power balance in the group, since power struggles in the group may hamper efforts to seek an integrative outcome. Mannix et al. (1989) found that packaged agendas resulted in higher group gains and more integrative agreements than did sequential agendas; decision rule by itself had no impact on outcomes but interacted with the type of agenda; and the more powerful the group member, the more the individual profited; however, power imbalances in the group did not influence the outcome or profit gains of the entire group.

Weingart, Bennett, and Brett (1993) found that four-person groups negotiating a multi-issue task had higher-quality outcomes when they used a packaged agenda and when the group members were instructed to be cooperative, rather than to seek individual gains in the negotiation. They also noted that cooperative groups were more trusting and engaged in less argumentation than did competitive groups. These findings agree with the results of Mannix et al. (1989) and studies of dyads (Erickson, Holmes, Frey, Walker, & Thibaut, 1974; Froman & Cohen, 1970; Kelly, 1966; Pruitt, 1981) that considering issues simultaneously significantly increases joint benefits.

As negotiating in global organizations becomes more group based, we suggest that the parties use a packaged agenda, so that items can all be discussed and then some can be logrolled or traded off as the negotiation proceeds (the exchange of information and options is essential for an integrative settlement); along with a unanimous decision rule, and encourage an integrative settlement by modeling a cooperative motivational approach to negotiating group tasks.

Almost all effective organizations have some system or procedure for resolving conflicts or grievances (Feuille & Hildebrand, 1995). In the absence of a labor union, the grievance process usually has a lower profile in the workplace, although a growing number of nonunion organizations are adopting grievance procedures, especially when the alternative is more costly grievance-resolution methods, such as lawsuits. Brett, Goldberg, and Ury (1990) identified six principles for designing systems for resolving disputes that can be applied in a wide variety of organizations. The conflict-resolution principles are intended to cut the transaction and outcome costs of conflict and to realize benefits like preventive measures, such as consultation between the parties before conflict erupts, coupled with timely and specific feedback after the consultation. Some of the other principles include fo-

cusing on interests, rather than positions, in negotiations and establishing a program for teaching negotiation skills. Brett et al. stated that conflict resolution is not just the job of a negotiator
or mediator (a neutral third party to a dispute),
but the responsibility of all organizational members.

NEGOTIATING AROUND THE WORLD

In the global marketplace, organizational negotiators are increasingly negotiating with persons
from many diverse cultures. Accordingly, there
is a greater need for strategies to guide negotiations in different cultural contexts and to promote efficient and integrative negotiated settlements (Bond & Smith, 1996).

GLOBAL NEGOTIATIONS

Weiss (1994a, 1994b) presented guidelines for
conducting negotiations in a culturally sensitive
and responsive manner. For example, to pursue
negotiations with parties from different cultures,
it is critical to have a sense of their concepts of
negotiations, ranging from distributive bargaining (fixed pie, split the settlement, zero sum) to
nondirective discussions in which settlements
emerge from exchanges of information and dialogue without a fixed agenda. It is important to
align such negotiations culturally, since the
closer the alignment, the more likely an integrative negotiated settlement will be reached
and the greater the gain for both parties. For example, if the parties are highly familiar with
each other's cultures (language, values, customs, humor, and educational-recreational activities), they can proceed to identify a negotiating script or set of guidelines that focuses more
on the parties and the issues than the broader
culture. If both parties have minimal knowledge
of each other's culture, however, then they probably should proceed with an agent or adviser,
which, of course, introduces formality and struc-

tured interactions, at least in the early phases of
the negotiations.

In cross-cultural negotiations as in within-cul-
tural negotiations, it is important to be a continuous learner, to appreciate that the guidelines
are suggestive, and that there is a great deal of
room for innovation and adaptability, depending on the parties and the situation.

Chinese Negotiations

Adler, Brahm, and Graham (1992) reported that
when negotiating with their cultural counterparts, both Chinese and American negotiators
were more successful when they used a problem-solving approach, which focuses on the
search for win-win solutions and the exchange
of information, than other bargaining strategies.
The finding that both American and Chinese
negotiators were successful with this approach
indicates that openness and trust-building behaviors can be powerful levers for developing
cooperative ventures between Chinese and
American businesspersons and governmental
officials.

In addition, when using a problem-solving approach to negotiation, it would be wise to be
aware of the centrality of Confucian philosophy
and ethics in all phases of the Chinese culture
(Westwood, Tang, & Kirkbride, 1992). Confu-
cianism focuses on relationships between humans and the universe and nature and, most important, between humans and humans. The
primary Confucian values are harmony; orientation to a social group, especially the family;
conformity to settled relationship structures, so
that a given role system, like that between a
manager and her or his subordinates is not challenged; face-saving or graciousness; reciprocity;
and *guanxi* (mindfulness of the longer-term and
extended implications of behavior in current interactions) (Westwood et al., 1992).

American and Chinese negotiators have a lot
to learn from each other. We hope the rate and
amount of mutual learning will accelerate with

increasing real and virtual contact between the two cultures.

SUMMARY

Conflict is global, lifelong, and neither intrinsically good nor bad; the key is how it is managed. Conflict arises from many sources (intra- and interpersonal, as well as intra- and inter-group), but usually involves two or more parties in a situation in which resources are finite and there are perceived or real incompatibilities or disagreements between the parties. People can respond to conflict with a variety of behavioral patterns, including integrating, obliging, dominating, avoiding, and compromising. How a person responds to conflict depends on the context and her or his level of concern (low to high) for self and others.

Negotiations are formal systematic processes for resolving conflicts, and involve transaction costs, satisfaction with outcomes, effect on relationship, and recurrence of disputes. As one noted global citizen once said, "It ain't over until it's over," which captures the importance of focusing on relationship issues and clearly indicates the inevitable interactions in a relationship that continue long after the negotiations are over. A central feature of negotiations is the importance of knowing yourself, so you can recognize the strengths and weaknesses of others. It is also necessary to know your BATNA, so you can decide when to walk away from a failing process or unacceptable outcome. Furthermore, we encourage you to choose, when possible, a principled, rather than a hard or soft, negotiated strategy. Principled negotiations involve separating the people from the problem, focusing on interests (a long-term perspective), rather than positions (a short-term, contextually bound perspective), generating options for mutual gain, and using objective standards to inform negotiations rather than relying on dogma, flimsy evidence, or hollow rhetoric.

We briefly reviewed the impact of gender, context, and dispositional forces on the process and outcomes of negotiation. Women have a greater inclination to engage in dialogue during negotiations than to persuade, argue, or debate. It has been suggested that more potential solutions to conflict are generated from dialogue than from entering a negotiating situation with a solution; dialogue seems to be a strategy that is suited to organizational settings that are complex and ambiguous in which a priori or up-front solutions may not be as effective or appropriate. Finally, we examined group-based negotiations and discussed the importance of agenda setting, decision rule, and power relationships in the groups. We also highlighted some key features of negotiating strategies around the world, particularly among American and Chinese parties.

CHAPTER REFERENCES

Adler, N. J., Brahm, R., & Graham, J. L. (1992). Strategy implementation: A comparison of face-to-face negotiations in the People's Republic of China and the United States. *Strategic Management Journal, 13*, 449–466.

Bach, S. (1985). *Final cut: Dreams and disaster in the making of Heaven's Gate.* New York: William Morrow.

Baranowiski, T. A., & Summers, D. A. (1972). Perceptions of response alternatives in a prisoner's dilemma game. *Journal of Personality and Social Psychology, 21*, 35–40.

Baron, R. A. (1990). Conflict in organizations. In K. R. Murphy & F. E. Saal (Eds.), *Psychology in organizations: Integrating science and practice* (pp. 197–216). Hillsdale, NJ: Lawrence Erlbaum.

Barrett, J. T. (1990). A win-win approach to collective bargaining: the PAST model. *Labor Law Journal, 41*, 41–44.

Bazerman, M. H. (1986). *Judgment in managerial decision making.* New York: John Wiley & Sons.

Bazerman, M. H., & Carroll, J. S. (1987). Negotiation cognition. In B. M. Staw & L. L. Cummings (Eds.), *Research in organizational behavior* (pp. 247–288). Greenwich, CT: JAI Press.

Bazerman, M. H., Magliozzi, T., & Neale, M. A. (1985). The acquisition of an integrative response in a competitive market. *Organizational Behavior and Human Decision Processes*, *35*, 294–313.

Blake, R. R., & Mouton, J. S. (1964). *The managerial grid*. Houston: Gulf.

Bond, M. H., & Smith, P. B. (1996). Cross-cultural social and organizational psychology. *Annual Review of Psychology*, *47*, 205–235.

Bottom, W. P., & Studt, A. (1993). Framing effects and the distributive aspect of integrative bargaining. *Organizational Behavior and Human Decision Processes*, *56*, 459–474.

Brett, J. M. (1986). Commentary on procedural justice papers. In R. Lewicki, M. Brazerman, & B. Sheppard (Eds.), *Research on negotiations in organizations* (Vol. 1, pp. 81–90). Greenwich, CT: JAI Press.

Brett, J. M., Goldberg, S. B., & Ury, W. L. (1990). Designing systems for resolving disputes in organizations. *American Psychologist*, *45*, 162–170.

Burton, J. (1990). *Conflict: Resolution and prevention*. New York: St. Martin's Press.

Carnevale, P. J., & Isen, A. M. (1986). The influence of positive affect and visual access on the discovery of integrative solutions in bilateral negotiations. *Organizational Behavior and Human Decision Processes*, *37*, 1–13.

Carroll, J. S., Bazerman, M. H., & Maury, R. (1988). Negotiator cognitions: A descriptive approach to negotiators' understanding of their opponents. *Organizational Behavior and Human Decision Processes*, *41*, 352–370.

De George, R. T. (1994). *Business ethics*. New York: Macmillan.

Economy, P. (1994). *Business negotiating basics*. Homewood, IL: Richard D. Irwin.

Erickson, B., Holmes, J. G., Frey, R., Walker, L., & Thibaut, J. (1974). Functions of a third party in the resolution of conflict: The role of a judge in pretrial conferences. *Journal of Personality and Social Psychology*, *31*, 864–872.

Feuille, P., & Hildebrand, R. L. (1995). Grievance procedures and dispute resolution. In G. R. Ferris, S. B. Rosen, & D. T. Barnum (Eds.), *Handbook of human resource management* (pp. 340–369). Cambridge, MA: Blackwell.

Fisher, R., & Ury, W. (1981). *Getting to yes: Negotiating agreement without giving in*. Boston: Houghton Mifflin.

Froman, L. A., Jr., & Cohen, M. D. (1970). Compromise and logroll: Comparing the efficiency of two bargaining processes. *Behavioral Science*, *15*, 180–183.

Hilty, J. A., & Carnevale, P. J. (1993). Black-hat/white-hat strategy in bilateral negotiation. *Organizational Behavior and Human Decision Making*, *55*, 444–469.

Johnson, R. A. (1993). *Negotiation basics: Concepts, skills, and exercises*. Newbury Park, CA: Sage.

Katz, N. H., & Lawyer, J. W. (1993). *Conflict resolution: Building bridges*. Newbury Park, CA: Corwin Press.

Kelly, H. H. (1966). A classroom study of dilemmas in interpersonal negotiations. In K. Archibald (Ed.), *Strategic intervention and conflict* (pp. 49–73). Berkeley: University of California, Institute of International Studies.

Kolb, D. H. (1993). Her place at the table: Gender and negotiation. In L. Hall (Ed.), *Negotiation: Strategies for mutual gain* (pp. 138–150). Newbury Park, CA: Sage.

Komorita, S. S., & Barnes, M. (1969). Effects of pressures to reach agreement in bargaining. *Journal of Personality and Social Psychology*, *13*, 245–252.

Kramer, R. M., Newton, E., & Pommerenke, P. L. (1993). Self-enhancement biases and negotiation judgment: Effects of self-esteem and mood. *Organizational Behavior and Human Decision Processes*, *56*, 110–133.

Lamm, H., & Kogan, N. (1970). Risk taking in the context of intergroup negotiations. *Journal of Experimental Social Psychology*, *6*, 351–363.

Lax, D. A., & Sebenius, J. K. (1986). *The manager as negotiator: Bargaining for cooperative and competitive gain*. New York: Free Press.

Lewicki, R. J., Bowen, D. D., Hall, D. T., & Hall, F. S. (1988). *Experiences in management and organizational behavior*. New York: John Wiley & Sons.

Lewicki, R., & Litterer, J. A. (1985). *Negotiation.* Homewood, IL: Richard D. Irwin.

Liebert, R. M., Smith, W. P., Hill, J. H., & Keiffer, M. (1968). The effects of information and magnitude of initial offer on interpersonal negotiation. *Journal of Experimental Social Psychology, 4,* 431–441.

Lind, E. A., & Tyler, T. R. (1988). *The social psychology of procedural justice.* New York: Plenum Press.

Mannix, E. A., Thompson, L. L., & Bazerman, M. H. (1989). Negotiation in small groups. *Journal of Applied Psychology, 78,* 504–517.

Neale, M. A., & Bazerman, M. H. (1985). The effects of framing and negotiation overconfidence on bargaining behaviors and outcomes. *Academy of Management Journal, 28,* 34–49.

Neale, M. A., Huber, V. L., & Northcraft, G. B. (1987). The framing of negotiation: Context versus task frames: *Organizational Behavior and Human Decision Processes, 39,* 228–241.

Neale, M. A., & Northcraft, G. B. (1991). Behavioral negotiation theory: A framework for conceptualizing dyadic bargaining. *Research in Organizational Behavior, 13,* 147–190.

Nirenberg, G. I. (1971). *Creative business negotiation: Skills and successful strategies.* New York: Hawthorn.

Pinkley, R. L., Neale, M. A., & Beggs, R. (1989). *The impact of alternatives to negotiation on the process and outcome of negotiation* (Working paper). Evanston, IL: Northwestern University.

Pondy, L. R. (1992). Reflections on organizational conflict. *Journal of Organizational Behavior, 13,* 257–261.

Pruitt, D. G. (1981). *Negotiation behavior.* San Diego, CA: Academic Press.

Pruitt, D. G. (1983). Achieving integrative agreements. In M. H. Bazerman & R. J. Lewicki (Eds.), *Negotiation in organizations* (pp. 35–50). Beverly Hills, CA: Sage.

Pruitt, D. G., & Carnevale, P. J. (1993). *Negotiation in social conflict.* Pacific Grove, CA: Brooks/Cole.

Pruitt, D. G., & Drews, J. L. (1969). The effect of time pressure, time elapsed, and the opponent's concession rate on behavior in negoti-

ation. *Journal of Experimental Social Psychology, 5,* 43–60.

Pruitt, D. G., & Lewis, S. A. (1975). Development of integrative solutions in bilateral negotiations. *Journal of Personality and Social Psychology, 31,* 621–630.

Pruitt, D. G., & Rubin, J. Z. (1986). *Social conflict.* New York: Random House.

Rahim, M. A. (1992). *Managing conflict in organizations* (2nd ed.). Westport, CT: Praeger.

Rahim, M. A., & Bonoma, T. V. (1979). Managing organizational conflict: A model for diagnosis and intervention. *Psychological Reports, 44,* 1323–1344.

Rekosh, J. H., & Feigenbaum, K. D. (1966). The necessity of mutual trust for cooperative behavior in a two-person game. *Journal of Social Psychology, 69,* 149–154.

Rigdon, J. (1994, April 12). Companies see more workplace violence. *Wall Street Journal,* p. 1.

Roby, T. (1960). Commitment. *Behavioral Science, 5,* 253–264.

Rubin, J. Z. (1993). Conflict from a psychological perspective. In L. Hall (Ed.), *Negotiation* (pp. 123–137). Newbury Park, CA: Sage.

Rubin, J. Z., & Brown, B. R. (1975). *The social psychology of bargaining and negotiation.* New York: Academic Press.

Saunders, H. H. (1985). We need a larger theory of negotiation: The importance of pre-negotiating phases. *Negotiation Journal, 1,* 249–262.

Smith, C. G. (1966). A comparative analysis of some conditions and consequences of interorganizational conflict. *Administrative Science Quarterly, 10,* 504–529.

Sondak, H., & Bazerman, M. H. (1989). Matching and negotiation processes in quasi-markets. *Organizational Behavior and Human Decision Processes, 44,* 261–280.

Teasdale, J. D., & Fogarty, S. J. (1979). Differential effects of induced mood on retrieval of pleasant and unpleasant events from episodic memory. *Journal of Abnormal Psychology, 88,* 248–257.

Thibaut, J., & Gruder, C. L. (1969). Formation of contractual agreements between parties of unequal power. *Journal of Personality and Social Psychology, 11,* 59–65.

Thomas, K. W. (1976). Conflict and conflict management. In M. D. Dunnette (Ed.), *Handbook of industrial and organizational psychology* (pp. 889–935). Chicago: Rand McNally.

Thomas, K. W. (1992). Conflict and negotiation processes in organizations. In M. D. Dunnette & L. M. Hough (Eds.), *Handbook of industrial and organizational psychology* (pp. 651–716). Palo Alto, CA: Consulting Psychologists Press.

Tidd, K. L., & Lockhard, J. S. (1978). Monetary significance of the affiliative smile: A case for reciprocal altruism. *Bulletin of the Psychonomic Society, 11*, 344–346.

Ting-Toomey, S., Gao, G., Trubisky, P., Yang, Z., Kim, H. S., Lin, S. L., & Nishida, T. (1991). Culture, face maintenance, and conflict styles of handling interpersonal conflict: A study in five cultures. *International Journal of Conflict Management, 2*, 275–296.

Ury, W. L., Brett, J. M., & Goldberg, S. B. (1988). *Getting disputes resolved: Designing systems to cut the costs of conflict.* San Francisco: Jossey-Bass.

Walton, R. E., & McKersie, R. B. (1965). *A behavioral theory of labor negotiations: An analysis of a social interaction system.* New York: McGraw-Hill.

Weiss, S. E. (1994a). Negotiating with "Romans"—Part 1. *Sloan Management Review, 36*, 51–61.

Weiss, S. E. (1994b). Negotiating with "Romans"—Part 2. *Sloan Management Review, 36*, 85–99.

Weingart, L. R., Bennett, R. J., & Brett, J. M. (1993). The impact of consideration of issues and motivational orientation on group negotiation process and outcome. *Journal of Applied Psychology, 78*, 504–517.

Westin, A. F. (1992). What can and should be done to protect whistle blowers in industry? In L. H. Newton & M. M. Ford (Eds.), *Taking sides: Clashing views on controversial issues in business ethics and society* (pp. 105–107). Guilford CT: Dushkin.

Westwood, R. I., Tang, S. F. Y., & Kirkbride, P. S. (1992). Chinese conflict behavior: Cultural antecedents and behavioral consequences. *Organization Development Journal, 10*(2), 13–19.

Yukl, G. A., Malone, M. P., Hayslip, B., & Pamin, T. A. (1976). The effects of time pressure and issue settlement order on integrative bargaining. *Sociometry, 39*, 276–281.

SUGGESTED REFERENCES

The first of the three suggested references, by Bunker, Rubin, and Associates, contains an excellent treatment of the constructs of conflict, cooperation, and justice by distinguished scholars and practitioners. The material focuses on conflict, cooperation, and justice in the global community and provides a sound grounding in these three important topics for individuals and organizations as the 21st century approaches. The book by Morrison, Conaway, and Borden provides specific tested strategies for negotiating in 60 countries around the world, from Argentina to China, Finland, Kuiwait, Singapore, and the United States and back to Venezuela, as well as the cognitive styles, value systems, and other useful information on these countries. The book by Engholm presents specific suggestions for negotiation strategies, conflict resolution, and decision-making processes in Vietnam, an emerging member of the global community.

Bunker, B. B., Rubin, J. Z., & Associates. (1995). *Conflict, cooperation, and justice: Essays inspired by the work of Morton Deutsch.* San Francisco: Jossey-Bass.

Engholm, C. (1995). *Doing business in the new Vietnam.* Englewood Cliffs, NJ: Prentice Hall.

Morrison, T., Conaway, W. A., & Borden, G. A. (1994). *Kiss, bow, or shake hands.* Holbrook, MA: Bob Adams.

PART III

ADAPTATION

10

Individual Change

CHAPTER OVERVIEW

Individual change can lead to the enhancement of a person's intellectual, emotional, physical, and psychological capacities that promote a healthy, productive, loving, and enjoyable life. Individual change involves the whole person, not just the enhancement of a skill, job, or career, and this development takes place in organizational contexts that change and challenge each person. Organizations must continue to accommodate a wide variety of individual changes to participate effectively in the global marketplace. Accordingly, we examine some of the major domains of change related to a variety of work-life issues.

Organizations, like families around the world, have experienced turbulent times and have been reconfigured in a variety of patterns over the past two decades. Therefore, the reconfiguration of relationships and the pursuit of new partnerships, both at work and at home, are central in everyone's life. In almost all organizations, job security has been traded for empowerment, and both organizations and employees are evolving new relationships that are grounded in a calculus of customers' demands and organizational loyalties. Around the world, but especially in the United States, Europe, and Japan, the workforce is aging, although a wide range of performance domains appear immune to aging and there is lower absenteeism, turnover, illness, and higher job satisfaction among older employees.

Women work longer hours than do men, juggle work and family needs and roles, and make up an increasingly larger proportion of the global workforce. Accordingly, organizations must target and promote opportunities for individual development that are unique to women, including effective and nurturing day care and professional development programs to expedite the deployment of women into increasingly stronger leadership positions.

Sexual harassment, which occurs in all organizations, can arrest the individual development of women at work and in other domains of life. Although progress has been made, we review specific organizational and legal actions to expunge harassment from the workplace. Sexual harassment is wrong, unacceptable, illegal, and counterproductive to wholeness and productivity.

Alcohol and drug use cost U.S. organizations about $85–$100 billion per year, so it is not surprising that many job-application procedures require blood and urine tests in addition to the usual interviews. Drug testing, policies, and responses to identified substance abusers are influenced significantly by procedural justice. Concrete, specific, and timely information, presented in a sensitive and compassionate manner, leads to greater individual acceptance and effective organizational drug testing and assistance programs.

In the global marketplace, justice for all parties at work is critical; it involves distributive justice (criteria for the allocation of finite resources), procedural justice (processes for distributing such resources), and interactional justice (how organizational members are treated). Organizational citizenship behaviors are discretionary or chosen, not position or mandated behaviors, and further strengthen the linkages between individual development and organizations. Organizations that value and care for their members by anticipating, rather than responding to, members' needs are generally perceived as highly supportive, which leads to enhanced organizational citizenship behaviors.

It is clear that individuals do not seek to work for organizations exclusively on the basis of pay and benefits, but also consider other important organizational features, such as values and organizational demographics. Given equal compensation among organizations, individuals align with those organizations that have employees and values that are similar to them and offer the greatest potential for individual development.

Slowly and inevitably, more and more organizations are operating 24 hours per day and hence have expanded opportunities for night work. If people choose to work continuously at night, there appear to be no performance decrements on or off the job that are due to day-night sleep cycles, as there are when individuals are required to work sporadically at night.

Regardless of when you work, there are certain core features of jobs that enrich individual development and yield higher performances. These features, outlined in the job enrichment model, include the degree of autonomy associated with a position and the timeliness and specificity of feedback regarding job performances. Organizations and managers will have to pay increasing attention to cultural sensitivity as the global workforce continues to diversify if they are to promote the development of all their members.

Last, we examine stress at work and organizational interventions to manage stress. We outline a modest and easily used coping strategy or program for personal discipline that focuses on the mind, body, and spirit that works at and away from work to enhance individual well-being and helps people deal more effectively with a wide variety of work-life issues.

LEARNING OBJECTIVES

After studying this chapter, you will be able to

- appreciate the many components of individual change and the wide variety of work issues arising in organizations
- identify organizational features, such as the aging workforce, harassment, and role juggling, that moderate individual development
- explain the changing agreement at work, the trade-off of job security for empowerment, and the pursuit of new partnership configurations between individuals and organizations
- describe the relationship between aging and performance at work and the benefits of an aging workforce
- discuss the challenges to individual development that women face, including role juggling and sexual harassment, and the imperative for development programs to place women in increasingly robust leadership positions
- identify the organizational costs of alcohol and drug abuse, describe drug-testing procedures and policies, and outline organizational options for substance abusers
- define distributive, procedural, and interactional justice and indicate clearly why each is critical for individual development
- define organizational citizenship behaviors and outline some of the emotional support that organizations can provide to enhance them
- describe the attraction-selection-attrition and organizational demography models that explain which important features beyond compensation and benefits moderate the relationship between individuals and organizations

- identify the impact of night work on job performance and the design of programs to promote individual development both at night and during the day

- describe the job enrichment model and identify core job features that promote individual development and productivity

- distinguish between objective and subjective stressors, describe organizational stress-management programs, and outline the important features of a coping strategy or personal discipline program to promote individual well-being.

Work and life are change issues for each of us.

THE ROLE OF WORK

We define work as the act of producing a useful product or providing a useful service for another person, group, or organization that yields appropriate compensation for the provider. Work is one integral part of life, along with sustained, healthy, and rewarding relationships with other emotionally important persons who are usually drawn from one's family and circle of friends. Just as there have been many reconfigurations of relationships in families because of divorce, single parenthood, and combined households over the past 20 years, there have also been changes in the configurations of the relationships between employers and employees (Basic Behavioral Science Task Force, 1996; O'Reilly, 1994). Accordingly, the reconfiguration of relationships and the pursuit of new partnerships are a major focus of life in workplaces and homes around the world.

The Changing Agreement

Both large and small organizations around the globe have been saying more frequently to employees something like this:

> Listen, we are in a different world now: We compete globally; the competition is fierce and relentless; and our old agreement, in which we promised you job security and asked for your loyalty in return, is now dead. Today, we want from you, our employees, nothing less than total dedication to our customers. You have to be creative, innovative, fast, and committed to our organizational goals. You are invaluable to us; you will be working in self-managed teams, will be more involved in decision making, and will have greater flexibility. Also, remember that you are expendable, so if we have to fire you, we will.

Downsizing, right sizing, or whatever you want to call reductions in the number of employees in organizations has been a major part of organizational life since the mid-1980s and has dramatically changed how individuals and organizations view individual or career development. Experienced middle managers, mostly white men, whose salaries used to be in the $45,000–$75,000 range, continue to be laid off in increasing numbers. These managers have reported a gamut of emotional experiences like these: "Losing my job is worse than the death of a loved one; you have to be very aggressive when looking for a new job; I was surprised to feel relief because I was working from 7:30 A.M. to 6:00 P.M. plus work at home" (Caminiti, 1994, p. 70). Thus, for a growing number of employees throughout the world, in both managerial and nonmanagerial positions, the pursuit of the goal of one marriage, one family, and one career is being replaced by the pursuit of new relationship patterns at home and at work.

Work and Time

The majority of adults around the world spend about 8–12 hours per day at work or in work-related activities, an average of about 6–8 hours in other activities, and about 8 hours sleeping. They all invest a great deal of their lives, time, and energy in their work and, increasingly, at least for the next three to five years, will be asked or required to work harder for fewer financial rewards. This chapter examines some of the specific ways that work in organizations affects the lives of different groups of individuals in the global workforce and then identifies specific strategies that individuals and organizations can use to enhance the capacities of individuals to deal with a wide variety of work-life issues.

WORK-LIFE ISSUES

We believe that work is an important, valuable, and meaningful activity and that organizations can enhance the quality of their products and the productivity of their services, as well as of the lives of their employees. Almost any healthy adult who could be a member of the workforce but who is unemployed owing to economic constraints or the lack of equal opportunity can readily testify to the economic and psychological benefits of work. In fact, some psychologists who are interested in the development of older persons (aged 60 and older) have argued (and the evidence is accumulating) that "being intellectually busy during one's life may well add an active decade to a life that might ordinarily have slowed to a near stop around age 70" (Shneidman, 1989, p. 693). Many of the pioneering psychodynamic psychologists, such as Sigmund Freud and Carl Jung, recognized the beneficent power of elected work and believed that one of the major challenges of adulthood is to integrate successfully the responsibilities and rewards of "love and work," or in Freud's words *"Lieb und Arbeit"* (Shneidman, 1989). Inasmuch as the

workforce is aging and almost all people derive many rewards and experience challenges and frustrations from work, we first examine the individual development of and challenges for older workers in the global workforce.

Aging

In general, people around the world are living longer; in the United States, for example, it has been estimated that by the year 2000, nearly 20% of the population (a subnation of 40 million people) will be aged 65 or older, compared with 11% in the late 1980s (Buie, 1987). It has also been projected that the number of U.S. workers aged 55 and older will increase 38% from 1993 to 2005, compared with 3% between 1979 and 1992. Thus, the fastest-growing segment of the U.S. workforce during the 1990s, more than either blacks or women has been older workers (Shellenbarger & Hymowitz, 1994). In addition, age-bias lawsuits, which are based on the protection afforded older people in the Age Discrimination in Employment Act (ADEA) of 1967 and the "Age" Act of 1986 (which all but eliminated mandatory retirement at age 70) increased 14% from 1992 to 1994 (Shellenbarger & Hymowitz, 1994). In the United States, as well as in Japan and Western Europe, there will be a growing number of older workers in the next 5–10 years, unless organizations fire them (as some organizations have attempted to do) and replace them with younger; less expensive; and, as some organizations have alleged, more productive workers.

The relationship, if any, between age and work performance is an important issue, but there has been little systematic empirical research on this relationship using measures of productivity (Cascio, 1992; McEvoy & Cascio, 1989; Waldman & Avolio, 1986). Despite the paucity of such research, there is widespread belief that work performance declines as age increases (Giniger, Dispenzieri, & Eisenberg, 1983; Mark, 1956; Shellenbarger & Hymowitz,

1994). According to the decremental theory of aging, general performance declines with age, and there is solid evidence that such abilities as dexterity, speed of responses, agility, hearing, and vision do, in fact, decline (Giniger et al., 1983). These findings, combined with the findings that ability is strongly and causally related to job performance, leads to the likely prediction that job performance will decline with age—not a bright picture for aging individuals or their employers (Schmidt, Hunter, & Outerbridge, 1986). On the other hand, many others (Pfeffer, 1994; Rhodes, 1983; U.S. Department of Commerce and Labor, 1993) have pointed out that older workers have lower absenteeism, turnover, illness, and accident rates, higher job satisfaction, and more positive work values than do younger workers. These latter findings provide support, albeit as indirect as that for the decremental theory of aging, that work performance may actually increase with age, not change, or increase with age up to a certain age and then decline.

In their meta-analysis of the relationship between age and job performance (the latter indexed by supervisors' ratings, productivity, or sales performance), McEvoy and Cascio (1989) did not find any evidence that age significantly influenced work performance across a broad cross section of jobs (professional and nonprofessional) and age groups (ages 17 to 60 or more). In fact, in their review of 96 independent studies involving a total sample of 38,983 persons, the correlation ($r = 0.17$ out of a possible 1.0) between age and work performance was the highest for the youngest subjects (aged 17–26 years), compared to a correlation of $r = 0.04$ for all other age groups, which agreed with earlier findings (McEvoy & Cascio, 1989; Waldman & Avolio, 1986).

Thus, the evidence suggests that each person should be evaluated on the merits of her or his performance and that the performance of some older persons may be lower than that of other employees (those who are younger, the same age, or even older). It is important to keep in mind that in the studies just cited, cross-sec-

tional sampling (different subjects for different age groups), rather than longitudinal sampling (the same subjects tracked across years and decades) was used. So the findings that performance does not decline on average among older workers may have been due to selective retention in that only above-average older workers are retained or choose to remain in the workforce. Therefore, to the extent possible, organizations can effectively harness the contributions of all employees by matching, as closely as possible, the individual to a particular range of jobs, and organizational members of all ages must be willing to learn constantly.

Since the workforce throughout the world is growing older, successful organizations and managers must develop strategies to promote the individual development of older workers. These workers, in turn, must be open to learning new procedures and practices as the functions of organizations likewise change.

Women

Since the beginning of the 20th century, women have been entering the labor force in increasing numbers. In addition, it is well established that around the globe, women work longer hours than do men (Tavris & Wade, 1984) and that mothers work longer hours than anyone else because fathers do not participate equally in household and primary parenting tasks (Scarr, Phillips, & McCartney, 1989).

In industrialized countries in the East and West, fathers devote an average of 50 hours per week to employment and household work, compared to 80 hours per week for mothers (Cowan, 1983). However, according to self-reports, many mothers who are also employees do not feel more stressed than do women with fewer roles and obligations (Crosby, 1987).

Juggling Roles

As a consequence of the decline in real family income in the United States from 1973 to 1988, most women go to work primarily because their families need the money and secondarily for their personal self-actualization (Congressional Budget Office, 1988; Scarr et al., 1989). Empirical psychological studies have found that maternal employment can be both a positive and negative experience (Gutek, Repetti, & Silver, 1988; Hoffman, 1989). Its positive effects include increased self-esteem, perceptions of efficacy, status, and life satisfaction (Gove & Zeiss, 1987; Kessler & McRae, 1982; Nieva & Gutek, 1981; Verbrugge, 1983); on the negative side, maternal employment may involve role conflict, stress, dissatisfaction with life, and tension in the family (Cooke & Rousseau, 1984; Kandel, Davies, & Raveis, 1985). Williams, Suls, Alliger, Learner, and Wan (1991) found that working mothers reported greater negative affect and less enjoyment of tasks when they had to juggle the demands of work and household roles than when no role juggling was necessary. In general, it appears that role juggling is a stressor, regardless of who is doing the juggling (Carver & Scheier, 1990; Kirmeyer, 1988). Williams et al. (1991) concluded that role juggling is an initial strain and that working mothers appeared to adapt to such conditions (at least for the eight days of their observation) because there did not appear to be any interaction between affect at work and satisfaction at home, and affect at home did not seem to influence job satisfaction. Further research of extended periods of role juggling and of the influence of other moderators, such as support from husbands and other family members and the availability of day care, is needed to understand more fully the long-term effects of role juggling on satisfaction at home and work.

Women indicate that an important key to the success of dual-career families is the cooperation of their partners, which includes positive attitudes toward maternal employment and greater participation in household and child care tasks (Bernardo, Shehan, & Lesile, 1987; Gilbert, 1985, 1988). Matthews and Rodin (1989) reported that from 1975 to 1986 the proportion of married working women increased from 44.4%

to 54.6% and that the most dramatic increase was in women with young children. From the perspective of children, in 1960, 38.8% of children under age 18 had mothers in the labor force, whereas compared to 58.2% (34 million) in 1986. Accordingly, in the 1990s we can expect the majority of children will have a mother in the labor force, and more than half the employed mothers will work nonday shifts other than from 8 A.M. to 4 P.M. (Presser, 1988).

Advancement

As more women enter the labor force, they are moving into more and more positions that previously had been male dominated such as executive and managerial, college-level teaching, engineering, and mathematics and natural science positions (Matthews & Rodin, 1989). Likewise, the number of females who were appointed to governing boards of global oriented U.S. business firms has increased dramatically from 1988 to 1993, and as one female board member put it "companies are looking to women for their expertise, not their gender" (Lopez, 1993). Also, the rate of growth of black professional women in U.S. business firms increased substantially from 1982 to 1992, with a compound annual growth rate of 8.4% compared to 6.4% for white women and 4.2% for black men (Gaiter, 1994). Despite this rate of growth, it is important to remember that the relative number of black professional women compared to white professionals—both women and men—is minuscule.

In the United States, women have made progress in developing their individual talents and interests, but many have paid a high price for doing so. With an increasing number of women in the workplace, organizations must take many specific steps to strengthen further the individual development of women: providing equal pay for equal work and opportunities to advance into leadership positions, child and elder care support programs, mentoring or nurturing aspiring women employees with key seasoned organizational members, and enhancing organizational cultures so that the individual development and organizational contributions of women are valued (Feinstein, 1987; Jelinek & Adler, 1988; Noe, 1988; Powell, 1988). The organizational wake-up call is clear: Global organizations that do not provide these opportunities for women will find it difficult to recruit female employees, and there will be an increasing exodus of women from such organizations (Morrison & Von Glinow, 1990; Taylor, 1986).

Sexual Harassment

Sexual harassment has been a feature of the workplace since women entered the workforce, was made illegal in the United States with the passage of the Civil Rights Act of 1964, and was not legally defined until 1980 by the U.S. Equal Employment Opportunity Commission (EEOC, 1980; Fitzgerald, 1993).

Legally, sexual harassment includes two broad classes of prohibited behavior: (1) efforts to extort sexual cooperation by subtle or explicit threats of job-related consequences, such as the loss of a job or promotion (quid pro quo harassment), and (2) pervasive sex-related verbal or physical conduct that is unwelcome or offensive (hostile environment) but without threats of job-related consequences (EEOC, 1980). Sexual harassment, as Fitzgerald (1993, p. 1070) noted, "has become increasingly understood as any deliberate or repeated sexual behavior that is unwelcome to its recipient, as well as other sex-related behaviors that are hostile, offensive, or degrading."

Sexual harassment arises in all organizations. It was estimated that half the women in the workforce have or will experience sexual harassment, and sexual harassment was a central focus of the confirmation hearings of U.S. Supreme Court Justice Clarence Thomas and the U.S. Navy Tailhook scandal (Fitzgerald, 1993; Martindale, 1990). The consequences of sexual harassment for the person filing a complaint may include one or some combination of the follow-

ing: job loss as a result of firing or resignation owing to stress (Coles, 1986), decreased morale and job satisfaction, increased absenteeism, and damage to interpersonal relationships at work (Fitzgerald, 1993; Gutek, 1985).

Fitzgerald (1993) suggested a number of legislative initiatives and legal reforms that are needed to emphasize the prevention of sexual harassment in the workplace, some of which are presented in Table 10–1. An important first step in prevention is the presence of a strong policy statement on sexual harassment that is distributed and discussed systematically throughout the organization (Hesson-McInnis & Fitzgerald, 1992). In addition, the potential to collect large damages may motivate employers to promote prevention, and in states that provide for the possibility of large awards, such awards are relatively rare so the preventive value of large rewards is not yet known (Fitzgerald, 1993). Last, the federal EEOC guidelines provide that a complaint of sexual harassment must be made within 180 days (300 days in some states) of the incident (Bravo & Cassidy, 1992). As Fitzgerald (1993) stated, strong affirmative action programs, together with the aggressive recruitment

Table 10–1. Suggested Legislative Actions and Legal Reforms to Prevent Sexual Harassment

- Require all employers by law to develop and notify all employees about a clear policy against harassment that includes sound grievance procedures and is posted prominently in the workplace and provide education and training about harassment.

- Remove caps on available damages and link the award of substantial punitive damages more closely to the seriousness of the offense.

- Reform unemployment statutes so that women who quit their jobs because of sexual harassment can receive unemployment compensation.

- Extend the statute of limitations for filing charges of sexual harassment.

Adapted from L. F. Fitzgerald, *Sexual Harassment: Violence Against Women in the Workplace*, pp. 1073–1074. Copyright 1993 by the American Psychological Association, Washington, DC.

and career advancement of women, are among the most powerful organizational strategies for eliminating sexual harassment in that work sites with a relatively equal number of men and women have substantially fewer problems with harassment (Gutek, 1985).

Work and Drugs

When you apply for a job or even if you are already employed, many organizations want not only your expertise and potential for individual professional development but samples of your urine or blood or a piece of your hair for their drug-testing programs (American Management Association, 1991; Rothman, 1988). Approximately half the U.S. medium and large organizations test current or prospective employees for drug use (Guthrie & Olian, 1989). One survey (Schuster, 1987) reported that 19% of employed Americans aged 20–40 had used an elicit drug during the month before the survey and 29% had used drugs at least once during the previous year. Drug use has long been linked to a variety of organizational costs, including accidents, reduced productivity, and increased health care costs (Berry & Boland, 1977; Trice & Roman, 1972). It has been estimated that employees' abuse of alcohol and drugs has cost organizations $85–$100 billion per year (Cohen, 1984; Newcomb, 1988). Thus, drug abuse is both an individual and a critical organizational issue that affects co-workers and constitutes a potential danger for the public and the environment, as in the case of passenger train and airline accidents and the alcohol-related Exxon Valdez oil spill. We now briefly discuss the benefits (increased safety) and the costs (invasion of privacy) of organizational drug-testing programs, starting with the impact of such programs on prospective and current employees.

Attitudes toward drug testing. Grant and Bateman (1990) studied the impact of the presence or absence of a drug-testing program on potential job applicants' attitudes toward companies and their intention to apply to the companies. The subjects were 163 upper-level undergraduate business students, many of whom were planning to seek employment on graduation. The subjects were randomly assigned to one of four groups and were given information about four simulated organizations that either had or did not have drug-testing programs and that had either a high or a low need for such programs. Grant and Bateman found that potential job applicants had more positive attitudes toward and were more likely to apply to companies that did not test for drugs than toward those that did, regardless of whether or not there was a high need (indexed by accident rates, absenteeism, and theft) to test for potential drug use. Thus, the existence of a drug-testing program or a high need for such a program (even if no program is in place), coupled with negative attitudes toward such organizations, is most likely to cause applicants to look elsewhere for jobs. In short, a "clean" workplace is an important organizational reality when people are seeking employment.

In a field-based study, Stone and Kotch (1989) examined the attitudes of 73 blue-collar employees of a manufacturing firm toward hypothetical drug-testing policies. The subjects were told either that advance notice of testing was or was not provided and that the consequences of positive drug tests were either termination of jobs or rehabilitation by means of employee assistance and related therapeutic programs. As might be expected, the subjects had significantly more positive attitudes toward drug-testing programs when advance notice of testing was given and rehabilitation was provided than when no notice was given and the consequence was being fired. Drug testing may well be perceived as fair and necessary to detect and deter the use of drugs by employees in safety-sensitive jobs (such as airline pilots or operators of nuclear power plants), yet still be considered an invasion of privacy when it is time to collect urine samples for testing. Thus, organizations must be more sensitive in implementing drug-testing programs, and all will be well served when employees are given advance notice of tests and when those who test positive are offered rehabilitation.

A continuing issue regarding drug testing is the scope of such programs across a wide variety of jobs within and across different types of organizations. Hence, there is substantial legal support for mandating drug testing for those in transportation jobs (such as airline pilots) and security-related jobs (police), but not for those in nonsensitive jobs, such as clerks and some professionals (Greenfield, 1989; Greenfield, Karren, & Giacobbe, 1989). For example, the U.S. Supreme Court upheld drug testing for railroad crews because of the potential public hazards if drug use remained unchecked (Murphy, Thornton, & Reynolds, 1990).

It appears as if most members of organizations do not object to drug testing per se, but object to testing programs that are not related to their ability to perform their jobs (Lumsden, 1967; Thorson & Thomas, 1968). On the basis of the responses to a questionnaire by undergraduate college students and older nontraditional students, many of whom had substantial work experience, Murphy, Thornton, and Prue (1991) concluded that judgments of the acceptability of drug-testing programs for employees are strongly related to the characteristics of particular jobs, especially when the impairment of job performance may increase the potential for danger to others. These findings make plain that the acceptance of or objection to drug-testing programs is grounded in a reasonable assessment of the need for such programs for reasons of safety. In addition, people appear to react less favorably to alcohol testing than to tests for other drugs (Murphy et al., 1990).

Procedural justice. Konovsky and Cropanzano (1991) examined the impact of procedural justice (procedures that provide opportunities for input from all affected parties and for appeals that are as accurate as possible, and are applied consistently) and perceptions of the fairness of drug-testing programs on employees' attitudes (job satisfaction, commitment, and trust of management), intentions to leave organizations, and job performance. The results of this field-based study of 195 employees of a pathology laboratory indicated that procedural justice significantly influenced employees' attitudes and behavior, which, in turn, influenced their perceptions of fairness. Specifically, employees with higher job satisfaction, loyalty or commitment to the organization, trust in their leaders, and higher performance evaluations also reported that they perceived the organizational drug-testing program and processes as fair and just. Although it is not possible to identify causal directionality from these correlational findings, it is clear that when planning a drug-testing program, an organization needs to pay particular attention to procedural justice by including advance-notice, employees' voice, and appeals features. The centrality of procedural justice in drug-testing programs parallels findings of the importance of procedural justice in other organizational contexts, such as decisions on granting pay raises (Folger & Konovsky, 1989), performance appraisals (Greenberg, 1986), layoffs (Brockner & Greenberg, 1990), and decision making on budgets (Bies & Shapiro, 1987). In short, in all important decisions and domains of organizational life, people generally seek fair and just processes, procedures, and practices, which, in turn, are related to enhanced commitment to organizations and trust in organizational leaders.

Tepper (1994) conducted a correlational field investigation of employees of a major airline and a medium-sized utility company and a telephone survey of the general public to determine a broader social range of attitudes toward drug-testing programs. The findings indicated that individuals who were not tested were more concerned than were those who were tested about distributive justice (the invasion of privacy; the financial costs of the program; and the benefits, especially increased safety for the public and for co-workers) in drug-testing programs. On the other hand, individuals who were tested were more concerned than were those who were not about procedure justice, and those who participated in punitive drug-testing programs (in which the consequence of positive results was termination) were primarily concerned about the consistency of the procedures in that they felt they had been singled out for testing (Tepper, 1994; see also Leventhal, 1980). The message to organizational drug-testing programs that is implied in the findings of studies is to identify and amplify the procedural justice features; choose rehabilitative, rather than punitive, outcomes; and pay attention to distributive justice (the extent to which outcomes are fairly distributed among participants).

Bans on smoking. Promotion of the acceptance of bans on smoking in the workplace is another important issue for all organizations around the globe, especially in countries with high rates of smokers. The evidence of the negative effects of tobacco smoking on employees' health and on the efficient functioning of the organizations is unequivocal (Aronow, 1978; Ockene, 1984). Specifically, it costs U.S. companies about $95 billion per year or about $2,000 to $5,000 annually per employee for illnesses (cardiovascular disease, lung cancer, strokes, and emphysema) that arise from the direct inhalation of smoke as well as the inhalation of side-stream smoke (Greenberg, 1994). It has been shown that the physical damage to nonsmokers who are exposed regularly to side-stream cigarette smoke is equivalent to the damage incurred from smoking 10 cigarettes a day (Wynder & Stellman, 1977). Accordingly, public and legal pressures influence U.S. organizations to implement nonsmoking programs if they have not already done so (Fielding, 1986; Schein, 1987; Sorensen & Pechacek, 1989). However, the potential violation of smokers' rights makes the implementation of bans on smoking in the worksite a high-profile controversial issue (Ludington, 1991).

Greenberg (1994) examined the impact of the amount and type of information presented (capsulated and poignant information on adverse effects versus brief factual statements) and the interpersonal sensitivity (recognition of how difficult it is to stop smoking and of behavioral adjustments needed to smoke only in designated areas versus brief comments about the behavioral changes that will be required of all employees) on acceptance of a smoking-ban program in a large financial services organization. Greenberg found that although heavy smokers were the least accepting of the ban, they exhibited the greatest incremental increase in acceptance when they received thorough information presented in a highly sensitive manner. These findings agree with the earlier findings of Greenberg (1990a, 1990b), discussed in Chapter 6, on the positive impact of the sensitive presentation of detailed information about the hardships of pay cuts for all employees; the findings of both studies making plain that when you have to present "bad news" in an organization, it is best to do it in detail and with compassion.

INDIVIDUAL-ORGANIZATIONAL LINKAGES

A person pursues her or his individual job and career (series of jobs over an extended period, usually leading to jobs with greater responsibilities and rewards) goals based on relationships with an organization or a series of organizations. In this section, we examine three important features of the individual-organizational linkage that can facilitate both individual and organizational development: justice, citizenship, and support for the individual.

Justice

Organizational justice in the workplace, like normative or social justice, arises whenever there is an allotment of something that is rationally regarded as disadvantageous or advantageous (Greenberg, 1987; Rawls, 1971). It involves issues like who gets promoted, fired (or euphemistically "separated" from the organization), recommended for further training, or relocated and who receives pay increases, new offices and/or equipment, or any other organizational resources that may be associated with individual development. As we indicated in Chapter 2, most organizational members want to be treated fairly and to be perceived as being fair or just (Greenberg, 1990b).

Initially, the systematic investigation of organizational justice was grounded in Adams's (1965) equity theory (briefly discussed in Chapter 6). As we noted, equity focuses on an explanation of behavior involving the cognitive and motivational processes of the individual organizational member. Thus, a member is said to experience a state of inequity whenever her or his perceived (not necessarily actual) ratios of outcomes to job efforts or inputs are unequal to the perceived ratios of some other comparison. Here the focus is on *distributive justice* (the fairness of outcomes). Overpayment is said to result in guilt and underpayment in anger; either state gives rise to tension that the individual attempts to ease by, for example, reducing inputs or changing the social comparison referent. A major drawback of an equity-grounded model of organizational justice is that equity theory is silent on how perceptions of justice are moderated or influenced by the procedures through which outcomes are determined (Leventhal, 1980).

As we mentioned earlier, the influence of *procedural justice* (fair procedures) has been established firmly for a number of organizational contexts. In general, Leventhal (1980) suggested that procedural justice is operative in an organization when

- affected parties have input
- procedures are applied consistently
- bias is minimized

- information and procedures are accurate
- procedures allow for appeals of a decision
- procedures are ethical

Therefore, if you want members of your organization to experience organizational justice for key decision contexts, it is critical to pay attention not only to the fairness of the outcomes, but to the fairness of the organizational procedures that are used to arrive at the outcomes that have an impact on the members. In addition, *interactional justice* (the fair interpersonal treatment members receive) is also important to promote a sense of organizational justice, as has been shown for decisions involving the perceived fairness of layoffs (Brockner & Greenberg, 1989), performance appraisals (Greenberg, 1986), and the acceptance or rejection of proposals (Bies & Shapiro, 1987). Thus, if as a manager you seek to promote economic productivity by *equitable* allocations of resources (each according to her or his merits), *equal* allocations (the same for all) to foster harmony, or *need-based* allocations (to each according to her or his legitimate needs) to nurture individual development, it is important to bear in mind the distributive, procedural, and interactional facets of organizational justice, so that regardless of your goal, your decisions or allocations will be perceived as fair.

Citizenship

To determine if organizational justice influences job performance, Moorman (1991) examined the relationship between distributive and procedural justice and organizational citizenship behaviors—work-related behaviors that are discretionary, rather than position mandated; that are unrelated to the organization's formal reward system, and that advance the organization's effectiveness (for a discussion of these behaviors, see Organ, 1988). Measures of distributive justice (from the five-item Distributive Justice Index; Price & Mueller, 1986) and procedural and interactional justice (indexed by a scale designed for the study and the Organizational Citizenship Behavior [OCB] Scale; Podsakoff & MacKenzie, 1989) were obtained for 270 employees of two organizations, with the responses of 225 employees usable for data analyses (Moorman, 1991). The findings indicated that interactional justice was the only form of organizational justice that was related to OCB, which included the behavioral domains of altruism, courtesy, fairness, conscientiousness, and civic virtue. Thus, the perception of the fairness of organizational procedures to determine organizational outcomes seems to depend largely on the manner in which managers implement the procedures. What you do as a manager strongly influences members' organizational citizenship behaviors.

Support

Member's commitment to their organization has been examined by assessing members' *affective attachment* (Mowday, Porter, & Steers, 1982) to the organization (for example, "Working here has a lot of meaning for me" or "This organization does not deserve my loyalty"), as well as their *calculative involvement* (perceptions of the economic advantages accrued in one's job compared to alternative employment opportunities) (Koslowsky, Kluger, & Yinon, 1988). Eisenberger, Huntington, Hutchison, and Sowa (1986) suggested that employees develop a general perception regarding the extent to which their organization values their contributions and cares about their well-being.

Thus, if an organization chooses, rather than responds to mandated governmental regulations or rules, to implement a program (such as on-site day care) that benefits employees, the affected employees are likely to conclude that their organization cares for them and can be depended on for future rewards and nurturance (Eisenberger, Fasolo, & Davis-LaMastro, 1990). This perception of organizational support of individual development, expressed as being cared for and valued by one's organization, may then be translated into enhanced job performance, affective attachment to the organization, and prosocial acts (such as speaking positively and enthusiastically about the organization to outsiders, helping associates beyond one's role requirements, and looking out for the organization's welfare). Eisenberger et al. (1990) found that increased perception of organizational support reduced the absenteeism and enhanced the job performance of employees in six occupations, including high school teachers, police officers, hourly manufacturing workers, and insurance personnel. They also found that enhanced organizational support was associated with increased affective attachment to the organization, as measured by Meyer and Allen's (1984) Affective Commitment Scale, and innovativeness, as measured by the constructiveness of anonymous employees' proposals to strengthen the organization for the 422 hourly and 109 managerial employees in a large steel plant. Similar findings were reported by Shore and Tetrick (1991) for a variety of members of a large multinational organization. Thus, organizations that increase their support for employees' individual development and needs can expect employees to be more conscientious and creative in performing their jobs and have a strong affective attachment to and calculative involvement in the organization without expecting direct rewards or personal recognition. In short, if an organization supports employees, then employees will support the organization in a variety of ways that are a reflection of the reciprocity of organizational commitment (Scholl, 1981).

A PLACE TO WORK

In general, when people look for a place to work, they must evaluate a number of facets of the organization whether they are searching for their first job or are changing jobs from one organization to another. As we already discussed, people seek out and stay with organizations when they sense there is a high level of organizational justice. Almost all organizational members want to be good citizens and are most likely to behave as such when they sense that their organization is fair, especially in difficult economic times. Also, job performance and innovativeness increase when organizational members sense that the organization provides, as best as possible, support for their individual needs and development. In addition, people seem to search for and stay with organizations when the other members have similar psychological and demographic characteristics to them.

We now briefly discuss the psychological (individual-level) and the demographic (group-level) features that draw people to or away from particular places of work. We also examine the impact of dispositional and situational forces on the selection of places to work and the growing number of night jobs in many global organizations.

Organizational Attractiveness

Assuming that salaries and benefits are equivalent, why is one organization more attractive to a potential employee than another, and why is an organization more attracted to one applicant than to other equally qualified applicants?

A psychological-level explanation of organizational attractiveness is Schneider's (1987) attraction-selection-attrition (ASA) model, which suggests that when current members screen applicants, they are attracted to similar others and so are more likely to admit applicants who are like them. Furthermore, if the match between new members and current members is not satisfactory, then pressures arise to encourage dissimilar members to leave the organization, which ultimately results in psychologically homogeneous work groups (George, 1990). According to the ASA model, personality, inter-

ests, and values are the focal influences on attraction to organizations and the people in them.

A group-level (demographic) explanation of organizational attractiveness is Pfeffer's (1983) model of organizational demography, which asserts that group or composite variables, such as the age, tenure in the organization, sex, race, and religion of current members, are key variables that influence the attractiveness of the organization to potential new members. According to the model, the more similar the match on significant demographic variables, the more likely a candidate will select and be selected by a particular organization.

Both the ASA and organizational demography models recognize the importance of personal attributes and the mix of attributes in the current membership of an organization that influence organizational attractiveness and attrition. Also, both models emphasize that similarity is one of the most central determinants of interpersonal attractiveness (Levine & Moreland, 1990; Lott & Lott, 1965). An extensive study of 93 top management teams (ranging from 3 to 18 members) in 51 bank holding companies found that turnover was predicted by the heterogeneity of the management teams (in terms of age, tenure, and educational levels), whereas promotion from within the organizations increased the teams' homogeneity (Jackson et al., 1991). Hence, the finding that a reliance on internal selection contributes to the creation of homogeneous top management teams, coupled with the finding that organizations headed by homogeneous top management teams are less innovative, supports the ASA model's predictions that recruitment and selection processes are key to creating organizations that are capable of change.

Finally, when seeking a position in the global marketplace, it is important to appreciate that techniques for selecting organizational members vary across cultures (Steiner & Gilliland, 1996). Thus, for example, many European organizations, particularly French ones, analyze handwriting samples to assess applicants' personal attributes, whereas many U.S. organizations rely heavily on biographical information, requesting specific information about applicants' work experience, education, skills, and hobbies or personal interests. In a laboratory-based study of American and French college students, Steiner and Gilliland (1996) reported that the selection techniques that both groups preferred were work-sample tests, interviews, and résumés. These findings are encouraging since the results of both work-sample tests (Schmitt, Gooding, Noe, & Kirsch, 1984) and structured interviews (Huffcutt & Arthur, 1994) are highly predictive of future work performance. It is interesting that the French students rated honesty testing and handwriting analyses negatively, despite the widespread use of handwriting analyses in French organizations (Lévy-Leboyer, 1994).

The Person or the Place?

Since the 1980s, many investigators of organizational behavior have again questioned whether dispositional traits (the person) or the organizational context (the place) primarily determine what members experience and do in a variety of organizational situations (Newton & Keenan, 1991). Schneider (1987), for example, in developing his ASA model of organizational attractiveness, asserted that "the attributes of people, not the nature of the external environment, or organizational technology, or organizational structure are the fundamental determinants of organizational behavior" (p. 437).

Staw and Ross (1985) found stable retest correlations with job satisfaction across time and job situations and concluded that job satisfaction may be determined mainly by the basic disposition of an individual, rather than by changing work contexts or situations. On the other hand, Davis-Blake and Pfeffer (1989) argued that high retest correlations do not prove that attitudes and affect have been stable across time or contexts because they indicate only the rela-

tive, not the absolute, position of individuals in a group. Thus, for example, at one point in time, measures of job satisfaction may all cluster around 1 (low) and at a later time around 5 (high) on a five-point job satisfaction scale, indicating a high retest correlation coupled with a marked change in the magnitude of the dependent measure. Accordingly, Newton and Keenan (1991) investigated the job satisfaction and affect, such as anxiety and alienation, of engineers when they were in their final year of university training (Time 1) and then after two years (Time 2) and four years (Time 3) of full-time employment. That is, they obtained measures of attitude and affect following situational changes from university studies to full-time employment and then a change of employers for some subjects. Their findings indicated that there was a general decrease in observed levels of job satisfaction and affect measures over time; hence, full-time employment was less satisfying, less alienating, and less anxiety provoking than was being a student. Although dispositional influences were stronger than situational influences, situational forces were also influential in that the respondents who had changed employers reported significantly greater job satisfaction than did those who had not. In sum, both people and the place seem to shape the job satisfaction and affect levels of organizational members.

Night Work

As the global economy continues to evolve and spread throughout the world, more and more organizations will be open 24 hours a day. The regular business hours of 8 A.M. to 5 P.M. have long disappeared for many organizations, and more employees are working shifts outside the normal human diurnal cycle of sleeping at night and being awake during the day (Barton, 1994).

Some of the problems experienced by individuals who are *required* to work nights include disturbances of the sleep-wake cycle (Akerstedt, 1990), physical and psychological ill health

(Bohle & Tilley, 1989; De Vries & De Vries-Griever, 1990), and social and domestic disruption (Colligan & Rosa, 1990). However, Barton and Folkard (1993) did not find an increase in sleep or social problems for a group of *permanent* night shift nurses in comparison with rotating shift nurses (who worked one to four weeks during the day and then at night work for the same interval). Some people may prefer night work for a variety of reasons, including time at home with young children during the day, interacting with fewer persons both at work and at home, since most family members, friends, and neighbors are at work or school during the day. On the basis of an extensive survey of 587 nurses and midwives, Barton (1994) found that fewer health, sleep, social, and domestic complaints were reported by permanent than by rotating night shift nurses and midwives, especially when the individuals had chosen to

work at night. Thus, if your organization is going to be open 24 hours per day, it is probably best to recruit and retain persons who prefer and choose night work and to institute a permanent schedule for the night workers (Barton, 1994).

Job Enrichment

No matter where or when you work outside the home, you are going to spend a lot of time on the job, as well as getting to and from your workplace. Therefore, it is valuable for your individual development, as well as for the organization's productivity, to have some index of what constitutes a good job, psychologically speaking.

Probably the most frequently cited job-enrichment model is that of Hackman and Oldham (1975, 1980), which is depicted in Figure 10–1. As can be seen in Figure 10–1, there are five

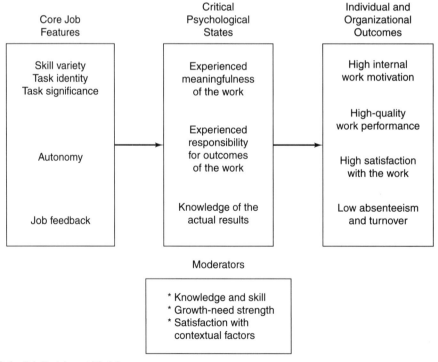

Figure 10–1 Job-Enrichment Model.
J. R. Hackman & G. R. Oldham, *Work Redesign* (fig. 4.6 from p. 90), © 1980 by Addison-Wesley Publishing Company, Inc. Reprinted by permission of Addison-Wesley Longman Publishing Company, Inc.

core job characteristics (left-hand column) that give rise to three fundamental psychological experiences that, in turn, lead to four basic outcomes for the individual and the organization (right-hand column). Table 10–2 presents brief definitions of each of the five core job characteristics. If you are searching for or designing a job, you are likely to find or build one that has a high amount of all five characteristics. In addition, as is shown at the bottom of Figure 10–1, three individual moderators influence the relationship between core job characteristics and individual-organizational outcomes: knowledge and skills, growth-need strength (the desire for individual development, growth, and learning), and satisfaction with contextual factors (such as personnel policies, organizational culture, and physical work environment).

Hackman and Oldham (1975) also developed the *job diagnostic survey* to measure the magnitude of each of the five job characteristics in any given job and the likely outcomes listed in Figure 10–1. The results of the survey yield the motivating potential score (MPS), which is calculated as follows:

$$\text{MPS} = \frac{\begin{matrix} \text{Skill} & \text{Task} & \text{Task} \\ \text{Variety} + \text{Identity} + \text{Significance} \end{matrix}}{3} \times \text{Autonomy} \times \text{Feedback}$$

Table 10–2. Definitions of the Five Core Job Characteristics

Skill Variety: the range of personal competencies and capabilities to perform the job
Task Identity: the degree to which the job is done by a single person and the extent of the discernible outcome
Task Significance: the extent to which the job has an impact on the lives of other persons within or outside the organization
Autonomy: the extent of one's freedom, discretion, and independence in scheduling and in the way in which one performs the job
Job Feedback: the degree of reported or measured performance outcomes

In general, a job or position that is high in variety, identity, and significance, together with autonomy and feedback on performance, is most likely attractive. To appreciate the psychological robustness of the job-enrichment model, think of the worst job you ever had or might have. Such a job or position probably would be extremely low on all or many of the components of the MPS formula, which can serve as a rough preliminary assessment of any future positions you may be contemplating.

Going Global

Some important features of a global manager's job include working with people of other cultures as equals and learning continuously to enhance the capability of the global organization (Adler & Bartholomew, 1992; Odenwald, 1993). To be an effective representative of the global organization, a culturally sensitive global manager tries to learn many of the facets that form the foundation of a culture (Fatiu & Rodgers, 1984), in addition to being competent in her or his field or area of work; in so doing, the manager will learn about herself or himself as well, which is the key to becoming and being a global citizen. A survey of the criteria that 50 participating multinational organizations use to select candidates for global assignments indicated that the most important criterion was technical expertise, followed, in order of importance, by managerial ability, and language skills (fifth) and cultural sensitivity (seventh) (Fatiu & Rodgers, 1984). Clearly, technical competence is critical to successful performance in the global marketplace and, if coupled with a knowledge of languages and cultural sensitivity, it can enhance a manager's effectiveness in the global economy. There is, of course, no place to hide from the realities of the global marketplace, so it is essential for all managers to enhance their cultural sensitivities by learning how to live and work effectively in a variety of cultural settings (Fowers & Richardson, 1996).

COPING STRATEGIES

Each person experiences problems at work and at home and attempts in her or his own way to cope with the problems. In most cases, stress is associated with problems; although a moderate level of stress is a valuable source of motivation, a high level of stress usually leads to deteriorating performance and may lead to dysfunction. An important part of individual change is to manage stress so that life can be enjoyable and fulfilling (Quick, Murphy, & Hurrell, 1992).

Stress

Although everyone knows what stress feels like and is aware of its impact on behavior, cognition, and emotions, there is no clear and generally accepted definition of stress in the management or psychological literature (Kahn & Byosiere, 1990). We define stress as a general reaction to an action or situation that places special (and usually sustained) physical and psychological demands (or both) on an individual (Beehr & Franz, 1986; Ivancevich & Matteson, 1986). People respond differently to various situational demands. Thus, it is difficult to identify a stress-management program at work that responds to the needs of all organizational members, although all stress-management interventions (health-promotion or wellness programs) focus on reducing the presence of work-related stressors or assisting individuals to minimize the negative consequences of stressors (Ivancevich, Matteson, Freedman, & Phillips, 1990).

Organizational Stress Management

In most instances, stress-management programs (SMPs) focus on individuals, most of whom are managerial and white-collar employees (Ivancevich et al., 1990). Furthermore, organizations consider stress to be a response of individual employees and hence support SMPs that teach individual responsibility and personal coping skills (Singer, Neale, Schwartz, & Schwartz,

1986). For example, because of extreme heat in the workplace (a situational stressor), an organization might install air-conditioning (an organizational intervention); the outcome would be the enhanced quality of work life (individual), productivity (organizational), and job satisfaction (individual-organizational interface).

Organizational SMPs in Europe are an outgrowth of the early work of the Tavistock Institute in England that extensively studied group processes in the 1950s and 1960s (Cooper & Payne, 1992). The focus of European programs has been more on identifying organization-wide stressors and implementing strategies for organizational change than on identifying stressors and implementing strategies targeted at the individual, as is characteristic of the American approach. The organizational approach is also widely used by Japanese firms (Nakajima, 1988). As Cooper and Payne (1992) noted a combined emphasis on individual and organization-wide SMPs is usually more effective than either program alone because stressors arise at both the micro- and macrolevels of organizations.

Individual features moderate the response to stress, regardless of the type of SMP. In general, women seem to report higher rates of psychological distress while men appear to be more prone to physical illness (Jick & Mitz, 1985). It has also been suggested that blacks adapt better to stress than do whites (Veroff, Douvan & Kulka, 1981) as demonstrated by the finding that John Henryism (the belief that psychological stressors can be controlled by hard work and determination) moderated stress for blacks but not for whites (James, Hartnett, & Kalsbeck, 1983; James, Strogatz, Wing, & Ramsey, 1987). Individuals differ in their hardiness (sense of commitment in various aspects of life, sense of control over life events, and search for and welcome challenge); hardy persons experience fewer dysfunctional outcomes under chronic stress than do less hardy ones (Kobasa, Hilker, & Maddi, 1980; Kobasa, Maddi, & Kahn, 1982).

Cooper and Payne (1992) suggested that although objective stressors (such as extreme levels of heat, cold, or noise) may be consistent across cultures, subjective stressors (individual appraisals of stress) probably vary across cultures. For example, according to Hofstede's (1991) measures of culture (such as individualism versus collectivism, masculinity versus femininity, and power distance), an organizational member may find it stressful to speak out in front of her or his superiors or answer questions in public in a culture with high power distance that promotes respect for and obedience to people in authority. Furthermore, as Angyal (1946) noted, mature individuals around the world constantly have to align the forces of autonomy (doing your own thing) with heteronomy, or integrating oneself with others (doing our thing), so that it may be less subjectively stressful to be heteronomous in a culture that is high in femininity on Hofstede's femininity-masculinity cultural dimension. Since what is subjectively stressful in one culture may not be so in another culture, managers must attend to both objective and subjective stressors by learning continuously about their own and other cultures.

Fitness, Wellness, and Discipline

In the global economy, change is constant, generating ambiguities of events and organizational uncertainties that can be stressful to organizational members at work and at home. Organizations need healthy and compassionate persons. There is a substantial amount of solid empirical data that fitness and wellness programs improve general health (Bowne, Russell, Morgan, Optenberg, & Clarke, 1984; Gebhardt & Grump, 1990), significantly reduce health care costs (Bly, Jones, & Richardson, 1986; Gibbs, Mulvaney, Henes, & Reed, 1985), increase job performance and morale (Gebhardt & Grump, 1990), and reduce absenteeism (Bowne et al., 1984).

We, along with others, believe that individual change involving a variety of work-life issues and coping strategies is advanced substantially by a discipline or a way to experience personal wholeness and uniqueness (Sinetar, 1986). According to Glasser (1976), a discipline must contain five facets to help a person grow, namely,

- An exercise (sitting quietly, walking, running, or whatever) that is done, for the most part, alone.

- An exercise that is easy to initiate and does not require much mental effort.

- An exercise done daily for at least 30 minutes to 1 hour.

- An exercise that the exerciser must believe will improve her or his mental and physical state and for which he or she can recognize experiential signs of improvement without the help of an expert or guru.

- An exercise that does not require inordinate self-criticism or comparison of one's progress to the progress of others (for instance, "I ran quickly today," rather than "I didn't run as fast as others").

We encourage you to pursue your own coping strategy or discipline, so you can learn to adjust effectively to the wide variety of work-life issues that you encounter at work and at home.

SUMMARY

We began this chapter with a holistic definition of individual change as the enhancement of a person's intellectual, emotional, physical, and psychological capacities. Organizations, like families, have experienced fundamental changes in the past 10 years, and new patterns of relationships are evolving at work as well as at home. Individual change does not occur in static organizational contexts, and each person has to deal at different levels with a wide variety of work-life issues, such as aging, sexual harassment, and role juggling.

We examined the relationship between aging and work, noting that older workers have lower rates of absenteeism, turnover, and illness and that aging does not negatively influence work performances. We also examined issues of role juggling between work and family and advancement patterns of women in a variety of organizations. We outlined specific steps that organizations can take to expunge sexual harassment from the workplace.

We then examined the tremendous financial and human-resource costs of alcohol and substance abuse and the profound truncation of individual development by substance abusers. Studies have found that drug-testing procedures, policies, and assistance programs that promote procedural justice are highly acceptable to organizational members and that justice in the workplace (distributive, procedural, and interactional) is essential for individual members and the organization as a whole.

Organizational citizenship behaviors that are chosen, rather than position mandated, strengthen the linkages between individuals and organizations and are influenced substantially by the level of proactive support for individual development.

We examined the ASA and organizational demography models of individual and organizational linkages, both of which indicate that shared values and demographic features (such as age and gender) are keys to enhancing the relationship between individuals and organizations.

Night work is growing around the world, and studies have indicated that when the night shift is chosen, rather than mandated, individuals work effectively and independently of the normal day-night cycle.

The job enrichment model identifies essential features of jobs that promote individual motivation, including the degree of autonomy and the timeliness of feedback on performance. Obviously, the higher both of these features are, the greater the enhancement of individual opportunities. Also, organizations need to pay increasing attention to cultural factors if they are to promote individual change across an increasingly diversified global workforce.

Finally, we defined objective and subjective stressors and identified stress-management interventions that are applied in a wide variety of organizations. We concluded with an outline of the critical features of a modest coping strategy to promote individual change that will help organizational members to be more authentic and resourceful at work and elsewhere.

CHAPTER REFERENCES

Adams, J. S. (1965). Inequity in social exchange. In L. Berkowitz (Ed.), *Advances in experimental social psychology* (Vol. 2, pp. 267–299). New York: Academic Press.

Adler, N., & Bartholomew, S. (1992). Managing globally competent people. *Academy of Management Executive, 6,* 19–27.

Akerstedt, T. (1990). Psychological and physiological effects of shift work. *Scandinavian Journal of Work and Environmental Health, 16,* 67–73.

American Management Association. (1991). *Drug abuse: The workplace issues.* New York: Author.

Angyal, A. (1946). *Foundation for a science of personality.* New York: Commonwealth Fund.

Aronow, W. S. (1978). Effect of passive smoking on angina pectoris. *New England Journal of Medicine, 299,* 21–30.

Barton, J. (1994). Choosing to work at night: A moderating influence on individual tolerance to shift work. *Journal of Applied Psychology, 79,* 449–454.

Barton, J., & Folkard, S. (1993). Advancing versus delaying shift systems, *Ergonomics, 36,* 59–64.

Basic Behavioral Science Task Force, National Advisory Mental Health Council. (1996). Basic behavioral science research for mental health:

Family processes and social networks. *American Psychologist*, *51*, 622–630.

Beehr, T. A., & Franz, T. M. (1986). The current debate about the meaning of job stress. *Journal of Organizational Behavior Management*, *8*, 5–18.

Bernardo, D. H., Shehan, C. L., & Lesile, G. R. (1987). A residue of tradition: Jobs, careers, and spouses' time in housework. *Journal of Marriage and the Family*, *49*, 381–390.

Berry, R. E., & Boland, J. P. (1977). *The economic cost of alcohol abuse*. New York: Free Press.

Bies, R. J., & Shapiro, D. L. (1987). Interactional fairness judgments: The influence of causal accounts. *Social Justice Research*, *1*, 199–218.

Bly, J., Jones, R., & Richardson, T. (1986). Impact of worksite health promotion on health care costs and utilization: Evaluation of Johnson and Johnson's live for life program. *Journal of the American Medical Association*, *256*, 3235–3240.

Bohle, P., & Tilley, A. J. (1989). The impact of night work on psychological well-being. *Ergonomics*, *32*, 1089–1099.

Bowne, D. W., Russell, M. L., Morgan, M. A., Optenberg, S., & Clarke, A. (1984). Reduced disability and health care costs in an industrial fitness program. *Journal of Occupational Medicine*, *26*, 809–816.

Bravo, E., & Cassidy, E. (1992). *The 9 to 5 guide to combating sexual harassment*. New York: John Wiley & Sons.

Brockner, J., & Greenberg, J. (1990). The impact of layoffs on survivors: An organizational justice perspective. In J. S. Carroll (Ed.), *Applied social psychology and organizational settings* (pp. 45–75). Hillsdale, NJ: Lawrence Erlbaum.

Buie, J. (1987, October). Available grants could shape care of the future. *APA Monitor*, p. 12.

Caminiti, S. (1994, June). What happens to laid-off managers. *Fortune*, pp. 68–78.

Carver, C. S., & Scheier, M. F. (1990). Origins and functions of positive and negative affect: A control-process view. *Psychological Review*, *97*, 19–35.

Cascio, W. F. (1992). *Managing human resources* (3rd ed.). New York: McGraw-Hill.

Cohen, S. (1984). Drugs in the workplace. *Journal of Clinical Psychiatry*, *12*, 4–8.

Coles, F. S. (1986). Forced to quit: Sexual harassment complaints and agency response. *Sex Roles*, *14*, 81–95.

Colligan, M. J., & Rosa, R. R. (1990). Shiftwork effects on social and family life. *Occupational Medicine: Shiftwork*, *5*, 315–322.

Congressional Budget Office. (March, 1988). *New report on family income*. Washington, DC: Author.

Cooke, R. A., & Rousseau, D. M. (1984). Stress and strain from family roles and work-role expectations. *Journal of Applied Psychology*, *69*, 252–260.

Cooper, C. L., & Payne, R. L. (1992). International perspectives on research into work, well-being, and stress management. In J. C. Quick, L. R. Murphy, & J. J. Hurrell, Jr. (Eds.), *Stress and well-being at work* (pp. 348–368). Washington, DC: American Psychological Association.

Cowan, R. S. (1983). *More work for mother: The ironies of household technology from the open hearth to the microwave*. New York: Basic Books.

Crosby, F. J. (Ed.). (1987). *Spouse, parent, worker: On gender and multiple roles*. New Haven, CT: Yale University Press.

Davis-Blake, A., & Pfeffer, J. (1989). Just a mirage: The search for dispositional effects in organizational research. *Academy of Management Review*, *14*, 385–400.

De Vries, G. M., & De Vries-Griever, A. H. G. (1990). The process of developing health complaints: A longitudinal study of the effects of abnormal, irregular and condensed working hours. In G. Costa, G. Cesna, K. Kogi, & A. Wedderburn (Eds.), *Shiftwork, health, sleep and performance* (pp. 290–296). Frankfurt am Main: Peter Lang.

Eisenberger, R., Fasolo, P., & Davis-LaMastro, V. (1990). Perceived organizational support and employee diligence, commitment, and innovation. *Journal of Applied Psychology*, *75*, 51–59.

Eisenberger, R., Huntington, R., Hutchison, S., & Sowa, D. (1986). Perceived organizational support. *Journal of Applied Psychology*, *71*, 500–507.

Fatiu, I., & Rodgers, I. (1984). A workshop on cultural differences. In *AFS Orientation Handbook* (Vol. 4). New York: American Field Service.

Feinstein, S. (1987, November 10). Women and minority workers in business find a mentor can be a rare commodity. *Wall Street Journal*, p. 39.

Fielding, J. E. (1986). Banning work site smoking. *American Journal of Public Health, 76,* 857–862.

Fitzgerald, L. F. (1993). Sexual harassment: Violence against women in the workplace. *American Psychologist, 48,* 1070–1076.

Folger, R., & Konovsky, M. S. (1989). Effects of procedural and distributive justice on reactions to pay raise decisions. *Academy of Management Journal, 32,* 115–130.

Fowers, B. J., & Richardson, F. C. (1996). Multiculturalism. *American Psychologist, 51,* 609–621.

Gaiter, D. (1994, March 8). The gender divide: Black women's gains in corporate America outstrip black men's. *Wall Street Journal*, p. B-1.

Gebhardt, D. L., & Grump, E. E. (1990). Employee fitness and wellness programs in the workplace. *American Psychologist, 45,* 262–272.

George, J. M. (1990). Personality, affect, and behavior in groups. *Journal of Applied Psychology, 75,* 107–116.

Gibbs, J. O., Mulvaney, D., Henes, C., & Reed, R. W. (1985). Work-site health promotion. *Journal of Occupational Medicine, 27,* 826–830.

Gilbert, L. A. (1985). *Men in dual-career families: Current realities and future prospects.* Hillsdale, NJ: Lawrence, Erlbaum.

Gilbert, L. A. (1988). *Sharing it all: The rewards and struggles of two-career families.* New York: Plenum Press.

Giniger, S., Dispenzieri, A., & Eisenberg, J. (1983). Age, experience, and performance on speed and skill jobs in an applied setting. *Journal of Applied Psychology, 68,* 469–475.

Glasser, W. (1976). *Positive addiction.* New York: Harper & Row.

Gove, W. R., & Zeiss, C. (1987). Multiple roles and happiness. In F. Crosby (Ed.), *Spouse, parent, worker* (pp. 125–137). New Haven, CT: Yale University Press.

Grant, J. M., & Bateman, T. S. (1990). An experimental test of the impact of drug-testing programs on potential job applicants' attitudes and intentions. *Journal of Applied Psychology, 75,* 127–131.

Greenberg, J. (1986). Determinants of perceived fairness of performance evaluations. *Journal of Applied Psychology, 71,* 340–342.

Greenberg, J. (1987). A taxonomy of organizational justice theories. *Academy of Management Review, 16,* 399–432.

Greenberg, J. (1990a). Employee theft as a reaction to underpayment inequity: The hidden cost of pay cuts. *Journal of Applied Psychology, 75,* 561–568.

Greenberg, J. (1990b). Looking fair vs. being fair: Managing impressions of organizational justice. In B. M. Staw & L. L. Cummings (Eds.), *Research in organizational behavior* (Vol. 12, pp. 111–157). Greenwich, CT: JAI Press.

Greenberg, J. (1994). Using socially fair treatment to promote acceptance of a work site smoking ban. *Journal of Applied Psychology, 79,* 288–297.

Greenfield, P. A. (1989). Drug testing and the law. *Employee Responsibilities and Rights Journal, 2,* 11–26.

Greenfield, P. A., Karren, R. J., & Giacobbe, J. K. (1989). Drug testing in the workplace: An overview of legal and philosophical issues. *Employee Responsibilities and Rights Journal, 2,* 1–10.

Gutek, B. (1985). *Sex and the workplace.* San Francisco: Jossey-Bass.

Gutek, B. A., Repetti, R. L., & Silver, D. (1988). Nonwork roles and stress at work. In C. L. Cooper & R. Payne (Eds.), *Causes, coping, and consequences of stress at work* (pp. 141–174). New York: John Wiley & Sons.

Guthrie, J. P., & Olian, J. D. (1989, April). *Drug and alcohol testing programs: The influence of organizational context and objectives.* Paper presented at the fourth annual conference of the Society for Industrial/Organizational Psychology, Boston.

Hackman, J. R., & Oldham, G. R. (1975). Development of the Job Diagnostic Survey. *Journal of Applied Psychology, 60*, 159–170.

Hackman, J. R., & Oldham, G. R. (1980). *Work redesign.* Reading, MA: Addison-Wesley.

Hesson-McInnis, H., & Fitzgerald, L. F. (1992, November). *Modeling sexual harassment: A preliminary analysis.* Paper presented at the APA/NIOSH conference on stress in the 90s: A Changing Workforce in a Changing Workplace, Washington, DC.

Hoffman, L. W. (1989). Effects of maternal employment in the two-parent family. *American Psychologist, 44*, 283–292.

Hofstede, G. (1991). *Cultures and organizations: Software of the mind.* New York: McGraw-Hill.

Huffcutt, A. I., & Arthur, W., Jr. (1994). Hunter and Hunter (1984) revisited: Interview validity for entry-level jobs. *Journal of Applied Psychology, 79*, 184–190.

Ivancevich, J. M., & Matteson, M. T. (1986). Organizational level stress management interventions: Review and recommendations. *Journal of Organizational Behavior and Management, 8*, 229–248.

Ivancevich, J. M., Matteson, M. T., Freedman, S. M., & Phillips, J. S. (1990). Worksite stress management interventions. *American Psychologist, 45*, 252–261.

Jackson, S. E., Brett, J. F., Sessa, V. I., Cooper, D. M., Julin, J. A., & Peyronnin, K. (1991). Some differences make a difference: Individual dissimilarity and group heterogeneity as correlates of recruitment, promotions, and turnover. *Journal of Applied Psychology, 76*, 675–689.

James, S. A., Hartnett, S. A., & Kalsbeck, W. D. (1983). John Henryism and blood pressure differences among black men. *Journal of Behavioral Medicine, 6*, 259–278.

James, S. A., Strogatz, D. S., Wing, S. B., & Ramsey, D. L. (1987). Socioeconomic status, John Henryism, and hyper-tension in blacks and whites. *American Journal of Epidemiology, 126*, 664–673.

Jelinek, M., & Adler, N. J. (1988, February). Women: World-class managers for global competition. *Executive, 2*, 11–19.

Jick, T. D., & Mitz, L. F. (1985). Sex differences in work stress. *Academy of Management Review, 10*, 408–420.

Kahn, R. L., & Byosiere, P. (1990). Stress in organizations. In M. D. Dunnette & L. M. Hough (Eds.), *Handbook of industrial and organizational psychology* (pp. 571–650). Palo Alto, CA: Consulting Psychologists Press.

Kandel, D. B., Davies, M., & Raveis, V. H. (1985). The stressfulness of daily social roles from women: Marital, occupational and household roles. *Journal of Health and Social Behavior, 26*, 64–78.

Kessler, R. C., & McRae, J. A., Jr. (1982). The effects of wives' employment on the mental health of married men and women. *American Sociological Review, 47*, 216–227.

Kirmeyer, S. L. (1988). Coping with competing demands: Interruption and the Type A pattern. *Journal of Applied Psychology, 73*, 621–629.

Kobasa, S. C., Hilker, R. R., & Maddi, S. R. (1980). Remaining healthy in the encounter with stress. In *Work, stress, health* (pp. 10–15). Chicago: American Medical Association.

Kobasa, S. C., Maddi, S. R., & Kahn, S. (1982). Hardiness and health: A prospective study. *Journal of Personality and Social Psychology, 42*, 168–177.

Konovsky, M. A., & Cropanzano, R. (1991). Perceived fairness of employee drug testing as a predictor of employee attitudes and job performance. *Journal of Applied Psychology, 76*, 698–707.

Koslowsky, M., Kluger, A. N., & Yinon, Y. (1988). Predicting behavior: Combining intention with investment. *Journal of Applied Psychology, 73*, 102–106.

Leventhal, G. S. (1980). What should be done with equity theory? In K. J. Gergen, M. S. Greenberg, & R. H. Willis (Eds.), *Social exchange: Advances in theory and research* (pp. 27–55). New York: Plenum.

Levine, J. M., & Moreland, R. L. (1990). Progress in small group research. *Annual Review of Psychology, 41*, 585–634.

Lévy-Leboyer, C. (1994). Selection and assessment in Europe. In H. C. Triandis, M. D. Dunnette, & L. M. Hough (Eds.), *Handbook of industrial and organizational psychology* (2nd ed., Vol. 4, pp. 173–190). Palo Alto, CA: Consulting Psychologists Press.

Lopez, J. A. (1993, January 22). Once male enclaves, corporate boards now comb executive suites for women. *Wall Street Journal*, p. B1.

Lott, A. J., & Lott, B. E. (1965). Group cohesiveness and interpersonal attraction: A review of relationships with antecedent and consequent variables. *Psychological Bulletin, 4,* 259–302.

Ludington, D. M. (1991). Smoking in public: A moral imperative for the most toxic of environmental wastes. *Journal of Business Ethics, 10,* 23–27.

Lumsden, H. (1967). The plant visit: A critical area of recruiting. *Journal of College Placement, 27,* 74–84.

Mark, J. A. (1956). Measurement of job performance and age. *Monthly Labor Review, 79,* 1410–1414.

Martindale, M. (1990). *Sexual harassment in the military: 1988.* Arlington, VA: Defense Manpower Data Center.

Matthews, K. A., & Rodin, J. (1989). Women's changing work roles. *American Psychologist, 11,* 1389–1393.

McEvoy, G. M., & Cascio, W. F. (1989). Cumulative evidence of the relationship between employee age and job performance. *Journal of Applied Psychology, 74,* 11–17.

Meyer, J. P., & Allen, N. J. (1984). Testing the "side-bet theory" of organizational commitment: Some methodological considerations. *Journal of Applied Psychology, 69,* 372–378.

Moorman, R. H. (1991). Relationship between organizational justice and organizational citizenship behaviors: Do fairness perceptions influence employee citizenship? *Journal of Applied Psychology, 76,* 845–855.

Morrison, A. M., & Von Glinow, M. A. (1990). Women and minorities in management. *American Psychologist, 45,* 200–208.

Mowday, R. T., Porter, L. W., & Steers, R. M. (1982). *Employee-organization linkages: The psychology of commitment, absenteeism and turnover.* New York: Academic Press.

Murphy, K. R., Thornton, G. C., III, & Prue, K. (1991). Influence of job characteristics on the acceptability of employee drug testing. *Journal of Applied Psychology, 76,* 447–453.

Murphy, K. R., Thornton, G. C., & Reynolds, D. H. (1990). College students' attitudes toward employee drug testing. *Personnel Psychology, 43,* 615–631.

Nakajima, S. (1988). *Introduction to total productive maintenance.* Cambridge, MA: Productivity Press.

Newcomb, M. D. (1988). *Drug use in the workplace.* Dover, MA: Auburn House.

Newton, T., & Keenan, T. (1991). Further analyses of the dispositional argument in organizational behavior. *Journal of Applied Psychology, 76,* 781–787.

Nieva, V. F., & Gutek, B. A. (1981). *Women and work: A psychological perspective.* New York: Praeger.

Noe, R. A. (1988). Women and mentoring: A review and research agenda. *Academy of Management Review, 13,* 65–78.

Ockene, J. (1984). Toward a smoke-free society. *American Journal of Public Health, 74,* 1198–1217.

Odenwald, S. (1993). *Global training: How to design a program for the multinational corporation.* Homewood, IL: Richard D. Irwin.

O'Reilly, B. (1994, June). The new deal: What companies and employees owe one another. *Fortune,* pp. 44–52.

Organ, D. W. (1988). *Organizational citizenship behavior: The good soldier syndrome.* Lexington, MA: Lexington Books.

Pfeffer, J. (1983). Organizational demography. In L. L. Cummings & B. M. Staw (Eds.), *Research in organizational behavior* (Vol. 5, pp. 299–357). Greenwich, CT: JAI Press.

Pfeffer, J. (1994). *Competitive advantage through people.* Cambridge, MA: Harvard Business School Press.

Podsakoff, P. M., & MacKenzie, S. B. (1989). *A second generation measure of organizational citizenship behavior.* Unpublished manuscript, Indiana University, Bloomington.

Powell, G. N. (1988). *Women and men in management.* Newbury Park, CA: Sage.

Presser, H. B. (1988). Shift work and child care among young dual-earner American parents. *Journal of Marriage and the Family, 50,* 133–148.

Price, J. L., & Mueller, C. W. (1986). *Handbook of organizational measurement*. Marshfield, MA: Pittman.

Quick, J. C., Murphy, L. R., & Hurrell, J. J., Jr. (1992). *Stress and well-being at work*. Washington, DC: American Psychological Association.

Rhodes, S. R. (1983). Age-related differences in work attitudes and behavior: A review and conceptual analysis. *Psychological Bulletin, 93*, 328–367.

Rothman, M. (1988, March–April). Random drug testing in the workplace: Implications for human resource management. *Business Horizons*, pp. 23–27.

Rawls, J. (1971). *A theory of justice*. Cambridge, MA: Harvard University Press.

Scarr, S., Phillips, D., & McCartney, K. (1989). Working mothers and their families. *American Psychologist, 44*, 1402–1409.

Schein, D. (1987). Should employers restrict smoking in the workplace? *Labor Law Journal, 38*, 173–188.

Schmidt, F. L., Hunter, J. E., & Outerbridge, A. N. (1986). Impact of job experience and ability on job knowledge, work sample performance, and supervisory ratings of job performance. *Journal of Applied Psychology, 71*, 432–439.

Schmitt, N., Gooding, R. Z., Noe, R. A., & Kirsch, M. (1984). Meta-analyses of validity studies published between 1964 and 1982 and the investigation of study characteristics. *Personnel Psychology, 37*, 407–422.

Schneider, B. (1987). The people make the place. *Personnel Psychology, 40*, 437–453.

Scholl, R. W. (1981). Differentiating organizational commitment from expectancy as a motivating force. *Journal of Applied Psychology, 59*, 603–609.

Schuster, C. R. (1987). *Strategic planning for workplace drug abuse programs*. (NIDA Publication ADM-87-1538). Washington, DC: U.S. Government Printing Office.

Shellenbarger, S., & Hymowitz, C. (1994, June 14). Over the hill? *Wall Street Journal*, p. A1.

Shneidman, E. (1989). The Indian summer of life: A preliminary study of septuagenarians. *American Psychologist, 44*, 684–694.

Shore, L. M., & Tetrick, L. E. (1991). A construct validity study of the survey of perceived or-ganizational support. *Journal of Applied Psychology, 76*, 637–643.

Sinetar, M. (1986). *Ordinary people as monks and mystics: Lifestyles for self-discovery*. New York: Paulist Press.

Singer, J. A., Neale, M. S., Schwartz, G. E., & Schwartz, J. (1986). Conflicting perspectives on stress reduction in occupational settings: A systems approach to their resolution. In M. F. Cataldo, & T. J. Coates (Eds.), *Health and industry: A behavioral medicine perspective* (pp. 162–192). New York: John Wiley & Sons.

Sorensen, G., & Pechacek, T. F. (1989). Implementing nonsmoking policies in the private sector and assessing their effects. *New York State Journal of Medicine, 89*, 11–15.

Staw, B. M., & Ross, J. (1985). Stability in the midst of change: A dispositional approach to job attitudes. *Journal of Applied Psychology, 70*, 469–480.

Steiner, D. D., & Gilliland, S. W. (1996). Fairness reactions to personnel selection techniques in France and the United States. *Journal of Applied Psychology, 81*, 134–141.

Stone, D. L., & Kotch, D. A. (1989). Individual's attitudes toward organizational drug testing policies and practices. *Journal of Applied Psychology, 74*, 518–521.

Tavris, C., & Wade, C. (1984). *The longest war: Sex differences in perspective*. New York: Harcourt Brace Jovanovich.

Taylor, A. III. (1986). Why women managers are bailing out. *Fortune*, pp. 16–23.

Tepper, B. J. (1994). Investigation of general and program-specific attitudes toward corporate drug-testing policies. *Journal of Applied Psychology, 79*, 392–401.

Thorson, H., & Thomas, W. (1968). Student opinions of the placement process. *Journal of College Placement, 29*, 80–84.

Trice, H. M., & Roman, P. M. (1972). *Spirits and demons at work: Alcohol and other drugs on the job*. Ithaca, NY: Hoffman Printing.

U.S. Departments of Commerce and Labor. (1993). *Workplace of the future: A report on the future of the American workplace*. Washington, DC: Author.

U.S. Equal Employment Opportunity Commission. (1980). Discrimination because of sex under

Title VII of the 1964 Civil Rights Act as amended: Adoption of interim guidelines—Sexual harassment. *Federal Register, 45,* 25024–25025.

Verbrugge, L. M. (1983). Multiple roles and physical health of women and men. *Journal of Health and Social Behavior, 24,* 16–30.

Veroff, J., Douvan, E., & Kulka, R. A. (1981). *The inner American: A self-portrait from 1957 to 1976.* New York: Basic Books.

Waldman, D. A., & Avolio, B. J. (1986). A meta-analysis of age differences in job performance. *Journal of Applied Psychology, 71,* 33–38.

Williams, K. J., Suls, J., Alliger, G. M., Learner, S. M., & Wan, C. K. (1991). Multiple role juggling and daily mood states in working mothers: An experience sampling study. *Journal of Applied Psychology, 76,* 664–674.

Wynder, E. L., & Stellman, S. D. (1977). Comparative epidemiology of tobacco-related cancers. *Cancer Research, 37,* 4608–4619.

SUGGESTED REFERENCES

Job Choices, a magazine published by the National Association of Colleges and Employers, contains timely information on the occupational needs anticipated by corporate and governmental employers that normally recruit college students. It provides detailed information about a specific employer, opportunities in a specific geographic location, and specific information for persons who have completed master's or doctoral degrees. *Job Web* is an electronic gateway to career planning and employment information and can be reached at

http://www.jobweb.org

or you can contact the

National Association of Colleges and Employers
62 Highland Avenue
Bethlehem, PA 18017
(phone 800-544-5272)

Another individual development resource is

Center for Creative Leadership
PO Box 26300
Greensboro, NC 27438
(phone 910-288-7210)

which provides a wide range of leadership and executive development programs for a variety of organizations around the globe.

11

Organizational Change

CHAPTER OVERVIEW

Organizational change focuses on changing the organization, rather than specific individuals, although individual change is essential for organizational change. Organizational development (OD, improving what an organization already does) is compared with organizational transformation (OT, changing what an organization does to something fundamentally different), and both OD and OT are presented as points along the planned-change continuum, indicating that each or both may be used during the life of an organization.

Organizational change is about planned changes, and we review a four-facet model of planned organizational change. The first facet is the change intervention that involves either OD or OT. Organizational target variables of the intervention (the second facet) include the organizational vision and work setting (for example, social interaction patterns and physical environment). The other facets driven by the target variables include cognitive and behavioral changes in individual members that result in improved organizational performance and enhanced individual development.

After we review the four-facet model, we briefly discuss Lewin's (1951) early foundational model of organizational change. Thereafter, we examine the specific steps involved in implementing an OD planned change intervention, ranging from the selection of a client (establishing a partnership between an appropriate consultant or change agent and the organization) to contracting (for the scope and cost of intervention), all the way to evaluation and stabilization. We also present some specific practices for organizational development at the micro, meso, and macrolevels of an organization. Research has suggested that members consider change interventions to be positive when physical settings, social factors, and organizing arrangements (such as the formal reward system) were changed.

We then review the sociotechnical systems (STS) approach to organizational change, which emphasizes the importance of changing jointly the social system (people piece, such as norms and rules moderating behaviors and interactions) and the technical systems (the tools, techniques, and technology piece) of the organization. Specific guidelines for implementing an STS program are described, and circular and parallel organizational strategies for implementing and evaluating organizational change are discussed.

We then turn to OT and present the four specific core components of an organizational vision that is the major lever for instituting OT—a more extensive change intervention than OD. We also review a basic framework for developing a global organization so that OD and OT strategies can be deployed in almost any organization that is or aspires to become a global organization. In addition, we examine guidelines for the new work culture that apply to any organization anywhere. Every organization must address the global-local dilemma, and specific features of the global and local axes are presented that need to be integrated and developed in an organization.

We discuss organizational change in relation to three systems found in almost all organizations: the technical, political, and cultural systems. Organization-wide change requires altering the behaviors and cognitive frameworks of organizational members so as to change these three fundamental systems.

Last, we present reengineering as an important and robust strategy for organizational change. The focus of reengineering is on organizational processes—a cluster of activities that takes input and creates outputs that are of value to the customer or client. A fundamental assumption of reengineering is that by emphasizing changing their processes, organizations can encourage new cognitive perspectives and behaviors along many vectors throughout the organization that lead to widespread organizational development.

LEARNING OBJECTIVES

After studying this chapter, you will be able to

- define organizational change as a process of planned change to enhance current organizational activities and functions

- define, compare, and contrast organizational development (OD) and organizational transformation (OT) as points along the continuum of planned organizational change

- describe a four-facet model of planned organizational change that accommodates the change interventions of OD and OT

- describe briefly Lewin's foundational model of planned organizational change

- identify specific steps to implement an OD strategy

- define the sociotechnical systems approach and circular and parallel strategies as exemplars of OD

- identify the four core components of an organizational vision, which is a basic tool for an OT intervention

- present a basic framework for developing a global organization and identify the features of the new work culture that apply to almost all organizations

- identify the global-local dilemma and the specific features of the global and local axes that must be integrated and developed in an organization

- identify three fundamental organizational systems and explain the necessity of aligning these systems for an effective OD intervention

- define reengineering and organizational processes and identify the symptoms of dysfunctional processes that require reengineering

- define benchmarking and explain the relationships between reengineering and quality-improvement programs as robust OD strategies.

Change happens and can be made to happen.

PLANNED CHANGE

Planned organizational change involves a relatively fluid set of processes, rather than rigid step-by-step procedures to enhance organizations, and the focus is on changing the organization, not specific individuals, although individual change is necessary for organizational change. In general, planned change involves the strategies of organizational development (OD) and organizational transformation (OT); to some extent, these strategies represent points on a continuum of change in that each may be appropriate at different times in the life of an organization. OD, which was popular in the 1960s and 1970s, to deal with the increasing size and complexity of organizations, focuses primarily on incremental change (improving what the organization already does). It is usually initiated to facilitate the solution of specific problems in particular organizational systems, such as poor communications, high absenteeism, or low morale, although other problems may emerge in the process, and the planned change intervention is usually terminated when the particular problems are resolved.

In general, OT, increasingly popular in the 1980s and today, involves quantum change in response to, for example, significantly increasing demands from customers or clients and the competitiveness of the global marketplace. It goes beyond incremental change and emphasizes dramatic changes in what an organization does—becoming different—rather than getting better at what one already does, which is the focus of OD. OT is initiated by senior executives of an organization, usually in anticipation of or response to dramatic changes in the external environment (global compared to domestic markets) or internal environment (increasing workforce diversity), revolutionary technological change, or some kind of major shift in a paradigm, such as from centrally planned economies to open-market economies. OT usually involves changes in both an organization's basic business strategy and organizational culture.

Action research is the primary method for planning organizational change interventions. It involves systematically collecting data about presenting organizational problems (such as too much conflict and animosity among colleagues or financial hemorrhaging), and then taking action on the basis of interpretations of the collected data (Burke, 1994). In general, planned organizational change is not about getting bigger but about sharpening or changing the organization's capacity to do whatever has to be done to participate effectively in the market-

place (Ackoff, 1981). Inasmuch as we extensively examined organizational culture and cultural change strategies (major OT strategies) in Chapter 3, we focus here on a model of planned change, associated empirical findings, OD, OT, sociotechnical systems (STS), the development of global organizations, strategic management, and reengineering.

Major features of planned organizational change are the movement from managing expansion to managing consolidation as a consequence of downsizing that results in flatter organizations (Brockner, 1988, 1992); an emphasis on self-managed groups (Hackman, 1990); and knowledge of the core businesses of the organization, including the larger economic and political contexts of the target organization (Burke, 1994). Organizations, like individuals, change, and change in organizations can be expressed at the individual (micro), group (meso), and organizational (macro) levels. A change intervention can be introduced at any one or a combination of these levels. However, in all cases, sustained organizational change is built on experiential and behavioral changes in individuals in the organization.

Organizational change comes in two basic varieties: *unplanned* change and *planned* change. Unplanned usually arises from a condition or event outside the organizational system and yields adaptive reactions by the organization that are focused on a clearly defined and often narrow segment of the organization (Porras & Robertson, 1990). It has been described as spontaneous, evolutionary, fortuitous, or accidental (Lippitt, Watson, & Westley, 1958).

Planned change is

> change that originates with a decision by the system to deliberately improve its functioning and (typically) to engage an outside resource to help in the processes of making these improvements. (Levy, 1986, p. 6)

It focuses on enhancing the organization's capacity to handle existing (OD) or anticipated (OT) fundamental shifts in environmental demands and almost always influences many components of the organization.

Lewin (1951) was a pioneer in the field of organizational change, and the spirit of organizational change can perhaps best be sensed in his two dicta: There is nothing as practical as a good theory and to truly understand something try changing it. Accordingly, we begin with a model of planned change and then review some empirical findings associated with planned change. Thereafter, we discuss organizational development issues for established or aspiring global organizations and conclude with the reengineering of organizational processes, which is an increasingly important strategy for OD.

Model of Planned Change

According to Porras and Silvers (1991), planned organizational change involves four fundamental facets: (1) a change intervention that modifies (2) the organizational target variables of vision and work setting that then influences (3) individual members of the organization and their on-the-job behaviors that, in turn, brings about change in (4) organizational performance outcomes. The basic assumptions of Porras and Silvers's planned process model are that individual work behaviors give rise to organizational outcomes, with the work behaviors driven by the work setting or social and physical context (the goals, reward system, culture, technology, and physical setting of the organization). In addition, the organizational vision provides the fundamental rationale or cognitive context for the design of the work setting. Enhanced organizational performances and individual development—the two major outcomes of the change intervention—arise from the collective behaviors of the members of the organization (Porras & Silvers, 1991).

Change Interventions

In most instances, someone or some group in the organization decides that the organization must pursue a path of planned change either in response to imposed changes from the external environment or in anticipation of potential changes in the external environment or in the organization. As we mentioned earlier, planned change interventions include OD or OT.

OD is defined as a set of behavioral science models, strategies, and techniques for changing work settings, which, in turn, alter the thoughts and behaviors of individuals, so as to create a better fit between the organization's capacities and current demands of the environment or a predicted future environment. The intent of OD is to bring about appreciable or discernable changes in the work behaviors of organizational members to assist an organization to do what it already does better, rather than to do something totally different (single-loop organizational learning, see Chapter 3).

In contrast, OT is designed to change the organization's vision, which represents the self-reflective cognitive and affective processes by which members and the organization view themselves, the processes required for change and learning, and what the organization does. It involves double-loop organizational learning (see Chapter 3) in that it is designed to make fundamental changes in what the organization does, not to help the organization improve the performance of its existing activities and practices.

Organizational Targets

The organizational vision and the work setting are the cognitive and social and physical manifestations of the internal organizational environment, respectively, and the primary targets of change intervention programs. The organizational vision includes the guiding beliefs and principles of the organization that give rise to the enduring organizational purpose or mission and directs the organization's movement toward the achievement of its purpose. The focus of the organizational vision is on psychic forces, rather than market forces, in that it provides the cognitive framework for the planned organizational change.

According to Porras (1987), the work setting consists of four major variables: organizing arrangements (such as goals and reward systems), social factors (like culture and norms), technology, and the physical setting. The organizational vision provides the rational for a particular array of these four variables and thus gives them coherence and direction.

Individual Members

This is the third fundamental variable of the planned change process model. Basically, before organizational change can occur, there must be changes in the job or work behaviors of individual members. In effect, change in individual members is the sine qua non for organizational change.

Organizational members detect cues for change in the work setting and reflect on these cues in relation to the organization's vision, which provides the cognitive framework for individual behavioral changes. In addition to behavioral change, there is also cognitive change, which reflects a new way of viewing oneself, other organizational members, and the organization as a whole.

Organizational Outcomes

In terms of Porras and Silvers's (1991) planned change model, the two major expected outcomes are the enhancement of organizational performances, such as productivity, profitability, efficiency, quality, and innovativeness, and individual development, including improved job skills and new learning strategies to adjust to the changing environments within and outside the organization. We now examine some of the unique features, processes, and outcomes of OD, followed by those of OT, as expressions of planned organizational change.

ORGANIZATIONAL DEVELOPMENT

Lewin (1951) proposed one of the early foundational models of planned organizational change. According to his model, organizations are structured by two forces expressed by organizational members—the force to maintain the status quo and the force to change the organization. When these forces are equal, the organization is in equilibrium, or stable. Hence, to initiate planned organizational change, it is first necessary to unfreeze the equilibrium by introducing information that indicates a discrepancy between the organization's performances and aspirations (its goals and/or vision). The next step is to alter the organizational members' behaviors, values, and attitudes by changing the organizational structures (such as divisions, departments, and teams) and processes (like service to customers). The final step is to refreeze the equilibrium by reinforcing the new behaviors and values, such as the organizational culture, policies, and reward systems. Clearly, this model provides a broad framework for OD, and subsequent work has focused on which specific behaviors can and do change as a result of OD and what specific practices are involved in implementing OD interventions.

If the behavior of individual members is the key link between change interventions and organizational outcomes, then it is useful to know what behaviors to change to bring about effective OD. Accordingly, Porras and Hoffer (1986) asked leading OD scholars and practitioners which behaviors they expected would change in a wide range of organizations as a consequence of an effective OD program. For all organizational members, the most frequently mentioned behaviors were communicating openly, collaborating, assuming responsibility, maintaining a shared vision, solving problems effectively, respecting and supporting others, facilitating interactions, asking questions, and trying new things. For managers, the behaviors cited the most were encouraging participation, leading by vision, functioning strategically, promoting the flow of information, and developing others. Although all these individual behaviors may not change in any given successful OD program, it is important to note that practitioners and scholars view individual behavioral change as essential to OD.

Implementation

Unlike organizational change theories that emphasize the underlying dynamics of the planned change process, OD theories focus more specifically on the actions that change practitioners choose when implementing planned change interventions. Table 11–1 presents the usual implementation steps found in most OD change programs.

Selection of the client involves matching the capabilities of the OD practitioner and the needs of the target organization, primarily by preliminary conversations between the parties by phone, fax, and E-mail, or in off-site meetings. *Entry* is concerned with the issues of which and how many persons the change agent will meet with if and when he or she is invited to the organization. *Contracting* focuses on a written estimate of the scope of the work and the costs of the project, including consultants' fees (anywhere from $50 to $500 per hour plus expenses or some negotiated package that is also an early indicator of the quality and focus of the relationship between the parties). In terms of *diagnosis*, three key diagnostic indicators are systematic observations of the organizing arrangements, social factors, and technology (Porras & Robertson, 1990). The diagnosis can be made by a gap-analysis survey (to determine the distance between actual and desired organi-

Table 11–1. Steps in Implementing OD

1. Selection of the client
2. Entry
3. Contracting
4. Diagnosis
5. Planning and intervention
6. Evaluation and stabilization

zational states). An example of an item in such a survey would be, "On a scale of 1 (not important) to 5 (very important), please rate the importance of team building in the current and then in an ideal organization." Also, through interviews and systematic observations, the consultant matches the readiness of groups and individuals for change with potential change programs, such as training in group dynamics, team building, conflict management, leadership training, and motivational programs. *Planning* involves the identification of specific action plans, as well as procedures for managing possible pockets of resistance, and *implementation*, which involves the execution of the plans. In the final stage, the actions are *evaluated* and then refined, if necessary, and mechanisms are developed to *stabilize* the change programs in the organization.

Praxes

Since there is an almost limitless inventory of specific OD practices or praxes, in this section we discuss only a few for which empirical evaluation data are available.

To implement change at the individual level, OD practitioners often use flexible working hours to alter organizational arrangements (Cohen & Gadon, 1978), T-groups (unstructured groups to enhance individuals' awareness of themselves by feedback from other group members) for social-factor change, and job design for technological intervention by modifying the variety and significance of tasks, skills needed to accomplish them, and feedback on and autonomy in performing tasks (Hackman & Oldham, 1975). To promote change at the group level, OD practitioners have instituted quality control circles (Steel & Shane, 1986), which focus on group problem solving and decision making by first-level people for changing organizational arrangements, team building for social factors (Patten, 1981), and autonomous work groups for technological change (Cummings, 1978).

To implement change at the organizational level, OD practitioners use open system planning for changing organizing arrangements (Porras & Robertson, 1990). This technique involves creating a view of the current organization and a realistic view of a future scenario for the organization, identifying discrepancies between these views, and deciding what actions need to be taken tomorrow, six months from now, and two years from now to resolve these discrepancies.

Research Findings

In general, the most positive changes resulting from OD interventions were observed in the physical settings (you can "see" the changes almost immediately), followed by social factors (like norms) and organizing arrangements (such as goals; see Porras & Robertson, 1990). Furthermore, organizational outcomes were reported as changed more often than individual development, whereas overall change, regardless of the level at which it was measured or the dependent variables that were used, was minimal or modestly positive (Porras & Robertson, 1990). It is difficult to assess clearly the outcomes of OD interventions because of the complexity of the independent variables, the possible interactions among them, and the likelihood that other robust variables that are outside the scope of the intervention will change in organizations that are nested within dynamic environments. Accordingly, we suggest that your initial aspirations for an OD change program should be modest, that you should intervene at the individual and organizational levels, and that you should monitor the dependent variables for three to six months and be open to recalibrating the intervention program.

Sociotechnical Systems

The sociotechnical systems (STS) approach to OD focuses on job enrichment at the group level,

rather than at the individual level, as in Hackman and Oldham's (1975) motivational approach to job enrichment. The central principles of STS are that an organization is a combined social (people and their interactions) and technical (instruments, machinery, things) system and that each subsystem is open relative to its environment.

Every organization has a social component, made up of people and the formal and informal rules governing their interactions, and a technical component, consisting of the tools, techniques, and methods for performing tasks (Cummings & Worley, 1993). An STS program aims to optimize the two components on the basis of the appropriate collaborative design of both of them. The second STS principle stresses that any organization or work unit interacts with its environment by receiving inputs, such as energy, information, and materials, and then outputting products and services. The challenge is to design the system so it has enough freedom to function well and to interact effectively with the environment. STS seeks to optimize boundary management by structuring environmental relationships to buffer the system from external environmental turbulence but to allow for effective and timely exchanges with the environment. The STS approach to organizational development has been used in a variety of global organizations in North America; Europe; and most actively in Norway, where national laws have been enacted on the basis of STS criteria; and in Sweden, such as at Saab-Sandia and Volvo's Kalmar, a world-class automotive plant (Gyllenhammar, 1977).

Table 11–2 presents some of the primary guidelines for implementing an STS approach to OD. In general, adherence to these guidelines will enhance the likelihood of achieving the major STS goals of joint optimization of the social and technical components and boundary management. Probably the most popular application of the STS approach has been the use of self-regulating or self-managing teams. A survey of

Table 11–2. STS Guidelines

Compatibility. Select an organization or unit that is committed to open participation by allowing all primary stakeholders (employees, managers, engineers, and staff) the opportunity to design the work system.

Minimal critical specification. Keep the guidelines for implementation to a minimum and focus on what is to be done, rather than how to do it.

Variance control. Seek to control technical variance as quickly and close to the source as possible. Operational employees must have authority, information, and skills to control technical variances.

Boundary location. Arrange organizational boundaries so that information, learning, and knowledge are shared readily among those who perform interrelated tasks.

Power and authority. Work groups must have timely access to resources, and members of the groups need cross-training in multiple skills and expertise to maintain group functioning in the absence of some group members.

Fortune 1,000 companies found that 47% of these organizations had self-managing work teams in 1992, compared with 28% in 1987 (Lawler, Mohrman, & Ledford, 1995). In general, the implementation of self-managing work teams usually yields economic benefits for the organization as a result of fewer middle managers and greater job satisfaction (Wall, Kemp, Jackson, & Clegg, 1986).

Circular and Parallel Organizations

An interesting approach to OD is the *circular organization*, which focuses on changing the organizational structure (Ackoff, 1989). The central idea of this organizational change intervention is that each manager reports to a board of directors, composed of her or his immediate supervisors, subordinates, and important peers or outsiders. The responsibilities of such boards may include planning and coordinating with other units in the organization and evaluating the managers' performance.

Parallel organizations represent the limited experimentation with OD interventions by creating a parallel organization in an organization that is designed to promote group problem solving and the empowerment of employees (Herrick, 1985). If OD interventions prove successful in the circumscribed parallel organization, then they are implemented in the entire organization; if they are unsuccessful, the change strategies are modified or abandoned. In general, parallel organizations interventions have led to the greater empowerment of certain groups of employees compared to other similar groups in the organization (Bushe, 1987) and have facilitated employees' involvement in discussing organizational issues and making suggestions for change (Shani & Eberhardt, 1987). The strategy of parallel organizations is similar to that of Deming-Shewhart's Plan-Do-Check-Act, discussed in Chapter 6, in that both emphasize the importance of initially focused change projects, but the former is concerned primarily with quality-of-work life issues, while the latter involves primarily quality-improvement tools. In both types of change programs, if the outcomes of the strategies are positive, then the strategies are deployed throughout the organization.

ORGANIZATIONAL TRANSFORMATION

OT is concerned with profound, rather than pragmatic change, which is the province of OD. It is targeted at a deeper level of the organization (organizational beliefs, values, and purpose, all of which are components of the organizational vision) than the work-setting variables of OD (Porras & Silvers, 1991). OD change is like moving an organization from New York to San Francisco, whereas OT change is like moving it from Burlington, Vermont, to Beijing, or vice versa, and requires the functional acquisition of a new language and cultural perspectives and perhaps changing the organization's products and/or services. At the heart of OT is the need to change the organizational vision, which leads to a major shift in the organization's paradigm, which results in a learning organization that is capable of continuous self-diagnosis and change (Levy & Merry, 1986; Porras & Silvers, 1991).

Organizational Vision

A change in the organization's vision is usually prompted by drastic environmental or internal disruptions and crises or changes in the life cycle of the organization (Cummings & Worley, 1993). Inasmuch as organizational vision provides the framework for organizational structures (groups, units, or departments) and processes (motivational systems, leadership, decision making, and conflict resolution), OT is a tectonic, rather than a trivial, modification of the organization.

Organizational vision consists of four interrelated components (Porras & Robertson, 1990):

- core values and beliefs
- an enduring purpose
- a highly compelling mission
- a vivid description that brings the mission to life

The organizational beliefs and values are the foundation of the vision; they are few in number, tend not to change over time, and are the platform for the organization's purpose. The enduring purpose is the reason for the organization's existence that the organization constantly tries to achieve and provides the rationale for the interactional linkages among individual members. Some (such as Selznick, 1957) believe that the constructs of purpose and mission are interchangeable, while others (like Barnard, 1938) think that the mission is the statement of a major goal that can be achieved in 5–20 years, focuses the organization's capabilities, and guides both strategic decisions and daily organizational activities. The vivid description of the mission affords a compelling picture of what the accomplishment of the mission would look like. The organizational purpose and mission guide decision making and help members interpret environmental changes (Porras & Robertson, 1990).

Global Organizations

The development of the global organization involves changes that affect the strategy, structure, culture, and individual members of an organization (Moran, Harris, & Stripp, 1993). Table 11–3 presents a basic framework for developing a global strategy for an organization. A global organization requires a high-performance and high-commitment work culture in which the leaders must articulate and enact the practices and values of the culture, which are summarized in Table 11–4. Global organizations are built on technical, financial, political, and cultural systems that can change rapidly but maintain the steady purpose articulated in the organizational vision (Sherwood, 1988).

A survey of 200 managers (O'Toole, 1985) indicated that a global organizational environment requires balance and attention to various stakeholders; a sense of vision and commitment to long-term performance; a program of continuous learning; an orientation to technology to improve products and services; and a passion for free enterprise, coupled with an openness to new ideas. We believe that the global organization must develop a mind-set like that of a team participating in a worldwide athletic competition involving team work, discipline, constant learning, and being open to developing, when appropriate, new alliances with other organizations, some of which may be or have been competitors.

The global organization must develop core competencies, defined as functions that provide access to a wide variety of markets, make a sig-

Table 11–3. Basic Framework for Developing a Global Organization

Component	Issue
1. General philosophy	What is the firm's basic reason for existence?
2. Analysis and diagnosis	
External	Are there opportunities outside the domestic environment that can benefit the organization?
Internal	Can the organization meet global opportunities if they are present?
3. Mission statement	What is the organization's vision for its future existence as a global enterprise?
4. Objectives	What outcomes does the organization desire to achieve?
5. Strategic alternatives	How can the organization take advantage of the global opportunities and avoid global threats?
6. Strategic choice	Which alternative is most appropriate for the organization's situation?
7. Contingency plan	Given the possibility of failing, which alternative should the organization fall back on?
8. Implementation	
Leadership	Who will be selected to implement the global strategy?
Personnel	How will personnel be chosen?
Logistics	How will the lines of global communication and supply be organized?
Tactics	How will global resources be deployed?
9. Evaluation	How does the organization know if its plan is working? What provisions are made to alter or realign the strategy on the basis of feedback or new input?

From *Developing the Global Organization*, p. 35, by R. T. Moran, P. R. Harris, & W. G. Stripp. Copyright © 1993 by Gulf Publishing Company, Houston, TX. Used with permission. All rights reserved.

nificant contribution to customers' perceptions of the benefits of the end product, and are difficult for competitors to imitate (Moran et al., 1993). Likewise, a global organization must

- be prepared to enter all three of the world's most important markets: North America, Europe, and Asia
- develop new products and services for the world
- focus on profit centers that are based on product lines, rather than geography
- make strategic decisions on products or services, capital, and research and allow local units to decide tactical issues about packaging, marketing, and advertising
- open the senior ranks to international employees.

In effect, the global organization must simultaneously promote corporation-wide strategies and core values and accomodate the distinctive practices and values of its international components. Applying global strategies to local situations requires deployment patterns that are responsive to the distinctive features of national laws, tax codes, customs, market characteristics,

Table 11–4. Values and Practices of the Work Culture of a Global Organization

The work culture of a global organization does the following:

- Provides improved and more open communication and information to personnel, customers, and suppliers.

- Creates more autonomy and participation, so workers have increasing control over their own work and opportunities for involvement in the enterprise. The democratization in the workplace ranges from sharing in planning, problem solving, and decision making to team management and profit-sharing.

- Promotes an entrepreneurial spirit in innovative ventures, especially of a technological or service nature.

- Enhances the quality of work life, so it is more meaningful, fulfilling, and psychologically rewarding.

- Generates innovative and high-performing norms and standards that foster competence and excellence as the means to productivity and profitability.

- Uses more informal and synergistic organizational relations, so cooperation and trust are reinforced among the work force.

- Advances technology transfer and venturing, as well as research and development.

From *Developing the Global Organization*, pp. 12–13, by R. T. Moran, P. R. Harris, & W. G. Stripp. Copyright © 1993 by Gulf Publishing Company, Houston, TX. Used with permission. All rights reserved.

and management practices of the countries in which managers are located.

Global-Local Dilemma

The rapid pace of changing telecommunications and computer technologies; customers' escalating concerns for quality, price, and value; and the economic integration of the international community by means of various agreements and treaties are the engines that drive the development of global organizations, whereas governments, resources, cultures, and customers' preferences represent the forces of local responsiveness that must also be a central part of global organizations (Humes, 1993). As organizations become more and more global, they will have to manage and coordinate more coherently the organizational structure, workforce, and culture in relation to three potential organizational strategies that are shaped by a focus on product, function, or location and be responsive to local practices and values (Humes, 1993).

Organizational structure represents the formal lines of command and communication systems; workforce issues focus on how and who the organization hires, educates, and promotes to manage the organization; and the organizational culture includes the shared assumptions, beliefs, and values that influence the organizational vision and mission. An organization may focus on a product strategy, in which different divisions or groups are responsible for different sets of products that may be related by technology or the customers or markets that are served. An organizational strategy built around functional units emphasizes an organization whose functions are manufacturing and sourcing; marketing and sales; research and development; and management services, such as finance, personnel, and public affairs. A location-based strategy results in an organization that is constructed to reflect national, regional, or continental affiliates and offices.

An important dynamic influencing the coordination process are the forces of globality and locality. An organization's movement along the global axis dictates the need for the organization-wide integration of organizational features—structure, workforce, and culture—while its movement along the local axis requires responsiveness to the diverse conditions of various geographic markets and local conditions (Prahalad & Doz, 1987). Table 11–5 presents a summary of some of the global and local forces that have an impact on established and aspiring global organizations.

In general, American global organizations tend to be built around product strategies and highly structured or hierarchical management specialists and to stress central organization-wide planning and control. European global organizations are constructed mostly as units defined by geographic location with less structure and are staffed by elite corps of managerial generalists. Asian (mainly Japanese) global organizations are constructed along functional lines, stress shared values and consensual decision

Table 11–5. Some Features of the Global-Local Dilemma

Global Axis	Local Axis
General	
Global competition	Domestic competition
Uniform products	Demand for diverse products
Marketing	
Transnational responsive marketing	Locally responsive marketing
The presence of multinational customers who wish to purchase on a multicountry basis leads to a more international approach.	Differences in distribution channels in various countries and differences in pricing and advertising require a local presence.
Marketing industrial products	Multiproduct customers
Introduction of new products	Sensitivity to local products
Manufacturing and Sourcing	
Transnational manufacturing	Local manufacturing/sourcing
Plants that meet multicountry needs encourage firms to manufacture in a few locations serving multicountry markets.	Local manufacturing/sourcing may be preferable when protectionism is strong and transportation costs are high.
Other	
Transnational financing	Local financing
Global professional and management resources	Host country personnel
It is important to be able to shift expertise among countries and foster intercultural mixing and blending.	Local staffing is critical for local acceptance.

Adapted from S. Humes (1993). *Managing the Multinational: Confronting the Global-Local Dilemma.* Prentice Hall Europe, Hemel Hempstead, UK.

making, and are managed by members who are educated by rotation through many segments of the organization (Humes, 1993).

ORGANIZATIONAL SYSTEMS

Organizational change focuses on systemic change, rather than change in specific individuals or small groups in the organization. Since systemic change is instituted in all the divisions and units of an organization, it is important to be aware of the major systems within an organization so as to maximize the leverage for change. Tichy's (1983) approach to organizational change focuses on three systems that are found in almost all organizations: technical, political, and cultural systems. The technical system represents the rational and data-based features of the organization, such as production or management information units. The political system reflects the activities of dominant groups and individuals, coalitions, and bargaining agreements among members of the organization. The cultural system includes the shared beliefs, values, and "cognitive schemes" (basic assumptions) about reality, human nature, and human relationships held by members of the organization.

According to Tichy (1983), organization-wide change requires the alignment of the three systems specifically by changing the norms and cognitive schemas of the organizational members. For example, the cultural system may be grounded in quality and driven by a customer service orientation that requires the appropriate alignment or modification of the technical system (improvements in customer relations-oriented telecommunications and computer-based systems) and the reconfiguration of various units or groups in the organization; thus, the customer service or marketing unit, rather than the finance or production unit, would guide the goals and operations of other units. The key point, according to Tichy, is that effective organizational change requires altering the guidelines for behavior and the cognitive schemes, coupled with the appropriate alignment of the three fundamental systems of any organization.

REENGINEERING

So far we have primarily examined top-down directive approaches to organizational change that generally promote consistent and organization-wide change programs and that require the organizational leaders' absolute commitment and dedication (Howard, 1992; Ulrich & LaFasto, 1995). Such programs run the risk of being perceived as isolated events if they are not clearly linked to specific, timely, and identifiable behavioral changes and measures of organizational performance.

A recently developed approach to organizational change focuses on reengineering business processes (Hammer, 1990; Hammer & Champy, 1993). Reengineering is defined as "the fundamental rethinking and radical redesign of business processes to achieve dramatic improvements in critical contemporary measures of performance, such as cost, quality, service, and speed" (Hammer & Champy, 1993, p. 32). In brief, process engineering examines how work is done and then systematically improves the processes by streamlining operations, leveraging automation, reducing redundancies, linking as much as possible the flow of work with customers' or clients' needs and requests. A fundamental assumption is that as processes are reengineered, the new processes will lead to new paradigms and perspectives about the organization and thus enhance organizational change (Ulrich & LaFasto, 1995).

A business process is a cluster of activities that takes one or more types of input and creates an output of value to the customer or client. For example, the input of order fulfillment is the order, the output is the delivery of the ordered goods, and the value created by the process is the delivery of the ordered items or services to the customer or client. In general, most members in most organizations know which processes need to be reengineered or dumped, so as we have learned from our consulting activities in this area, we just need to ask people about processes and encourage them to speak up. Some symptoms of dysfunctional processes are the extensive exchange of information; redundant data; rekeying (keying data from one computer into another); a high ratio of checking and control to value-adding (a $10,000 inspection to save $10 of defects); and lots of complexity, exceptions, and special cases (Hammer & Champy, 1993).

As we indicated in Chapter 6, benchmarking, a major tool of reengineering, is an ongoing and systematic way of measuring and comparing the processes of organizations by bringing an external focus on internal activities, functions, or operations. For example, competitive benchmarking uses process data (such as the number of steps, time per step and total time, and number of people involved in a given process) from a few select direct competitors or peers as comparisons to identify specific reengineering actions for the target process. Best-in-class benchmarking searches across industries or business domains for new innovative processes, regardless of their source.

In a reengineering project, we benchmarked a number of organizational processes and reengineered many of them. As a result, the organization created a standing innovation team to promote organizational development beyond the specific reengineering projects.

According to Hammer and Champy (1993), both reengineering and quality-improvement programs recognize the importance of processes, start with the needs of the customer, and work backwards from there (right-to-left thinking). However, quality-improvement programs operate within the current processes by *kaizen*, or continuous incremental improvement (single-loop learning—members getting better and bet-

ter at what they already do) while reengineering seeks to develop new processes (double-loop learning—doing different things, rather than the same thing better). Clearly, reengineering and quality-improvement programs are not necessarily mutually exclusive, since once you implement a new organizational process, you can continue to refine it until it is appropriate to move on to a new process.

Reengineering requires patience, the clear identification of processes to be reengineered, the skills and authority to make changes, and the political sensitivity to make the development programs endure beyond specific reengineered projects.

SUMMARY

We started with a definition of planned change as a decision to improve or enhance an organization. We then compared OD and OT as examples along a continuum of planned change. OD focuses on incremental change, whereas OT focuses on quantum change. Organizational change can only occur if individuals change.

We reviewed a four-facet model of planned change that includes the type of intervention, organizational target variables (vision and work settings, the independent variables), and individual behaviors and cognitions (the dependent variables) that lead to improvements in the performance of the organization and its individual members.

We presented six specific steps in the implementation of a planned organizational change program, so organizational development can be operationalized and made visible. We then reviewed research findings at the micro, meso, and macrolevels of an organization that indicate the importance of changing the physical setting, social factors, and organizing arrangements so organizational development will be positive and effective. We also presented specific guidelines for implementing an STS approach to organizational development.

We discussed the four specific components of an organizational vision, which is a robust tool for OT programs. Next, we examined a basic framework for developing a global organization, along with a series of issues related to global and local development in the global marketplace every organization must address. We also indicated that effective organizational change must involve fundamental systems that are found in all organizations in the world: the technical, political, and cultural systems.

We concluded with a brief treatment of reengineering as a strong and concrete organizational change strategy that focuses on changing specific organizational processes, which, in turn, results in widespread organizational change.

CHAPTER REFERENCES

Ackoff, R. L. (1981). *Creating the corporate future.* New York: John Wiley & Sons.

Ackoff, R. L. (1989). The circular organization: An update. *Academy Management Executive, 3,* 11–16.

Barnard, C. I. (1938). *The functions of the executive.* Cambridge, MA: Harvard University Press.

Brockner, J. (1988). *Self-esteem at work: Research, theory, and practice.* Lexington, MA: Lexington Books.

Brockner, J. (1992). Managing the effects of layoffs on survivors. *California Management Review, 34,* 9–28.

Burke, W. W. (1994). *Organization development: A process of learning and changing* (3rd ed.). Reading, MA: Addison-Wesley.

Bushe, G. R. (1987). Temporary or permanent middle-management groups? Correlates with attitudes in QWL change projects. *Group Organizational Studies, 12,* 23–37.

Cohen, A. R., & Gadon, H. (1978). Changing the management culture in a public school system. *Journal of Applied Behavioral Science, 14,* 61–78.

Cummings, T. G. (1978). Sociotechnical experimentation: A review of sixteen studies. In W. A. Pasmore & J. J. Sherwood (Eds.), *Sociotechnical systems: A sourcebook* (pp. 259–270). San Diego, CA: University of Associates.

Cummings, T. G., & Worley, C. G. (1993). *Organization development and change* (5th ed.). Minneapolis, MN: West.

Gyllenhammar, P. G. (1977). *People at work.* Reading, MA: Addison-Wesley.

Hackman, J. R. (1990). *Groups that work (and those that don't): Creating conditions for effective teamwork.* San Francisco: Jossey-Bass.

Hackman, J. R., & Oldham, G. R. (1975). Development of the job diagnostic survey. *Journal of Applied Psychology, 60,* 159–170.

Hammer, M. (1990). Reengineering work. *Harvard Business Review, 68,* 93–111.

Hammer, M., & Champy, J. (1993). *Reengineering the corporation.* New York: Harper Business.

Herrick, N. Q. (1985). Parallel organizations in unionized settings: Implications for organizational research. *Human Relations, 38,* 963–981.

Howard, R. (1992). The CEO as organizational architect: An interview with Xerox's Paul Aliaire. *Harvard Business Review, 70,* 106–123.

Humes, S. (1993). *Managing the multinational: Confronting the global-local dilemma.* Englewood Cliffs, NJ: Prentice Hall.

Lawler, E., Mohrman, S., & Ledford, G. (1995). *Creating high performance organizations: Practices and results of employee involvement and Total Quality Management in Fortune 1000 companies.* San Francisco: Jossey-Bass.

Levy, A. (1986). Second-order planned change: Definition and conceptualization. *Organizational Dynamics, 15,* 4–20.

Levy, A., & Merry, U. (1986). *Organizational transformation: Approaches, strategies, theories.* New York: Praeger.

Lewin, K. (1951). *Field theory in social science.* New York: Harper & Row.

Lippitt, R., Watson, J., & Westley, B. (1958). *Planned change: A comparative study of principles and techniques.* New York: Harcourt, Brace, & World.

Moran, R. T., Harris, P. R., & Stripp, W. G. (1993). *Developing the global organization.* Houston: Gulf Publishing.

Herrick, N. Q. (1985). Parallel organizations in unionized settings: Implications for organizational research. *Human Relations, 38,* 963–981.

O'Toole, J. J. (1985). *Vanguard management: Redesigning the corporate future.* New York: Doubleday.

Patten, T. (1981). *Organizational development through team building.* New York: John Wiley & Sons.

Porras, J. I. (1987). *Stream analysis: A powerful new way to diagnose and manage change.* Reading, MA: Addison-Wesley.

Porras, J. I., & Hoffer, S. J. (1986). Common behavior changes in successful organization development. *Journal of Applied Behavioral Science, 22,* 477–494.

Porras, J. I., & Robertson, P. J. (1990). Organizational development: Theory, practice, and research. In M. D. Dunnette & L. M. Hough (Eds.), *Handbook of industrial and organizational psychology* (Vol. 3, pp. 51–78). Palo Alto, CA: Consulting Psychologists Press.

Porras, J. I., & Silvers, R. C. (1991). Organization development and transformation. *Annual Review of Psychology, 42,* 51–78.

Prahalad, C. K., & Doz, Y. (1987). *The multinational mission: Balancing local demands and global vision.* New York: Free Press.

Selznick, P. (1957). *Leadership in administration.* New York: Harper & Row.

Shani, A. B., & Eberhardt, B. J. (1987). Parallel organization in a health care institution. *Group Organizational Studies, 12,* 147–173.

Sherwood, J. (1988). Creating work cultures with competitive advantages. *Organizational Dynamics, 16,* 5–26.

Steel, F., & Shane, G. S. (1986). Evaluation research on quality circles: Technical and analytical implications. *Human Relations, 39,* 449–468.

Tichy, N. M. (1983). *Managing strategic change: Technical, political, and cultural dynamics.* New York, John Wiley & Sons.

Ulrich, D. O., & LaFasto, F. (1995). Organizational culture and human resource management. In G. Ferris, S. D. Rosen, & D. T. Barnum (Eds.), *Handbook of human resource management* (pp. 317–336). Cambridge, MA: Blackwell.

Wall, T., Kemp, N., Jackson, P., & Clegg, C. (1986). Outcomes of autonomous work groups. A long-term field experiment. *Academy of Management Journal, 29,* 280–304.

SUGGESTED REFERENCES

Some governmental sources of economic information about doing business in different parts of the world to assist OD programs can be obtained from the following:

U.S. Commerce Department (14th Street, Washington, DC 20230), especially *Global Market Surveys*, *Country Market Sectorial Surveys*, *Overseer Business Reports*, *Foreign Business Trend Reports*, and *Market Share Reports.*

U.S. International Trade Commission (500 E Street, SW, Room 112, Washington, DC 20436).

Bureau of Economic and Business Affairs, U.S. Department of State (2201 C Street, NW, Room 6822, Washington, DC 20520).

Office of International Trade, U.S. Small Business Administration (409 Third Street SW, Room 501A, Washington, DC 20416.

United Nations (46th Street and First Avenue, New York, NY 10017), especially *The Statistical Yearbook*, *The Demographic Yearbook*, and *Yearbooks of Industrial and Labor Statistics.*

The World Bank (1818 H Street, NW, Washington, DC 20433), especially *The World Development* and *The World Bank Tables.*

Some selected private commercial organizations that provide economic information for different parts of the world are

Business International Corporation (Dag Hammarskjold Plaza, New York, NY 10017).

Euromonitor (18 Doughty Street, London, WC IN2 PN, England), which publishes a wide variety of regional economic reports.

12

Summary

We thank you for using our book. We hope it has added to your knowledge and appreciation of organizations around the world and has enhanced your understanding of others and yourself.

We believe that many of the established and emerging leaders of the global generation are clever and pragmatic and relentlessly pursue not only profit and power but fairness, accountability for organizational and personal actions, enhancement of the local and global environment and community, and a commitment to a peaceful world order for all. We see the future as bright and challenging. We believe that many diverse kinds of organizations will continue to work to minimize the severely erosive forces of poverty and ignorance on human potentialities that lurk everywhere around the globe. Just as some sectors of the world are expanding their populations exponentially without the capacity to carry such a load, in other sectors, the rate and magnitude of consumption reflect the impoverishment of the human spirit and denial of environmental degradation. Put simply, we are all part of the same world, and firmly believe that effective and humane organizations are a fundamental engine for enhancing the global marketplace and all members of the global community as the 21st century approaches. We wrote this book because we have faith in the goodness of humanity and the promise of the future.

We hope this book will help you further develop your knowledge and appreciation of organizations and the people around the world who work in them. Who knows with precision and clarity what the future will hold other than change, possibilities, problems, and death? In shaping and working in organizations in various countries, we encourage you to aspire to make them more productive and wholesome by adopting some of the specific information and guidelines presented in this book. We now provide a brief summary and an 11-step guide for working in organizations throughout the world.

Awareness

We began with a brief summary of some of the major forces of the global environment that shape almost all organizations and provide a framework for understanding and leading organizations. It is important to have some sense of the people and context of the target organization of interest, as well as some framework for understanding the major features of and processes in organizations around the world. Look around and get a feel for the people and the place.

Plan

Organizations, like people, are born, grow, mature, and eventually die or are transformed into new and different organizations. We examined five fundamental features of individuals and organizations that influence their functioning and development over time. We also reviewed specific strategies for studying and understanding organizations. An appreciation of the fundamental features of and methods of inquiry about organizations provides a firm foundation for understanding, leading, and working in organizations. Look for the expression of the fundamental features of an organization and have a systematic method to assemble your observations.

Culture

Every organization has a culture that is a shared pattern of learned assumptions to solve the problems of external adaptation and internal integration. Organizational culture can significantly enhance the adaptability, profit, productivity, and wholesomeness of individual members and entire organizations. An appreciation and understanding of organizational culture is critical because organizational culture affects all members of an organization and is a pervasive and potentially robust force for shaping organization's present and future. Get a sense of the culture of an organization by meeting with as many people from as many parts of the organization as possible.

Diversity

We clearly stated the contributions of workforce diversity, pointing out the legal, moral, and strategic imperatives for a diverse workforce. We also looked at programs and specific steps to enhance and harness the advantages and address the problems of a diversified workforce. All organizations around the globe have to work constantly to fix the mix that is an enduring and engaging challenge for all. Meet with as many different people in the organization and spend time with different people to understand the similarities and differences that separate and unite members of an organization.

Groups and Teams

Almost no one works completely alone anywhere in the world, and all organizations are relying more and more on teamwork to do more with less. Therefore, it is important to have a solid grounding in how groups and teams function, the forces that enhance their effectiveness, and how to work with teams. A group or a team can be a powerful force for implementing a specific project or program, and in almost every instance, represents years of cumulative organizational experience, wisdom, and invaluable resources.

Motivation

We examined the construct of motivation at the individual and organizational levels and outlined specific strategies and tools to increase motivation and productivity at each level. We also indicated how these motivational tools need to be adapted to specific cultural contexts. It is important to remember that most people respond positively to specific and challenging goals no matter where they work. Implement goal setting; it works.

Leadership

Leadership is about stewardship, caring, nurturing, and learning continuously about oneself and others in organizations. We examined trait, behavioral, and situational approaches to leadership, influence, power, and politics, as well as charismatic and transformational leadership styles. Leadership is a relational process, so keep an eye out for how and with whom a leader interacts over time.

Decision Making

In most organizations around the world, decisions are made by groups and teams, which makes decision making a social process. We examined the decision-making process, the forces that contribute to effective and defective decision making, and some specific strategies to increase the generation of creative ideas or alternatives for decision making. Effective organizations and individuals implement their decisions; thus, it is important to observe if decision loops are closed or left open.

Conflict and Negotiation

There is no shortage of conflict in organizations around the world. Conflict is inevitable, potentially constructive as well as destructive, and can be managed. We examined the nature and sources of conflict and various negotiation strategies, especially principled negotiations. Conflict is part of life. When it is not managed properly, it can be nettlesome and even deadly, but if it is managed properly, it may open up new opportunities.

Individual Change

Every organization wants, at some level, to grow and nurture individual members, anticipating that there will be a value-added payback to the organization. We looked at a variety of timely work-life issues that influence individual change and identified specific guidelines for enhancing

organizational citizenship behaviors and for developing an increasingly diversified workforce. Look for organizations that nurture their members.

Organizational Change

Finally, organizations, like individuals, change and can pursue a path of planned change. We outlined a model of planned change, and presented some specific guidelines for organizational development, including a sociotechnical model of planned change. We also outlined the major features of organizational transformation and examined the reengineering of business processes as a timely and robust strategy for organizational change. Organizations, like individuals, must continue to learn, and continuous learning gives new life and vitality to the organization, its members, and the larger community.

We believe that the systematic application of competence, grace, and compassion in organizations can lead to more effective, efficient, and noble organizations. We would appreciate hearing from you about any experiences you have had while applying the material in this book. We wish you enlightenment, peace, and a wholesome life, no matter where you work or live in the global marketplace.

Index